CLINICAL APPLICATIONS OF ISLAMIC PSYCHOLOGY

In the Name of Allāh
the Most Gracious, Most Merciful

CLINICAL APPLICATIONS
OF ISLAMIC PSYCHOLOGY

Edited by

Amber Haque

and

Abdallah Rothman

INTERNATIONAL
ASSOCIATION OF
ISLAMIC PSYCHOLOGY

This book first published 2023
International Association of Islamic Psychology Publishing
Seattle, Washington, USA
Copyright © 2023 by International Association of Islamic Psychology

All proceeds of this book go to the IAIP Fazal Haque Scholarship Fund. Reprinting and translation of the text in any form will carry the same conditions.

DEDICATION

The first editor would like to dedicate this book to his deceased parents

Syed Fazal and Safia Haque

May the contribution of my efforts increase their ranks in Jannah!

CONTENTS

ACKNOWLEDGMENTS

The editors wish to acknowledge each author's contributions to this volume from chapter one on preventive approach of Islamic Psychology to chapter twelve on Tazkia Therapy. Jamilah Hanum Abdul Khaiyom, Alizi Alias, Ahmad Nabil Md. Rosli, Khadijah Hasanah Abang Abdullah, Zul Azlin Razali, Nadzirah Ahmad Basri, Tuti Iryani Mohd Daud, Mohamed Hatta Shaharom (Malaysia), Fahad Khan (USA), Sena Aycan, Hooman Keshavarzi (Turkiye), Masoud Janbozorgi, Masoud Azarbayejani, Hamid Rafiei-Honar (Iran), Nazila Isgandarova (Canada), Filius F. Iakhin and Olga S. Pavlova (Russia), Amber Haque (USA), Venus Mahmoodi, Lindsay White, Zarnab Virk, Anna Akhavan (USA), Mustafa Merter, Nursena Balatekin, Lütfiye Söğütlü (Turkiye), Mohammad Omar Salem, Khalid Elzamzamy (Qatar), Sarah Mohr and Latifat I. Ahmed (USA), Halim Krausen and Rabia Malik (UK), and Bagus Riyono (Indonesia).

Finally, we acknowledge the works of Musa Abdul Mateen, editorial assistant, and Raabia Haque, typesetter and book cover designer. It is only the sincerity and hard work of everyone involved in this project that brought this book to fruition.

We are deeply grateful to all of you!

Amber Haque and Abdallah Rothman

Book editors

INTRODUCTION

Abdallah Rothman and Amber Haque

Islamic Psychology (IP) is rapidly developing and growing in public interest, with more academic and clinical training programs around the world (Haque & Rothman, 2021). Yet, it is still a nascent field and requires much development to be considered a fully-fledged and well understood discipline. Over the past decade, a great deal of work has gone into creating theoretical frameworks and therapeutic modalities for applying Islamic psychology principles in clinical settings. Much of that work has been dispersed throughout the world in isolated settings as individuals or groups of practitioners develop and implement their own models. Without a broader sense of what that work has entailed, what has worked and what has not worked in practice as clinicians experiment with creative adaptations within contemporary contexts, it is hard to get a collective sense of the field and its development. This edited volume provides a window into some of that work from clinicians around the world attempting to put Islamic psychology concepts, principles, and frameworks into therapeutic practice. The authors present their own professional experiences, ideas, methods, and evidence-based research, giving a broad view of the current state of affairs in the clinical applications of Islamic psychology.

Since the release of Malik Badri's seminal work, the Dilemma of Muslim Psychologists, where Dr. Badri laid out some of the philosophical considerations in approaching psychology from within a uniquely Islamic paradigm, the field of Islamic psychology has formalized into a recognized discipline globally. With the establishment of the International Association of Islamic Psychology

1

(IAIP) in 2017 and the subsequent publications of many books on the subject, as well as the recent establishment of academic programs in IP offered at Islamic institutions in the United Kingdom, Pakistan, Australia and soon to come to Qatar, IP is fast moving from the fringe to the mainstream. However, the contemporary field in its current iteration is still relatively young and may even be growing faster than it is ready for. Many aspiring psychologists are looking to learn the fundamentals of IP and are eager to jump into practice. Yet the field is still far off from being in such a state as to offer a solid foundational footing with clear guidelines. Within this period of rapid growth, what is needed is an organized effort to assess what developments have happened, pool collective experiences, and create an alliance among IP practitioners to establish a precedent for ongoing sharing, dialogue, and collaboration to advance our collective understanding properly and formally move into the next phase of the development of the field. This is why Dr. Malik Badri established the IAIP: to facilitate the networking of seasoned and aspiring Islamic psychologists to advance the field for future generations. There are a number of talented and hard-working professionals who have been doing incredible work in the integration of Islamic psychology into clinical practice that need to be highlighted and benefitted from.

In the review of literature in the field of IP, Haque et al. found in 2006 that the least amount of research and development, in terms of academic publications in English, was in clinical applications. Out of the five categories they identified in the literature on integrating Islamic traditions in modern psychology, only three publications were found in the category "development of interventions and techniques". Since then, within the past seven years, more studies and reports that are focused on therapeutic methods have been published as the field has continued to grow. In 2019, Elzamzamy & Keshavarzi explored the considerations and challenges in navigating ethical dilemmas in mental health practice between professional ethics and Islamic values. While this article did not offer therapeutic techniques, these ethical considerations are more and more critical as clinical methods that honor religious beliefs are applied in secular clinical contexts. In 2020, the team at Khalil Center in North America and colleagues published the book *Applying Islamic Principles to Clinical Mental Health Care: Introducing Traditional Islamically*

Integrated Psychotherapy (Keshavarzi et al., 2020), which includes both a theoretical framework and a model for their clinical approach TIIP. In 2021, Rothman & Coyle (2021) published the third article from their research, this one building on the theoretical framework that they laid out and presenting a model of the "clinical scope of Islamic psychotherapy", which outlines the distinctions between Islamically integrated therapy and religious guidance and provides parameters for clinicians. In 2022, Saged et al. (2022) published an article that reports evidence-based findings on implementing their "Islamic-Based" intervention in the treatment of depression and anxiety. In the somewhat different context of coaching rather than psychotherapy, Kamel & Nieuwerburgh (2023) recently published an article introducing a therapeutic framework that they call the "Ershad Framework," which references much of the past literature from the field of Islamic psychology as it focuses on practical applications of Islamic psychology theory.

To add to this growing body of literature in the development of interventions and techniques, most recently, in 2023, in the APA journal *Spirituality in Clinical Practice,* a special issue on Islamic spirituality in clinical contexts brought forth several studies in this specific area of focus. Weisman et al. (2023) contributed an article titled "A pilot study to assess the feasibility and efficacy of a transdiagnostic, religiously/spiritually integrated, culturally informed therapy". Mahmoodi, Akhavan & Virk (2023) contributed an article titled "Integration of Islamic spirituality in the treatment of grief for pregnancy loss: A case series of loss during early, mid-, and late pregnancy." Bagasra (2023) contributed an article titled "Religious interpretations of mental illness and help-seeking experiences among Muslim Americans: Implications for clinical practice". And Abdul Majid & Laird (2023) contributed an article titled "Encountering god, accompanying others: Spirituality and Theology among Muslim health care chaplains," among others, published in the special issue. All this new literature is a testament to the robust growth of applied Islamic psychology and the importance of studies that help us understand the various ways Islamic principles can and are being integrated and implemented into clinical applications.

As Haque et al. (2006) aimed to highlight, there is a particular approach to the integration of Islamic principles that distinguishes it from what was previously more commonly known as "Islamization". The accounts of clinical applications that are reported in this book were selected due to their attempt to approach therapeutic methods from within a uniquely Islamic paradigm, using what is commonly referred to as bottom-up approaches rather than top-down (Kaplick, Loucif & Rüschoff, 2021) approaches. The inclusion criterion used in this regard was authors with experience working within an Islamic framework in clinical practice and explicitly attempting to approach clinical interventions from within these Islamic frameworks rather than adapting Islamic principles to otherwise secular frameworks. This made the task a more difficult, as while there are a multitude of efforts to integrate Muslim beliefs and culture with secular mental health, there are fewer practitioners versed in the theological foundations of the Islamic tradition to approach the task from the "bottom-up". As the field of IP gains in popularity and begins to encroach on the mainstream, it is ever more critical to distinguish between conventional mental health practice with Muslim populations, which generally tends to adopt an otherwise secular paradigm of psychology, versus approaches that are solidly grounded in the epistemological and ontological foundations set out in Islamic theology and various Islamic traditions. This is a part of the growing effort to delineate a distinct field of Islamic psychology that is separate from but related to that of Muslim Mental Health.

The editors of this books' volume, titled "Islamic Psychology Around the Globe" (Haque & Rothman, 2021) highlighted the developments in IP in 17 countries and demonstrated the wide diversity of efforts among a growing community of Islamic psychologists globally. This presented a view of the state of affairs in the development of theory, the establishment of programs, and the general efforts to bring IP into the consciousness of the Muslim community and the field of psychology more broadly. As a result of all those efforts that the authors reported on, as well as a great deal more not represented in the book, practitioners around the world have been developing and testing their own theories and putting into practice their own models and methods in their local contexts, often in isolation from the larger network of IP internationally. More familiar to those following the development of IP is that of the larger institutions that have been able to gain credibility and recognition for their efforts. Khalil Center in North America has been widely successful in galvanizing its efforts in providing clinical services and offering training for practitioners. With their publication of *Applying Islamic Principles to Clinical Mental Health Care* (Keshavarzi et al. 2021) and their subsequent launch of the TIIP (Traditional Islamically Integrated Psychotherapy) training courses, Khalil Center has helped to bring IP as a clinical modality into reality on a wider scale than previously existed. At the same time, Cambridge Muslim College has made advancements in Islamic Psychology graduate education by launching the postgraduate Online Diploma in Islamic Psychology, a yearlong academic program that gives practitioners a grounding in the theory and practice of Islamic psychology. While these are the largest and most public advancements in the clinical application of IP, there are a number of efforts that have been happening on a smaller scale off the radar of the public that are important to understand for the advancement of the field.

The following is an overview of the chapters in this book, which gives insight into a cross-section of some of the clinical work that has been going on quietly out of the public eye, which can help to give a better picture of the current state of affairs with regards to the clinical application of Islamic psychology.

Chapter one is about defining mental health to its management and how Islam promotes good mental health. The chapter authors illustrate the model of Islamic-scientific Psychology in three stages of clinical prevention. Examples are used primarily from authors' clinical practice, giving the readers firsthand experience in delivering IP in clinical settings.

Chapter two discusses a case study using the TIIP Model developed earlier by chapter authors. After a brief discussion on the concept of the self, the authors indicate that the Islamic scholarly tradition is an inclusive epistemology that considers scriptural, rational, and empirical data as equally admissible sources of information in developing psychological knowledge. The chapter covers seven underlying principles of TIIP, a model of human ontology, and discusses the case of a client who successfully used the model to overcome her challenges. The authors claim that TIIP is helpful for everyone and not just Muslims.

In chapter three, the authors discuss the God-Oriented Spiritual Psychotherapy Multidimensional Model, which activates the spiritual dimension in a person by correcting an individual's relationship with God. Using clinical research methods for clients given spiritual interventions in psychotherapy, the authors conducted a qualitative analysis of religious texts. This method has been used in Iran for more than fifteen years and is now used toward developing a more comprehensive treatment methodology unknown in other parts of the world.

Chapter four discusses the spiritual tradition of Islam and how mindfulness-based therapy models are a part of Islamic tradition. Sufi psychology trains the seekers of knowledge to take responsibility for connecting with God through training of temptations, whims, thoughts, emotions, behaviors, etc. This chapter focuses on incorporating murāqaba as a therapeutic tool in clinical settings with Muslim clients.

Chapter five is about Ayah Therapy based on the divine signs given in the Qurʾān, as understanding ayah or signs in the Qurʾān can create a deep connection of humans with their inner world and a comprehensive impact on their intellectual and spiritual development. The authors point out that the symbols in the Qurʾān reveal the quintessence of the methods of intervention and goals of therapy. The Qurʾānic text is intended to affect mental processes and states by reflecting on symbolic images, which can help transform dysfunctional beliefs. Similarly, visualization of images that have many contextual meanings can facilitate therapy. Also, visualization of parables and stories, listening to audio recordings with a translation of ayah, and comparing psychological states in each session can be highly beneficial for Muslim clients.

Chapter six discusses the integration of Thanvi's Islamic-based techniques into therapy. The author contends that because mainstream counseling techniques lack in addressing the conditions of the spiritual heart, therapies remain largely ineffective for Muslims. Thanvi's views on personality, psychological disorders and healing, therapeutic objectives, and methods are outlined. A detailed description of various types of spiritual hearts and the factors affecting them are discussed as gleaned from the Qurʾān. While there are some commonalities between Thanvi's methods and the secular approach, Thanvi's Islamic concept of human nature and treatment of psychological disorders are highlighted. The qualities of a Muslim counselor, the steps in Thavi's counseling, and what not to expect from therapies are also laid out for practicing clinicians.

Chapter seven addresses grief treatment from an Islamic spiritual perspective in perinatal loss. A pregnancy loss can cause traumatic experiences and positively and negatively impact one's Muslim identity and relationship with Allāh. The authors outline an Islamically integrated approach to treating grief and point out that instilling hope in God's plan (*qadr*) and teaching reliance on Allāh's plans (*Tawakkul*) are essential in Islamic-based therapy. The chapter covers much research and analysis on concepts of motherhood in Islam, death and grief, and an Islamic Psychology approach to coping with perinatal loss.

The authors of chapter eight introduce Nafs Psychotherapy based on the ancient Sufi Muslim system taught by the first author in Turkey, the Netherlands, and Germany. The chapter outlines the therapy process using *'ayn-al-yaqīn* and *haqq-al-yaqīn*, leading to *'ilm-al-yaqīn*. The authors believe that the most effective way to do this is through dream analysis but caution that therapists must undergo their own nafs analysis to study others. Nafs psychotherapy can be used with people of any belief system. Client assessment and treatment methods are outlined with case reports.

In chapter nine, the authors present an Islamic-based cognitive behavioral therapy, which can be tailored to the client's needs and applicable across various psychopathologies. Derived from Propst's Model of Religious CBT, the first author developed and used strategies including religious and spiritual guidance, spiritually oriented support groups, religious self-help tools, prayers, and seeking support from the religious communities in many countries. A multi-station protocol is outlined, aiming to enhance spirituality within an Islamic cognitive-behavioral framework.

The authors of chapter ten offer *jihād-an-nafs* as a paradigm to treat the problems of drug addictions in Muslims. The works of Al-Ghazali on *'ilm-un-nafs* are used to address the treatment of the components of personal change and character refinement in combination with religiously integrated cognitive behavioral therapy.

Motivational interviewing is discussed as an adjunct of RCBT for those suffering from addictions and clinicians attempting to relieve the impact of addictions on others.

Chapter eleven discusses the Divine Names of Allāh as a source of healing. One or a cluster of Divine names are prescribed to awaken the client's consciousness of God and for inner reflection and self-knowledge. The chapter draws on the depth of psychological and spiritual dimensions of the meaning and effects of the Divine Names. The authors also provide a theological overview of Divine Names and their relevance for our self-understanding of God, followed by a case example drawing on the Divine qualities of mercy, forgiveness, and recommendations for practitioners.

Chapter twelve is about Tazkia therapy, which the authors explain is a Qur'ānic-based intervention to purify and develop the human soul from problematic conditions towards peace. An orientation towards eternal life is essential in Tazkia therapy, leading to peace. The counselor facilitates the client's understanding of the signs through reason, empathy, and spirituality. A set of theories and approaches of Tazkia are outlined through a successful case study.

It is the hope of the editors of this volume that it can serve to mark a milestone in the next stage of advancement in the developing field of Islamic psychology. This second offering by these editors builds upon the first, moving from institutional, organizational, and theoretical initiatives toward the further development of practical therapeutic interventions grounded in Islamic psychological frameworks. As new generations of young aspiring practitioners enter the field through the growing number of IP programs, this book provides several diverse accounts of the variety of ways that IP can be creatively integrated within clinical settings. It is up to the new generation of practitioners to respond to the current times and circumstances and find creative solutions to new problems, using the foundations of knowledge and guidance from the Islamic tradition to inform best practice aligned with an Islamic paradigm. This creative integrative response to our current times is what is most needed in the continued development of clinical applications of Islamic psychology.

References

Abdul Majid, S., & Laird, L. D. (2023). Encountering God, accompanying others: Spirituality and theology among

Muslim health care chaplains. *Spirituality in Clinical Practice, 10* (1), 74–88. https://doi.org/10.1037/scp0000315

Badri, M. (1979). *The Dilemma of Muslim Psychologists.* Kuala Lumpur: Islamic Book Trust.

Bagasra, A. (2023). Religious interpretations of mental illness and help-seeking experiences among Muslim Americans: Implications for clinical practice. *Spirituality in Clinical Practice, 10* (1), 20–31. https://doi.org/10.1037/scp0000299

Elzamzamy, K. & Keshavarzi, H. (2019). Navigating ethical dilemmas in mental health practice between professional ethics and Islamic values. *Journal of Islamic Faith and Practice, 2* (1), 40–71.

Haque, A. & Rothman, A. (2021). Islamic Psychology around the Globe. International Association of Islamic Psychology, Seattle: USA.

Haque, A., Khan, F., Keshavarzi, H., & Rothman, A. E. (2016). Integrating Islamic Traditions in Modern Psychology: Research Trends in Last Ten Years. *Journal of Muslim Mental Health*, 10 (1).

Ismail, G., Shealy, C., & Nahas, Z. (2023). Psychotherapy through a Sufi Islamic lens: A dialectic of transcendence and acceptance. *Spirituality in Clinical Practice*, 10(3), 200.

Kamel, M. & van Nieuwerburgh, C. (2023). How Muslims in the UK Experience Coaching using the Ershad Framework: An Interpretative Phenomenological Analysis. International *Journal of Evidence Based Coaching & Mentoring*, 21 (2).

Kaplick, P., Loucif, A. & Rüschoff, I. (2021) Islamic Psychology in Western Continental Europe: A Top-down Approach. In Haque, A. & Rothman, A. Eds. *Islamic Psychology Around the Globe*. Seattle: International Association of Islamic Psychology.

Keshavarzi, H., Khan, F., Ali, B. & Awaad, R. (2020). *Applying Islamic principles to clinical mental health care: Introducing traditional Islamically integrated psychotherapy*, Routledge.

Mahmoodi, V., Akhavan, A., & Virk, Z. (2023). Integration of Islamic spirituality in the treatment of grief for pregnancy loss: A case series of loss during early, mid-, and late pregnancy. *Spirituality in Clinical Practice*, 10 (1), 52-61.

Rothman, A. & Coyle, A. (2021), The clinical scope of Islamic psychotherapy: A grounded theory study. *Spirituality in Clinical Practice*, online first publication.

Saged, A.A.G, Sa'ari, C.Z., Abdullah, M., Al-Rahmi, W.M. Ismail, W.M., Zain, M.I.A., Al-Shehri, N. (2022). The Effect of an Islamic-Based Intervention on Depression and Anxiety in Malaysia. *Journal of religion and health, 61* (1), p.79-92.

Weisman de Mamani, A., Lopez, D., McLaughlin, M. M., Ahmad, S. S., & Altamirano, O. (2023). A pilot study to assess the feasibility and efficacy of a transdiagnostic, religiously/spiritually integrated, culturally informed therapy. *Spirituality in Clinical Practice, 10* (3), 233.

CLINICAL PREVENTIVE APPROACH OF ISLAMIC PSYCHOLOGY

Jamilah Hanum Abdul Khaiyom, Alizi Alias, Ahmad Nabil Md. Rosli, Khadijah Hasanah Abang Abdullah, Zul Azlin Razali, Nadzirah Ahmad Basri, Tuti Iryani Mohd Daud & Mohamed Hatta Shaharom

Introduction

Mental Health and the Management of Mental Illness

Mental health is often perceived as a condition free from psychiatric symptoms, but the scope is much broader due to many factors surrounding it. These include socio-economic conditions, relationships, past adverse events, physical or organisational environment, and individuals' intrinsic factors. Jamaiyah (2000) defined mental health as "the capacity of the individual, the group, and the environment to interact with one another in ways that promote subjective wellbeing, optimal development of mental abilities, and the achievement of individual and collective goals" (p.156).

The integration of these multifactorial causes contributes to mental illness. At some point, they must be addressed, while managing mental illness is best done using a biopsychosocial-spiritual approach, which includes both pharmacotherapy and psychotherapy.

Mental health management has now evolved from face-to-face sessions to using facilities of technological advancement such as telemedicine, e-health, artificial intelligence platforms, therapeutic apps, and socially assistive robots. Robots are helpful for self-help interventions, moving towards an interactive therapeutic experience while addressing the fear and stigma associated with seeking treatment at a psychiatric center (Fiske et al., 2019).

Mental health management also incorporates the support of significant people around individuals with mental illness, including family members, peers, employers, and teachers. A study that combined collaborative care from a generic, clinician-administered peer-led self-management group to intervene with individuals with serious mental illness demonstrated improved self-management and functioning up to 6 months follow-up (Lawn et al., 2007).

Promotion of Psychological Health from the Perspective of Islam

Human beings differ in their perception and worldviews of life. For instance, the differences in worldviews between Westerners and East Asians are due to the differing ecologies, social structures, educational systems, and philosophies that date back, respectively, to the ancient Greek and Chinese civilizations (Nisbett, 2004). Similarly, the orientations and thus preoccupations of Westerners and Eastern Muslim men are distinct and are pictured as having a disposition to either "looking down at his feet to the ground, or to raise his eyes towards the heavens" (Bennabi, 2010, p. 3). Therefore, these two groups of men would differ in their conception of the self and how they think, feel, and behave. Their ideas of happiness and misery, the purpose and meaning of life, and wellbeing or good health would also differ.

Etymologically, health means wholeness. It is also associated with happiness, prosperity, and safety. Technically, the World Health Organization (WHO) has defined health as a state of complete physical, mental, and social wellbeing and not merely the absence of disease or infirmity (WHO, 2020). However, due to its inadequacy, another practical definition has been proposed, which states health is

12

the ability to adapt and self-manage in the face of social, physical, and emotional challenges (Huber et al., 2011). This new definition has a broader outlook where it considers the limitations of the human being, treats a person as more than his illness, and focuses on one's strengths rather than his weakness (Huber et al., 2016). Nevertheless, the spiritual domain is not clearly spelled out in both definitions.

From the perspective of Islam, psycho-spiritual health is related to one's ability to actualize one's primordial spiritual purpose (Keshavarzi & Ali, 2019). It is important to note that the three key terms frequently mentioned in the Qur'ān are closely related to the essential meaning of health. The word *īmān*, often translated as faith, is derived from a root word that means 'to be at peace' and 'to be safe.' *Islām* is from a root word that means 'to be safe' and 'to be whole and integral.' *Taqwā* means 'to protect from getting lost or wasted' and 'to guard against peril' (Rahman, 1998). Happiness or *sa'ādah* is the goal of every living being. Islam views happiness as having a dual dimension: the one experienced in the present world, and ultimately the one experienced in the hereafter (al-Attas, 2001). In elucidating this further, al-Attas explains:

> Enduring happiness in life refers not to the physical entity in man, not to the animal soul and body of man; nor is it a state of mind, or feeling that undergoes terminal states, nor pleasure nor amusement. It has to do with certainty (*yaqin*) of the ultimate Truth and fulfilment of action in conformity with that certainty. And certainty is a permanent state of consciousness natural to what is permanent in man and perceived by his spiritual organ of cognition, which is the heart (*qalb*). It is peace and security and tranquillity of the heart (*tuma'ninah*); it is knowledge (*ma'rifah*) and knowledge is true faith (*imān*). (al-Attas, 2001, p. 108)

The study of the soul, the promotion of psychological wellbeing, and the prevention of psychological ill-health require the understanding of the heart (*qalb*), as al-Ghazali explains:

> The heart (*qalb*) is that which, if a man knows it, he knows himself, and if he knows himself, he knows his Lord. It is that which, if a man knows it not, he knows not himself, and if he knows not himself he knows not his Lord... Whoever does not know his heart, to be mindful of it, to be watchful over it, and to observe what shines

over it and through it of heavenly treasures, he is one of those about whom Allāh Almighty said: And do not be like those who forgot Allāh so He made them forget themselves. It is they who are truly rebellious (Al-Qur'ān, 59:19). Thus, knowledge of the heart, its realities, and its qualities is the foundation of the religion and the basis of spiritual seeking. (al-Ghazali, 2010, pp.2-3.)

Many Islamic classical writings by the likes of al-Ghazali give utmost importance to the knowledge of the self. In one of his basic texts on psychology, al-Ghazali writes about the nature of one's *qalb*, its properties, and its relation to knowledge.

Among various internal activities of the soul that are discussed are the following: (i) effects of external and internal senses or the effects of imagination on the *qalb*; (ii) various sources of *khawāṭir,* which in modern psychology are unhelpful negative automatic thoughts; and (iii) the devil's stratagem to prevent one's true perception and understanding of reality, and the eventual bad intention and behavior that result from this misunderstanding.

In contrast to conventional psychology or psychotherapy, this approach targets a problem, e.g., *muhlikāt* (vices), from the very beginning at its root and whether it disrupts one's daily functioning that would warrant a psychiatric diagnosis. Another example that can be a subject of discussion is anger (*ghaḍab*). Through a multi-perspective analysis, a theological, cognitive, emotional, and behavioral understanding becomes the basis for holistic *sharī'ah*-compliant management.

Definitions of Islamic Psychology

It would be worth noting that there are active debates on the use of the following terms: Islamic Psychology, Psychology of Islam, Psychology from an Islamic perspective, and Islam and Psychology. In this chapter, Islamic psychology is used.

Malik Badri, the father of modern (or postmodern) Islamic psychology, did not provide a clear definition of Islamic psychology, perhaps because of the complexity of its subject. However, his major writings (Badri, 1979, 2000a, 2000b, 2009) revealed two major themes: i) the absent dimension in Western psychology, i.e., the soul, and ii) the importance of Islamic empirical methods in the study of psychology. His writings and thoughts influenced Muslim and non-Muslim scholars who attempted to define Islamic psychology, albeit not without criticism.

We want to quote two examples of the definition of Islamic psychology that highlights the soul:

1. The first is by Utz (2011): "The study of the soul; the ensuing behavioural, emotional, and mental processes; and both the seen and unseen aspects that influence these elements" (p. 34); and

2. The second is by the International Association of Islamic Psychology (2022): "A holistic approach that endeavours to better understand the nature of the self and the soul and the connection of the soul to the Divine."

An example of a definition of Islamic psychology that highlights the inclusion of Islamic methodology is by al-Karam (2018): "An interdisciplinary science where psychology subdisciplines and/or related disciplines engage scientifically about a particular topic and at a particular level with various Islamic sects, sources, sciences, and/or schools of thought using a variety of methodological tools." (pp. 101-102)

Alias (2018) defined Islamic psychology as "The scientific study of the manifestation of the soul in the form of behaviour and mental processes." This definition includes the soul element and the term 'scientific study', which implicitly refers to both empirical methods (quantitative and qualitative) and Islamic methods (*uṣūl al-fiqh, uṣūl al-tafsīr,* and *uṣūl al-ḥadīth*). The focus on studying the 'manifestation of the soul' rather than the soul itself is to accept the fact that humans are not given knowledge about the spirit except very little (al-Qur'ān 17:85). This definition might be most suitable for both Muslim psychologists and non-Muslim psychologists who believe in the soul. Another definition is "the study of the human being based on revealed text and empirical investigation" (Hasan & Alias, 2019). The subject of 'human being' (which includes the soul) is broader than 'human behavior,' yet the methods of 'revealed text' (Qur'ān and *al-Sunnah*) and 'empirical investigation' (quantitative and qualitative) are more specific. This definition might be most suitable to scholars trained in Islamic studies and psychologists trained in scientific methods. In other words, the former definition can be considered the realistic definition, whereas the latter definition can be regarded as the idealistic definition of Islamic psychology.

Regarding the clinical applications of Islamic psychology, this chapter offers the following definition for Islamic clinical psychology: A study of the manifestation of the soul in the form of behavior and mental processes and its applications in clinical settings based on revealed text and empirical investigation.

Clinical Applications of Islamic Psychology from the Perspective of Qur'an and Hadith

Human life is full of the blessings of Allāh SWT. But life is also about facing and surmounting hardships. In so doing, we can become better people and understand that Allāh SWT is the ultimate helper when we are faced with physical, mental, emotional, and spiritual challenges. Allāh SWT said: *"Whatever blessings you have are from Allāh. Then whenever hardship touches you, to Him alone you cry for help"* (Qur'ān, 16:53). And although Allāh said: *"Indeed, We have created humankind in constant struggle"* (Qur'ān, 90:40), He also said: *"Indeed, We created humankind in the best form"* (Qur'ān, 95:4).

All human beings face mental health issues at various points in their life. Having mental health issues does not mean having mental illness. Prophet Muhammad SAW had shown normal worry during a crisis, such as amid the Battle of Badr when he prayed to Allāh SWT: *"O Allāh, accomplish for me what Thou hast promised to me. O Allāh, bring about what Thou hast promised to me. O Allāh, if this small band of Muslims is destroyed, Thou will not be worshipped on this earth* (Recorded by Muslim: 1763). The Prophet Muhammad SAW had also shown normal sadness during the demise of his son when he said: *"The eye weeps and the heart grieves, but we say only what our Lord is pleased with, and we are grieved for you, Ibrahim"* (Reported by Abū Dāwud: 3126. Graded authentic by al-Albānī).

It is interesting to note that Islamic *fiqh* (jurisprudence) has always considered human needs (which include mental health needs) based on the *al-Maqāṣid al-Sharī'ah* (the objectives of Islamic law) put forth by early Muslim scholars such as al-Shāṭibī and al-Ghazālī.

The objectives of Islamic Law (*al-Maqāṣid al-Sharī'ah*) are meant to safeguard the tranquility of human life. The range of objectives are *al-ḍarūriyyāt* (the essential needs), *al-ḥajjiyyāt* (the complementary needs), and *al- taḥsīnīyyat* (the embellishment needs) (Kamali, 1991). Kamali (1991) provided the definition for all three terms. Needs grouped in *al-ḍarūrīyyāt* are those on which the lives of people depend and whose neglect leads to total disruption and chaos. Needs grouped in *al-ḥajjīyyāt* are interests whose neglect leads to hardship in the community's life, although it does not amount to its total collapse. Finally, needs grouped in *al- taḥsīnīyyat* are interests whose realization leads to improvement and to the attainment of that which is desirable.

Essentials needs, or *al-ḍarūrīyyāt,* are further divided into five needs that are to be protected: i) the religion or *al-dīn,* ii) the life or *al-nafs,* iii) the intellect or *al-'aql,* iv) the lineage or *al-naṣl,* and v) the property or *al-māl* (Kamali, 1991). One might think that only the first three essentials are related to mental illness, which are religion (to protect from spiritual emptiness), life (to protect from untimely death), and intellect (to protect from mental disorders). However, mental illness can also be related to lineage (to protect family and offspring from the risk of mental illness) and property (to protect from poverty which increases the risk of mental illness). Refer to Table 1 for some examples of psychological prevention, both clinical and non-clinical, in relation to the five *al-ḍarūriyyāt.*

Table 1. *Some examples of primary, secondary, and tertiary psychological prevention (clinical and non-clinical) in relation to the five al-ḍarūriyyāt*

Maqāṣid al-Sharīʿah	Primary Prevention	Secondary Prevention	Tertiary Prevention
Religion	• Faith-based psychoeducation • Ritualistic *ʿibādah*	• Ritualistic *ʿibādah* • *Ruqyah al-Shar ʿiyyah*	• Ritualistic *ʿibādah* • *Ruqyah al-Shar ʿiyyah*
Life	• Psychological first aid • Mental health first aid • Mental health self-care activities • Individual counseling	• Pharma-cotherapy • Psychotherapy	• Pharma-cotherapy • Psychotherapy
Intellect	• Mental health self-care activities • Stress management	• Pharma-cotherapy • Psychotherapy • Islamic cognitive therapy	• Pharma-cotherapy • Psychotherapy • Islamic cognitive therapy
Lineage	• Work-family balance policies & culture • Islamic family counseling	• Islamic family therapy	• Islamic family therapy
Property	• Employee salary & benefits	• Return-to-Work counseling • Behavior therapy & behavior modification	• Return-to-Work counseling • Behavior therapy & behavior modification

Models for Clinical Applications of Islamic Psychology

Several contemporary scholars like Keshavarzi and Haque (2013), al-Karam (2018), Rothman and Coyle (2018), and Skinner (2020) have attempted to provide an Islamic model of psychology. From Malaysia, Alias (2021) uses the term Islamic-scientific approach, which integrates traditional Islamic methods and contemporary scientific methods in understanding psychology. In this approach, all biological, psychological, socio-cultural, and spiritual (soul) elements play their respective roles in both normal and abnormal behaviors. When this model is adapted to clinical applications of Islamic-scientific psychology, particularly in clinical prevention, the soul is seen to play a central role in the explanation of abnormal behaviors. It is not just a common factor like other various biological, psychological, and social factors or domains. It plays important and numerous roles as the main variable, moderator variable, and mediating variable that influence the relationship between various biopsychosocial factors and abnormal behaviors. With proper prevention and clinical interventions, the spiritual (soul) element or factor helps one to achieve a good life (Figure 1). "Whoever works righteousness, man or woman, and has Faith, verily, to him will We give a new Life, a life that is good and pure, and We will bestow on such their reward according to the best of their actions" (Qur'ān, 16: 97).

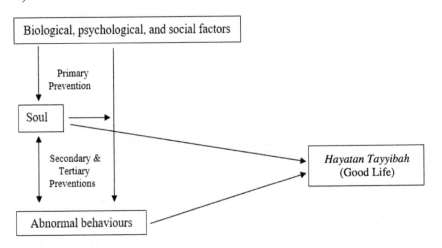

Figure 1. *A biopsychosocial-spiritual approach to clinical application, particularly clinical preventions, of Islamic-scientific*

psychology.

The model is adapted from Alias (2021). The terms "primary prevention" and "secondary & tertiary preventions" are added, and the word "behavior" from the original model is changed to "abnormal behaviors".

Alias (2021) also introduces a methodological model for Islamic psychology addressing the integration between revealed texts and empirical methods. In this model, Alias differentiates between *al-dalīl al-qat'īy* (definitive Islamic evidence) in the Qur'an and the *mutawātir* Hadith and *al-dalīl al-ẓannīy* (interpretable Islamic evidence) in the Qur'an, Hadith, and early Muslim scholars' opinions. Interpretable Islamic evidence or *al-dalīl al-ẓannīy* can be integrated with psychological theories derived from empirical studies that will guide psychological research and interventions (Figure 2).

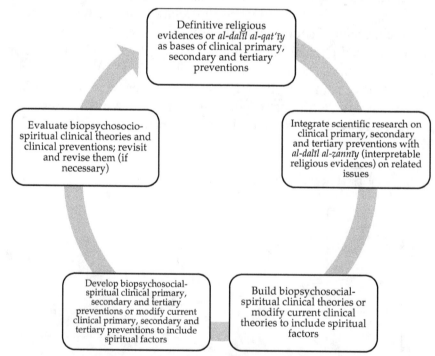

Figure 2. *Evidence-based model for evaluating clinical applications, particularly clinical preventions, in Islamic-scientific psychology.*

The model is adapted from Alias (2021). The terms "clinical primary, secondary, and tertiary preventions" are added.

The two models above provide a guide on the relationships between various variables and the methodological steps of clinical prevention in Islamic-scientific psychology.

Clinical Applications of Islamic Psychology

Prevention of mental disorders aims to reduce symptoms and occurrence of mental disorders. One strategy used is mental health promotion, i.e., increasing psychological wellbeing, enhancing competencies and resilience, and improving living conditions and environments (WHO, 2004).

There are three levels of mental disorders prevention: primary, secondary, and tertiary (WHO, 2004). The Summary Report of Prevention of Mental Disorders: Effective Interventions and Policy Options (WHO, 2004) reviews different primary prevention of mental disorders (i.e., universal, selective, and indicated prevention) as below:

> Universal prevention is defined as those interventions that are targeted at the general public or to a whole population group that has not been identified based on increased risk (Mrazek & Haggerty as cited in WHO, 2004, p. 17).

> Selective prevention targets individuals or subgroups of the population whose risk of developing a mental disorder is significantly higher than average, as evidenced by biological, psychological, or social risk factors (Mrazek & Haggerty as cited in WHO, 2004, p. 17).

> Indicated prevention targets high-risk people who are identified as having minimal but detectable signs or symptoms foreshadowing mental disorder or biological markers indicating predisposition for mental disorder but who do not meet diagnostic criteria for disorder at that time (Mrazek & Haggerty as cited in WHO, 2004, p. 17).

The stigma that is attached to mental illness is real and debilitating. It is related to a lack of awareness and understanding of mental health conditions. Repeated anti-stigma and mental health awareness initiatives with a variety of strategies would increase familiarity and improve acceptance of mental disorders (Shahwan et al., 2022).

In the Muslim community, there is a strong culturally influenced belief that symptoms of mental illnesses are related to supernatural beings or phenomena like the *jinn*, evil eye, and magic (Lim et al., 2018; Abdullah et al., 2017). Lack of spirituality or poor adherence to religion has also been thought of as a cause of mental illness. To some, seeking the aid of spiritual healer help would suffice in the effort to treat mental disorders, leading to the refusal to seek medical help, delayed diagnosis, and non-compliance with medical treatment (Lim et al., 2015; Javed et al., 2021). Even highly educated persons with mental illness may solely attribute their symptoms to supernatural causes, which leads them to confine their need for help to traditional or spiritual healers (Abdullah et al., 2016). Educating Muslims about the need to be holistic in their approach improves their acceptance of the neurobiological cause of mental illnesses. It is a religious duty to guide fellow Muslims on the correct method of reliance on Allāh. Some of the so-called traditional or spiritual healers are known to have used methods that are harmful to a diverse clientele and influenced by polytheism or *shirk* (شرك), the ascribing partners to Allāh (Razali & Tahir, 2018).

Clinical applications of Islamic psychology at the primary-universal prevention stage should involve preventing or reducing mental illness risk factors and promoting physical, mental, emotional, and spiritual needs. The Prophet Muhammad SAW said, "A Muslim is a brother of another Muslim, so he should not oppress him, nor should he hand him over to an oppressor. Whoever fulfilled the needs of his brother, Allāh SWT will fulfil his needs; whoever brought his (Muslim) brother out of a discomfort, Allāh will bring him out of the discomforts of the Day of Resurrection, and whoever screened a Muslim, Allāh will screen him on the Day of Resurrection" (Reported by al-Bukhari, no. 2442).

The incidents of Prophet Muhammad SAW experiencing emotional distress during the earliest encounters with the Angel Jibril (Gabriel) can be used to illustrate the importance of the primary-indicated prevention stage. It was narrated by Aishah RA: Then Allāh's Messenger SAW returned with that experience, and the muscles between his neck and shoulders were trembling till he came upon Khadijah (his wife) RA and said, "Cover me!" She covered him, and when the state of fear was over, he said to Khadijah, "O Khadijah!

What is wrong with me? I was afraid that something bad might happen to me." Then he told her the story. Khadijah said, "Nay! But receive the good tidings! By Allāh, Allāh will never disgrace you, for by Allāh, you keep good relations with your kith and kin, speak the truth, help the poor and the destitute, entertain your guests generously, and assist those who are stricken with calamities." Khadijah RA then took him to Waraqah bin Naufal, the son of Khadijah's paternal uncle. Waraqah had been converted to Christianity in the Pre-Islamic Period and used to write Arabic and write the Gospel in Arabic as much as Allāh wished him to write. (Reported by al-Bukhari, no. 4953). What Khadijah RA did during this vital moment of the prophecy were the strategies normally used in the primary-indicated prevention stage. She listened attentively without interruption, avoided denying the negative emotion or adding the feeling of guilt, and strengthened the self-concept. She also knew her own limitation, and she had referred the matter to the expert, who, in this matter, was her own paternal cousin. One should also be able to manage the physical and physiological symptoms of a person in distress. This was well demonstrated by the Hadith when the Prophet Muhammad SAW was covered in a blanket as one of the ways to manage the symptoms of a panic attack. Some of the mentioned strategies could also be used in the secondary-prevention stage when someone is diagnosed with a mental disorder.

Clinical Application of Islamic Psychology from Malaysian-Historical Context

Alias (2021a) outlined the establishment and growth of Islamic psychology in Malaysia and divided it into three eras: i) Early contributions to Islamic psychology since the 1950s, ii) the establishment of Islamic psychology in the 1990s, and iii) the growth of Islamic psychology in the 2000s. For this chapter, only the writings related to the clinical aspects of Islamic psychology in Malaysia will be outlined, which include the field of psychiatry, clinical psychology, and counseling. And due to the limited space, only books and book chapters are reviewed and cited.

According to Alias (2021a), probably the earliest writings on Islamic psychology (which include the clinical aspects) are the series of articles written by Yusoff Zaky Yacob published in *Majalah Dian* or the Dian (pronounced: di-yān) Magazine in 1961 discussing 1,001 psychological problems faced by human beings. About two decades later, Langgulung (1983) wrote a book on the theories of mental health and compared the forms, concepts, and theories of Western mental health from the perspective of modern psychology and Islamic educationists' approach.

Book publications on Islamic counseling in Malaysia were more active compared to Islamic psychology or Islamic psychiatry. Most writings cover many aspects of Islamic counseling, but each contributes significantly to specific aspects of Islamic counseling such as Islamic counseling theory (Malek, 1992), family counseling (Nor, 1992), Islamic counseling process (Ismail, 1993), Islamic counseling techniques (Salleh, 1993), Islamic counseling method (Kadir,1994), comparison between Western and Islamic counseling (Manaf, 1995, 2000), counseling from the perspective of Islamic morality (*akhlāq*) (Omar, 2005), and counseling from the perspective of Islamic call (*da'wah*) (Rahman, 2008). All these are related to the clinical applications of Islamic psychology.

The establishment of Kulliyyah of Islamic Revealed Knowledge and Human Sciences (KIRKHS) (currently known as AbdulHamid Abu Sulayman KIRKHS), International Islamic University Malaysia (IIUM) in 1990 saw the growth of book publications by IIUM academic staff on clinical-related Islamic psychology in Malaysia such as a chapter on *'ibadah*-based therapy (Badri, 2000a), contemplation as a form of both method and therapy (Badri, 2000b), Islamic perspective of abnormal psychology (Iqbal, 2009), a chapter on the Islamic perspective of psychotherapy (Sipon & Hussin, 2010), *Īmān* -Restoration Therapy (Razak, 2018, 2019a), therapy from Qur'an and Hadith by Hussain (2011), early Muslim scholars' contribution to the psychology of mental illnesses (Badri, 2013), a compilation of Questions-and-Answers using Islamic counseling approach (Badri, 2015), and a chapter of counseling and psychotherapy from Islamic perspective (Badri, 2017).

A few books on Islamic-oriented psychiatry were also published, such as Islamic family psychology/psychiatry (Shaharom, 1989), Islamic adolescent psychology/psychiatry (Hatta, 1994), Islamic psychological medicine (Hatta, 1995), psychospiritual contemplation on Allāh's Names (Shaharom, 2009), *al-ruqyah al-shar'iyyah* (*sharī'ah*-compliant incantation) (Shaharom & Razali eds, 2018), and ethics in Islamic medicine and psychiatry (Shaharom, 2020). All these various publications on Islamic counseling Islamic clinical psychology, and Islamic psychiatry combined have contributed to clinical applications of Islamic psychology, particularly on clinical prevention.

Other than the above, below are some of the selected examples of primary-prevention activities utilizing the model of Islamic psychology. The prevention exercises consider the spiritual (soul) as a central role in explaining the behaviors and helps one to achieve a good life (refer to Figures 1 and 2).

Primary-Universal Prevention Using Islamic Psychology

Example 1: International Islamic University Malaysia Framework for Mental and Spiritual Health (The IHSĀN - IIUM Haikal li al-Ṣiḥḥah al- 'Aqliyyah wa al-Nafsiyyah)

The International Islamic University Malaysia (IIUM) views a person with good mental health as an individual who exhibits characteristics of *insan sejahtera* – one whose physiological, psychological, and spiritual dimensions are balanced and harmonious. It describes the status of *sejahtera* as a balanced and harmonious way of life that is underpinned by the promotion and preservation of life, intellect, lineage, wealth, and faith, which is in accordance with *al-Maqāṣid al-Sharī'ah*. By enhancing the person's awareness of their relationship with Allāh, the *sejahtera* way of life promotes and preserves *al-Maqāṣid al-Sharī'ah*. This, in turn, enables the person to function well with their ecological, cultural, and socio-economical surroundings (Razak, 2019b). The concept of *insan sejahtera* is in line with WHO's constitution, whereby "health is a state of complete physical, mental, and social wellbeing and not merely the absence of disease or infirmity" (WHO, 2022).

IIUM ensures the sustainability of mental health coordination through the IIUM Framework for Mental and Spiritual Health (i.e., The *IHSĀN - IIUM Haikal li al-Ṣiḥḥah al- 'Aqliyyah wa al-Nafsiyyah*) (IIUM, 2022a). Under this framework, there are the IIUM Employee Mental Health Policy 2021, the IIUM Student Mental Health Policy 2021, and the Standard Operating Procedures for Emergency Cases. The framework outlines mental health areas of action with a wide range of commitments: i) preventive initiatives and promotion of mental wellbeing, ii) providing services for those in need of mental health help, iii) advocacy of mental health issues, iv) training and research, and v) governance of the mental health agenda within the University (IIUM, 2022a).

One of the unique features of *IHSĀN* and in line with the model of Islamic psychology (refer Figure 1 and 2) is the incorporation of Centre for Islamization (CENTRIS) as one of its permanent agencies (IIUM, 2022a). CENTRIS plays a role in enhancing the mental health needs of the IIUM community members in the preventive, post-standard intervention stages, and advocacy. CENTRIS has also established an *'Ilāj* and *Irshād* Unit (i.e., Treatment and Guidance Unit) to cater to spirituality-related illnesses attributed to supernatural causes, which are beyond medical or scientific investigation processes. Other permanent agencies of *IHSĀN* are i) Counselling and Career Services Centre, Department of Educational Psychology; and ii) Counselling, Department of Psychiatry and Mental Health, Department of Psychology, and IIUM Health and Wellness Centre (IIUM, 2022a).

Example 2: IIUM Sejahtera Profiling by the IIUM's Counselling and Career Services Centre Counseling and Career Services Centre of IIUM uses IIUM Sejahtera Profiling (ISP), a screening tool to detect early mental health symptoms.

It has three dimensions that indicate one's psychological condition: i) integrated mind (I-mind – mental health), ii) coping, and iii) propensity towards spirituality. It is a web-based application that is easily accessed by the IIUM community and takes approximately 10 to 15 minutes to complete all questions with quick results (IIUM, 2021).

New students are invited to fill out the ISP, and the results will be emailed to them. Students may discuss the results with a psychology officer by booking an appointment through the student portal (IIUM, 2021). For students who need urgent attention, a psychology officer will reach out to them within a week to confirm their *sejahtera* status and provide psychosocial support for five-to-six sessions, including crisis management for self-harm and suicidality. The support that is in line with the model of Islamic psychology (refer to Figures 1 and 2) includes a discussion on Islamic spiritual-based coping (i.e., the relationship between the individual person with themselves, with Allāh, with other human beings, and the world at large). The team plans to translate the ISP into both the Arabic and Malay languages and develop a preventive intervention module that is based on the various ISP domains (N. S. M. Munir, personal communication, June 29, 2022).

Example 3: Other Islamic Religiosity/Spirituality Measurements

Assessment tools measuring a person's religiosity/spirituality provide an objective measure of a subjective experience. Researchers can assess the relationship between spirituality and religion with mental health or general wellbeing (Hill & Pargament, 2008). In line with the model of Islamic psychology (refer to Figures 1 and 2), this can help guide prevention strategies, be it in primary, secondary, or tertiary. At an individual level, the ability to assess one's religiosity or spirituality level would be helpful, especially during counseling or therapy sessions. There has been an increase in measurements of Islamic religiousness in the last three decades. Most measures are theoretically sound and reliable but in need of further work to achieve good external and predictive validity (Abu-Raiya & Hill, 2014). Table 2 below provides examples of Islamic religiosity/spirituality measurements.

Table 2. *Examples of measurements of Islamic religiosity/spirituality*

Scale	Year	Authors	No of item	Country	Remarks
Hatta Islamic Religiosity Scale (HIRS-96)[a]	1996	Shaharom	27 items	Malaysia	Islamic knowledge and practice
Muslim Attitudes Toward Religion Scale (MARS)[b]	1997	Wilde & Joseph	14 items	UK	Islamic tenets, beliefs, and practices

Attitudes Towards Islam Scale[b]	2002	Sahin & Francis	23 items	UK	Based on Attitude towards Christianity Scale (Francis, 1987) - affective response to Islamic religiosity
Islamic Religious Orientation Scale (IROS)[b]	2003	Azarba ijani	70 items	Iran	Creeds/ rituals and morals
Pakistani Religious Coping Practices Scale (PRCPS)[b]	2006	Khan & Watson	8 items	Pakistan	Religious coping
Muslim Religiosity-Personality Inventory (MRPI)[b]	2006	Krauss, Azimi, Rumay a & Jamalia h	102 items	Malaysia	Islamic worldview and religious personality
The Religiosity of Islam Scale (RoIS)[b]	2007	Jana-Masri & Priester	19 items	USA	Belief and behaviour
Islamic Doctrinal Orthodoxy[b]	2007	Ji & Ibrahi m	8 items	Indonesia	Central belief of Islamic dogma intrinsic-extrinsic religious orientation concept and religious quest

The Psychological Measure of Islamic Religiousness (PMIR)[b]	2007	Abu-Raiya et al.	60 items	Israel/ USA	Multi-item (Belief, ethical conduct, religious conversion, coping, punishing & reappraisal, struggle, duty)
Sahin Index of Islamic Moral Values (SIIMV)[b]	2008	Francis et al.	17 items	UK	*Akhlāq* or *adab* (moral values)
Knowledge-Practice Measure of Islamic Religiosity (KPMIR)[b]	2008	Alghorani	100 items	USA	Knowledge and practice
Brief Arab Religious Coping Scale (BARCS)[b]	2008	Amer, Hovey, Fox & Rezcallah	15 items	USA	Religious coping
Short Muslim Belief and Practice Scale (Short-MBPS)[b]	2009	AlMarri, Oei & Al-Adawi	13 items	Australia	Belief and practice
Islamic Religiosity Scale (IRS)[b]	2009	Tillioui ne, Cummi ns & Davern	11 items	Algeria	Religious practice and religious altruism

Five Dimensions of Muslim Religiosity Scale[c]	2014	El-Menouar	22 items	German	Glock's multidimensional concept of religiosity
Multidimensional Measure of Islamic Spirituality (MMS)[d]	2014	Dasti & Sitwat	75 items	Pakistan	Multidimensional (self-discipline, quest, behaviour, self-aggrandizement, connectedness, meanness-generosity, tolerance, and practices).
IIUM Religiosity Scale (IIUMReIS) [c]	2016	Mahudin, Noor, Dzulkifli, & Janon	10 items	Malaysia	Iman, Islam, Ihsan
Muslim Daily Religiosity Assessment Scale (MUDRAS) [c]	2016	Olufadi	21 items	Nigeria	Religious behaviour
Spiritual Health Questionnaire[d]	2021	Jaberi, Momennasab, Cheraghi,	47 items	Iran	Connectedness, moderation, spiritual striving, transcendence, purpose

Yektat alab, & Ebadi	seeking, faith

Notes:
[a](Salleh& Hatta, 2000)
[b](Abu-Raiya & Hill, 2014)
[c](Mahudin et al., 2016)
[d](Jaberi et al., 2021)

Example 4: Mental Health Promotion during COVID-19 by IIUM Mental Health and Psychosocial Care Team (IMPaCT)

The compulsory lockdown during the COVID-19 pandemic contributes to various mental health issues, such as social isolation, fears and rumination, stress, anxiety, depression, and trauma. The IMPaCT was established to help reorient the IIUM community towards the application of psychosocial-spiritual knowledge and skills in responding to COVID-19 (Global RCE Network, 2020) in line with the model of Islamic psychology (refer to Figure 1 and 2). Psychosocial-spiritual education helped to develop awareness of good healthcare to reduce the transmission of COVID-19 and to cope psychologically. This was delivered through infographic posters, comic art illustrations, articles, videos, and web content (refer IMPaCT, n.d.a), which includes Islamic spiritual fitness (refer IMPACT, n.d.b).

Distressed staff and students were offered e-psychosocial support and peer support groups. Until October 2020, about 300 e-psychosocial support sessions were conducted through various online platforms, with WhatsApp, Telegram, and Google Meet being the most used medium (refer IMPaCT, n.d.a). Because of this initiative, IMPaCT was awarded the Honourable Mention RCE Recognition Award 2020 by the Regional Centre of Expertise on Education for Sustainable Development, acknowledged by the United Nations University (IIUM, 2022b).

Example 5: Universiti Teknologi MARA (UiTM) Mental Health Promotion Activities

Mental health awareness needs to reach all levels of society. Outreach efforts include carnivals, mass event gatherings, public/online talks, and social media engagement (Shahwan et al., 2022). A hybrid health

31

carnival was organized by the Universiti Teknologi MARA (UiTM) based on the Health Belief Model, where they focused on the perceived susceptibility (mental illness knows no boundaries), severity (mental illness is a silent killer), benefits (productivity with good mental health), and barriers (It's OK to seek help). Almost 80% of the 515 participants were virtual participants. They broadcasted the opening and closing ceremony speech, which included positive messages about mental health, a forum featuring a mental health professional and a Muslim scholar to understand mental illness from a more holistic perspective (in line with the model of Islamic psychology – refer Figure 1 and 2), educational posters, videos on social media, and quizzes. There were screening opportunities available for a free online therapy session. They reported 5,585 hits on Facebook for all activities. Participants completed a baseline self-assessment of their mental health knowledge before and after the 2-day event demonstrating a significant improvement in the mean knowledge scores (p=0.001), with a mean paired difference of 2.56 (CI: 1.90, 3.23) (Ruzlin et al., 2021).

Example 6: Mental Health Awareness Through Literature

Creative ways of mental health promotion should continue to be encouraged. The 1980s saw Malaysian Muslim mental health professionals writing non-fiction academic-professional books related to psychology and psychiatry. Issues related to mental health and mental disorders are discussed, along with their prevention and management. By the 1990s, creative writing related to Islamic psychology and psychiatry started to appear on the horizon of the landscape of Malay Muslim literature. The momentum picked up by the turn of the century. Reports and articles on psychological issues in mainstream media became a rising trend well accepted by the reading public. One of the many examples is Hamid (2019), who published in a local newspaper his article on pseudo-psychology by traditional healers.

These efforts are meant to attract the younger generation and the learned community to the realities, challenges, and hope in managing mental health and illness. The latest books of non-fiction and creative writing are listed below (Table 3). Creative writing, like poetry (*puisi* in Malay), which includes *pantun* (a Malay verse form, also imitated in French and English, with a rhyme scheme a-b-a-b), is among the many ways to promote mental health.

Table 3: *Sample of literature with mental health messages and in line with model of Islamic psychology (refer to Figure 1 and 2)*

Majnun	A story about espionage with a mental health message (Razali, 2020).
Depresi	A book that discusses depression in layperson language and addresses the myths and misunderstandings pertaining to religion and depression (e.g., weak *Īmān* as a cause of mental illness, *jinn* possession, and traditional healing vs. Islamic medicine) (Razali, 2018).
Medical Wisdom & Ar-Ruqyah Ash-Shar'iyyah	An academic book based on studies that elucidate spiritual issues related to mental health and ill health. It includes the integration of spiritual intervention, namely *sharī'iah*-compliant incantation and contemporary psychiatric intervention (Shaharom & Razali, 2018).
Istiqāmah: Jalan Ke Arah-Nya	This book discusses 11 praiseworthy characteristics of the soul on the path to God, including the way to cleanse the soul (Shaharom, 2018).
Etika Perubatan Islam dan Isu-isu Psikiatri	A book on Islamic medical ethics and psychiatric issues which includes Islamic psychology, psychiatry, and medical law (Shaharom, 2020).
Saudara Sedarah Satu Sejarah	A book of 101 poems and 101 colored photos taken by the author that includes four poems on psychology, five poems on psychology-related medicine, and a few other psychology-related verses (Shaharom, 2022).

Examples of Primary-Selective Prevention using Islamic Psychology

Example 1: Customized Suicide-Prevention Programmes in Muslim Communities

The Muslim Mental Health and Islamic Psychology Lab, Stanford University School of Medicine, developed the Muslim Community – Suicide Response Manual (Stanford Medicine, 2022). The initiative was in response to the high suicide attempt rate among Muslims in the US because they are a religious minority group at risk of religious discrimination but may access mental health services more infrequently than other faith communities (Awaad et al., 2021a).

The Manual is customized for the Muslim community and covers the spectrum of prevention, intervention, and postvention of managing suicide, and it is in line with the model of Islamic psychology (refer to Figures 1 and 2). The manual incorporates Qur'anic verses, and some topics include the value of human life in Islam, balancing science, and faith, addressing cultural mental health stigma, the Islamic mandate to intervene, and the Islamic responsibility of the community member (Awaad, 2021b).

Focusing on the prevention domain, Maristan.org (i.e., institution of healing), a non-governmental organization supported by the Stanford Muslim Mental Health & Islamic Psychology Lab's research work, advocates on the Muslim community suicide response. Based on the evidence-based Suicide Response Manual, they conducted Suicide Response Training for 500 Religious Leaders (via 500 Imam Campaign 2021) and Suicide Prevention Sermons/Khutbah (Awaad, 2021b; Maristan, n.d.).

Example 2: Designing and Evaluating Mental Health Prevention Programme for At-Risk Populations as part of the Teaching and Learning of PSYC 4240 Clinical Psychology, Bachelor of Human Sciences in Psychology (Honours), IIUM.

Part of the assessment for PSYC 4240 Clinical Psychology is to develop and conduct a community-based mental health prevention program among people who are identified to be at risk of developing mental health issues in the population, e.g., young adults, and women. The assessment is designed to achieve the learning outcomes of the course, i.e., organize various assessment and intervention methods in clinical psychology and propose solutions to current mental health problems by utilizing Islamic principles (Iqbal, 2017).

The design and evaluation of the prevention program followed the guidelines by Lee and Hunsley (2018), and it is integrated with the model of Islamic psychology (refer to Figures 1 and 2).

1. Identify the target. What do you want to prevent?
2. Determine how serious the problem is. How many people are affected? What are the costs of the problem, in human suffering, health care costs, etc.?
3. Review the research evidence about the problem. What do you know about how the risk factors develop? What variables make it more likely that a problem will develop?
4. Identify high-risk groups.
5. What is known about protective factors? These are the factors that have been shown to moderate risk.
6. Design the intervention. How will the target condition be prevented? Is there an evidence-based prevention program for this problem? If so, does it need to be modified for your community?
7. Design the study. How will you know if the intervention is efficacious?

(Lee & Hunsley, 2018, p. 219)

During the COVID-19 pandemic, there were concerns about the increasing distress among all levels of the population. The restrictions on public gatherings led to innovative approaches to conducting prevention programs online. Below are some of the highlighted prevention programs designed and evaluated since 2020.

Table 4: Selective prevention program utilizing Islamic psychology designed and evaluated:

Authors (Year)	Title of the Programme	Findings
Aziz et al. (2020a)	The effectiveness of an online psychospiritual gratitude-listing prevention program on young women's stress during COVID-19 Malaysia.	Intensive two-week daily gratitude listing integrated with Islamic spiritual elements brought a significant impact in reducing stress among targeted participants during the pandemic and further highlights the utility of incorporating spirituality into traditional prevention interventions.
Aziz et al. (2020b)	The effectiveness of psychospiritual mindfulness strategies in enhancing psychological flexibility & self-compassion and reducing psychological distress among young Muslim adults during COVID-19.	Intensive two-week intervention of psychospiritual mindfulness strategies is effective in enhancing psychological flexibility and self-compassion and reducing psychological distress. Qualitative analysis found that the program was labeled as a helpful stress management strategy, enhancing mental wellbeing, and relaxation.

Examples of Primary-Indicated Prevention utilizing Islamic Psychology

Example 1: Developing and Evaluating Effectiveness of Islamic Spiritual Enhancement Module (ISEM) among University Students Who Are Stressful

Faris et al. (2021) and Khaiyom et al. (2021a) developed and ran the Islamic Spiritual Enhancement Module (ISEM) among IIUM university students who were stressed. The module comprised seven different topics covering stress from psychological perspectives and ways to manage it from Islamic spiritual perspectives. Referring to Table 4 for the information on ISEM program, the effective ways to manage stress from Islamic spiritual perspectives include i) psychoeducation on stress and mental health from the Islamic perspective, ii) *dhikr*, *Qur'ānic*, and *awrād* recitation practices, iii) conducting *khalwah* and *muhāsabah*. The modules were delivered in six 2.5 hours sessions weekly. Twenty-one students with mild to severe levels of stress attended the program. Measures used to assess the effectiveness were the Stress Scale from Depression Anxiety and Stress Scale-42 (DASS), Perceived Stress Scale-10, WHO Quality of Life-BREF, and IIUM Religiosity Scale. The assessment was conducted using all the measures before and after the program, except DASS-Stress was measured in every session to monitor the process of change. The results found that only the scores of the DASS-Stress Scale were significantly reduced, and the effect size was large ($d=1.38$). The starting and continuous reductions of stress symptoms were clear after the Islamic spiritual components were delivered to the participants in Session 2 (i.e., psychoeducation on stress and mental health from the Islamic perspective and *dhikr* recitation) (refer to Figure 4). Based on the participants' subjective feedback, the three most effective strategies in alleviating stress using ISEM are the recitation of *dhikr*, *awrād*, and Qur'anic verses. Psychoeducation of stress and mental health from the Islamic perspective was also found to assist the participants in accepting that stress and struggles are part of life and, therefore, it is normal to feel stress. Despite the promising results, future research is suggested to improve the program by incorporating more sensitive outcome measures on spirituality and quality of life as part of the psychoeducation component.

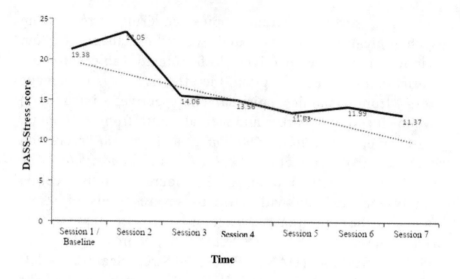

Figure 3. *Estimated Marginal Mean Scores of the DASS-Stress Scale for Seven Sessions of the Program*

Example 2: Developing and Evaluating Integrated Islamic Psychospiritual Acceptance and Commitment Therapy (i-ACT For Life) for At-Risk Young Adults during COVID-19 Pandemic

Khaiyom et al. (2022) developed i-ACT for Life, an integrated Islamic psychospiritual Acceptance and Commitment Therapy-based prevention program to reduce psychological distress in at-risk young adults in Malaysia during the COVID-19 pandemic. The contents of the module are outlined in Table 5. The study was also preregistered at ClinicalTrials.gov (NCT04870385). Purposive sampling was used to recruit university students studying in Malaysia (*N*=93, 78% female) aged 18-29 years old. Participants were randomized to either receive the prevention program (*n*=46) or be wait-listed (*n*=47). The contents were delivered online using a cloud-based instant messaging service. The participants were contacted once to twice daily (except on Sunday) for five weeks, using micro-content messages in infographic and audio-visual materials. The outcomes assessed were anxiety, stress, depression, self-compassion, psychological flexibility, and resilience. They were asked to complete assessments at pre-intervention, mid-intervention, post-intervention, and 1-month follow-up. Based on the intention-to-treat analyses using the last observation carried forward, significant between-group effects at post-intervention and follow-up ($p<.05$), and a significant overall effect of time across the four time points ($p<.001$) was found. Findings suggest that web-based prevention programs are effective in preserving the mental health of young Muslim adults in Malaysia during the pandemic and support the integration of Islamic spiritual elements into traditional cognitive-behavioral and mindfulness techniques to improve the acceptability of mental health interventions.

Table 5: *Information on the ISEM Program summarized from Khaiyom et al. (2021b)*

Week	Module	Content	Activities	Homework
1	1. Psychoeducation on Stress	• Definition of Stress • Types of Stress • Symptoms of Stress • Coping Strategies	• Stress Tracker • Stress Symptoms Checklist • Mindful Breathing	Complete Stress Tracker Table developed based on Cognitive-Behavioral Approach, daily
2	2. Stress and Mental Health from Islamic Perspective	• Main Tenets in Islamic Spirituality • Illnesses and Mental Health Problems from Islamic Perspectives • Treatments of Mental Health Issues from Islamic Perspectives	Assessing Positive and Negative Qualities from a Situation	-
	3. *Dhikr* (Remembrance of Allāh)	• Definition of *Dhikr* • Forms of *Dhikr* • *Dhikr* as a Protective Factor of Stress	*Dhikr* Recitation Practice	Recite selected *Dhikr* every day based on the recommendations/ guideline provided Complete *Dhikr* Checklist

3	4. Qurān	• Qurān and Heart Purification • Reciting Qurān and its Importance	Qurānic Recitation Practice	On top of continuing the previous homework. Participants also: • Recite selected Qurānic verses every day based on the recommendations/ guideline provided • Complete Qurān Checklist
4	5. *Awrād* (Spiritual Litany)	• Definition of *Awrād* • *Awrād* and *Dhikr*: What is the Difference?	*Awrād* Recitation Practice	On top of continuing the previous homework. Participants also: • Recite selected *Awrād* every day based on the recommendations/ guideline provided • Complete *Awrād* Checklist
5	6. *Khalwah* (Seclusion/ Solitude)	• Definition of *Khalwah* • Benefits of *Khalwah* and Its Relation to Stress	• Discussion on What Do We Do during *Khalwah* • Discussion on *Khalwah's* Condition	On top of continuing the previous homework. • Participants also: Practice *Khalwah* based on the recommendations/ guideline provided • Complete *Khalwah* Checklist
6	7. *Muhāsabah* (Self-Introspection)	• Definition of *Muhāsabah* • Visiting the Sick and its *Adab* • Visiting the Graves and its *Adab*	• Listening to Tazkirah at the Graveyard • Doing Reflections on the Activity	On top of continuing the previous homework. Participants also: • Write down their reflections on the activity conducted
7	-	-	• Reflect-ions on the ISEM Program • Sharing of Results on their weekly stress level	-

			• Discussion on the plan to continue the skills learned

Table 6: *Summary of i-ACT For Life Module*

No.	Module	Summary/ Aim	Example of ACT Exercise	Example of Islamic Psychospiritual Elements
1.	Grounding	Noticing thoughts and feelings, slowing down, and connecting with the body, and paying attention to the present moment.	Mindful breathing exercises	*Khushu'* mindful *dhikr* and mindful wuḍū exercises
2.	Unhooking	Noticing and naming difficult thoughts or feelings and then distancing from them.	Notice, Name, and Refocus 3-step exercise	Reflections on relevant Qur'ānic verses (al-Baqarah 2:216) and authentic hadith (Sahih al-Bukhari, Hadith 2528)
3.	Acting on Your Values	Choosing important values and picking one small way to act according to these values.	Improving an existing personal relationship by acting on a chosen value	Reflections on relevant Qur'ānic verses (al-Baqarah 2:177) and value-setting as a Muslim
4.	Being Kind	Noticing pain in the self and others and responding with kindness.	Self-talk kindness exercise	Reflections on relevant Qur'ānic verses (Maryam 19:47) and authentic hadith (Sahih al-Bukhari, Hadith 13 & Sunan Abi Dawud, Hadith 494)
5.	Making Room	Noticing and naming difficult thoughts or feelings	Making room exercise	Reflection on authentic hadith (al-Nawawi, Riyad al-

41

| and allowing them to come and go. | Salihin, 927 & Sahih Musli, 924) |
| | Reflection on Rumi's *The Guest House* |

Clinical Applications of Islamic Psychology in Secondary Prevention

Secondary prevention aims to lower the rate of illness in the population or established cases of the disorder (prevalence) through early detection and treatment of diagnosable diseases (WHO, 2004). The manifestation and progression of a mental disorder can be halted by secondary preventions. The main components of this phase of public health intervention include screening, early identification or detection, and prompt intervention. As far as mental health service is concerned, in general, the existing clinical methods to implement secondary prevention are considered beneficial and sufficient. When Islamic psychology is brought into the discussion of secondary prevention, the utmost priority is not to reinvent the methods but to analyze and criticize the current 'un-Islamic' mentality and behaviors which are camouflaged by 'Islamic' labeling.

This section of the chapter aims to highlight several issues pertaining to secondary prevention strategies, namely screening, early detection, and prompt intervention within the context of Islamic psychology. In some of the sub-headings, a case report is included. Important propositions are made and, albeit bold and radical, merit honest assessment and critical discussion.

Screening

General practitioners and primary healthcare providers are the gatekeepers for mental healthcare services. The rise of psychiatric cases in primary health care and the increasing trend of referral to tertiary specialist centers were thought to be partly because of the increased awareness among primary healthcare personnel and their capability to detect mental health disorders. The ever-improving psychiatric screening scales and the rigorous effort of academics to validate Western-based instruments in local languages contribute to this feat.

There is also increased awareness among the general population, to some extent, thanks to the efforts in primary prevention. The fight against stigmatization continues in various areas, such as in education (i.e., programs in schools, colleges, and universities), in media (i.e., engagement with reporters, integrative workshops with filmmakers, etc.), in various industries (i.e., as part of corporate social responsibilities), and in religious institutions.

In any Muslim society, as in Malaysia, a group of well-intending pious men and women will practice faith healing. This form of service caters to symptoms that represent mental health issues, among other things. As Razali and Tahir (2018) discussed, this service would never be short of patrons but inevitably will lead to more confusion among the public because of the vague definition of what constitutes 'Islamic Medicine' and the lack of proper regulations. However, faith healers, for their sheer popularity and accessibility, can play an important role in the screening of mental health issues. With the awareness and the acceptance that mental illnesses need proper immediate treatment, faith healers would fulfill the required *Maqasid al-Shari`iyyah* to preserve life and sanity by being the valuable gatekeepers (i.e., screening agents). The main challenge, though, is to get the religious authorities, under whom jurisdiction the faith healers belong, and the modern psychiatry practitioners, to agree and accept one ultimate definition of Islamic psychology.

Early detection

Early treatment of severe mental illnesses such as schizophrenia and bipolar mood disorder makes up for a good prognosis. The longer the delay of the first treatment of the illness, the worse the outcome. Similar to screening, faith healers play a profound role in preventing delay in seeking mental health treatment.

When a 40-year-old lady developed symptoms of Major Depressive Disorder and sought the assistance of multiple faith healers, to no avail, the illness escalated to psychosis after a year duration. Only then she became in contact with psychiatric service, and she went into remission after a few months of adequate treatment. In the early phase of her psychiatric care, she was fortunate to meet a faith healer who encouraged her to do *Ar-Ruqyah Ash-Shar'iyyah* on her own and motivated her to comply with the hospital treatment (Razali, Rahman, & Husin, 2018). A prevalence study by Abdullah et al. (2017) demonstrated a marked percentage of undiagnosed mentally ill clients who had faith healers as their first point of treatment-seeking endeavors. Most of the clients attributed their illnesses to supernatural, demonic causes.

The above case report and prevalence study demonstrated the significant influence faith healers exerted in the Muslim community. They can tip the scale considerably, and it is paramount for the psychiatric fraternity to investigate this untapped strength in the realm of mental health care promotion. The knowledge, attitude, and practice of the faith healers impact Muslim decision-making to get help for their mental illness symptoms. There was a study on this, and the attitude toward mental illness among Muslim faith healers was mixed at least (Saad, Razali, Sanip, & Rani, 2018).

Prompt Intervention

As discussed previously, what Khadijah RA did during the vital moment of the prophecy can be considered prompt intervention (i.e., the basic secondary interventions). Khadijah RA listens attentively without interruption, avoids denying the negative emotion or adding the feeling of guilt, and strengthens the self-concept. She also knew her limitation, and she referred the matter to the expert, Waraqah bin Naufal.

Some Malaysian universities incorporate Islamic psychology during the training of medical and psychology students at the undergraduate and postgraduate levels. Among the topics discussed are stigma and religio-cultural misunderstandings of mental illness. Controversial issues like the role and management of weakness of *īmān* (faith), demonic possession, and suicide that are associated with mental illness are addressed.

These efforts would prepare a future generation of Muslim doctors and mental health professionals who are grounded in *naqlī* (divine) and *'aqli* (scientific) knowledge. They would hopefully be confident to address the religio-cultural quandaries that are faced by their patients and clients (Shaharom & Razali, 2018). Muslim mental health practitioners who are holistic and integrated in their knowledge and training would be competent enough to manage their patients appropriately, at least during the earliest phases of the illness. They would not waste time and be lost in the choices of faith healers that they want to refer their patients to.

In applied Islamic psychology, one would benefit from the application of *al-dalīl al-qat'īy* and *al-dalīl al-ẓannīy*. While believing in the existence of the *jinn* is definitive (i.e., *qat'īy*), understanding and perceiving how the *jinn* disturbs humans has been debatable in Islamic history. There were many reputable scholars, such as Fakhruddin ar-Razi, who believed that the human being could not be possessed by the *jinn*. In this context, the *dalīl* is *ẓannīy*.

However, some Muslims, including contemporary influential shaikhs, believe that the phenomenon of *jinn* possession is indisputable (Shaharom & Razali, 2018). Evidence-based medicine and psychiatry have demonstrated that antipsychotics could effectively treat a disorganized and agitated patient suffering from schizophrenia. Instances of *dalīl naqlī* like this would help the Muslim ummah to consider the other causes of abnormal behavior. Believing that the *jinn* is the only agent that wreaks havoc in the lives of righteous members of the ummah is a parochial attitude that must be debunked. Instead, the holistic approach to mental disorders must be pursued. This includes focusing attention on the neurobiological (e.g., the treatment of a diseased brain) and psychospiritual (the reinforcement of the defense against Satan) domains of life.

It must be mentioned that one of the authors (Shaharom, M. H.) had the experience of treating Muslim patients (including those who appeared to be influenced by spiritual beings or were charmed) with Islamic psychospiritual therapy (Islamic PST) without the use of drugs. On other occasions, Islamic PST was instituted as an adjunct therapy to pharmacotherapy.

With a clear definition and practical application, Islamic psychology would continue to be the essential component of psychiatry and clinical psychology. The series of intellectual discourses that have commenced involving the clinicians (i.e., Islamic psychiatrists and clinical psychologists) and the *shaikhs* (i.e.,

Islamic scholars and faith healers) must be further improved for Islamic psychology to be an effective reality. There must be sincerity and humility on all sides. Arrogance and haughtiness, a blameworthy characteristic of Satan, will only devastate the *ukhuwwah* among the various parties of Muslims concerned. It would also render Islamic psychology devoid of its psychospiritual, neurobiological, and social credibility needed by the *ummah*.

Clinical Applications of Islamic Psychology in Tertiary Prevention

Tertiary prevention includes interventions that reduce disability, enhance rehabilitation, and prevent relapses and recurrences of the illness. The socio-environmental determinants involve social participation, social responsibility and tolerance, social support, and community networks (WHO, 2004).

During the time of the Prophet Muhammad SAW, Anas RA reported that a woman had a partial derangement in her mind, so she said. "Allāh's Messenger, I want something from you." He said: "Mother of so and so, see on which side of the road you would like (to stand and talk) so that I may do the needful for you." He stood aside with her on the roadside until she got what she needed (Reported by Muslim, no. 2326).

As illustrated in the Hadith, providing support for a mental health survivor is an important factor in mental illness prevention in a community setting. Another example is providing support for survivors of suicide. Previous studies have indicated that suicide attempts and rates among Muslims are low (Lester, 2006), and Islam has been identified as a protective factor against suicide. However, recent studies have suggested the contrary. Awaad et al. (2021a) reported suicidal attempt was higher among American Muslims compared to other faith communities. Eleven out of forty-six Muslim-majority countries had an age-adjusted suicide rate above the global average (Lew et al., 2022). It has been suggested that suicide rates in Muslim-majority countries have been underreported due to the stigma attached to suicide (Lester, 2006).

Postvention in the Muslim Community Suicide Response Manual refers to interventions conducted after a suicide, aiming to reduce suicide contagion and support the bereaved (Awaad et al., 2021c). A vital aspect of postvention is understanding suicide in Islam. Although Islam condemns suicide as mentioned in the Qur'ān (4: 29-30), suicide referred to in these verses is suicide conducted with hostility and a will to do wrong (Awaad et al., 2021c). On the other hand, the minds of most individuals who die by suicide are often unclear, compounded further by mental illness. Hence, the fate of the deceased is only known to Allāh and is not for others to judge. Thus, the focus during such challenging times should be on healing and preventing suicide contagion. The manual further recommends the postvention process based on the timing from the day of the suicide event, as summarised in Table 7.

Table 6. *The postvention process from the day of suicide event*

Day	Actions
0 (day of the event)	Express sympathy when meet the family of the deceased. Listen to the family's emotions. Offer referrals to mental health service providers. Offer to provide food.
1	Look out for other individuals at risk of suicide. Dissemination of information (information that family allows being shared while avoiding exact details of suicide)
2-14	Informing the broader community (draft letter) Arrangement of *janāzah* Healing circles separated by age and gender. Postvention *khutbah*

| Long term | Memorialization of the deceased - similar to when the dead had died through other means |
| | Community healing sessions - attended by individuals aged 10 and above. |

Another area in tertiary prevention reported by Ardinata et al. (2021) was for individuals with schizophrenia. Schizophrenia is a chronic illness associated with substantial disability and has a worldwide prevalence ranging between 4 and 7 per 1,000 persons (Saha et al., 2005). Charlson (2018) reported an increased disease burden for schizophrenia, particularly in middle-income countries. The non-adherence rate to pharmacotherapy among individuals affected by the disease was as high as 56% (Semahegn et al., 2020).

To address this problem, Ardinata et al. (2021) conducted an intervention study of Islamic Spiritual Mindfulness Therapy delivered through an Android-based app for improving drug adherence among patients with schizophrenia. The adherence rate for individuals in the intervention group was significantly higher compared to the control group. The intervention comprised three Islamic spiritual mindfulness sessions conducted in 6 weeks, focusing on training the study participants to be fully aware of the body, mind, feeling, and behaviour through *murāqabah*, *muhasabah*, repentance, and *tawakkul*. Problem solving, being calm, having compassion, and respecting himself were some of the elements of the intervention. Information about schizophrenia and drug adherence was also incorporated into the intervention.

Conclusion

Before further concluding remarks are made, it is essential that Freudian principles and Western psychology are briefly commented upon. The anti-God and anti-religion psychology of Freud eradicates any possible understanding of the self's ability to achieve the *maqām* (station) of *al-qalb al-salīm* (the sound heart), i.e., the heart that is sound and unblemished which is indicated in the Qur'ān (26:89). As compared to half a century ago, today many contemporary Malaysian Muslim mental health workers view Freudian psychology with great reproval. In the future, the influence of Freudian psychology among these critical Muslims would be negligible or even be reduced to naught.

A number of approaches in Western psychology that are silent about God and Godliness can be a benefit to Muslims. However, great caution must be taken not to compromise Islamic principles that enrich the self and society.

As has been mentioned above, the objectives of the Islamic Law (al-Maqāṣid al-Sharī'ah) are meant to preserve and protect (i) the religion (al-dīn); (ii) the life (al-nafs); (iii) the intellect (al-'aql); (iv) the lineage (al-naṣl); (v) the wealth (al-māl).

Although all these five objectives (maqāṣid) are related to the human self or soul, the first three are related directly to the way humans think, feel, and know God. The promotion, preservation, and enhancement of mental health is the core business of Islamic psychological theory and practice. The future of psychology will continue to be related to these maqāṣid.

Psychology, or 'ilm al-nafs (علم النفس), is a field of knowledge governed by the religious sciences or 'ulūm al-dīn (علوم الدين). It is infused with the principle of God's Oneness or al-tauḥīd (التوحيد) within the confines of the Law of Islam, al-Sharī'ah al-Islāmiyyah (الشريعة الإسلامية).

This Oneness of God principle permeates through the whole God-conscious state of a Muslim and a believer, and with it comes the state of khushu' (خشع) which means humbled attentiveness. Thus, the believer is conscious and mindful of Allāh coupled with the praiseworthy characteristic of humility.

The conscience in the self is derived from this khushu'. This gives rise to the feeling of guilt when a wrong is done, and with the alertness of the intellect, there is a yearning of the emotion to seek forgiveness from Allāh al-Ghafūr (The Forgiving) and return to the teaching of the Prophet of Allāh SAW.

In Islamic psychology, true success is when the self can wrestle its way up from the basest station of al-nafs al-ammārah bi al-su' (the badness-commanding soul) and ascends to the station of al-nafs al-lawwāmah (the self-criticizing soul), to finally reach the peak of al-nafs al-muṭma'innah (the tranquil soul).

49

The future of Islamic psychological practice in multi-ethnic and multi-religious Malaysia depends on factors that are directly related to available governmental and private services. These, in turn, are related to the various national Acts concerning mental health services. Counseling and the various accepted modes of psychotherapy would be expected to be further advanced in the fields of behavioral and psychological medicine.

It is essential that dominant theories in Islamic psychology be generally agreed upon by the practitioners of Islamic psychology in counseling, psychological therapies, and psychiatry. This convergence in thinking would help unite the various schools of psychological thought into a cohesive front. The positiveness that is incumbent in Islamic psychology makes this universal psychology positive.

The application of psychological knowledge in the arts, nay, in all spheres of life, must be the catalyst for the flowering of true human development. By the late 1990s, multi-genre writers among Malaysian psychologists, psychiatrists, and mental health workers have published works that range from academic-professional books to creative writing, including novels, short stories, and poems. This would be expected to progress further.

While psychospiritual therapy and *al-Ruqyah al-Shar'iyyah* (الرقية الشرعية) are practised, the relevance of psychophysiology and neuropharmacology must not be overlooked. Continuous efforts at the prevention of social conflicts involving the knowledge of organizational and social behaviors would be part of the future practice of psychology.

The application of psychological methods and procedures for interviews would consist of contents that are suitable for the times and in the future. The administration or interpretation of value-laden tests of intelligence, mental abilities and disorders, neuropsychological functioning, and personality characteristics would be executed in accordance with Islamic principles.

Mental health awareness campaigns that are not directly associated with the prevention of individual and community mental illness are pointless. Psychological theories that are divorced from the skills and enhancement of healthy and balanced living would remain as assignments in academic exercises. They would not benefit the individual or society at large.

Human resilience and hope flourish with the guidance and blessing of Allāh *al-'Alīm* (The Knowing), *al-Ḥakīm* (The Wise). Blessed human life means the prevention of a hedonistic and Godless lifestyle and the total rejection of Satan. Muslim mental health workers must be able to separate the wheat from the chaff. They must have the knowledge and skills to differentiate the influence of the divine from the influence of Satan in psychology. Through divine guidance, the *ummah* would flourish and be safeguarded from anti-Islamic elements that are detrimental to its enhancement.

References

Abdullah, K. H. A., Saini, S. M., Sharip, S., & Shaharom, M. H. (2016). Seeking help at an Islamic spiritual healing centre: Malaysia's perspective. *Mental Health, Religion and Culture, 19*(7), 742–751. http://doi.org/10.1080/13674676.2016.1277986

Abdullah, K. H. A., Saini, S. M., Sharip, S., & Shaharom, M. H. (2017). Psychiatric morbidities among attenders of an Islamic spiritual healing centre in Malaysia. *International Medical Journal Malaysia, 16*(1), 75–82. http://doi.org/10.31436/imjm.v16i1.360

Alias, A. (2018, October 26-28). *Islamisation, releventisation, and integration: A guide for Islamic psychology curriculum* [Guest speaker]. The IAIP Inaugural Conference Evolving Islamic Psychology: Past, Present & Future, Istanbul Zaim University, Istanbul, Turkey.

Alias, A. (2021a). The establishment and the growth of Islamic psychology in Malaysia. In

Haque, A. & Rothman, A. (Eds.). *Islamic psychology around the globe*. International Association of Islamic Psychology. Alias, A. (2021b). Islamic-scientific social research: Philosophy, methods, issues and a proposed model. In Ariffin, A. (Ed.). *Enriching the Islamic tradition in research inquiry: Some practical guidelines in using qualitative data collection techniques* (pp.1-16). International Institute of Islamic Thought (IIIT).

Ardinata, N. A., Dwidiyanti, M., Cider, S. P., Rizki, F., Andika, T. H., Jamal, M. A., Huda, M., Maseleno, A., & Point, S. (2021). The effect of Islamic Spiritual Mindfulness Therapy on the drugs adherence of schizophrenia patients through SI-POS Android application. *International Journal of Grid and Distributed Computing, 14*(1), 305–312.

Awaad, R., El-Gabalawy, O., Jackson-Shaheed, E., alBilal, Z., Keshavarzi, H., Mogahed, D., & Altalib, H. (2021a). Suicide attempts of Muslims compared with other religious groups in the US. *JAMA Psychiatry, 78*(9), 1041-1044. doi:10.1001/jamapsychiatry.2021.1813

Awaad, R. (2021b, December 27-28). *The mental health crisis among Western Muslims* [Keynote address]. International Conference on Islamic Spiritual Care (INSPIRE) 2021, Online via Zoom. https://conference.iium.edu.my/inspire/index.php/videos/

Awaad, R., El-Gabalawy, O., Kouser, T., & Zia, B. (2021c). *The Muslim community suicide response manual: on suicide prevention, intervention and postvention, for community and religious leaders.* https://maristan.org/muslimsuicieresponse

Aziz, A. F. A., Ramizu, F. M., Aziz, A. K. A. & Khaiyom, J. H. A. (2020a). *The effectiveness of an online psychospiritual gratitude-listing prevention programme on young women's stress during COVID-19 Malaysia.* [Unpublished manuscript]

Aziz, N.N.A., Choo, S. Z. R., Faudzi, F. H. A., Amiruddin, M. M., Zaki, N. S. M., Hosna, I. N. I. M., Zulkifli, F. W., Khan, A. S. & Khaiyom, J. H. A. (2020b). *The effectiveness of psychospiritual mindfulness strategies in enhancing psychological flexibility and self-compassion and reducing psychological distress among Muslim young adults during COVID-19.* [Unpublished manuscript]

Abu-Raiya, H., & Hill, P. C. (2014). Appraising the state of measurement of Islamic religiousness. *Psychology of Religion and Spirituality, 6*(1), 22–32. http://doi.org/10.1037/a0035082

Al-Attas, S. M. N. (2001). The meaning and experience of happiness in Islam. In *Prolegomena to the metaphysics of Islam: an exposition of the fundamental elements of the worldview of Islam* (2nd ed., pp. 91-110).

International Institute of Islamic Thought and Civilization (ISTAC).

Al-Ghazali, A. H. (2010). *Kitāb sharh ʿajāʾib al-qalb* [The marvels of the heart] Book 21 of the Ihyāʾ ʿulūm al-dīn [The revival of the religious sciences] (W. J. Skellie, Trans). Fons Vitae

Al-Karam, C. Y. (2018). Islamic psychology: towards a 21st century definition and conceptual framework. *Journal of Islamic Ethics, 2*(1-2), 97-109. doi:10.1163/24685542-12340020

Badri, M. (1979). *The dilemma of Muslim psychologists.* MWH London Publishers.

Badri, M. (2000a). *The AIDS crisis: A natural product of modernity's sexual revolution.* International Institute of Islamic Thought and Civilization (ISTAC-IIUM).

Badri, M. (2000b). *Contemplation: An Islamic psychospiritual study.* Medina Books.

Badri, M. (2009). The Islamization of psychology: its "why," its "what," its "how," and its "who". In N. M. Noor, (Ed.), *Psychology from an Islamic perspective: A guide to teaching and learning* (pp. 13-42). IIUM Press.

Badri, M. (2013). *Abu Zayd al-Balkhi's sustenance of the soul: The cognitive behaviour therapy of a ninth century physician.* The International Institute of Islamic Thought (IIIT).

Badri, M. (2015). *Cyber-counselling for Muslim clients.* The Other Press.

Badri, M. (2017). *Cultural and Islamic adaptation of psychology: A book of collected articles.* Human Behaviour Academy Ltd.

Bennabi, M. (2010). *The question of ideas in the Muslim world.* Islamic Book Trust.

Charlson, F. J., Ferrari, A. J., Santomauro, D. F., Diminic, S., Stockings, E., Scott, J. G., McGrath, J. J., & Whiteford, H. A. (2018). Global epidemiology and burden of schizophrenia: findings from the Global Burden of Disease Study 2016. *Schizophrenia Bulletin, 44*(6), 1195–1203. doi:10.1093/schbul/sby058

Faris, W. F, Abdullah, F., Bahari, C. A., Mohamad, M., Abdul Razak, A. L., Abdul Khaiyom, J. H., & Abdullah Zawawi, N. A. I. (2021b). *Spiritual therapy: Islamic perspective.* International Institute for Muslim Unity, International Islamic University Malaysia, and Islamic Book Trust Kuala Lumpur.

Fiske, A., Henningsen, P., & Buyx, A. (2019). Your robot therapist will see you now: Ethical implications of embodied artificial intelligence in psychiatry, psychology, and psychotherapy. *Journal of Medical Internet Research, 21*(5), e13216. doi:10.2196/13216

Global RCE Network. (2020). RCE Greater Gombak 2020 - IIUM Mental Health and Psychosocial Care Team (IMPaCT). https://www.rcenetwork.org/portal/rce-greater-gombak-2020-14?user=1034&year=2020

Hamid, H. S. (2019, April 7). Sudut puisi: Sihir Alkemi. *Berita Harian.*

Haque, A. (Ed.). (2001). *Mental health in Malaysia: issues and concerns.* University of Malaya Press.

Hasan, A., & Alias, A. (2019, December 22). *Definition of Islamic psychology.* In Hasan, A (Chair), The Anatomy of Islamic Psychology and Counselling [Symposium], London, United Kingdom.

Hatta, S. M. (1994). *Psikologi dan kaunseling remaja.* Pertubuhan Jamaah Islah Malaysia.

Hatta, S. M. (1995). *Perubatan psikologi Islam.* Dewan Bahasa dan Pustaka.

Hill, P. C., & Pargament, K. I. (2008). Advances in the conceptualization and measurement of religion and spirituality: Implications for physical and mental health research. *Psychology of Religion and Spirituality, S* (1), 3–17. http://doi.org/10.1037/1941-1022. s.1.3

Huber, M., André Knottnerus, J., Green, L., van der Horst, H., Jadad, A. R., Kromhout, D., Leonard, B., Lorig, K., Loureiro, M. I., van der Meer, J. W. M., Schnabel, P., Smith, R., van Weel, C., & Smid, H. (2011). How should we define health? *BMJ, 343,* d4163. https://doi.org/10.1136/bmj.d4163

Huber, M., van Vliet, M., Giezenberg, M., Winkens, B., Heerkens, Y., Dagnelie, P. C., & Knottnerus, J. A. (2016). Towards a "patient-centred" operationalisation of the new dynamic concept of health: a mixed methods study. *BMJ Open, 6*(1), e010091. doi: 10.1136/bmjopen-2015-010091.

Hussain, F. (2011). *Therapy from the Qur'an and ahadith: a reference guide for character development.* Darussalam Publishers.IIUM Mental Health and Psychosocial Care Team

(IMPaCT). (n.d.a). *Emotional and psychosocial support.* https://flagship.iium.edu.my/eps/IIUM Mental Health and Psychosocial Care Team (IMPaCT). (n.d.b). *Emotional and psychosocial* *support.* https://flagship.iium.edu.my/eps/category/spiritual/

International Association of Islamic Psychology. (2022, June 24). *What is Islamic psychology?* https://www.islamicpsychology.org/what-is-islamic-psychology

International Islamic University Malaysia. (2021). *IIUM Sejahtera Profiling (ISP).* https://isp.iium.edu.my/index.php/about-isp/

International Islamic University Malaysia. (2022a). *IIUM Framework for Mental and Spiritual Health: The IHSĀN - IIUM Haikal li al-Ṣiḥḥah al- 'Aqliyyah wa al-Nafsiyyah.* International Islamic University Malaysia.

International Islamic University Malaysia. (2022b). *RCE Recognition Award 2020.* https://www.iium.edu.my/page/RCE-Recognition-Award-2020

Iqbal, M. I. M. (2009). Abnormal psychology. In N. M. Noor, (Ed.), *Psychology from an Islamic perspective: A guide to teaching and learning* (pp. 217-236). IIUM Press.

Iqbal, M. I. M. (2017). *Course outline.* In J. H. A. Khaiyom (Ed.), PSYC 4240: Clinical psychology course pack (p. 3). International Islamic University Malaysia.

Ismail, I. (1993). *Panduan asas kaunselor Muslim.* Aras Mega Sdn. Bhd.

Jaberi, A., Momennasab, M., Cheraghi, M., Yektatalab, S., & Ebadi, A. (2021). Development and psychometric evaluation of the Spiritual Health Questionnaire among Iranian Muslim adults. *Nursing and Midwifery Studies, 10*(3), 194–202. http://doi.org/10.4103/nms.nms_35_20

Jamaiyah, H. (2000). Community mental health in Malaysia: marriage of psychiatry and public health. *Jurnal Kesihatan Masyarakat, 6*(S), 155-166.

Javed, A., Lee, C., Zakaria, H., Buenaventura, R. D., Cetkovich-Bakmas, M., Duailibi, K., Azeem, M. W. (2021) Reducing the stigma of mental health disorders with a focus on low- and middle-income countries. *Asian Journal of Psychiatry, 58,* 102601. http://doi.org/10.1016/j.ajp.2021.102601

Kadir, W. H. A. A. (1994). *Kaunseling dan psikologi menurut Islam.* Kuala Lumpur: Dewan Bahasa dan Pustaka.

Kamali, M. H. (1991). *Principles of Islamic jurisprudence.* The Islamic Text Society.

Keshavarzi, H. & Ali, B. (2019). Islamic perspectives on psychological and spiritual wellbeing and treatment. In H. S. Moffic, J. Peteet, A. Z. Hankir, & R. Awaad (Eds.), *Islamophobia and psychiatry: recognition, prevention, and treatment.* Springer.

Keshavarzi, H., & Haque, A. (2013). Outlining a psychotherapy model or enhancing Muslim mental health within an Islamic context. *International Journal for the Psychology of Religion, 23,* 230-249. https://doi.org/10.1080/10508619.2012.712000

Khaiyom, J. H., Abdullah Zawawi, N. A. I, Faris, W. F, Bahari, C. A., Abdul Razak, A. L., Mohamad, M. & Abdullah, F. (2021a). *Exploring the effectiveness of Islamic Spiritual Enhancement Module (ISEM) in reducing stress among university students* [Manuscript submitted for publication]. Department of Psychology, International Islamic University Malaysia.

Khaiyom, J. H., Bahari, C. A., Abdul Razak, A. L., Faris, W. F, Mohamad, M., Abdullah, F. & Abdullah Zawawi, N. A. I. (2021b). *A manual of spiritual therapy: Islamic perspective.* International Institute for Muslim Unity, International Islamic University Malaysia.

Khaiyom, J. H., Abdul Aziz, A. F., Md. Rosli, A. N., Bahari, C. A., & Thomas Abdullah, N. S. (2022). *A randomized controlled trial to evaluate the effectiveness of an Islamic psychospiritual Acceptance Commitment Therapy-based prevention program for at-risk young adults during the COVID-19 pandemic* [Manuscript submitted for publication]. Department of Psychology, International Islamic University Malaysia.

Langgulung, H. (1983). *Teori-teori kesihatan mental: perbandingan psikologi modern dan pendekatan pakar-pakar pendidikan Islam.* Penerbit Pustaka Huda.

Lawn, S. J., Battersby, M. W., Pols, R. G., Lawrence, J. S., Parry, T., & Urukalo, M. (2007). The mental health expert patient: findings from a pilot study of a generic chronic condition self-management programme for people with mental illness. *International Journal of Social Psychiatry, 53*(1), 63-74. https://doi.org/10.1177/0020764007075010

Lee, C. M. & Hunsley, J. (2018). *Introduction to clinical psychology: an evidenced-based approach* (4th ed.). Wiley.

Lester, D. (2006). Suicide and Islam. *Archives of Suicide Research, 10*(1), 77–97. https://doi.org/10.1080/13811110500318489

Lew, B., Lester, D., Kõlves, K., Yip, P. S. F., Chen, Y.-Y., Chen, W. S., Hasan, M. T., Koenig, H. G., Wang, Z. Z., Fariduddin, M. N., Zeyrek-Rios, E. Y., Chan, C. M. H., Mustapha, F., Fitriana, M., Dolo, H., Gönültaş, B. M., Dadfar, M., Davoudi, M., Abdel-Khalek, A. M., ... Ibrahim, N. (2022). An analysis of age-standardized suicide rates in Muslim-majority countries in 2000-2019. *BMC Public Health, 22*(1), 882. https://doi.org/10.1186/s12889-022-13101-3

Lim, A., Hoek, H. W., & Blom, J. D. (2015). The attribution of psychotic symptoms to *jinn* in Islamic patients. *Transcultural Psychiatry, 52*(1), 18–32. http://doi.org/10.1177/1363461514543146

Lim, A., Hoek, H. W., Ghane, S., Deen, M., & Blom, J. D. (2018). The attribution of mental health problems to *jinn*: An explorative study in a transcultural psychiatric outpatient clinic. *Frontiers in Psychiatry, 9*, 1–7. http://doi.org/10.3389/fpsyt.2018.00089

Mahudin, N. D. M., Noor, N. M., Dzulkifli, M. A., & Janon, N. S. (2016). Religiosity among Muslims: a scale development and validation study. *Makara Human Behavior Studies in Asia, 20*(2), 109. http://doi.org/10.7454/mssh.v20i2.3492

Malek, N. A. A. (1992). *Konsep manusia menurut pandangan Islam: satu pemikiran ke arah pembentukan teori kaunseling Islam.* Arena Ilmu.

Manaf, K. A. (1995). *Kaunseling Islam: Perbandingan antara amalan dan teori kaunseling Barat.* Utusan Publications & Distributors Sdn Bhd.

Manaf, K. A. (2000). *Kaunseling Islam: Satu alternatif baru di Malaysia.* Utusan Publications & Distributors Sdn Bhd.

Maristan. (n.d.). Why religious leader training in suicide response? https://maristan.org/muslimsuicideresponse

Nisbett, R. E. (2004). *The geography of thought: how Asians and Westerners think differently and why.* Free Press.

Nor, S. Z. M. (1992). *Kaunseling perkahwinan menurut perspektif Islam.* Angkatan Belia Islam Malaysia.

Omar, M. N. (2005). *Akhlak dan kaunseling Islam.* Utusan Publications & Distributors Sdn. Bhd.

Rahman, A. B. (2008). *Perkhidmatan kaunseling: Pendekatan dalam hikmah berdakwah.* Utusan Publications & Distrubutors.

Rahman, F. (1998). *Health and medicine in the Islamic tradition: change and identity (health/medicine and the faith traditions).* ABC International Group.

Razak, A. L. A. (2018). *Terapi kesihatan mental: Teknik rawatan mental berdasarkan pengukuhan iman.* Telaga Biru.

Razak, A. L. A. (2019a). Spiritual health: Conceptual, philosophical, and practical aspect of *Īmān* Restoran Therapy. IIUM Press.

Razak, D. A. (2019b). Introduce 'sejahtera' values in education. https://www.nst.com.my/opinion/letters/2019/05/493104/introduce-sejahtera-values-

Razali, Z. A. (2018). *Depresi: terpuruk rasa ingin mati.* DuBook Press.

Razali, Z. A. (2020). *Majnun.* Buku Fixi.

Razali, Z. A., & Tahir, M. F. (2018). The role of psychiatrists and Muslim faith healers in mental health issues. *International Medical Journal Malaysia, 17*(Special Issue 1), 31–35. http://doi.org/10.31436/imjm.v17i1.1037

Razali, Z. A., Rahman, N. A. A., & Husin, S. (2018). Complementing the treatment of a major depressive disorder patient with *Ruqyah Shar 'iyyah* therapy: a Malaysian case study. *Journal of Muslim Mental Health, 12*(2). https://doi.org/10.3998/jmmh.10381607.0012.204

Rothman, A., Coyle, A. (2018). Toward a framework for Islamic psychology and psychotherapy: An Islamic model of the soul. *Journal of Religious Health, 57,* 1731–1744. https://doi.org/10.1007/s10943-018-0651-x

Ruzlin, A. N. M., Chen, X. W., Yunus, R. M., Samsudin, E. Z., Selamat, M. I., & Ismail, Z. (2021). Promoting mental health during the COVID-19 pandemic: a hybrid, innovative approach in Malaysia. *Frontiers in Public Health, 9,* 747953. http://doi.org/10.3389/fpubh.2021.747953

Sa'ad, R. A. A. M., Razali, Z. A., Sanip, S., & Rani, M. D. M. (2017). Knowledge and attitude of Malaysia's Muslim faith healers in dealing with the mentally ill. *Mental Health, Religion & Culture,* *20*(10), 1015-1027. https://doi.org/10.1080/13674676.2018.1428793

Saha, S., Chant, D., Welham, J., & McGrath, J. (2005). A systematic review of the prevalence of schizophrenia. *PLoS Medicine,* *2*(5), e141. https://doi.org/10.1371/journal.pmed.0020141

Salleh, A. (1993). *Kaunseling Islam Asas.* Utusan Publications & Distributor Sdn. Bhd.

Salleh, H., & Hatta, M. (2000). Hatta Islamic Religiosity Scale 1996 (HIRS96): a reliability and validity study. *Malaysia Journal of Psychiatry, 8*(1), 5–14.

Semahegn, A., Torpey, K., Manu, A., Assefa, N., Tesfaye, G., & Ankomah, A. (2020). Psychotropic medication non-adherence and its associated factors among patients with major psychiatric disorders: a systematic review and meta-analysis. *Systematic Reviews, 9*(1). https://doi.org/10.1186/s13643-020-1274-3

Shaharom, M. H. (1989). *Psikologi keluarga ke arah rumahtangga bahagia.* Pustaka Salam.

Shaharom, M. H. (2009). *Allāh: A psychospiritual contemplation on His names.* CERT Publications.

Shaharom, M. H., Sidi, H., Tan, M. K., Che Ngah, A., & Abdul Rahman, A.H. (2020). *Etika perubatan Islam dan isu-isu psikiatri.* Dewan Bahasa dan Pustaka.

Shaharom, M. H., & Razali, Z. A. (Eds.) (2018). *Medical Wisdom & Ar-Ruqyah Ash-Shar'iyyah.* Universiti Islam Malaysia.

Shaharom, M. H. (2018). *Istiqāmah: jalan ke arah-Nya.* Risalah Harmoni.

Shaharom, M. H. (2020). *Etika perubatan Islam dan isu-isu psikiatri.* Dewan Bahasa dan Pustaka.

Shaharom, M. H. (2022). *Saudara sedarah satu sejarah.* Dewan Bahasa dan Pustaka.

Shahwan, S., Goh, C. M. J., Tan, G. T. H., Ong, W. J., Chong, S. A., & Subramaniam, M. (2022). Strategies to reduce mental illness stigma: perspectives of people with lived experience and caregivers. *International Journal of Environmental*

Research and Public Health, 19(3), 1632. http://doi.org/10.3390/ijerph19031632

Sipon, S., & Hussin, R. (2010). *Teori kaunseling dan psikoterapi.* Universiti Sains Islam Malaysia (USIM).

Skinner, R. (2020). A beginner's guide to the concept of Islamic psychology. *Journal of the British Islamic Medical Association, 3,* 1-5.

Stanford Medicine. (2022). Muslim Mental Health and Islamic Psychology Lab - Projects. https://med.stanford.edu/mmhip/projects.html

Utz, A. (2011). *Psychology from Islamic perspective.* International Islamic Publishing House.

World Health Organization. (2004). Prevention of mental disorders: effective intervention and policy options – summary report. https://apps.who.int/iris/handle/10665/43027

World Health Organization. (2017). Mental health ATLAS 2017- member state profile – Malaysia. https://www.who.int/publications/m/item/mental-health-atlas-2017-country-profile-malaysia

World Health Organization. (2020). Basic documents. http://apps.who.int/bookorders.

World Health Organization. (2022). Constitution https://www.who.int/about/governance/constitution#:~:text=Health%20is%20a%20state%20of,belief%2C%20economic%20or%20social%20condition

CLINICAL APPLICATIONS OF TRADITIONAL ISLAMICALLY-INTEGRATED PSYCHOTHERAPY (TIIP) MODEL: CASE OF A TURKISH FEMALE

Fahad Khan, Sena Aycan,

and Hooman Keshavarzi

Introduction

Traditional Islamically-Integrated Psychotherapy (TIIP)

An Islamically integrated psychotherapy approach was initially presented in a publication by Keshavarzi and Haque, outlining a model of care based on the contributions of early Muslim scholars (Keshavarzi & Haque, 2013). Keshavarzi and Khan further developed this model and termed it "Traditional Islamically-Integrated Psychotherapy (TIIP)", with the term 'traditional' used as a qualifier for its grounding in traditional Sunni theology (Keshavarzi & Khan, 2018). A more comprehensive discussion of the epistemological and ontological foundations and TIIP's practical applications to clinical mental health practice was provided in TIIP's first major book publication with the contributions of other like-minded experts and scholars (Keshavarzi et al., 2020). TIIP has become the dominant modality of psychotherapy used in the treatment of patients for various types of problems, such as Trauma, Depression, Anxiety, Obsessive-Compulsive Disorder, and marital discord at Khalil Center, an Islamically-oriented outpatient mental health center with its international headquarters near Chicago, USA. Data collected at the Khalil Center supports its efficacy in reducing symptoms of psychological and functional distress (Keshavarzi, 2022). Under the umbrella of Khalil Center, a three-level training curriculum has been developed, with Level I as an introduction to TIIP's foundations, Level II exploring advanced application, Level III offering clinical supervision, and finally, certification. TIIP training has become hugely popular with international demand, and Levels I & II trainings have been conducted in the United States, Canada, Türkiye, and Pakistan.

Epistemology

Although the term "psychology" literally translates to the study of spirit or soul, the theoretical as well as practical aspects of the field have been far from discussions of metaphysics and its implications on spiritual psychology. In fact, upon the establishment of the American Psychological Association (APA) in the early 1900s, Stanley G. Hall and his associates decided that they would revoke their membership in the Society for Psychical Research (SCR), which focused on studying metaphysics to stay true to an empirical science created in the image of the hard sciences. Furthermore, until the last few decades, modern psychology largely ignored significant contributions of Muslim scholars or any scholarly literature outside of the Western world. Often courses or works discussing the history of psychology start from the early Greeks in the 300s BC and jump to the Renaissance in the 14th century to the development of modern psychology in the late 19th century (Khan et al., 2021). The divorce of the sacred from scientific reflects European history that separated the church from state, science, and academia from religion. This was similarly reflected in the modern movements of psychology as seen in the emergence of behaviorism, an ultra-reductionist approach to human behavior that further marginalized the spiritually minded. However, recent attempts have led to the revival of age-old debates such as the mind-body, re-exploring the role of the spirit in psychology, and increasing diverse contributions to the field. This is evidenced by the increasing literature published on spirituality and psychology and through the inclusion of Eastern practices (mindfulness, acceptance) or the role of virtues and character development in psychology as witnessed by Positive Psychology.

Given the newfound interest in diverse methods and theories in psychology, the presentation of a more inclusive approach that provides a broader epistemology is needed. The Islamic scholarly tradition provides a more inclusive epistemology that considers scriptural, rational, and empirical data as all equally admissible sources of information in developing any psychological knowledge. Islamic scholars have generally agreed upon these three sources of knowledge (Al-Taftazani, 2000).

All three sources of knowledge are also subject to a system of gradation and are evaluated in accordance with the strength of their truth value. Knowledge is thus graded as either definitive/certain (*qat'i*) or probabilistic/inferential (*dhanni*). While only *qat'i* knowledge can be considered hard facts, such as the outcome of definitive empirical lab experiments or clear-cut scripture that leaves no shadow of doubt on the reality of some phenomenon, the spectrum of probabilistic knowledge opens up the space for the inclusion of discussion of various ideas, techniques, and studies in psychology upon the condition of acknowledging the ambiguity or uncertainty contained within this knowledge. This system of gradation in knowledge facilitates a reconciliatory approach to the construction of the psychological sciences by providing a mechanism for the appropriate placement of information irrespective of whether it is 'western' or 'eastern' in origin or which source it is derived from (i.e., scriptural, empirical, or rational). Though the American Psychological Association's (2006) publication on the various methodologies that can be considered empirical provides such a flexibility, an Islamic epistemology may be considered to contain even more robustness through its additional inclusion and gradation of scripture and rational methods (American Psychological Association, 2006). Moreover, this enables reconciliation and construction of a framework of the human psyche that can effectively and systematically integrate the sacred and psychological sciences. The TIIP model has adopted this epistemological framework in the construction of the human ontological model by drawing upon empirical truths, scholarly literature, both Islamic and contemporary, and Islamic scripture (Keshavarzi & Ali, 2020).

Underlying Assumptions of TIIP

Consistent with Islamic values and traditional views on health and well-being, the TIIP model rests upon the following underlying assumptions (Keshavarzi et al., 2020):

- While hierarchically graded according to the strength of evidence, empirical, rational, and scriptural sources of knowledge are all equally valid and admissible for utilization in the science of human psychology.

- Though there exists a state of inner intrapsychic tensions, all human beings are born with a predisposed primordial inclination and recognition of universal good and connection with the Divine (*Fiṭrah*).

- Mere presence or absence of a diagnosable psychological disorder or measurement of external functioning are not indicators of overall health and well-being, rather complete health is seen on a continuum, and all individuals may have some degree of subclinical 'ailments' in some capacity. While some may suffer from psychological illnesses, others may contain within themselves spiritual ailments.

- Consistent with the previous assumption related to health and wellness, the internal psychological and spiritual condition of the practitioner is just as important as the patients in the facilitation of the process of change. As the Arabic saying goes, "one who does not possess something cannot give it."

- Since our existence does not solely begin at birth and does not truly end upon death, all aspects of the therapeutic process (assessment, evaluation, and treatment) must take into consideration the primordial existence of the human soul as well as post-mortem considerations and their associated assumptions.

- The human psyche is a multidimensional ontological essence whereby all of its elements are intricately tied to each other. A change in one element will result in a change in other aspects of the psyche. Therefore, treatment must address specific aspects while also keeping the complete system in mind.

- Since human beings are a complex creation of God and there is so much variability about the expressions of psychopathology, no single therapeutic approach can be equally applicable to all human beings, and treatment goals must be constructed bearing the variability of clinical expressions in mind.

TIIP Model of Human Ontology

The human being is primordially born upon a good essence known as the 'Fiṭrah.' The fiṭrah is explicitly mentioned in the Qurʾān, "... this is the natural disposition given to you by God, upon which He originated all humankind..." (Qurʾān, 30:30) and Hadith, "every child is born upon the fiṭrah..." (Al-Bukhārī, 2010, Book 23, Hadith 137). Fiṭrah stems from the primordially endowed human faculty to recognize good and evil and distinguish truth from falsehood (Yasin, 1996). Modern research also suggests that children as early as age two can learn to recognize and practice prosocial behaviors, and these behaviors increase in frequency and sophistication as they age (Eisenberg et al., 2006; Svetlova et al., 2010). Experiments conducted at Yale's Infant Cognition Center showed preverbal infants as young as 6-10 months being able to socially evaluate the actions of others and preferring individuals who were helpful rather than those who were hindering (Hamlin et al., 2007).

Where the Fiṭrah may stem from the human soul's primordial covenant with the divine, the soul's encounter with the temporal material world gives rise to the four competing drives: 1) appetitive (shahwah), 2) aggressive (ghaḍab), 3) satanic, and 4) angelic. While the appetitive and aggressive drives are natural survival drives and not inherently bad, the satanic drives emerge if these two drives are not kept within moderation (Al-Ghazālī, 1990, p. 137). The human soul, or rūḥ, also carries a tension between the metaphysical divine essence desiring reconnection with the divine (rūḥ ʾulwī samāwī) and the metaphysical life force (rūḥ ḥayawānī) grounded in the world (Al-Suhrawardī, 1993, p. 247). Because the human being is composed of two parts, the physical and metaphysical or the body and soul (Al-

Bajūrī, 2002), the metaphysical entity is referred to as the *latīfah rabānniyah* by (Al-Ghazāli, 1990; Al-Bājuri, 2002) or the human-divine subtle essence (Al-Bajūrī, 2002; Al-Ghazālī, 1990). While it is a single unitary essence, it has various expressions (*i'tibārāt*). These expressions are referred to as 1) *'aql* (cognition), 2) *nafs* (behavioral inclinations), 3) *rūḥ* (spirit), and 4) *qalb* (heart). The TIIP

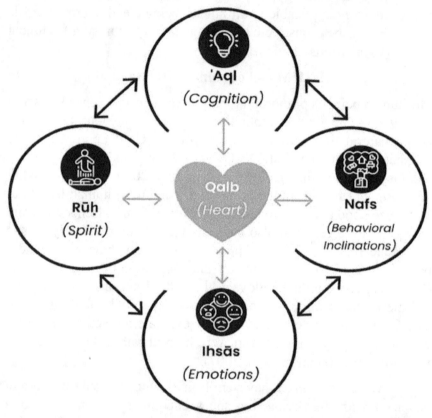

model, for the purposes of psychological conceptualization and treatment, draws upon this classification and adds a secondary element of *iḥsās* (emotion) which is not an independent entity, but simply a result of the interaction between the *'aql, nafs,* and *rūḥ.*

Figure 1. *Composite elements of the internal human psyche (Keshavarzi & Khan, 2018).*

Therefore, in sum, the TIIP model divides the elements of the human psyche into (1) *'aql* (cognition), (2) *nafs* (behavioral inclinations), (3) *rūḥ* (spirit), (4) *iḥsās* (emotion), and (5) *qalb* (metaphysical heart). The heart essentially refers to the spiritual/metaphysical heart that serves as a homeostatic receptacle of health and pathology. Changes in other components will positively or negatively affect the heart (Keshavarzi & Ali, 2020). Lastly, human existence is seen within the context of relationships with its external aspects as well. This includes a relationship with God that can be developed internally but also externally through the relationship with the social and natural environment. This is referred to as the *ijtimā'i* aspect of the model.

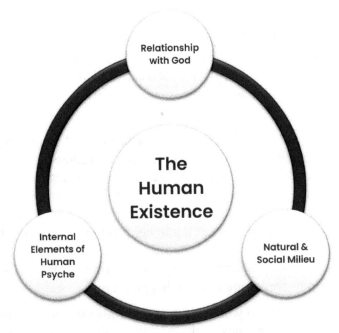

Figure 2. *Social contextual existence of the human being.*

With this explanation in mind, a case will be presented, and the ontological aspects of the human psyche will be discussed accordingly along with the process of treatment according to TIIP.

The Case of Aylin

This is based on a real case treated by a TIIP clinician in Türkiye. All identifiable data has been changed to protect the privacy and confidentiality of the patient.

Introduction and Presenting Problems

Aylin is a 47-year-old Turkish housewife who has been married for 27 years; she has no children. She sought therapy after her father's death and utilized antidepressants conjunctively. She sought out psychotherapy due to feelings of loneliness and anger outbursts. She specifically requested a female therapist who identifies strongly with her faith and can skillfully integrate Islamic spirituality into the therapeutic process.

Precipitating Events

Aylin was a member of an intimate religious congregation (*jamā'ah*) and had to leave because she reported that they violated some of her core values. After this separation, she socially isolated herself and neglected her religious practices leading to her feeling more spiritually and socially disconnected.

Shortly afterward, Aylin's spouse retired and began spending all his time at home, which led to constant arguments. Aylin felt resentment towards her husband because of his desire to have a second marriage due to her infertility. She felt rage towards him for even making this suggestion. These anger outbursts were further accompanied by days of not talking to her husband. She also reported being easily irritable on account of this and losing control over small things, such as her husband refusing to turn on the air conditioning on a road-trip or forgetting to fix a dripping tap.

Aylin wished to work on her anger outbursts and improve her relationship with her husband and other family members. She mentioned having high expectations of others and imposing strict rules upon them. She realized that she could be controlling and demanding at times, leading her to argue with others, stonewalling them, or even cutting ties with them until her demands were met. She additionally reported being afraid of "aging and becoming a grumpy and lonely lady that everyone is afraid to approach".

Early Life Experiences and History

Aylin was born and raised in Türkiye in a religious/tradition-bound Muslim household. She grew up in a small village and was the oldest of seven siblings. Given her mother's struggle with ongoing depression, Aylin reported being a parentified child taking on significant family responsibilities at a young age, including taking care of her siblings, doing household chores, and working at a local farmers market to earn extra pocket money for school.

Aylin reported growing up in an unloving home where neither her mother nor her father ever provided any affection or attention. She also reported listening to her mother talk about how much she did not want to be married to her father, and how inept he was (i.e., physically, sexually, etc.), along with other private thoughts and matters that were shared that Aylin stated, "were not appropriate for a 9-year-old child to hear." She added that her mother had a difficult time making friends due to her depression and that she experienced a role reversal such that her mother would use her as her confidant to discuss her private marriage problems while neglecting Aylin's needs for love, play, and attention.

Aylin reported feeling resentment toward her mother, and to add to her sense of isolation, Aylin reported that her mother expressed positive emotions around her cousins' children and made them feel at home. She could not recall a single event in childhood wherein her mother showed any kind of affection toward her. She recalled an especially painful memory from her childhood where her mother didn't show up to a class play because it was "a waste of time."

She mentioned that her mother compared her to her father when she made any mistakes on a task because they were both "useless." Aylin mentioned that she was relieved of her duties whenever her father was around and that "she could just be a kid who wasn't responsible for taking care of others."

When Aylin was 16, her mother gave birth to her youngest brother. At the time, there had been a lot of financial struggles in the family, so her mother started working two jobs immediately after giving birth, and all the responsibility of the child-rearing of her younger brother was passed on to Aylin. On account of this, she started to have trouble with her attendance at school, negatively affecting her academic performance and resulting in her dropping out of high school. Aylin reported feeling sad about never being able to fulfill her desire to go to college and become a nurse.

69

Aylin was married to her now-husband at the age of twenty and had to move far away from her hometown, leaving behind her family and friends. When they got married, Aylin's husband had been working as a military officer. However, during the 1997 Turkish military memorandum, her husband was expelled from the army due to his and Aylin's strong religious beliefs and orientation. After this, her husband remained unemployed for a significant period, which led to many financial and emotional challenges.

Other Significant History

Aylin's family from her mother's side has a long history of mental illness. Her mother experienced postpartum trauma in most of her childbirths. Aylin's grandmother suffered from delusional psychosis and had attempted to kill her baby (Aylin's mother) twice until she was admitted to a psychiatric hospital, where she took her own life.

TIIP Conceptualization

As stated above, TIIP case conceptualization is holistic and comprehensive. In most cases, one area of the psyche presents as the predominant locus and source of imbalance and dysfunction. Therefore, intervention often initiates with that component of the psyche first while transitioning to the other elements gradually, given that all elements are interconnected, and dysfunction in one area ultimately affects the entire system.

After the initial assessment, emotional disturbances (*ihsās*) were found to be the primary area of Aylin's dysfunction. Aylin's experiences of emotional trauma were internalized as emotional schemes that led to primary maladaptive feelings of sadness and negative thoughts (*'aql*) about herself and others (e.g., "I mean nothing to my husband," "No one cares about me"). On account of being sensitive to rejection, she would become extremely angry, especially when criticized by her husband, and either lash out at him or stop talking to him. This would also cause her to stop taking care of the house and indulge in unproductive activities, such as binge-watching (*nafs*). Being resentful towards God because of all the trials He put her through had caused Aylin to neglect most of her spiritual and religious practices, which increased her feelings of loneliness and led her to feel a spiritual void (*rūḥ*). For Aylin, the dysfunctions in her emotions (*iḥsās*), cognitions (*ʿaql*), manifestations of behavioral inclinations (*nafs*), and spiritual despondency and distress (*rūḥ*) had led to her heart (*qalb*) being in a state of sickness.

Emotion (Iḥsās)

While there are different views regarding emotions, among the most dominant theories is the emotion theory championed by Emotion focused psychotherapists (Greenberg, 2015). While they posit that emotions are rooted in biological drives having evolutionary origins designed for survival and adaptation, more cognitive approaches view emotions as top-down processes that are modulated through the cognitive appraisals of one's instincts for survival. On the other hand, Muslim scholars view emotions more as having multiplex origins. These include biological and cognitive origins as well as those potentially arising out of spiritual origins. Thus, they present emotions as both bottom-up, process-based, that are biologically or spiritually rooted as well as top-down mental processes that are influenced by cognitions (Keshavarzi & Keshavarzi, 2020). For example, Sufi poets have attributed a sense of divine connection through human emotions; where Muhammad Iqbal associates the depression and anxiety in this world to the pain and longing for reunification with the Creator, Rumi considers positive and negative emotions as "guests" from the divine (Helminski, 2005; Iqbal, 2014).

Since *iḥsās* is considered a secondary element of the human psyche resulting as a byproduct of the interaction between other aspects of the psyche (*ʿaql, rūḥ, nafs*), emotions may arise as a result of underlying or covert thoughts/beliefs or overt thinking (*ʿaql*) or from the primitive drives of the *nafs* or simply emotions that arise on account of spiritual experiences or divine castings (*rūḥ*).

Within the psychotherapeutic context, emotions may be seen as alarm signals that draw the patient's attention to inner experiences. It signals that something is 'off' and that some potential underlying needs of the self are not being met. Since all emotions have associated needs (e.g., anger needing justice or sadness needing meaning or connection), in the absence of pathology, emotions may emerge naturally, leading one to meet their needs. However, emotions become maladaptive when those emotions do not provide or lead to those underlying needs. These maladaptive emotions may either be under- or over-regulated. The patient may thus be dissociating and not experiencing emotions, having a flood of emotions, unhealthy expressions of these emotions, or experiencing secondary emotions that cover up the primary emotions, all of which continue to leave the underlying emotional needs unsatisfied. Thus, it is important for patients to uncover the underlying needs of their primary emotions. Once needs are uncovered, an evaluation of those needs must be made within the context of the patient and whether those needs must be modified or can be attained within one's social context without the violation of values.

Aylin's early experiences with emotional abuse and neglect were internalized as emotional schemes that led her to growing up and developing primary maladaptive feelings of sadness related to being unloved and unworthy. Her unhealthy emotional schemes were further reinforced by her husband's desire to enter another marriage, triggering her sense of worthlessness and being unloved. Given that expressing sadness would lead to the further risk of being hurt in the context of a relationship, she would often instead experience secondary maladaptive emotions of extreme anger and frustration accompanied by feelings of shame and guilt afterward only exacerbating her sadness and worthlessness.

Cognition ('Aql)

'Aql is human cognition responsible for acquiring information or knowledge, decision making, understanding through thought processes, orientation to appreciate the future consequences of one's actions, and the ability to self-reflect and self-direct. Furthermore, it has the potential to gain realizations and intuition regarding human senses and perception and their functioning at optimal capacity (Al-Ghazālī, 1993; Al-Taftazani, 2000). According to Islamic spiritual conceptualization, a fully developed 'aql provides the faculty of rationality, knowledge attainment, appreciation of consequences, ability to distinguish right from wrong, and even regulate emotions (Al-Bajūrī, 2002; Al-Ghazālī, 1990).

In psychotherapy, a sound 'aql can lead to a healthy cognition with the ability to think reasonably, rationally, and interpret the world through Islamic belief. However, irrational or unhealthy thought processes can lead to a pathological lens by which one views the world, leading to unhealthy emotions, behavioral actions, and ultimately diminished spirituality. Thus, individuals may catastrophize and harbor negative thinking regarding others, themselves, or their environments.

For Aylin, the emotional abuse and neglect experienced in her early childhood caused her to develop schemas that led to negative thoughts about herself and others. Aylin perceived herself as unlovable, incompetent, and unworthy, and others as unreliable, neglectful, and hurtful. Her maladaptive schemas of mistrust, abandonment, and emotional deprivation further played out in her relationship with her husband. Negative internal dialogues originating through demonic whispers causing accompanying cognitive distortions, including mind-reading ("I mean nothing to my husband") and catastrophizing ("No one cares about me"), were activated whenever she felt unheard and disapproved of. This led her to either argue with her husband or punish him silently. In addition, Aylin had thoughts that questioned divine wisdom. Her inability to see everything as a manifestation of Allāh's will lead Aylin to resent towards God and distance herself from spiritual and religious practices.

Behavioral Inclinations (Nafs)

Nafs, or 'lower ego,' is among the most ignored aspects of the human psyche in contemporary psychology (Williams, 2019). This may be due to the emphasis of *nafs* on controlling desires, something that is not consistent with an increasingly post-modern or 'value-free' discipline such as modern psychotherapy. Although *Nafs* is sometimes compared with the Freudian conceptualization of the psyche (id, ego, and superego), from an Islamic perspective, it is not considered to be inherently evil (Rothman & Coyle, 2020). The two types of drives embedded within the *nafs* (*shahwah* and *ghaḍab*) in their primitive expression, engaging in over-indulgence, leads to the state known as *nafs ammārah bi al-su'* (Qur'ān, 12:53) or commanding towards evil. However, through awareness, training, regulation, and rejection of its desires for overconsumption, the *nafs* can grow and elevate with the emergence of elevation and growth, entering the state of *nafs lawwāmah* (Qur'ān, 75:2) or the reprimanding self. Lastly, through consistent, successful training and extinguishing of the desire for overindulgence, the *nafs* enters a state of calm and serenity known as *nafs mutma'innah*, (Qur'ān, 89:27) (Hammad, 2009). At its highest state, the *nafs* is no longer shackled by the dictates and drives of the carnal desires as they relate to this temporal world, and there is relief in its inner struggle and tension.

In the TIIP model, we have opted to translate *nafs* as "behavioral inclinations" due to its automatic, instinctual impulse to act on its drives that often occur 'thoughtlessly,' unless a process of opposition and training takes place. It can thus be seen as habituated behaviors acquired over time and through passive or active training. In the context of psychotherapy, nafs can be considered as all of those habituated or automated actions that serve either a pleasure-seeking need or avoidance of discomfort. Individuals who engage in such pleasure-seeking activities or avoidance behaviors typically experience some temporary comfort that leads to a vicious cycle of pathology that sustains an overall sense of dysfunction. This may include compulsive, addictive, or avoidance behaviors.

Aylin's unhealthy controlling behaviors, lashing out at her husband and others, and stonewalling or even cutting ties completely appear to have been related to her *Nafs*. The lashing out would often be accompanied by the sadness of being criticized which would lead Aylin to stop taking care of responsibilities resulting in unproductive activities such as binge-watching or even self-gratification through unhealthy eating habits.

Spirit (Rūḥ)

Where *rūḥ 'ulwī samāwī* is the primordial soul that possesses an inherent inclination toward the sacred and longs for reconnection with and remembrance of God, *rūḥ ḥayawānī* contains the human life force with animalistic tendencies and survival inclinations (Al-Ghazālī, 1993; al-Suhrawardī, 1993).

Aḥmad Sirhindī (d. 1012), an Indian Muslim Sufi jurist, posits that the *rūḥ* can see truth through the inner eye; however, it must subdue the physical sensory drives such that it is not driven by them to fully unlock this inner potential of the spirit (Er, 2016, p. 83). In the TIIP model, the *rūḥ* is developed through various religious acts (such as prayer, fasting, charity, and intimate contemplation); the most essential is the divine remembrance or *dhikr*. These mind-body synchronizations can potentially synchronize the frontal cortex and the limbic system, resulting in the activation of the parasympathetic nervous system, a heightened state of calmness and relaxation (Saniotis, 2018).

Aylin's spiritual functioning was impacted immensely by her negative experiences. She had abandoned voluntary prayers, supplicating to Allāh, reading the Qur'an and religious literature, and attending religious gatherings. Aylin's abandonment of spiritual and religious practices increased her loneliness. It led her to feel a spiritual void in which she felt that her life became absent of any deeper meaning. Distancing from the religious and spiritual side of her life, which used to serve as a core coping mechanism for all kinds of challenges, left her with fewer resources to cope with her current difficulties. Additionally, Aylin abandoned her spiritual lens upon her world, which she would use to connect with Allāh daily. This made her feel discontent and grow apart from Allāh, increasing a sense of spiritual "death."

Heart (Qalb)

The heart is the receptacle and a metaphysical balance for all the aspects of human ontology. Imam al-Ghazālī and others have proposed that there are two types of hearts: the physical heart, which is necessary for physical functioning, and the metaphysical heart, which is separate yet interacts with the physical heart (Al-Ghazālī, 2008). This metaphysical heart, referred to in the TIIP model, is the locus of human beings and the container of health and dysfunction (Al-Suhrawardi, 1993). The *qalb* becomes sick or healthy by virtue of or due to the actions of other elements of the psyche. In the TIIP model, the ultimate goal is the nurturance of balance across all components of the human psyche that lead to an integrative whole or unity of being (*ittiḥād*) (see below) that consequently results in a sound heart (*qalb salīm*) (Keshavarzi & Ali, 2020).

For Aylin, the dysfunctions in her emotions (*iḥsās*), cognitions (*ʿaql*), manifestations of behavioral inclinations (*nafs*), and spiritual despondency and distress (*rūḥ*) had led to her heart (*qalb*) being in a state of sickness.

Social (Ijtimāʿi)

Muslim communities, in general, place a great deal of emphasis on community. Ibn Khaldun (d. 1406), a Middle Age sociologist and philosopher, posited that compassion and a sense of social cohesion amongst one's relatives and social group (*asabiyya*) is not only part of human nature but also a "divine gift put into the hearts of men" (Rosenthal, 1969, p. 98; Sümer, 2012). Islam further encourages the believer to become a meaningful part of the community by emphasizing the rights of family members, neighbors, and community members. The TIIP model assumes that a healthy individual living a holistic life will focus not only on their internal framework of psycho-spiritual functioning but will also consider their relationship with others around them and The Creator. Modern psychotherapies, at times, tend to place more emphasis on individualistic values. Much like the internal aspects of the psyche, these external aspects are also interconnected. The individual's relationship with God can be strengthened through direct worship and following the tradition of His Prophet (peace and blessings be upon him) and through living a moral and responsible life in the natural and social environment. Moreover, influences from external aspects can lead to a positive or negative change in inner functioning. Al-Ghazālī posits that society exerts an influence on the inclinations that are intrinsic in human nature and that these communally influenced inclinations are constantly interacting with human feelings, thoughts, and behaviors (Al-Ghazālī, 1998).

At a young age, Aylin had to let go of her social connections to care for her family. She also lost her father and recently left the congregation she was a member of. Her stonewalling also led to decay in her relationships, leaving her with no friends and a husband with whom she does not have a healthy relationship. Aylin often described feeling "completely alone." Expressing that it was a great disrespect to her father's memory, Aylin stopped visiting and calling her mother, who remarried after Aylin's father's death. Upon these incidents, Aylin socially isolated herself and stopped talking to most of her friends. Moreover, her negative outlook on others and difficulty controlling her anger impaired her relationships with friends and family. Her overall low engagement in the community caused Aylin to lose all access to social support, further exacerbating feelings of loneliness and worthlessness.

Application of the TIIP Model

The TIIP model presents the processes of change in four stages containing the mechanisms of change initiated by the practitioner and principles of change as resultant features instilled in the patient.

Table 1. *TIIP Process of Change*

	Stage 1	Stage 2	Stage 3	Stage 4
Principles of Change (Patient)	Compliance (*Inqiyād*)	Introspective Self-Awareness (*Inkishāf*)	Psycho-spiritual Equilibrium (*I'tidāl*)	Integrative Unity (*Ittiḥād*)
Mechanisms of Change (Clinician)	Alliance (*Murābatah*)	Uncovering (*Mukāshafah*)	Intervention (*Mu'ālajah*)	Continuity (*Muwāsalah*)

Stage 1: Building Alliance and Attaining Compliance

The first stage in the change process in TIIP is the clinician's attempt to create a working, therapeutic relationship/alliance (*murābatah*) with the patient, leading the patient to respond with greater compliance (*inqiyād*) and motivation to work. This stage requires using empathic following techniques in therapy with an emphasis on empathic presence while simultaneously assessing the psyche within the TIIP ontological framework. One's assessment is an evolving process starting with tentative hypotheses in formulating the nature of the patient's dysfunction. Psycho-spiritual assessment and initial case formulation have six major goals:

1. Building a therapeutic alliance

2. Assessing the patient's motivation to change

3. Assessing the religiosity (both overt through quantitative methods and covert through qualitative methods)

4. Psycho-spiritual diagnosis and conceptualization

5. Assessing internal and external psycho-spiritual functioning

6. Orienting the patient to the psychotherapy process by way of psychoeducation, discussing prognosis, and setting therapeutic goals (Khan, 2020).

At the initial stages, it is also important to formulate a conceptualization regarding which aspect of the human psyche seems to be the primary source of dysfunction (*'aql, nafs, iḥsās,* or *rūḥ*). Through the formation of the therapeutic connection, the patient will be more likely to accept the demands of the process, which is presumed to enhance the overall treatment outcomes (Keshavarzi & Ali, 2020).

After developing a preliminary conceptualization, the therapist may provide psychoeducation to the patient, introducing her to the ontological domains of the human psyche as it relates to the holistic well-being of an individual. For Aylin, the therapist illustrated the conceptualization using a TIIP diagram displayed each situation's problematic cognitive, emotional, behavioral, spiritual, and social processes. The therapist held her formulation tentatively and worked collaboratively with the patient soliciting her feedback regarding whether the model and the conceptualization resonated with her. While providing psychoeducation, the therapist used a Socratic method of teaching to create an open dialogue with the patient and bring her to make connections for herself rather than simply presenting the information. The patient affirmed the conceptualization and stated she felt much more hopeful upon having a clear and thorough understanding of her situation. She verbalized her motivation to start working on her therapy goals.

Stage 2: Uncovering and Awareness

In this stage, the goal is for the patient to develop introspective self-awareness (*inkishāf*). This is an important aspect in this process of change since human behavior is the product of inner mechanisms, and research has indicated that people are generally unaware of why they engage in certain behaviors, have certain thoughts, or experience certain emotions (Blakemore & Frith, 2003). This deep awareness of the self and insight into deficiencies is considered a noble task that Imam Ghazālī attributes as significantly important in one's personal psycho-spiritual development. The role of the clinician in this stage is to enhance self-examination (*mukāshafah*), beginning with the experiential unveiling of the patient's internal psychological worlds, thereby creating increased awareness for the patient. The higher aspiration of this stage is for the patient to understand how, when, where, and which part of the psyche are activated from moment to moment as the individual is engaged emotionally, cognitively, spiritually, and behaviorally (Khan & Keshavarzi, 2022). It also allows the patient to have a better appreciation of the multiplexity of the inner psyche and how it creates or removes distress from the individual.

The stage of *Inkishāf* requires a strong psycho-spiritual bond between the clinician and the patient. The TIIP practitioner, referred to as a *Rafīq*, or a *Khalīl*, serves as a mirror for the patient to help facilitate this awareness of the workings of the metaphysical inner world (Khan et. al., 2020). Muslim scholars like Imam al-Ghāzalī, Abū Zayd al-Balkhī (d. 322), Abū Bakr al-Razī (d. 313), and others emphasize the importance of having another who can help the individual in uncovering one's deficiencies (Al-Ghāzalī, 1990). This self-awareness shares many elements that have been identified in mindfulness literature (Brown & Ryan, 2003). This includes having open, receptive awareness of the surroundings and their experiences (Martin, 1997) as encouraged by the Qu'ran (3:191), increased emotional intelligence through perceptual clarity about internal emotional states as well as external manifestations (Mayer et. al., 2004), active wakefulness to cognitive tasks in an open and assimilative manner (Bodner & Langer, 2001), internal state awareness and self-reflectiveness leading to private self-consciousness (Fenigstein et al., 1975), and self-monitoring and the ability to self-reflect (Snyder, 1974).

Inkishāf or introspective self-awareness facilitated Aylin becoming aware of her emotional patterns, their origins, relationship with her thoughts and underlying beliefs, as well as manifestations of cognitive distortions, need for control, and aggression manifested through behavioral inclinations, spiritual functioning causing a rupture in her relationship with God, and unhealthy social functioning having no social support or meaningful connections.

Stage 3: Psycho-spiritual Balance Through Intervention

In this stage of the TIIP process of change, the main goal is to facilitate a state of psycho-spiritual equilibrium or balance across all composite parts of the psyche (i.e., *'aql, rūḥ, nafs, iḥsās,* and *qalb*). Because creating equilibrium may often require adding or removing a construct, more directive interventions are expected while keeping in mind that a strong alliance has been created and the patient has increased awareness and insight. This requires the clinician to focus on one or more of the elements based upon determining where the primary sources of dysfunction are rooted. The TIIP model aims to engender a psycho-spiritual balance through directive interventions (*mu'ālajah*). The interventions vary depending on which domain of the psyche is being intervened. Given that each of the domains has accompanying overarching goals, the intervention with *'aql* is intended to engender an actively contemplative mind through reflection, restructuring, and psychoeducation; intervention with *Iḥsās* will help facilitate the expression of maladaptive emotions followed by transformation to more balanced adaptive expressions that meet underlying needs; the intervention with the *nafs* will require the confrontation and resistance of discomfort often characterized by avoidance behaviors that enables a vicious pathological cycle, intervention with spirit will focus on ridding spiritual diseases and filling the void and emptiness with the remembrance of God and virtuous characteristics.

Contemporary psychological literature also recognizes the importance of healthy psycho-spiritual balance in the nurturance of health and wellness (Seligman et al., 2004). This includes balance in thoughts (Tsai, 2013), emotions (Gross, 2014), resisting desires and temptations (Hofmann et al., 2012), and even spirituality (Lukoff, 2019). Islamic spirituality emphasizes but does not require, the clearing out of that which is unhealthy before attempting to implant praiseworthy traits as they require the preparation of the fertile psychic ground.

Iḥsāsi I'tidāl (Emotional Equilibrium): In the preliminary sessions, Aylin talked about the emotional challenges she has been facing in her relationship with her mother. She tearfully remembered her childhood memories, reporting not being able to recall any incidents where her mother expressed any affection towards her. Subsequent sessions emphasized emotional work focused on helping Aylin access and express her core pain, uncover, and meet unmet childhood needs, and transform maladaptive emotional responses. These sessions involved re-enacting through chair work, a technique derived from EFT with Islamic adaptation where the *mizāj* or experiencing self is placed in one chair and the other (inner critic, an individual with unfinished business, etc.) is placed on the second chair facing each other. For Aylin, the other chair occupied the image of her invalidating mother, allowing her to access the core painful emotions, retrieve the unmet needs, and activate adaptive emotions to change the maladaptive ones by helping the patient make sense of her past and present experiences (Figure 3). The goal was primarily to find healthier and more appropriate ways of expressing emotions and emotional needs and to reduce the unhealthy ways of attempting to meet the needs to achieve a *I 'tidāl*. Throughout the process of emotional work, the therapist's rolewas to heighten, facilitate and stay empathically attuned to the patient.

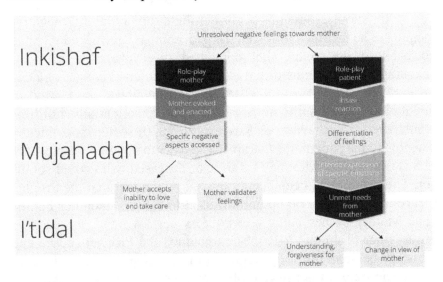

Figure 3. *EFT two-chair enactment of unfinished business toward mother*

Aylin initially found it difficult to stay with her core pain as the memories and feelings associated with it were overwhelming for her. During the chair work in session, she quickly changed the subject and expressed secondary maladaptive emotions of hopelessness. While staying empathically attuned as the patient moved towards her core emotional pain, the therapist utilized several interventions such as empathic reflection, empathic affirmation, evocative responding, and empathic conjecture or interpretation to facilitate the emergence of adaptive needs (Elliott et al., 2004). After accessing and deepening experiences related to her core emotional wound, Aylin recognized that her emotional need was to be loved and acknowledged by her mother. As adaptive needs emerged, the therapist's empathic validation of them permitted the patient to be more aware of and be more able to express her emotions and needs. Through the process of switching between the chairs and expressing emotional needs, the resentment, sadness, and hurt that was dominant in the early phases of the chair work left its place to the expression of adaptive anger. The expression of adaptive underlying anger helped Aylin be more assertive, defend herself, and feel more deserving of love and care. Feelings of being worthy of love and care shifted her negative beliefs about herself.

In another session, Aylin brought up a painful negative memory. The therapist followed the pain compass and asked Aylin to go back to the image that contained this vulnerable memory, encouraging her to transform this using a technique known as guided imagery or *tasawwur*. This technique functions as a way of facilitating a deep spiritual connection and experientially fulfilling unmet needs (Keshavarzi & Keshavarzi, 2020). After empathically listening to the patient, the therapist asked her to imagine the presence of a caring figure, who may be alive or deceased, who could soothe her. The patient had been deeply moved by the fact that the Prophet (peace and blessings be upon him) used to call his daughter Fatima 'The Mother of her Father' to express her love and appreciation towards her (Tabrani, 2016). She imagined the Prophet (peace and blessings be upon him) in a vague form, showing up at her doorstep where she watched her little brother and mother, and telling her that *"she was the mother of her mother, even though her mother was not aware of it."* After the exercise, the patient reported an immense peace and an expansion in her chest. The therapist reminded the patient that she could access such guided imagery whenever she felt like she needed a tool to soothe herself. In the proceeding sessions, Aylin was also able to feel empathy and compassion for her mother during subsequent chair work enacting her mother.

'Aqlāni I'tidāl (Cognitive Equilibrium): Positive effects were also seen on Aylin's cognitive functioning. After some emotional work was successfully provided, cognitive processing naturally emerged. Aylin held newly formed healthy thoughts regarding herself and her significant others. Aylin had developed negative schemas as a result of her past experiences. The beliefs stored in her schemas had strengthened over time due to the reinforcement of beliefs through similar repetitive experiences and her negative interpretations of these events. After the abovementioned emotional work, the therapist began to help Aylin challenge her negative thought processes by evaluating them with more balanced thoughts. Her negative thought patterns further manifested with her religious beliefs, where she still experienced spiritual depletion and displayed a lack of reliance on God, discontentment, and jealousy, indicating the need to focus on improving her spiritual functioning. As a result of the chair work, Aylin had more neutral emotions towards her mother, thereby allowing her to re-assess the relationship in a more balanced manner, keeping her religious duty to her mother in mind.

Ijtimāʿi Iʿtidāl (Interpersonal Equilibrium): After working on her emotional wounds and making sense of her interpersonal experiences, the patient could access adaptive and healthy ways of expressing her emotions and emotional needs. Consequently, this positively influenced her relationship with her husband and other family members. However, even though Aylin forgave her mother regarding her treatment of herself as a child, she refused to forgive her for getting married right after her father's death. She started seeing her mother again but told her openly that she was not ready to meet her husband and wasn't sure if she would ever be. In the proceeding sessions, Aylin informed the therapist regarding her relationship with her husband, stating that she was not afraid of being vulnerable with him anymore, which improved their relationship as he gradually started becoming more expressive of his feelings. She stated that this reciprocation helped them become more compassionate towards each other and improved their intimacy.

Rūhāni Iʿtidāl (Spiritual Equilibrium): According to the TIIP, psycho-spiritual dysfunctions can be demonstrated by a sense of spiritual depletion, exhaustion, fatigue, hopelessness, and deliberately refusing to comply with religious principles (Keshavarzi & Khan, 2018). Spiritual work aimed to assist Aylin in her spiritual development by integrating the signature spiritual interventions of TIIP into the therapy sessions (Keshavarzi et al., 2020). The focus of spiritually based interventions was to fulfill the spirit's innate affinity for divine connection and nourishment through remembering Allāh (*i.e., dhikr of gratitude*), doing contemplative reflection (*tafakkur*) on the purpose and meaning of life, and taking value-based actions.

Aylin was then advised by her therapist to keep a diary where she highlighted her good qualities, blessings, values, and her purpose in relating to these. Aylin identified her values as spirituality, compassion, helpfulness, contribution, supportiveness, fairness, forgiveness, and persistence, along with others. The therapist and the patient went over these values and discussed their importance in the patient's life more thoroughly. Together with the therapist, they turned these into value-based goals and created action items.

The therapist also helped Aylin consider the importance of taking values-based actions to contribute toward behavior change. She talked about the importance of opposing the negative inclinations of the *nafs al-ammārah* and provided psychoeducation as an entrance for working with the patient's *nafs*. The clinician introduced the concept of disciplining the *nafs* (*tahdhīb al-nafs*) by embracing the discomfort in the process of reformation of the nafs. The treatment utilized behavioral interventions as they moved forward to help Aylin stick to her therapy goals, repel avoidance behaviors, and embrace any uncomfortable feelings that arose. In order to do that, the therapist introduced Aylin to The Six M's of behavioral change, which is derived from the literature in Islamic spirituality on behavioral modification (Keshavarzi & Haque, 2013). The six M's in the model corresponds to (1) *Mushāratah* or goal-setting, (2) *Murāqabah* or self-monitoring, (3) *Muhāsabah* or self-evaluation, (4) *Mu'āqabah* or consequences, (5) *Mu'ātabah* or self-reprimand, and (6) *Mujāhadah* or exertion (Al-Ghazālī, 1993). The therapist shared with the patient a printout of these Six M's along with a behavioral log that monitored her progress on her goals and asked her to fill them out on a daily basis. The therapist and the patient worked towards the spiritual goals while utilizing the Six M's method to help achieve these goals.

Stage 4: Integrative Unity through Continuity

The final stage in the TIIP process of change arises as the successful completion of the previous three stages. After an individual goes through developing a strong alliance with the clinician, increasing introspective self-awareness, and instilling psycho-spiritual balance

84

in all areas of their psyche, work is then transitioned into ensuring that all elements are working congruently and in unison towards their overall goals, leading to an inner integrative unity (*ittiḥād*). In this stage, there is also a focus on identifying overall meaningful goals in the form of focusing on the acquisition of virtues and resiliency development. The term *ittihad* here also alludes to the internal unity of the individual with the divine and a return to the primordial nature (*fiṭrah*). The primary goal of this stage is the alignment of the elements of the psyche with each other such that there does not remain any dissonance between them. This alignment requires all parts to work collectively and cohesively in an integrative, holistic experience. At this stage, the individual may be able to take on higher-level spiritual practices to elevate themselves and further protect themselves by instilling psycho-spiritual resilience.

For Aylin, the positive effects of treatment manifested themselves in a healthier way of expressing her emotions and a healthier mindset that entailed adopting a positive lens through which she looked at trials and tribulations and life overall. She viewed adversity as an opportunity to learn the virtues of patience and steadfastness, which led to an overall lessening of previously reported feelings of resentment and hurt, and an increased sense of contentment and spiritual rejuvenation that strengthened her psycho-spiritual resilience. Aylin reported that by taking value-based action, she felt she was fulfilling the purpose of her life and had a renewed sense of purpose. In order to maintain her therapeutic gain, Aylin and her therapist decided to further strengthen her relationship with God through inculcating virtuous behaviors. They identified and discussed the possible outcomes of acting in accordance with certain virtues, such as positive evaluation of others *(husn al-dhan)* and compassion and found additional strategies to undertake good deeds in harmony with her faith and religion.

Conclusion

The TIIP model is primarily designed to reform epistemology and ontology from an Islamic perspective, which is holistic and allows the clinician to be integrative. This model can be applied to Muslims and non-Muslims. The case of Aylin is a specific demonstration of the utility of Traditional Islamically Integrated Psychotherapy (TIIP) in practice with a Muslim patient. The specific display of a case with a predominant emotionally based problem that led to her depressive feelings, relationship problems, and psychological distress helps provide a roadmap for students of TIIP and practitioners interested in a structured and consistent Islamic model of psychotherapy that provides an integrative alternative to secular modalities that may not be as effective in working with Muslim populations. Perhaps the most important part of TIIP is its ability to provide a formulation of a patient that helps practitioners think about and explain psychopathology in a way consistent with Islamic thought. Furthermore, an accurate and thorough conceptualization of the patient allows for the natural progression through the processes of change, permitting practitioners to be able to draw upon the variety of therapeutic tools available to them in helping their patients reach *i'tidāl* or equilibrium and ultimately *ittiḥad*, integrative unity. Although the model is still in its early stages, it is being further developed through a practice-based evidence approach.

References

Abu-Raiya, H. (2014). Western psychology and Muslim psychology in dialogue: Comparisons between Qura'nic theory of personality and Freud's and Jung's ideas. *Journal of Religion and Health, 53*(2), 326-338.

Al-Bajūrī, A. (2002). *Hashiyat al-Imam al-Bajuri 'ala Jawharat al-Tawhid.* Cairo: Dar al-Salam.

Al-Bukhārī (2010). *Sahih al- Bukhari.* Riyadh: Darussalam.

Al-Ghazālī, A. H. (1990). *Mukhtasar: 'Ulum al-Din,* Beirut: Mua'ssas al-Kutub al-Thaqafiyyah.

Al-Ghazālī, A. H. (1993). *Revival of Religious Learnings: Imam Ghazzali's Ihya Ulum-id-Din* trans. F. Karim. Karachi: Dar ul Ishaat

Al-Ghazālī, A. H. (1998). *Minhajul 'Abideen,* trans. I. H. Ansari. Karachi: Dar ul Isha'at.

Al-Ghazālī, A. H. (2008). *Al- Maqṣad al- Asnā fī Sharḥ Ma'ānī Asmā' Allāh al-Ḥ usnā.* Cairo: Dār al-Salām.

Al-Suhrawardī, S. (1993). *'Awdrif al-Ma'arif.* Cairo: Dar al-Ma'arif

Al-Taftazānī, A. H. (2000). *Sharfr al-'Aqd'id al-NasaftJ!Yah.* Karachi: Maktabat al-Bushra.

American Psychological Association (2006). Evidence-based practice in psychology. *American Psychologist, 61*(4), 271-285.

Blakemore, S. J., & Frith, C. (2003). Self-awareness and action. *Current opinion in neurobiology, 13*(2), 219–224. https://doi.org/10.1016/s0959-4388(03)00043-6

Bodner, T. E., & Langer, E. J. (2001, June). *Individual differences in mindfulness: The Mindfulness/Mindlessness Scale.* Poster presented at the 13th annual American Psychological Society Conference, Toronto, Ontario, Canada.

Brown, K. W., & Ryan, R. M. (2003). The benefits of being present: Mindfulness and its role in psychological well-being. *Journal of Personality and Social Psychology, 84*(4), 822–848. https://doi.org/10.1037/0022-3514.84.4.822

Elliott, R., Watson, J. C., Goldman, R. N., & Greenberg, L. S. (2004). *Learning emotion-focused therapy: The process-experiential approach to change.* Washington American Psychological Association.

Eisenberg, N., Fabes, R. A., & Spinrad, T. L. (2007). Prosocial Development. *Handbook of Child Psychology.* https://doi.org/10.1002/9780470147658.chpsy0311

Er, M. E. (2016). *al-Mukhtdrdt min Maktubdt al-Imam al-Rabbdni al-Sirhindi.* Istanbul: ISAR.

Fenigstein, A., Scheier, M., & Buss, A. (1975). Public and private self-consciousness: Assessment and theory. *Journal of Consulting and Clinical Psychology, 43*, 522-527.

Greenberg, L. (2015). *Emotion Focused Therapy: Coaching clients to work through their feelings, 2nd edition.* American Psychological Association.

Gross, J. J. (2014). Emotion regulation: Conceptual and empirical foundations. In J. J. Gross (Ed.), *Handbook of emotion regulation* (pp. 3–20). The Guilford Press.

Hamlin, J., Wynn, K. & Bloom, P. (2007) Social evaluation by preverbal infants. *Nature, 450*, 557–559

Hammad (2009). *The Gracious Qur'ān: A modern-phrased interpretation in English.* Trans. A. Z. Hammad. Lisle, IL: Lucent Interpretations.

Helminski, K. (2005). *The Rumi collection.* Shambhala Publications.

Hofmann, W., Baumeister, R. F., Förster, G., & Vohs, K. D. (2012). Everyday temptations: An experience sampling study of desire, conflict, and self-control. *Journal of Personality and Social Psychology*, *102*(6), 1318–1335. https://doi.org/10.1037/a0026545

Iqbal, M. (2014) *Gabriel's Wing*. Trans. D. J. Matthews, N. Siddiqui, Shah, S. A. Lahore: Iqbal Academy Pakistan.

Keshavarzi, H., & Haque, A. (2013). Outlining a psychotherapy model for enhancing Muslim mental health within an Islamic context. *The International Journal for the Psychology of Religion*, *23*(3), 230–249. https://doi.org/10.1080/10508619.2012.712000

Keshavarzi, H., & Khan, F. (2018). Outlining a case illustration of Traditional Islamically Integrated Psychotherapy. In Al-Karam, C. Y. (Ed.). *Islamically Integrated Psychotherapy: Processes and outcomes with Muslim clinicians.* (175-207). West Conshohocken, PA: Templeton Press.

Keshavarzi, H., & Ali, B. (2020). Foundations of traditional Islamically integrated psychotherapy (TIIP). In H. Keshavarzi, F. Khan, B. Ali, & R. Awaad (Eds.), *Applying Islamic principles to clinical mental health care*. Routledge. https://doi.org/10.4324/9781003043331-3

Keshavarzi, H., & Keshavarzi, S. (2020). Emotionally oriented psychotherapy. In H. Keshavarzi, F. Khan, B. Ali, & R. Awaad (Eds.), *Applying Islamic principles to clinical mental health care* (pp. 171–208). Routledge. https://doi.org/10.4324/9781003043331-12

Keshavarzi, H., Khan, F., Ali, B., & Awaad, R. (Eds.) (2020). *Applying Islamic principles to clinical mental health care: Introducing Traditional Islamically Integrated Psychotherapy.* New York: Routledge.

Keshavarzi, H., Yusuf, A., Kaplick, P., Ahmadi, T., & Loucif, A. (2020). Spiritually (Rūḥānī) focused psychotherapy. In H. Keshavarzi, F. Khan, B. Ali, & R. Awaad (Eds.), *Applying Islamic principles to clinical mental health care* (pp. 266–290). Routledge. https://doi.org/10.4324/9781003043331-15

Keshavarzi, H. (2022, March 25-26). *Exploring Islamically integrated psychotherapy for addressing Muslim mental health within an Islamic context: Preliminary data from a study* [Conference session]. 14th Annual Muslim Mental Health Conference, Yale University, New Haven, CT, United States. https://muslimmentalhealth.psychiatry.msu.edu/projects/14th -annual-muslim-mental-health-conference-2022

Khan, F. (2020). Quantitative and Qualitative Assessment of the Ontological Domains of the Psyche in TIIP. In Keshavarzi, H., Khan, F., Ali, B., & Awaad, R. (Eds.) *Applying Islamic principles to clinical mental health care: Introducing Traditional Islamically Integrated Psychotherapy.* New York: Routledge.

Khan, F., Keshavarzi, H., & Rothman, A. (2020). The Role of the TIIP Therapist: Scope of Practice and Proposed Competencies. In Keshavarzi, H., Khan, F., Ali, B., & Awaad, R. (Eds.) *Applying Islamic principles to clinical mental health care: Introducing Traditional Islamically Integrated Psychotherapy.* New York: Routledge.

Khan, F., Keshavarzi, H., Elzamzamy, K., & Awaad, R. (2021, August 12-15). *Omission of Muslim/Arab Contributions to Psychology from Research and Academia: Systemic Injustice?* [Conference presentation]. APA 2021 Convention, Virtual.

Khan, F. & Keshavarzi, H. (2022). Theoretical Foundations and Clinical Applications of Traditional Islamically Integrated Psychotherapy (TIIP). In Richards, Kawika, G., & Judd, D. (Eds.) *Handbook of Spiritually Integrated Psychotherapies.* American Psychological Association Press (*In Press*).

Lukoff, D. (2019). Spirituality and extreme states. *Journal of Humanistic Psychology, 59*(5), 754–761. https://doi.org/10.1177/0022167818767511

Martin, J. R. (1997). Mindfulness: A proposed common factor. *Journal of Psychotherapy Integration, 7,* 291–312.

Mayer, J., Salovey, P., & Caruso, D. (2004). Emotional Intelligence: Theory, findings, and implications. *Psychological Inquiry, 15*(3), 197-215.

Mohamed Y. (1996). *Fitrah: The Islamic concept of human nature.* Ta-Ha.

Rosenthal, F. (1969). *Ibn Khaldun, the muqadimah.* N. J. Davor d (Ed.). Princeton, NJ: Princeton University Pre ss, Bollinger Series.

Rothman, A., & Coyle, A. (2020). Conceptualizing an Islamic psychotherapy: A grounded theory study. *Spirituality in Clinical Practice,* 7(3), 197–213. https://doi.org/10.1037/scp0000219

Saniotis A. (2018). Understanding Mind/Body Medicine from Muslim Religious Practices of Salat and Dhikr. *Journal of religion and health,* 57(3), 849–857. https://doi.org/10.1007/s10943-014-9992-2

Seligman, M. E., Parks, A. C., & Steen, T. (2004). A balanced psychology and a full life. *Philosophical transactions of the Royal Society of London. Series B, Biological sciences,* 359(1449), 1379–1381. https://doi.org/10.1098/rstb.2004.1513

Sümer, B. (2012). Ibn Khaldun's asabiyya for social cohesion. *Turkey: Electronic Journal of Social Sciences.* http://dergipark.ulakbim.gov.tr/esosder/article/viewFile/5000 068522/5000063584

Svetlova, M., Nichols, S. R., & Brownell, C. A. (2010). Toddlers' prosocial behavior: from instrumental to empathic to altruistic helping. *Child development,* 81(6), 1814–1827. https://doi.org/10.1111/j.1467-8624.2010.01512.x

Snyder, M. (1974). Self-monitoring of expressive behavior. *Journal of Personality and Social Psychology,* 30(4), 526–537. https://doi.org/10.1037/h0037039

Tabrani, S. (2016). *Al Mu'jam Al Kabir* (G. D. Chishti Trans.), Islamabad, Pakistan: Millat Publications

Tsai, K. C. (2013). Being a Critical and Creative Thinker: A Balanced Thinking Mode. *Asian Journal of Humanities and Social Sciences, 1*(2), 1-9.

Williams, D. (2019). *Darwinian Hedonism and the Epidemic of Unhealthy Behavior.* Cambridge: Cambridge University Press. doi:10.1017/9781316275047

GOD-ORIENTED SPIRITUAL PSYCHOTHERAPY: A MULTIDIMENSIONAL MODEL BASED ON HOLY QUR'AN AND HADITH

Masoud Janbozorgi, Masoud Azarbayejani,

and Hamid Rafiei-Honar

Introduction

God-oriented Spiritual psychotherapy (God-OSP) is designed to help clients who want and follow spiritual help and resist current psychotherapies by activating the spiritual dimension based on the religious model. This model mainly began in the clinic and during work with clients after current psychotherapies looking for transcendence and spiritual needs. For the first time, Janbozorgi (2000) discussed this idea as a doctoral dissertation under the supervision of several clinical psychology professors. Then, by studying religious sources and matching them in the therapeutic process, it was used as independent and entirely spiritual therapy (Janbozorgi, 2016a, 2016b, 2017 and 2019).

The God-OSP should be considered in the framework of the fourth wave of psychology. Based on a transdiagnostic view, this therapy model is based on the belief that forgetting, denying, or cutting off the relationship with God removes a part of a person's identity due to cutting off the relationship with reality and truth. This phenomenon occurs as a result of psychological trauma or wrong learning. The monotheistic meaning-making system is then damaged, and the ground is set for persistent perceptual error. Psychologists have already recognized this phenomenon as negative schemas (Young, J E; Klosko, J S; Weishaar, M E, 2003) or insecure attachment (Bowlby, J. 2012, Brown, and Elliott, 2016. Greenberg, M. 2019) while this is a person's natural monotheistic meaning system that is damaged. This therapeutic model has set its operative field as the "action" of man. The action here is any internal or external psychological activity that the beginning and end of which is voluntary, and the quality of its implementation can be measured. The effort to create coherence in the action and its monotheism, which is related to the activation of the relationship with God, brings back the person's natural meaning system and mental health. This effort and spiritualization of the action constitute the primary mechanism of God-OSP. Although this therapy model was first developed to help people with anxiety (Janbozorgi, 2000, 2016b), it is used for various disorders and psychological problems. Such as depression (Mohamadi, 2018), psychological well-being of patients with depression (Rohani et al., 2019), Psychological Disorders and Post-Traumatic Stress Disorder (Faraji et al.), Emotional Stability, Self-Control, and Body Mass Index in Overweight Women (Shamsolahrari et al., 2021), stress and heart rate variability after bypass surgery (Nequee,2021), and psycho-spiritual development (Janbozorgi & Janbozorgi, 2020).

Theoretical framework

According to this model, a person is born with pure nature. The core tendency of this nature is to achieve complete human action and seek God and happiness. The different dimensions of human existence are unified due to the fundamental meaning-making capacity given to human beings by God in the form of innate force (*Fitrat*). Although they create different perceptual spaces for their performance, humans may use this space in a limited way in processing their actions under the influence of experiences, needs, external pressure, and psychological traumas (Janbozorgi, 2019). Psychological traumas, wrong learning, negative experiences, and wrong role models have caused damage to the fundamental semantic capacity. Thus, it creates a conflict between a person's self-definition, fundamental concepts, and what he perceives, and the perceptual field has been reduced to a natural dimension with limitations in processing actions. This issue has been shown by today's psychology under the title of injuries related to attachment and identity (Greenberg et al., 2019; quoted by Janbozorgi, 2019) or moral injury (Litz et al., 2009). As a result of repetition, this issue reduces the flexibility of humans against truth and reality.

Therefore, we have two existential dimensions (natural and spiritual) and four perceptual domains (self, objective world, origin, and resurrection). In the field of spiritual perception, humans consider the "origin and resurrection" of their action, and by processing it in the field of natural perception, that is, "self and the objective world," he seeks to prepare the best action. Complete perception occurs when all relevant data from these four domains are processed together. It means that the action has a specific origin and resurrection and is meaningful to the person. Regarding meaningful action, there is the highest compatibility (goodness) and permanence outcome for the person. Therefore, spirituality in multidimensional God-OSP means the *wise action adjustment between origin and resurrection.*

Wise regulation indicates a self-regulating action that divides human actions into three characteristics: meaningful, valuable, and purposeful. In this therapy, the *innate intellect (II)* forms the core structure of the human personality, which is an innate structure that God placed in the core of human beings, based on the verses of the Qur'an (Shams: 8-12) and hadiths (citation required). Its main action is distinguishing right from wrong and identifying the best action in each situation. For this reason, God expects human beings to choose the best action in every situation (referring to verse 2 of Sura Mulk of the Qur'ān). Over time, man realizes his need for external guidance, providing the ground for *empirical intellect (EI).* Therefore, human beings use two loci of control systems to regulate themselves: internal (II) and external (EI) (Janbozorgi & Gharavi, 2018).

Human health is guaranteed when the EI is in contact with the II and harmonizes. The heterogeneity of the data and the human's compliance with the invalid external system on the one hand and ignorant action on the other are the basis of psychological problems. The foundation of II recognizing is the meaningfulness of action within the framework of the divine creation system. Therefore, the most reliable source of EI (or external locus of control) is what God has planned for humans (revelation). The two primary ways of distinguishing the II system according to this framework are, Peity or *Taqwa* (God-oriented self-regulation) which means coherence of action, and wickedness (wrong or *Fojur*) (non-God-directed self-regulation) which means separation of action. The function for accurate action processing of this nuclear system, in addition to diagnosis, is the integration of all perceptual domains. Our action is dependent on our perception of reality. Action refers to any voluntary function in which a person can start and stop it.

Therefore, the basic principle of the God-OSP is that psychological unity represents mental health, and psychological disorder results from the loss of this unity. The factor that can create this psychological unity cannot be non-monotheistic. Therefore, only God can cause this psychological integration in the strict sense of the word.

Since, according to Qur'anic verses, human actions create human identity, conscious management of action is the most critical function of human health. Voluntary motivation and intention manage the intention during the action. It helps to choose the most valuable form of action. It also enables one to voluntarily end the action and receive feedback on its effect, indicating a healthy action cycle. If this cycle is God-oriented, the action is formed in the highest degree of its compatibility because the measure of its internal (intellect) and external sources (God's plan) provides the most consistent form of action together with human nature (the fungus or *Fiṭrah*). If each action step, such as the action's beginning, end, or management, is out of the person's control, or the final goal is not applicable, the action cycle takes on a pathological form. Therefore, in the treatment, an attempt is made to change the pathological action cycle to the adaptive and competent action cycle.

During psychotherapy, the de-imagination of perceptual domains and the activation of II and EI are always considered. It is essential to be aware that the action starts in the natural and objective sphere, settles in the inner and spiritual world, and often affects other human actions. The legality of the external and internal psychological world and its similarity to the world and the hereafter significantly affects the conceptualization of some therapeutic mechanisms such as forgiveness, compassion, care, and faith.

Therefore, the mechanism of the effect of multidimensional spiritual therapy is related to several things; activating the intellect for realism, processing the righteous action, being aware of the intention (origin) and the effects and feedback of the action (resurrection), creating a monotheistic attitude, internal refinement of actions that are inconsistent with human nature, self-differentiation, and saving the action (Janbozorgi, 2019). This process is conceptualized in Figure 1.

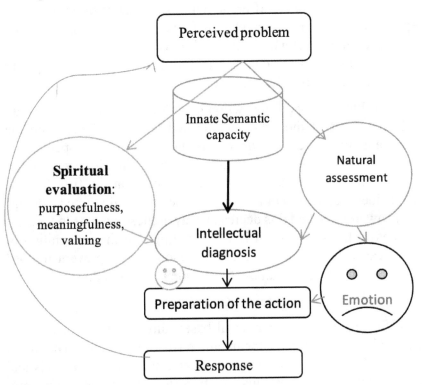

Figure 1: *An integrated model for explaining the process of spiritual action.*

This model explains human reaction to psychological problems on six levels. At the first level, the problem is perceived by the person. This problem may have an internal or external stimulus.

At the second level, the "semantic capacity system" checks it. If its meaning is obvious, it is sent to the internal diagnostic system (II), and the best possible reaction is checked, and it goes on to the next steps. But if it is inconsistent with the innate semantic system, it may be evaluated in a non-spiritual dimension and take the next path to action, or it may take the emotional path. In the spiritual cycle, the value, meaning, and purpose of the action are verified.

In the third level, the internal and external actions of a person are observed by the innate intellect, and after confirming the heart, it enters the next level. At this stage, in any case, the natural mind evaluates the correctness and harmony of that action with the overall psychological system of the person. In the fourth level, how to perform the action and different options for decision-making are prepared according to other internal forces, including emotions and time-space situation, and other conditions for action. At the fifth level, the action is prepared in its final form, and the volitional system comes into action after the decision.

At the sixth level, the action is performed, and at the seventh level, the effect of the action is checked, and it is faced with the action, and this effect (feedback) is again sent to the perceptual system for correction or follow-up or stopping. In all these stages, a human being is aware of his actions. However, at the fifth level, a person does not have control over some of his disturbed actions, despite awareness, and this decrease in awareness extends to the next stages as well. Of course, it is worth noting that the recognition of innate reason is not optional, and a person cannot prevent himself from recognizing reality unless the person is antisocial.

Intervention process

God-OSP can be applied manual-based directly and can be used analytically and indirectly for treatment-resistant clients. The initial protocol of the God-OSP was set under four treatment rounds and between 60 and 70 sessions (Janbozorgi, 2019), but short-term treatment protocols consisting of 10 to 20 sessions were also designed for various psychological problems, including depression (Rohani et al., 2019, Mohammadi, 2018), personality anxiety (Janbozorgi, 2000), mental health and religious adherence in addiction (Haqmohamadi, et al. 2021), post-traumatic stress disorder (Faraji , et. al. 2021), stress management after bypass surgery (Nequee,2021), Weight Loss and its effect on Emotional Stability, Self-Control, and Body Mass Index in Overweight Women (Shamsolahrari, et al. 2021), lifestyle regulation based on GOD-OSP for management of anxiety (Janbozorgi, A and Janbozorgi, M. 2021).

The process of psychotherapy evaluated and formulated a **preliminary round** to introduce and define spirituality and the spiritual conceptualization of actions. The **first-round** deals with the activation of the II, in which, while increasing insight, the function of II and its obstacles are examined, and with awareness of the learning that they hinder the operation of the II, it increases the trust to II.

In the **second round**, insight into the origin of action brings the clients closer to the activation of the spiritual dimension, the function of faith in God, considering him as the only facilitating factor for internal integration. At this stage of treatment, the following items are considered; developing a monotheistic attitude, de-imagery from the origin (distinguishing the real image of God from the images that are the result of parents' projection), feeling valuable to God as the creator of man, awareness of God's lordship and his care for man, and exploration the best plan of God's well-being for Man. In this round of therapy, the clinical symptoms of clients are usually significantly reduced.

In the **third round**, based on the choice of God's plan/story (from my story and your story) as his lifestyle, he connects his empirical intellect to an authentic source. Now II and EI work together to find the true identity. According to this program, human beings are naturally flexible towards perfection (God/Allāh) and show humility and reverence towards it. It is assumed that this flexibility towards injustice, meaninglessness, and oppression removes the human being from wholeness or monotheism. Therefore, in this round, firstly, self-image is analyzed, and is validated and checked. Secondly, according to the known point of the world, which is God, the definition of man and the general identity of man, i.e., slavery (flexibility to the righteousness), is revived, that is usually its function in life is examined.

The index of gratitude is followed, which is the most important index of change and the path of spiritual health (direct path). In this round, the most important areas of human vulnerability are examined, and the topic of spiritual care is followed based on verse 17 of Sura Al-Araf, which is called Vulnerable spiritual four-sidedness: Firstly, the human being from the goal or what he faces (the front). Secondly, the support or what relies on them or is attached to them (back). Thirdly, by creating doubt in correct performance and exaggeration in integrity, and fourthly (right), emotional impulses that cause emotional and sensual behaviors are investigated (left), and spiritual self-care is practiced from these four angles.

One of the important therapeutic mechanisms to enter the third round of psychotherapy is to recover spiritual identity and consciousness of lost innocence. According to verse 12 of Surah Shams from the Holy Qur'an, a person suffers psychologically and spiritually when he stores incongruent actions in a mental frame as a private event with his pure nature and protects them as private events. Because these actions are emotional and especially produce a sense of guilt, they affect the human action plan in different areas and divert him from the path of health or innocence. Reviewing them in his mind causes a drop in his motivation and performance quality. Resolving these actions or at least identifying their function is an important issue for therapy.

In the **fourth round**, the spiritual therapist deals with saving the action and transforming the ineffective action into a good and lasting action based on the verses of Surah Al-A'laa. Searching in the mind of clients for the exact meaning and conceptualizing of Images, the world, and the others, exchange negative actions into positive and positive actions into transcendence action, practicing gratitude, practicing forgiveness, and letting go are all pursued in this round.

In the **last round**, titled "Return to authentic life", the concept of death and the Hereafter, and one's ideas and image about them, are investigated, and its relationship with one's problems. Modifying these perceptions expands one's relationship with real life.

In the **follow-up** phase, the two concepts of remembrance of God or God-fulness (*Dhikr*) and asking forgiveness from God (*'istighfār*) as two mechanisms that maintain the results of the therapy are discussed and practiced and this completes the treatment (Janbozorgi, 2019).

Diagnosis and formulation process

Therapy begins with the reception phase. In this phase, the spiritual clinical psychologist tries to check the index to begin the intervention where severe emotional disorder such as II is not accessible, organic symptoms of the disorder, severe obsession, complete and deliberate disbelief in the existence of God with age less than 12 years and simultaneously psychotherapy is among the factors that prevent the acceptance of clients. Then, to diagnose the disorder, a conventional clinical interview is conducted. In the next step, a spiritual clinical interview is performed. In the field of spirituality, ten problems are examined: the individual's worldview, religious beliefs and their validity, religious and spiritual coping, the God-Image, psycho-spiritual development, conversation with God, religious behavior and rituals, religious adherence, measuring intellect and lifestyle/Values system. The results of these assessments are important in determining the therapeutic program. A person may be given direct or indirect treatment, and according to the symptoms and condition of the person, a short-term or long-term program may be considered. The choice of therapeutic regimen depends on the severity of the disorder and the psychological and spiritual evolution of the person (Janbozorgi, 2019; Janbozorgi and Janbozorgi, 2020).

After informing clients with God-OSP and evaluations, extracting psychotherapy and monitoring indicators, we formulate the individual's problem in the framework of the intervention method. In the formulation, after summarizing and diagnosing the disorder, the following process is performed:

- Analyzing the individual's data in a collaborative way and examining background factors (especially during innocence or childhood), revealing factors (especially factors that have affected the person's semantic capacity, changed the attachment styles, and changed the person's definition of himself), maintaining factors (the person, the environment, especially the image of God).

- Definition of the problem based on the integration and analysis of the information obtained from the recent process.

- Determining and clarifying the final therapeutic goals.

- Analyzing a person's problem, obtained from objective and suitable data, within the framework of psychotherapy goals and methods.

- Setting the basic hypotheses of psychotherapy based on the dimensions of the person's problem in the form of an intervention method, as well as determining the mandatory consultations that may be necessary to facilitate and speed up the psychotherapy (such as the use of medication).

- Final analysis of the problem with and without the spiritual cycle and considering the change of the problem.

- Arranging the psychotherapy program and work contract.

The goal of psychotherapy here is to restore psychological balance and facilitate a person's path to transcendence based on the innate meaning system. These general goals are pursued through the activation of innate intellect, the recovery of lost innocence, the reduction of clinical symptoms, the activation of wise spiritual practice, and the differentiation of traumatic events in the life of clients.

Therapeutic principles

The mechanisms and principles of the therapy here are based on the theoretical framework (Janbozorgi & Gharavi, 2018). The program of therapy is set based on the principle that the interaction of II and EI provides the basis for self-regulation. A person's God-oriented interaction saves him from a mental disorder. When this system is not accessible and active, man becomes vulnerable. Therefore, it is important to activate this system and trust it.

Transforming images into real concepts in perceptual domains is the basic principle in God-OSP. Among the most important are Image of God, Self- Image, World-Image, Others-Image, Death-Image, and Image of hereafter. The real concepts of each of these remove the disordered image from the mind and provide emotional regulation by God-oriented intellect.

In different sessions of psychotherapy, about 50 different techniques, along with operational worksheets, provide the possibility of realizing change. In addition to the general techniques common with other psychotherapies, some special techniques are as follows: activation of II, activation of God-oriented intellect, analysis of the period of spiritual innocence (before puberty), recovery of spiritual identity, analysis of images and the history of their formation and dysfunction, a walking daily with II, regulating action between origin and resurrection, God-oriented self-care, choosing the best life plan and God recommended life plan, action saving, and experiencing authentic life. These techniques have obtained an acceptable score in evaluating the coefficient of clinical effectiveness. These techniques are used in research with clinical psychology experts and have also treated clients who are under follow-up (Janbozorgi, 2019).

In this treatment, the basic assumption is that God is the main healer, and the only therapist has the role of facilitator. The mechanism of receiving real concepts is exploratory, and the therapist trusts the individual's internal diagnostic system (II). Therefore, in the initial stages of intervention, the therapist is active and gradually allows the client to reach the main path.

Case report

Mojtaba, a 35-year-old married man with a child, suffered from anxiety and some obsessions for six years. He had a difficult childhood, lost his father at 8, and was sexually abused by three young men in primary school. He was anxious about expressing himself in social situations. He has a religious orientation, but he had many conflicts with God and his current religious duties. *Mojtaba* was not successful in his work due to anxiety and obsession. He was unhappy with his marital relationship and saw himself as an unworthy father. Although his family was satisfied with him and he achieved relatively good financial success, he had been undergoing various psychotherapies for five years, three of which were psychoanalysis, but symptoms returned quickly. Short-term treatments such as cognitive behavioral therapy could not reduce *Mojtaba*'s symptoms and discomfort. He consulted a famous Tehran psychiatrist, who suggested spiritual therapy. *Mojtaba* was first clinically interviewed and evaluated. The data showed that he has high anxiety, mild obsessions, emotional instability, a little pessimism, perfectionism, and nervous tension. His worldview is conflicting and negativistic, and despite being religious and showing interest in it, his lifestyle contradicts his religious interest, and he was not religious. The conception of the image of God and reality caused mental confusion and emotional instability. According to the conceptual model, he did not trust his inner source (innate intellect), and most decisions were emotional and influenced by others.

In his assessment, *Mojtaba* considered himself extremely guilty and worthless and felt that he was losing control with each passing day. He felt that God had forgotten him, and that the world had not left him any chance. When he was introduced to the logic of God-OSP, he was asked to re-evaluate his internal and external actions by assuming the existence of God and his help. Thus, he came up with a different analysis. He realized that none of his disordered thoughts, problematic behaviors, or anxiety, had any meaning, purpose, or value. When the underlying, revealing, and maintaining factors of the problem were processed in the spiritual field, the cycle of spiritual action was explained to him. He realized his problem was a lack of psychological coherence and not truly seeing things. He realized mental problems seem much worse and unsolvable without considering the spiritual dimension.

After the contract to start psychotherapy and the preparation of the monitoring tool, the initial sessions begin by establishing a therapeutic relationship. The work with him began with a de-imagination of the concept of spirituality. The therapeutic challenges started with the difficulty of controlling the mind and the action to adjust them between origin and resurrection. The client became aware of the lack of mastery over his actions, the meaninglessness of many pathological actions, and the pragmatic nature of psychotherapy. Usually, each concept is followed by creating a challenge and doing an activity.

In the next stage, the innate intellect was activated under the title of the internal expert diagnostic system by practicing the metaphor of the island. This enables us to understand its innate function by reviewing it in real life, acutely identifying its obstacles, and pursuing ways to strengthen it. *Mojtaba* was then asked to examine his perception of his parents and important people and their function in his life. It was important to determine the effect of parents on the formation of *Mojtaba's* intentions and motives by analyzing *Mojtaba's* actions. The hypothesis of this intervention was that if anyone, or anything, except God, is the origin of the action, that action will not be fully functional. He became aware of this effect.

Furthermore, to increase the purity of his action, he began to practice being conscious of God's presence in his action and passively observed the effect of others on his action. By activating his natural intellect, he realized that his previous learning prevented him from believing in God and always doubted His existence. Now, to be aware of the image of God, he was asked to tell his ideas about God. Then he analyzed these images, their function, and the history of their formation and realized the similarity between the image of his parents and the image of God. After the de-imagination of God in the light of the holy Qur'an through his search and discovery, his feelings towards God and its effect on his actions caused many of the symptoms of the disorder to subside. The work on the signs of obsession and anxiety had not yet started. He reported no signs of other symptoms, especially the relentless anxiety. Spiritual identity was created by performing the treatment steps of the third stage protocol that examined the history of self-images and validated them. When he defined himself as a servant of God and flexibility towards God, there was a negative self-image change to correct self-concept.

In addition, *Mojtaba* considered self-care (based on verses 16 and 17 of Sura A'raf of the Qur'ān). God-oriented self-care practice made him sensitive to emotional actions, aggressions, and anxious decisions and helped him to seek ways to control them. It was interesting for *Mojtaba* to practice gratitude and to distinguish the mood of being thankful from being ungrateful, which balanced his mood. In the next round of treatment, *Mojtaba* made significant progress by saving his actions and establishing a real relationship with others and the world. He managed to forgive all the cruel people in his life, including himself, have a compassionate look at others, and regulate his emotions and desires towards worldly possessions.

Now he gently defends his right and can easily express his feelings to others. After passing more than 20 intervention sessions, he no longer reports any signs of disorder. In the last stage, *Mojtaba* managed to change his perception of death. The anxiety of death was changed to the concept of transition to a wider life and the fear of calculating the afterlife to the love of meeting God (based on the verses of the Holy Qur'ān). The fact that whatever God wills is good for us, his acceptance of any difficulty increased. *Mojtaba* was terminated by practicing the seeking forgiveness from God (*'istighfār*) and God-fulness (*dhikr*) for the lasting results of the treatment.

How to evaluate changes

Changes were tracked in two ways: one, through indicators selected for psychotherapy that were aimed at the beginning of each round. Other, through various valid tests, such as Beck's anxiety inventory (Kaviani, et. Al, 2008) and a religious adherence questionnaire (Janbozorgi, 2010). Pre-tests were taken at the beginning of intervention and were repeated at the end of each round. Although Janbozorgi (2019) reported the statistical results of a group of clients, clinical changes show that the target client (*Mojtaba*) not only achieved sufficient balance in various indicators but was also able to excel in indicators such as helping others, forgiving people, transcending situations, and managing unproductive efforts.

It should be noted that in Mojtaba's case, five years have passed since the termination of the therapy. He has had more than eight follow-up sessions and has not reported any signs of relapse. He still reports that he is improving and making more progress and that some of the repeated past experiences have become new experiences for him. For example, he said, "For the first time, I enjoyed the worship of the holy month of Ramadan." For him, the relationship with his wife and children are the best moments of his life.

Conclusion

To conclude, psychological injuries and traumas break the meaning-making capacity. This causes the deactivation of the Innate intellect, trusts in invalid external sources, collects and internalizes actions inconsistent with nature. This makes the basis for future life planning imaginative processing (unreal or only mental) rather than real processing. The lack of a monotheistic attitude causes the inability to self-regulate and regulate action between the origin (intention) and resurrection (goal and feedback) providing the context of psychological vulnerability by reducing integration. God-OSP seeks to activate this spiritual self-discipline and restore the person's mental health. If a person can adjust his actions between two valid internal and external guidance forces (innate reason and empirical reason with the priority of God's plan for man), it integrates his psychological system as a light from inside and outside.

With a God-oriented approach, the spiritually multidimensional therapy draws the person's attention from his problems to the open paths that God has given him. God-oriented self-regulation allows a person to keep himself on a safe and healthy path by managing the beginning and end of his actions. Allāh is the light of heaven and earth that enlightens and guides all creatures, concepts, and obscure phenomena of the world. With Him, we perceive the facts as they are. Therefore, the spiritual treatment is summarized in a few basic steps:

1. Spiritual conceptualization of the perceived problem.

2. Activation of intellect

3. De-imagination of the perceptual domains.

4. Revival of spiritual identity and self-care, overcoming self-image, and opening with self-concept.

5. Rescue the Action for building spiritual identity, differentiation, and diffusion (God-self, other-self, self-world, self-thought, self-emotion, and self-behavior), inner cleansing from heterogeneous actions, and psychological spiritual capitalization.

6. Returning to real life, well-being, and benevolence with the company of God.

7. Experiencing integrity, staying in real life with God's help, and caring to prevent recurrence.

God-OSP is applied for some psychological disorders and has the necessary empirical evidence. This model of therapy follows its own developmental process.

References

Ansari, H., Janbozorgi, M., et al. (2019). Design an Islamic approach of CBT in the treatment of OCD, *Clinical Psychology Studies [Persian]*, 34, 167-196.

Bowlby, J. (2012). *A secure base: Clinical Applications of Attachment The*ory. London: Routledge.

Brown, D. P., Elliott, D. S. (2016). *Attachment Disturbances in Adults: Treatment for Comprehensive Repair*. New York: W.W. Norton.

Faraji. F, Sh. Nouhi., A. PiadeKoohsar., M.Janbozorgi. (2021). The Effectiveness of God-inclined Spiritually Multidimensional Psychotherapy (SMP) in Improving Symptoms of Psychological Disorders and Post-Traumatic Stress Disorder. Journal of Assessment and Research in Counseling and Psychology Vol 3/No 1(7), 1-16.

Haqmohamadi, Sh.G. & Janbozorgi, M (2021). Comparison of the effectiveness of 12-step addiction treatment and Spiritually Multidimensional Psychotherapy on mental health and religious adherence in Substance Dependents. *Cultural Psychology [Persian]*, 5(1), 61-86.

Janbozorgi, M. & Dastani, M. (2014). An Overview on the Experimental Situation of Psychotherapy in Iran, *Studies in Islam and Psychology [Persian], 8(15)*, 145-190.

Janbozorgi, M. & Gharavi, S.M. (2013). *Theories of psychotherapy and counseling (principles, techniques, and cultural adaptations) [Persian]*. Qom: RIHU.

Janbozorgi, M. (2010). Construction and Validity of Religious Adherence Test on the Basis of the Statements of Qurʾān and Nahjul Balaghah. Studies in Islam and Psychology, 3(5), 79-105.

Janbozorgi, M. (2016a). Principles of Spiritually Multidimensional Psychotherapy (SMP). *Journal of Islamic Psychology [Persian]*, 1, 9-45.

Janbozorgi, M. (2016b). Spiritually Multidimensional Psychotherapy (SMP): Activation of spiritual action and its effectiveness on psychological problems of anxious clients, *Journal of Islamic Psychology [Persian]*, 3, 8-39.

Janbozorgi, M. (2017). Spiritual Multidimensional Therapy: Explanation of Psychological Phenomena (Health and Disorder) with Spiritual Constructs of Personality Based on Religious Resources, *Biannual Journal of Clinical Psychology & Personality [Persian]*, 14(2), 173-189.

Janbozorgi, M. (2019). *Spiritually multidimensional psychotherapy: a God-oriented approach [Persian]*. Qom: RIHU.

Janbozorgi, M., & Gharavi, S. M. (2018). *Principles of psychotherapy and counselling: an Islamic approach.* 2nd eds *[Persian].* Tehran: SAMT and RIHU.

Janbozorgi, M., Janbozorgi, A. (2020). The effect of God-Oriented Spiritual psychotherapy (GOSP) on Psycho-spiritual development. *Clinical Psychology Studies [Persian],* 11(41), 1-16.

Janbozorgi, M., Pasandideh, A., & Azarbayejani, M., (2022). **God-Oriented Family Therapy** [Persian]. Qom: RIHU.

Janbozorgi. M. (2000). Investigation the effectiveness psychotherapy with and without Islamic religiosity orientation on anxiety and stress. *J Psychology [Persian],* 2 (4), 343-68.

Jnbozorgi, A., & Janbozorgi, M. (2021). Therapeutic Lifestyle regulation: A Short-Term Intervention to Prevent and Treat Anxiety Based on Multidimensional God-oriented Spiritual Therapy1. Journal of Lifestyle, 6(2), 125-141.

Kaviani H, Mousavi A. Psychometric properties of the Persian version of Beck Anxiety Inventory (BAI). Tehran University Medical Journal 2008; 65:136-140 [Persian]

Litz, B. T., Stein, N., Delaney, E., Lebowitz, L., Nash, W. P., Silva, C., & Maguen, S. (2009). Moral injury and moral repair in war veterans: A preliminary model and intervention strategy. Clinical psychology review, 29(8), 695-706.

Mohammadi, J. (2018). Adaptation of spiritually multidimensional psychotherapy for Depression. (*Unpublished PhD thesis* [Persian-Unpublished]). Tehran: Tarbiat Modares University.

Nequee F. (2021) Effect of multidimensional spiritual intervention on stress and heart rate variability after bypass surgery. Islam and Health Journal. 2021; 6(2): 12-23.

Rohani, M, Janbozorgi, M., Ahadi, H. & Beliad, M. (2019). The Effectiveness of the Short-Term Pattern of Spiritually Multidimensional Psychotherapy (SMP) on Increasing Psychosocial Well-Being of Patients with Depression Syndrome, *Journal of Applied Psychology Research [Persian],* 10(3), 27-45.

Shamsolahrari, M., Nouhi, S., & Alipor, A. (2021). Effectiveness of Multidimensional Spiritual Therapy with a Focus on Weight Loss and its effect on Emotional Stability, Self-Control, and Body Mass Index in Overweight Women. Knowledge &

Research in Applied Psychology, 22(3), 62-70. doi: 10.30486/jsrp.2020.1901566.2465.

Young, Jeffrey E; Klosko, Janet S; Weishaar, Marjorie E (2003). Schema therapy: a practitioner's guide. New York: Guilford Press. ISBN 9781593853723. OCLC 51053419.

CHAPTER FOUR

MURĀQABA AS A MINDFULNESS-BASED THERAPY IN ISLAMIC PSYCHOTHERAPY

Nazila Isgandarova

With modifications and revisions, this article is based on the original article that was published by the *Journal of Religion and Health* in 2018.

Introduction

Mindfulness-based therapy models such as Mindfulness-based stress reduction (MBSR), Mindfulness cognitive-behavioral therapy (MBCT), Dialectical behavior therapy (DBT), Acceptance and commitment therapy (ACT), and Mindfulness-based relapse prevention (MBRP) are usually viewed as an integration of Buddhist psychology and Western psychology. In the 1980s, Jon Kabat-Zinn used MBSR as a psychotherapeutic tool for stress reduction in a general hospital setting and to treat relapse in cases of depression. The techniques combined sitting meditations, body scans, and hatha yoga. In MBCT, for example, the focus is to identify negative thoughts and beliefs that cause emotional problems. The goal of the therapy is to challenge these thoughts and beliefs and change them through acceptance. A review of the Islamic tradition, particularly the

Islamic theological and psychological sources, reveals that many aspects of mindfulness-based therapy models also existed in the Islamic tradition and were an integral part of Sufi psychology. The aim of Sufi psychology was not only to treat the "soul" and improve their relationship with God, but also to train the seeker to take responsibility for their *khawāṭir* and *wasāwis* (inner temptations or whims), thoughts, emotions, and behaviors with compassion and forgiveness.

Many Muslim psychiatrists, clinical psychologists, counselors, social workers, and spiritual caregivers integrate classical Sufi psychology with mainstream therapeutic approaches such as MBSR, MBCT, DBT, ACT, and MBRP in their clinical settings. The interest in both Muslim and non-Muslim meditation practices is especially growing in Islamic psychotherapy because of multiple clinical research studies that show that mindfulness-based therapy helps with multiple physical and mental health issues (Simkin & Black, 2014). In this regard, *murāqabah* is widely used as an Islamic contemplative exercise (Haque et. al, 2016). Although *murāqaba*-based/mindfulness-based therapy can be used by non-Muslim therapists with proper training, Muslim psychotherapists can mainly benefit by practicing it in their attempt to treat mental, emotional, and spiritual health issues expressed by their Muslim clients.

This article aims to highlight this psychotherapeutic technique in Islamic counseling by exploring the traditional sources of *murāqaba* (meditation) as a tool for Islamically oriented psychotherapy. First, I argue that *murāqaba* is a beneficial spiritual and psychological tool that has a therapeutic implication for Muslims in clinical settings. Although Muslim clinicians look to the classical Sufi tradition for this rich spiritual practice, they also need to adapt it to treatment context, diagnoses, and interventions. I will first describe Sufism, the mystical/spiritual tradition of Islam, then move to define Islamic psychotherapy and the various aspects of *murāqaba* by providing an overview of the Sufi literature. I will also highlight how the techniques used in *murāqaba* can be adapted and used as mindfulness-based stress reduction, mindfulness-based cognitive therapy, meditation, transcendental meditation, mind-body techniques (meditation, relaxation), and body-mind techniques. Although *murāqaba* might not be effective for all mental health issues, I suggest a possible value of *murāqaba* for treating symptomatic anxiety, depression, and pain. Furthermore, Muslim clinicians must be properly trained in classical Sufi traditions before using *murāqaba* techniques in their clinical practice. Although the application of *murāqaba* in therapy requires knowledge and training in Sufism, both Muslim and non-Muslim therapists can also benefit from the application of some elements of this therapy in their practice.

Sufism: Islam's Mystical/Spiritual Tradition

Sufism provides an essential foundation for Islamic psychotherapy as it has been recognized as the life-giving core since the emergence of Islam (Chittick, 2007; 2001; Murata and Chittick, 1994; Nasr, 2007; Ernst, 2011; Rahman, 1979; Schimmel, 2011; Sells, 1996). Sufi concepts have provided a strong foundation for Islamic psychotherapy in the past and continue to do so in the present. For example, the emphasis on the training of *nafs* (ego, self, soul) in Sufi psychology and its approaches to emotional and spiritual diseases have proved helpful in reducing stress and treating depression and anxiety. The word *nafs* refers to the "soul" or "the self". It is described as the spiritual reality of all living beings. In the Islamic tradition, it is also interpreted as the human potential to actualize the fullness of self-awareness, *'aql* (the intellect), or the "lower self", referring to spiritual impulses (Esposito, 2016). Therefore, many Muslim counselors, spiritual caregivers, and psychotherapists recommend certain spiritual practices such as *dhikr* (the rhythmic repetition of ' 'God's names) prescribed by the Sufi masters. As a ritual activity, *dhikr* is mentioned in the 'Qur'an (i.e., Q. 33: 41-42). It is either performed in a group or individually.

Although there is no consensus on what the name Sufism refers to, and it is beyond the scope of this study to present the diverse theories of Sufism's nature and origins, it is helpful to mention here that there are various explanations for the etymology of the term *tasawwuf* (Sufism). Some believe it is derived from *suf,* the word describing the rough woolen garments worn by many Sufis. Others draw a connection between the term and the *suffa,* an ascetic group of the Prophet's companions known as the People of the Bench. Due to the influence of Greek philosophy, the term is often associated with *sophos* (wisdom). It is also possible that the term is connected to the Syrian Sufi, Abu Hashim al-Sufi (d. 767). And finally, there may be a connection between the term and the *safwa* (chosen ones) who practiced *tasfiyat al-qulub* (the purification of the heart) (Ernst, 2008). Despite some controversies about the legitimacy of Sufism as part of the Islamic tradition, abundant examples show that prominent Muslim scholars such as Imam al-Shafi'i, Imam Ahmad ibn Hanbal, and ibn Qayyim al-Jawziyah followed the Sufi path. Also, many *shaikhs* (Sufi leaders) were prominent Hanbali jurists; for example, 'Abd al-Qadir al-Jilani (d. 1166) founded the Qadiri Sufi order, one of the largest Sufi orders in the Muslim and the Western world. Therefore, Muslim psychotherapists use Sufi practices as a legitimate tool in their clinical practice to help their clients not only improve their relationship with God but also address their mental and emotional health problems through their devotional rituals and practices.

Nevertheless, many Sufi writers, including a famous 13th century Sufi leader Muhyiddin Ibn' Arabi (d. 1240), prescribed four levels of understanding to be reflected in Sufi practice: *shari'ah* (exoteric religious law), *tariqah* (the mystical path and a term that was used to refer to the Sufi orders), *haqiqah* (truth), and *ma' rifah* (gnosis) (Frager, 1999). Shari'*ah* provides the foundation for the practice because it offers genuine guidance for living ethically and morally in this world. Without it, one cannot move to the higher levels.

Sufism represents a unique branch of the Islamic tradition that embraces "the earlier exemplary life of the Prophet Muhammad" (Green, 2012, p. 4). By integrating *shari' ah* and *tariqah,* it supports the *salik* or *murid* (follower of a spiritual path) to discover esoteric knowledge, to experience God directly, and to follow the practice of *awliya Allāh* (God's prophets and friends) in their private and public lives.

Although in the West, not many Muslims currently follow the traditional Sufi orders, some of the most popular Sufi orders are the Qadiriyah, the Rifa'iyah, the Shadhiliyah, the Suhrawardiyah, the Jerrahi Sufi order, the Naqshibandi, the Tijaniyah, and the Mawlawiyah in Anatolia and the Aḥmadayah in the Nile Delta. The Qadiriyah order was established around the teachings of 'Abd al-Qadir al-Jilani (d. 1166) in Baghdad; the Suhrawardiyah is based on the teachings of Abu al-Najib al-Suhrawardi (d. 1168) and his nephew Shihab al-Din al-Suhrawardi (d. 1234); the Rifa'iyah was founded by Aḥmad al-Rifa'i (d. 1182); the Shadhiliyah was founded by Abu al-Ḥasan al-Shadhili (d. 1258) in Egypt and North Africa; and the Chishtiyah by Mu'in al-Din Chishtui (d. 11420) in Central and South Asia. What differentiates these Sufi orders is their distinctive identity in terms of some Sufi concepts, i.e., *'fanaa'* (passing away) and *'baqa'* (abiding or remaining in God), or *sukr* (drunkenness or intoxication) and *sahw* (sober). For example, some Sufi orders, such as the Yasawiyah and the Naqshibandiyah, followed Abu Yazid al-Bistami (d. 874), who was famous for saying ecstatic utterances; whereas others (i.e., the Kubraqiyah and the Mawlawiyah) follow Abu al-Qasim al-Junayd (d. 910) emphasized sober Sufism, external aspects of the Shari' ah such as ritual purity and fasting.

The Overview of Islamic Psychotherapy

Islamic psychotherapy is a process that engages in assessing and treating cognitive, behavioral, emotional, and spiritual disturbances using Islamic and Western psychological interventions. Also, Islamic psychotherapy provides information, advice, encouragement, and instruction to the client using sources in the Islamic tradition. Those who provided Islamic psychotherapy used the Qur'an and the Prophetic tradition as the original foundation of their practice. However, during the period when Islamic sciences became diversified under the influences of Indian, Greek, Christian, and other thoughts, Islamic psychotherapy also became a highly complex field. For example, Islamic psychology, known as *'ilm-al nafsiat* (the science of the soul/self or psychology), became a unique branch of Islamic sciences and explored the self or psyche in the context of psychology, psychiatry, and the neurosciences (Ashy, 1999; Deuraseh & Abu Talib 2005). Gradually, Muslim clinicians and therapists, or *al tabib al-rūḥani or tabib al-qalb* (spiritual physician), also developed *al-'ilāj al-nafsy* (psychological therapy) to cure or treat the soul and mind (Haque, 2004). Muslim clinicians and therapists successfully used the work of Muhammad Ibn Sirin (d. 728) on dreams, the psychotherapy and music therapy of Abu Yusuf Yaqub ibn Ishaq as-Sabbah al-Kindi (Alkindus) (d. 873), the clinical psychiatry of Ali ibn Sahl Rabban al-Tabari (d. 870), cognitive therapy and psychosomatic medicine of Abu Zayd Ahmed ibn Sahl al-Balkhi (d. 850), physiological psychology of Ibn Sina, and the concept of spiritual diseases of Harith b. Asad al-Muhasibi (d. 857) and Abu Hamid al-Ghazali (d. 1111).

Nowadays, Islamic psychotherapy is becoming an independent discipline but is related to other forms of Islamic studies such as Islamic psychology, education, preaching, theology, Sufi tradition, and ethics. Islamic psychotherapy literature usually focuses on the interpretation and application of different Western-based counseling theories and techniques along with sources in the Islamic tradition (Abdullah, 2007; Dharamsi & Maynard, 2010; Sabry & Adarsh, 2013; Keshavarzi & Haque, 2013; Hodge, 2005; Abu-Ras, 2011; Isgandarova, 2008; Isgandarova & O'Connor, 2012; Isgandarova, 2012; Badri, 2000; Podikunju-Hussain, 2006; Badri, 2000). In this regard, those who prefer an integrative approach in Islamic psychotherapy came up with a few recommendations on how to use compatible Western approaches with traditional Islamic techniques. For example, some of them recommend Cognitive Behavior Therapy (Awaad & Ali, 2015), Family Therapy (Isgandarova & O'Connor, 2012), or other short-term approaches like Solution-Focused and Narrative Therapy (Valiante, 2003). Manijeh Daneshpur (2012) also suggested that the family systems theory can be used as a framework for understanding Muslim family behaviors and dynamics because it holds similar values to Islam about family relationships and identifies family interactions as milestones for emotional development, behavioral patterns, values, and loyalties for the individual members. However, a considerable number of psychotherapy books also pay attention to the careful use of Western psychological approaches (Dwairy, 2006).

The Overview of *Muraqaba* in the Sufi Tradition

Sufi practices are abundant. Therefore, there are major methodological differences between Sufi orders (i.e., Naqshi, Qadiri, Mawlavi), including in the practice of *muraqaba*. However, almost all Sufi orders agree that *muraqaba* is the most common mindfulness tool in the Sufi tradition.

In Arabic, *muraqaba* derives from the word "*raqeeb*", meaning "to watch over," "to take care of", or "to keep an eye." In the 'Qur'an (i.e., 4:1), it is also one of the names/attributes of the Creator, referring to ' 'God's role as a protector or caretaker. In Sufi practices, *muraqaba* is translated as "meditation" (Ernst, 2011) or contemplation (Azeemi, 2005). Regardless of how it is translated into English, in Sufi practice, it also refers to a certain type of meditation. In this type of meditation, the *salik* (one who follows the spiritual path) watches over or takes care of his *nafs* (soul) and acquires knowledge about it and its relationship with the Creator by being mindful of his/her feelings and outer surroundings. The individual performed the traditional *muraqaba* without the physical presence of his master or in the presence of the master. During the *muraqab*a, the *salik* needs to observe *batin* (inner), *zahir* (outward), and *ghayb* (hidden) states of being. The whole purpose of this important spiritual practice is to focus on thoughts, feelings, and sensations with openness, curiosity, gratitude, and acceptance.

Generally, *muraqaba* practice also has certain levels: beginning, middle and higher stages. During these stages, the *salik* observes/watches over certain signs such as *ihsan, nur, haatif-e ghabi* (subtle sounds of the cosmos, manifestations of the attributes of God), reflection on life after death, the spiritual heart, the purpose of life, nothingness, and the non-material universe.

Practicing *Muraqaba* in Clinical Settings

As previously outlined, *muraqaba* can be used as a meditation-based therapy in Islamic psychotherapy solely based on the Islamic tradition. It can be incorporated into Mindfulness-based stress reduction (MBSR), Mindfulness cognitive-behavioral therapy (MBCT), Dialectical behavior therapy (DBT), Acceptance and commitment therapy (ACT), and Mindfulness-based relapse prevention (MBRP). Taking into consideration that *muraqaba* also contains the same ideas with a variation of meditation style, this section describes the classical techniques in *muraqaba,* and they can be used regarding therapeutic goals such as spiritual, mental, and emotional well-being (See Table 1).

Table 1. *Techniques of Muraqaba and its use in therapy*

Meditation-based therapy	
Techniques of *Muraqaba*	Therapeutic/Clinical Implications
Mushahada (Observation)	Presence
Tasawwur (Imagination)	Focused attention and open monitoring
Tafakkur (Contemplation of Creation)	Creativity
Tadabbur (Contemplation of God's Names/Attributes	Connecting with Self, Nature, and Higher Power
Muhasaba (Self-Assessment)	Clarity, Serenity

The Preparation Stage

In the preparation stage, the Muslim psychotherapists prepare the client before the therapy by setting up rules to follow. Similarly, the *salik* needs to be mindful of the first stage or *maqam* of this type of spiritual practice. The Muslim therapist can apply the rules of the Naqshibandi Sufi orders, where it is the responsibility of the *shaikh* to provide clear instruction and guidance to prepare the client for the therapy. Similarly, in mindfulness-based therapies, the role of the guide/*shaikh*/therapist as a role model is important. Generally, in Islam, such a preparation starts with bodily purification which is called '*wudu*' or ablution. Therefore, the Muslim psychotherapist should ask the client to begin the preparation by taking ablution. Then the client is asked to enter *muraqaba*, or the stage of observation of feelings, thoughts, and bodily sensations. This stage usually lasts 5-15 minutes in the beginning, but then it can be increased to longer time periods. For this purpose, in the traditional settings, the *salik* usually sits in a dark room, kneeling in front of his *shaikh* (Sufi master) with his eyes and mouth closed and focusing on the inner aspects of self and his presence before his *shaikh*. The *shaikh* also makes sure that the *salik* follows the instructions by "checking the 'attendants' attentiveness by rapidly rolling his eyes over all of them" (Hussein, 2018, p. 30). In contemporary clinical settings, the therapy room does not need to be dark; a dimly lit room is sufficient to produce greater levels of relaxation and positive feelings. Also, the client does not need to kneel but needs to sit in such a way that he remains motionless and still to relax more. In mindfulness-based therapy, this is like the process of a body scan.

At the preparation stage, breathing is an important stage of preparation. The Muslim psychotherapist needs to teach the client how to exercise slow and deep breathing. For example, in the Naqshibandi way of *muraqaba* practice, the *salik* imagines white light entering through the stomach when he/she inhales through the nose and says *dhikr*. The common *dhikr* is "Allah Hu" which is considered one of the most sacred chanting in the Sufi tradition. For example, according to Hazrat Inayat Khan (1983), the *Hu* is also the most sacred sound referring to the Divine. When one chants the name of Hu, he/she imagines the blackness of carbon monoxide when he/she exhales through the nose. Depending on the orientation, the Sufi orders developed two categories of *dhikr*: the verbal *dhikr* (*dhikr jali*) and *dhikr* of the heart (*dhikr kafi*) (Saniotis, 2018). The hand position should follow certain positions. This special hand positioning represents the 99 Names of God. If the client is comfortable with this format, the Muslim psychotherapist can use these traditional elements at this stage. In the Sufi tradition, the special way of deep breathing along with a *dhikr* helps the *salik* to progress. 'Sa'di Shirazi (d. 1292) states that "Every breath taken in replenishes life, and once let go it gives joy to the soul. So, each breath counts as two blessings, and each blessing requires thanksgiving" (Chittick, 2008, p. 73; also see Shirazi, 2003). The Muslim psychotherapist can use this citation to encourage the client to reflect on the ability to breathe.

For a deeper reflection and contemplation in *muraqaba*, the Muslim psychotherapist can also prepare the physical environment by using candles, roses/flowers, and turning off any devices that prevent concentration and cause distraction and interference. This practice will boost mindfulness of sensory experiences such as sound, vision, etc.

Further, traditional Sufi writers believe that an effective *muraqaba* is possible through practicing the five pillars of Islam, including daily prayers, charity, social responsibility, kindness, and good manners (al-Ghazali, 1993). They also taught that it is important to be in a state of *'wudu'* (ablution, physical cleanliness) all the time to attain spiritual purification. They also recommended practicing *tafakkur* (contemplation) on the creation and ' 'God's 99 names/attributes, and exercise *muhasabah* (self-assessment) before and after prayers to prepare the self for *muraqaba*.

The stage of preparation should also involve a discussion of attitudes toward treatment. A famous 10th-century Muslim psychologist and founder of Cognitive Behavioural Therapy, Abu Zayd Ahmed ibn Sahl al-Balkhi (d. 934), offered sociological explanations as to why people do not seek help when they experience extreme fear and worry. For example, he mentions three major barriers that prevent the person from actively seeking treatment: 1) cultural beliefs about obsessions, 2) attitudes towards seeking treatment, and 3) loss of hope in finding a treatment (Awaad & Ali, 2015, p. 187). This kind of preparation allows the client to address unconsciousness and defensive attitudes toward treatment, to find a resolution and reduce *ghaflat* (heedlessness). In this regard, by giving an example of a drunk driver, Keshavarzi & Haque (2103) state, "The ' 'driver's condition—drunk, tired, angry, sleepy—will greatly influence his or her ability to operate the vehicle. Thus, one is encouraged to always be in a self-reflective state, to monitor ' 'one's day-to-day actions, views, cognitions, and behaviors as to whether one is attempting to truly live as a Muslim" (p. 236).

The Stage of Mushahada

One of the important therapeutic/clinical implications of *muraqaba* is to help the client to improve their ability to concentrate and focus. In this regard, according to Khwaja Shahsuddin Azeemi, who is the leader of the Azeemia Order, the Indian Sufi Syed Shah Waliullah Dehlawi (d. 1762) mentioned that the *salik* needs to use "the force of perception to concentrate on an object or idea, whether it is Divine

Attributes or on the separation of body and soul or any other topic" (Azeemi, 2005, p. 71). However, the role of the Muslim psychotherapist is to help the client to achieve the desired level during the *muraqaba*, which is being attentive to God. In this stage, Muslim psychotherapists teach the client to be mindful of whims and undesired thoughts and control them during the *muraqaba*. However, unlike the contemporary Western practice of mindfulness, as Syed Ghauth Ali Shah (1804-1880), traditional *muraqaba* encourages to attain "a point where the person himself becomes the meaning and becomes unaware of self" (Ali Shah, cited by Azeemi, 2005, p. 70).

For ibn 'Arabi, this aspect of *muraqaba* is the stage of *mushahada* (witnessing; observing) when "the individual self is annihilated" (Chittick 2008, p. 72). As Ali Shah mentioned, the Sufis believed that when "the heart is attentive to God or anything other than God then all internal organs follow its command, because they are all obedient to the heart" (cited by Azeemi, 2005, p. 70). This means that if a person is able to achieve an increased awareness/mindfulness of the Creator, all his/her mental and physical organs will achieve the state of mindfulness. Ibn 'Arabi's student, Muhammad ibn Ishaq Sadr al-Din al-Qunawi (d. 1273) (1949), even likened this process to achieving a total emptiness, which is compatible with similar contemporary ideas of optimal states of mindfulness that encourages freeing of the mind from unnecessary thoughts and being aware of the moment. Similarly, in mindfulness therapies, the concept of decentering is used to help the client remove the focus of attention from the self toward others. In cognitive therapy, it is expressed in terms of "cognitive shifting" that refers to "re-directing one's focus of attention away from a fixed idea or recurring thought, and toward a different focus of attention" (Mirdal, 2012, p. 1209).

In the classical Sufi tradition, the object for contemplation includes various subjects such as the face of the *shaikh*, the Prophet Muhammad, the Qur'an, and God. In Sufi psychology, thorough, focused attention on these objects by the person does not allow the mind to wander. Similarly, a Muslim psychotherapist can use various objects, such as elements of nature, etc., to help the client focus on and observe the flow of emotions, feelings, and thoughts without being stuck, reactive, or distracted. Proper practice of *mushahada* should help the client to remain still and motionless and endure the burden of emotions without being reactive. Sufis believe that letting go of whims and unwanted thoughts should produce more positive feelings and thoughts in the end. After 3-5 minutes of *mushahada*, the Muslim psychotherapist can ask the client to describe his/her experience of both pleasant and unpleasant bodily sensations, feelings, and emotions in a non-judgmental manner. Also, the client should be instructed that there may be times when they cannot control unwanted thoughts, whims, and memories, and they should not be discouraged. Sufi literature also includes stories of well-known and master Sufis who admitted that there are whole ranges of spiritual, emotional, and mental states or *hal* (plural *ahwal*) that can be beyond the control of the individual (Ernst, 20011, p. 115). For this purpose, the Muslim psychotherapist can, for example, use the key concepts in Mevlana Jalal-ad-Din Rumi (d. 1273), such as "acceptance and acknowledgement of both positive and negative experiences, unlearning of old habits and looking at the world with new eyes; decentering, changing one's focus from Self to Other; and attunement of body and mind" (Mirdal, 2012, p. 1208). In this regard, Rumi emphasized the "experiential approach" versus "experiential avoidance" (Mirdal, 2012). Therefore, at this stage, the Muslim psychotherapist can help the client to accept whatever comes to the client during the process of *muraqaba* and reflect on them in order to gain insight.

The Stage of Tasawwur

In classical *muraqaba*, the stage of *tasawwur* (imagination) usually involved feeling the presence of God, but since the 18th century, it also included the spiritual presence of Prophet Muhammad and the *shaikh* (Esposito, 2010). In some settings, i.e., for Indo-Muslims, the holy Ka'ba located in Mecca represents the symbol of imagination. The masters of the Sufi orders, i.e., Nakhshibandi, also encouraged the *salik* to "let the Shaikh enter your heart". In the Sufi terminology, this aspect of *muraqaba* is also called *"fana fi Shaikh"*. Become One or Annihilated in or with the Master. Gradually, the *salik* also learns how to practice the following:

- *Fana fi Shaikh - Fana Fi Rasul sm* - Become One and Annihilated in or with Muhammad.

- *Fana Fil Qur'ān*- Become One and Annihilated with or in the 'Qur'an and its commandments.

- *Fana fillah* - Become One and Annihilated in or with God.

Regardless of the variety of the symbolic elements in the Sufi traditions, the main idea is the center/ritual symbol for intensive concentration or archetypal imagery linked to the sacred. In the contemporary practice of *muraqaba*, it is not necessary to imagine the master, but the person can imagine a light that spreads the whole body (Azal, 2015). However, the Muslim psychotherapist in the clinical settings plays the role of guide, teacher, and leader. Sufi psychology and contemporary psychology both emphasize the role of the therapist in the therapeutic relationship. For example, when al-Ghazali prescribed intervention in cases where the patient rejects or is unable to stick to the opposite behavior, he suggested that the "shaikh should lead him from that greatly undesirable habit to another one, less desirable" (al-Ghazali, 1993, pp. 56-59). Similarly, Mirdal (2012) outlines, the "attainment of these psychological and spiritual states requires a facilitator or a teacher just as mindfulness training necessitates a person in authority to whom the patient turns for help" (p. 1207). Keshavarzi & Haque (2013) describe the crucial role of the therapist and compares them to the role of *shaikh* (master, guide, leader, spiritual healer). They state, "A shaikh, or spiritual doctor of sorts, has acquired and incorporated this experiential form of education (*tassawuf*) in the spiritual practices. They have been given permission to initiate others into the spiritual path by their s*haikh*. These spiritual healers have been the source of treating mental illness for generations in the Muslim community" (Keshavarzi & Haque, 2013, p. 236).

In addition to fulfilling the tasks of a modern psychotherapist, the Muslim psychotherapist should encourage the client to see through "the eyes of the heart". On higher stages of *muraqba*, the *salik* practices *tasawwur* or imagination for the transference of spiritual knowledge from master to student, spiritual knowledge from Prophet to student, experiencing the *tajalli* (manifestation) of God's attributes. Similarly, in the clinical setting, the client learns how to acknowledge the unpleasant and painful internal states, thoughts, sensations, and emotions from his/her therapist. The Muslim psychotherapist should create an environment where the client imagines openness to all forms of his/her experiences.

The Stage of Dhikr

As a traditional Sufi practice, *muraqaba* involves *dhikr* or chanting of divine names or certain prayers. Among the Haraghe Oromo who follow the Qadiriyya order, this stage also involves invoking the sacred by chanting the blessings and supplication on the Prophet Muhammad and asking forgiveness (Hussein, 2018). During this stage, the Muslim psychotherapist can give the special prayers or *dhikr* to the client and teach them how to use it properly. In *Muraqaba*, *dhikr* is recited with the combination of certain body postures, i.e., closing the eyes and taking a deep breath in and out. The Muslim psychotherapist can also use the classical Sufi ideas of the importance of *dhikr*. For example, for 'Ibn Arabi, the prayers and chanting are the conversations that start with God's invitation or request to dialogue/conversation or union, which is approved in the Qur'an: „Call upon Me, and I shall answer you "(40: 60). There are other verses, too, which emphasize this dialogue: "I am close, I respond to the call of the caller when he calls upon Me" (2:186); „I am closer to mankind than his jugular vein "(50:16); "Remember Me, and I shall remember You "(2:152). This process is reffered to as asking and asked for (*tâlib wa matlûb)* and involves the essential elements such as invocation and remembrance (*dhikr*) of God. This aspect of *muraqaba* is also "an act of the Heart" (Azeemi, 2005, p. 70).

In the Islamic tradition, *qalb,* or the heart, is the seat of spiritual knowledge that is learned through *dhikr* and *fikr*. In this regard, al-Ghazali stated "Oh friend, do not think that the door of the heart toward the spiritual realm does not open before death. This idea is wrong. When a person during his wakefulness, prays and abstains from immoral behavior, seeks solitude, closes his eyes and after suspending the outward senses turns his heart towards Gnosis. And then instead of using the tongue, invocate (*dhikr*) the Divine Name of Allah, with his heart and then loses himself and surrenders from all the physical things of this world. Then after reaching this station, the door of his heart opens even during wakefulness. Moreover, what other people see in their dreams he sees with his open eyes. He sees angels, he meets prophets of God and receives their blessing (*faidh*)"

(Azeemi, 2005, p. 71). For this purpose, the Muslim psychotherapist can use the classical prayer and *dhikr* manuals that classify God's names as *jalal* (majesty) and *jamal* (beauty) to reflect on God's grace, generosity, compassion, and mercy. The traditional *dhikr* practice encourages "expelling form consciousness of everything but God, reinforce the conviction that God is responsible for everything in creation" (Ernst, 2011, p. 97). Like in the Sufi tradition, using the *dhikr* as a clinical intervention should be accepted as a multileveled process which means that it should engage the heart, the soul, the spirit, the intellect, and the innermost conscience called the secret" (Ernst, 2011, p. 93).

The Stage of Tafakkur and Tadabbur

Muraqaba is contemplation and mental activity or state for further outward and inward inspirations (Azeemi, 2005). In traditional *muraqaba*, *dhikr* (remembrance) and *fikr* (contemplation) are important elements of spiritual awareness and mindfulness. For example, *dhikr* culture among the Hararghe Oromo is "a hermeneutic exercise that involves cognitive and analytical engagement with the exoteric meanings as well as the esoteric meanings of the world" (Hussein, 2017, p. 26).

Generally, *muraqaba* can also be translated as contemplation which "means to think or to focus on a given object" (Azeemy, 2005, p. 66). However, this aspect of *muraqaba* is reflected in the process of *tafakkur* and *tadabbur,* which I will translate as a theological reflection in this section. *Tafakkur* literally means to think on a subject deeply, systematically, and in great detail, and *tadabbur* means contemplation, remembrance of God, or thoughts of God. Both words are used often in the Qur'an. *At-tafakkur wat-tadabbur* (remembrance of God, thought of God) (3:191, 4:82) establishes the process of meditation. Imam Ahmad al-Haddad (Key to the Garden) defines *tafakkur* as follows: the focus and movement of the heart and mind through the meaning of things in order to reach the underlying intention. He also stated that "Knowledge comes from *tafakkur.*"

The Muslim psychotherapist can use the Qur'an, the Hadith (Prophetic narrations), and social sciences to instruct the client to reflect and contemplate at this stage. For example, the Qur'an states, "Surely in the creation of the heavens and the earth and the rotations of the day and night are signs for the *ulul al-bab*. Those who remember (*dhikr*) Allah, the Most High, standing, sitting and whilst reclining on their sides and who think (*tafakkur*) about the creation of the heavens and the earth, [They say] O our Lord You have not created this in vain, Glory be to Thee and protect us from the fires of hell" (3:190-191). The Prophet Muhammad (pbuh) encouraged reflection, and ibn Abbas and Abu Darda reported from him that *"Tafakkur* for an hour is better than a whole nights salah ". Muslim scholars and Sufi practitioners used various methods to enhance *tafakkur* and *tadabbur*. For example, Muhammad ibn Zakariya ar-Razi (Rhazes) (d. 925)considered theological reflection (*naz'ar*) obligatory (*waajib*). For Razi, theological reflection is a kind of attaining knowledge which aims at happiness or *sa'ada* and perfection or *kamal*. For this purpose, the person who tries this method affirms: (*a*) the existence of the rational human soul, separate from the body; (*b*) an intellectual pleasure that man may experience at the spiritual, rather than the bodily, level; and (*c*) a spiritual afterlife, in addition to the physical one (Shihadeh, 2005). For al-Ghazali, *kalam* (theology) was a theological speculation or *'naz'ar* for recognizing the validity of Revelation and religious belief. Therefore, he considered it obligatory upon everyone. For him, theology was not as the critical inquiry or *tahqiq* but as a means to seek a true knowledge of God or *ma'rifa*. Ibn Arabi also mentioned the ways of practicing it that include prayers, which should not be understood in the ordinary sense as communal recitation, but rather as theological reflection and a spiritual union and conversation with the Divine Beloved. Al-Suhrawardi (1975) stated that theological reflection occurs in *qalb* (the heart), which goes beyond basic anatomical functions. It becomes a pure soul and is illuminated by a shining light.

A contemporary Sudanese Muslim psychologist, Malik Badri (2000), states that the Islamic concept of *tafakkur* is different from Eastern contemplation or meditation because it encourages conscious sober thinking during the meditative practice. He states that *tafakkur* is a "cognitive spiritual activity in which the rational mind, emotion, and spirit must be combined" (Badri, 2000, p. xiv, 1). Moreover, *tafakkur* is "a refined form of worshipping God by appreciating His creating in this vast Universe" (Badri, 2000, p. xiv). Therefore, *tafakkur* in *muraqaba* should involve "a mixture of thought, cognition, imagination, sentiment, emotions and above all, spirituality" (Badri, 2000, p. 29).

During the stage of *mushahada*, theological reflection allows the elaboration of and reflection on the feelings, emotions, and bodily sensations observed. The Muslim psychotherapist can ask the client to start with identifying five feelings such as sadness, grief, anger, joy, etc. Second, he/she might ask the client to select a story in the 'Qur'an or *hadith* for theological reflection. For example, the story of Yusuf (Joseph) in the case of adoption or loss and depression might be used as a clinical example for theological reflection. During the process of *tafakkur*, the Muslim psychotherapist should instruct the client that he/she will go through four stages: (1) knowledge (via sight, hearing, touch, smell, and taste); (2) inspection of aesthetic aspects and qualities of data which yield fine appreciation, delicate feelings, and powerful passion; (3) crossing the boundary beyond or relating the object of contemplation to the Creator; and (4) spiritual cognition or *shuhud* (Badri, 2000, pp. 30-31). In this regard, the Muslim psychotherapist can use *Masalih al-Abdan wa al-Anfus* (*Sustenance for Body and Soul*) by Abu Zayd Ahmed ibn Sahl al-Balkhi (d. 934), the Muslim psychologist who discussed common mental disorders such fear, depression, and anxiety. For example, during the reflection process, the client can contemplate how their anxiety fits into the four main categories which al-Balkhi discussed in his book (al-Balkhi, 2013). These four main categories of anxiety are: *al-ghadab* (anger); *al-'jaza'* (sadness and depression) ; *al-faza' al-faza' al-faza'faza'* (fears and phobias); and, *wasawes al-sadr* (obsessional disorders) (Awad & Ali, 2015). The client can also be encouraged to reflect on al-' 'Balkhi's thoughts on how their thoughts prevent individuals from enjoying life, performing daily activities, and concentrating on other aspects of life. For example, al-Balkhi states that under the influence of intrusive, recurrent, and persistent thoughts, the person expects that the worst will happen soon.

Ibn Qayyim al-Jawziyah (d. 1350) described the importance of notions, reflections, and ideas in the mind because they become drives and incentives that lead to habits (al-Jawziyyah, 1994). He also described the nature of internal cognitive activity which is unceasing, i.e., they are continued and uninterrupted cognitive processes even during sleep (Badri, 2000, p. 22). Therefore, *tafakkur* is cognitive activity which starts with *khawāṭir* (the plural of *khatirah*) which means "an inner thought, a concealed speech or an internal dialogue" or "a fast, inner, concealed reflection, notion or unvocal thought, which may come fleetingly" (Ibn Qayyim al-Jawziyah, cited by Badri, 2000, p. 22). In contemporary psychology, it is like Aaron Beck's (1970) "automatic thoughts".

During this stage, the client needs to reflect on these inner thoughts because they later formulate human actions that can be harmful and sinful and strong emotions or *shahwah* (lust). In this regard, Ibn Qayyim al-Jawziyah stated.

You should know that the beginning of any voluntary act is *khawāṭir* and *wasāwis* (an inner temptation of Satan or whims) these *khawāṭir* and *wasāwis* lead to conscious thinking. Next, thinking will be transferred to or stored in the memory and the memory will transform into volition and a motive that will be acted out in real life as an action. Repeating the action leads to a strong habit. So, eliminating an emotional or lustful habit is easier at an early state before it gains strength (al-Jawziyah, 1981, p. 173).

Although these fleeting thoughts are as irresistible as breathing, the client can avoid them and accept the good *khawāṭir* and control harmful ones. During this stage, the client practices how to engage in good thoughts and spiritual contemplation. In this regard, as Badri states, this concept of Ibn Qayyim is similar to the concepts of the cognitive behavioral therapy and a systematic desensitization, a therapy that instructs the patient to relax and imagine themselves in a relaxing and beautiful place until the tranquil feelings replace the evoked anxiety (Badri, 2000, p. 25). In this regard, al-Ghazali offers a gradual approach in stimulating the opposite in internal cognition because he believes that "illness can only be treated with its opposite, like treating heat with cold, and cold with heat... the malady of ignorance is treated with learning, that of avarice with generosity, pride with humility, greed with abstinence and all by assuming the contrary" (al-Ghazali, 1993, pp. 56-59).

The Stage of Muraqabah (self-monitoring) and the Stage of Muhasabah (self-evaluation)

Many Sufi writers contributed to the exploration of this important concept in the Sufi tradition. However, it is a well-known fact that no one was able to present the details of *muhasabah* from a spiritual and psychological perspective like al-Harith al-Muhasibi (d. 857). It is no wonder that this famous 8th-century Sufi scholar became known as al-Muhasibi due to his contributions. During this stage of *murqabah*, the client is introduced to the Sufi idea of how to identify and bring under control the positive and negative potentialities within the human soul. With regard to negative aspects or weaknesses of the soul, the classical Sufi masters paid attention to *dhamm al-nafs,* or the dispraisal of the soul for its evil actions and intentions and the pursuit of its desires. Al-Muhasibi, for example, extensively emphasized the importance of the accusation of the soul or *ittiham al-nafs.* He drew attention to the deceptive and deceitful nature of the base self and even described it as the 'enemy within' (Picken, 2011). Although it needs thorough and careful consideration whether it is beneficial to have the 'broken 'soul', or *inkisar al-nafs,* through imposing punitive measures upon it. The Muslim psychotherapist can help the client to identify the weakness of the soul and ways to reform it. Further, the Muslim psychotherapist can help the client explore compulsive and unhelpful coping mechanisms that prevent the client from achieving optimum levels of *muraqabah.*

Incorporating *Muraqaba* into MBSR, MBCT, DBT, ACT, and MBRP

Contemporary Western psychotherapy has used various concepts of Buddhist meditation as stress-reduction techniques since the 1990s. For example, MBSR was developed by Kabat-Zinn (2003) for stress reduction, whereas MBCT was specifically designed by Segal (2002) to treat clinical depression. Both approaches aim to enable people to train the mind in presence and "recognize early warning signs and to engage in actions that prevent the return of the full-blown condition" (Marzillier, 2014, p. 167). Marzillier summarizes Kabat-Zinn's perspective of mindfulness as "paying attention in a particular way: on purpose, in the present moment, and non-judgmentally. This definition contains two features, present awareness, and the suspension of judgment, or acceptance (2014, p. 167).

MBIs have been proven to be more effective in comparison to conventional psychotherapeutic modalities. Later, Linehan (1993) developed DBT for treating patients with borderline personality disorder and as a tool for behavioral control, and Hayes (2004) developed the ACT for a range of mental and emotional issues encouraging commitment and behavior change to increase psychological flexibility and MBRP to address substance use (Simkin and Black, 2014). All these techniques use Buddhist meditation techniques such as *Sahaha* meditation, *Sahaja Sadadhi* meditation, *Sahaja yoga* meditation, *Tai Chi, Qi Gong, Yoga*, etc., that encourage self-management, self-control, and self-improvement (Simkin and Black, 2014). A practitioner does not need to become fully fluent with Buddhist teachings or study Buddhism or obliged to agree with all fundamental tenets of Buddhism in order to practice mindfulness-based interventions.

Like the implementation of Buddhist practices in contemporary Western psychotherapy, the application of classical Sufi understanding of human nature and mental and spiritual health issues has stimulated a new and dynamic discourse about the use of the Sufi practice of mindfulness in contemporary Islamic psychotherapy (Chishti, 1985; Hussein, 2018; Saniotis, 2018). The meta-message of the Islamic teachings is similar to the Buddhist philosophy expressed by Marzillier, "It is not your fault that you are the way you are. But you are still responsible for your actions and, with help, can escape the trap you find yourself in" (p. 177). In the Qur'an, we read: "Allah will never change a grace which He has bestowed on a people until they change what is in their own selves" (Q. 8:53). In this respect, post-treatment follow-ups, spiritual/religious practices and procedures are important to maintain the benefits of the therapy.

Muslim therapists need to engage in a deeper and more meaningful discourse about the implications of Sufi practices. The practice of *muraqaba* particularly can be used in mindfulness-based Islamic psychotherapy. I personally prefer to integrate this technique with the social sciences, such as family therapy, psychology, etc., and one of these techniques, i.e., MBSR, MBCT, DBT, ACT, and MBRP, to help the client understand the problem from their point of view. The benefit of such integration is that it provides a direct, whole body-spirit-mind awareness of the present moment. However, it requires the Muslim therapist to adapt MBSR, MBCT, DBT, ACT, and MBRP in efforts of acquiring mindfulness and complete relaxation drawn from within the Islamic tradition. Such integration allows for enhancing the therapeutic efficacy of mindfulness-based therapies. For example, depending on the need of the client, the Muslim therapist can choose the 'Qur'anic verses (i.e., "The likeness of the life of the present is as the rain which We send down from the skies: by its mingling arises the produce of the earth- which provides food for men and animals: (It grows) till the earth is clad with its golden ornaments and is decked out (in beauty): the people to whom it belongs think they have all powers of disposal over it: There reaches it Our command by night or by day, and We make it like a harvest clean-mown, as if it had not flourished only the day before! Thus, do We explain the Signs in detail for those who reflect "(Q. 10: **24**)) for a deeper contemplation.

In the context of Sufism, *muraqaba* is the most important technique to provide such a framework for body-spirit-mind awareness. It allows the person to learn new ways to detach from negative thoughts/feelings and become calm, peaceful, and accept change. Also, if taught properly, the client can practice it in day-to-day healing practice. In addition, like the traditional Sufi shaikhs, the therapist can choose various *dhikr* texts to reflect the mental, emotional, physical, and spiritual situation of a person who "is in a state of struggle against sources of uncertainty, instability and insecurity and reinforces the view that believers gain a sense of meaning, coherence and purpose from spirituality" (Hussein, 2018, p. 35). In this regard, if performed accurately, it can elicit psychological equilibrium and produce a state of calmness, altered states of consciousness, and intensify the state of communion with the sacred other (Saniotis, 2018).

However, it should be noted that the classical Sufi orders encouraged practicing *muraqaba* under the direct leadership of shaikh in order to avoid unpredictable unhealthy experiences such as *waswasa* (i.e., whispers, obsessions, etc.), disturbing or frightening experiences. Similarly, the Muslim therapist should also pay attention to the importance of the guiding context of *muraqaba* to avoid negative feelings such as anger and resentment or hallucinations. Therefore, the therapists, both Muslim and non-Muslim, who want to use this practice in therapy should be trained properly in Sufi psychology. Similarly, to the contemporary approach to the mindfulness therapies, in a secular context, a non-Muslim client can use *muraqaba* without accepting the whole Islamic teachings because the teachings of Islam, like other religious and spiritual traditions, such as mercy, compassion, love, justice, non-materialism, right livelihood, and dignity, are universal. Such an approach aligns well with Kabat-Zinn's position who, stated that, "One intention of MBSR was to recontextualize mindfulness within science, medicine, and healthcare "so that it would be maximally useful to people who could not hear it or enter into it through the more traditional dharma gates" (Baer, p. 102).

Nevertheless, as recommended in mindfulness-based interventions, the *muraqaba* technique in Islamic psychotherapy should be incorporated into practice, rather than a "cherry-picking" method. Proper training in Sufism and *muraqaba* is required to be effective. With proper training in both classical Sufi psychology and one of the mindfulness-based therapies, the therapist can help their clients develop self-awareness, loving-kindness, compassion, and empathy in their journey of healing. Furthermore, we need more evidence-based research to obtain empirical evidence on best practices and benefits of *muraqaba* and potential harms, such as relaxation-induced anxiety and fear of losing control, in clinical settings.

Conclusion

The practice of *muraqaba* is recommended not only for spiritual purposes but also for mental and emotional disturbances such as severe depression, anxiety, bipolar disorder, personality disorders, attention-deficit disorders, etc. Some even advocated the physical benefits of *muraqaba,* such as control of blood pressure, increase in life expectancy, improvement of vision, reduction of fat in blood, improvement in the performance of heart, hearing, increased immunity, increase of red blood corpuscles, end of insomnia, etc. (Azeemy, 2005, pp. 84-85). Many Sufi writers also reflected on the benefits of meditation and contemplation. Also, the concepts and practices in classical Sufi psychology have universal value and can easily be adapted to the challenges of the clinical settings. However, many also struggle with how to incorporate a spiritual dimension in their professional practice. In this article, I have attempted to use the concept of *muraqaba* to demonstrate how to incorporate it into mindfulness-based therapy with Muslim clients. Nevertheless, more research is required to enhance evidence-based *muraqaba* in Islamic psychotherapy practice and find out the positive correlation with mental and emotional health, stress reduction, and managing behavioral issues and emotional reactivity. However, the limited research in this area demonstrates how the concept of *muraqaba* can be a source of inspiration for not only Muslim but also non-Muslim therapists.

References

Al-Balkhi, Abu Zayd (2013). *Sustenance of the soul: The cognitive behavior therapy of a ninth century Physician.* Edited by Malik Badri. Herndon, VA: International Institute of Islamic Thought, 2013.

Al-Jawziyah, Muḥammad ibn Abī Bakr Ibn Qayyim. (1994). *Miftāḥ dār al-saʿādah wa-manshūr wilāyat   al-ʿilm wa-al-irādah.* Bayrut: Dasr al-Jil.

al-Jawziyah, Muḥammad ibn Abī Bakr Ibn Qayyim. (1981). *al-Fawaʾid.* Beirut: Dar al-Nafaʾis.

al-Ghazali, Abu Hamid. (1993). *Revival of religious learning* (Ihya Ulum-id-Din). Translated by Fazl ul-Karim. Karachi: Darul-Ishaat.

al-Suhrawardi, Abu al-Najib. (1975). A Sufi rule for novices (Kitāb ādāb al-murīdīn of Abū al-Najīb al-Suhrawardī). An abridged translation and introd. by Menahem Milson. Cambridge, Mass.: Harvard University Press.

Awaad, R. & & Sara Ali. Obsessional disorders in al-Balkhi's 9th century treatise: Sustenance of the body and soul. *Journal of affective disorders* 180, 185-189.

Azal, Roya. (2015). *Healing with Islamic meditation (Muraqaba).* Retrieved   from http://www.theartofislamichealing.com/healing-with-islamic-meditation-muraqaba/

Azeemi, K. (2005). *Muraqaba: The art and science of Sufi meditation.* Houston: Plato.

Badri, M. (2000). *Contemplation: An Islamic psychospiritual study.* London, UK: IIIT.

Baer R. & Crane, C. & Miller, E. & Kuyken, W. (2019) Doing no harm in mindfulness-based programs: Conceptual issues and empirical findings. University of Kentucky & University of Oxford: Clinical Psychology Review 71.

Chishti, A. G. M. (1985). *The book of Sufi healing.* New York: Inner Traditions International, Limited.

Chittick, W. C. (2005). *Sufism: Beginners guide.* Oxford: Oneworld.

Chittick, W.C. (Ed.). (2007). *The inner journey: Views from the Islamic tradition.* Sandpoint, Id.: Morning Light Press.

Chittick, W.C. *Sufism: A short introduction.* Oxford: Oneworld Publications, 2001.

Daneshpur, M. (2012). Family systems therapy and postmodern approaches. In S. Ahmed & M.

M. Amer (Eds.), *Counselling Muslims: Handbook of mental health issues and interventions* (pp. 119-134). New York, NY: Routledge, Taylor, and Francis Group.

Dharamsi, S. & Abdullah, M. (2012). Islamic-based interventions." In Sameera Ahmed and Mona M. Amer (Eds.). *Counselling Muslims: Handbook of Mental Health Issues and Interventions,* 135-160. New York, NY: Taylor and Francis Group.

Ernst, C.E. (2011). *Sufism: An introduction to the mystical tradition of Islam.* Boston: Shambhala.

Green, N. (2012). *Sufism: A Global History.* Oxford: Wiler-Blackwell.

Haque, A., Khan, F., Keshavarzi, H. & Rothman, A.E (2016). Integrating Islamic traditions in modern psychology: Research trends in last ten years." *Journal of Muslim Mental Health* 10(1), pp. 75-99. http://dx.doi.org/10.3998/jmmh.10381607.0010.107

Haque, A. (2004). Psychology from Islamic Perspective: Contributions of Early Muslim Scholars and Challenges to Contemporary Muslim Psychologists. Journal of Religion and Health, Vol. 43, No. 4, 357-377.

Hayes, S.C. (2004). Acceptance and commitment therapy and the new behavioral therapies: mindfulness acceptance and relationship. In Hayes, S.C., Follette V.M., Linehan M., editors. *Mindfulness and acceptance: expanding the cognitive behavioral tradition.* Pp. 1-29. New York: Guilford.

Hussein, J. W. (2018). The social–psychological and phenomenological constructs of spirituality in the culture of dhikr in eastern Ethiopia. *Culture & Psychology, 24*(1), 26-48. doi:10.1177/1354067X16672415

Isgandarova, N. (2012). *Effectiveness of Islamic Spiritual Care: Foundations and Practices of Muslim Spiritual Care Givers. The Journal of Pastoral Care & Counseling, 66*(3): 1-14.

Kabat-Zinn, J. (2003). Mindfulness based interventions in context: past, present, and future. *Clinical Psychological Science Practice* 10, 144–156.

Keshavarzi, H. & Haque, (2013). A. Outlining a psychotherapy model for enhancing Muslim mental health within an Islamic context. *The International Journal for the Psychology of Religion* 23, 230-249.

Khan, Hazrat Inayat. (1983). *The Music of Life*. Santa FE, N.M.: Omega Publications.

Linehan, M. (1993). *Cognitive behavioral treatment of borderline personality disorder*. New York: Guilford Press.

Marzillier, John. 2014 Trauma Therapies. New York, NY: Oxford University Press,

Mirdal, G. (2012). Mevlana Jalāl-ad-Dīn Rumi and Mindfulness. *Journal of religion and health, 51*(4), 1202-1215.

Murata, S. & Chittick, W.C. (1994). *The vision of Islam*. New York Paragon House.

Nasr, S.H. (2007). *The garden of truth: The vision and practice of Sufism*. San Francisco: Harper San Francisco.

Picken, G. (2011). *Spiritual purification in Islam: The life and works of al-Muhasibi*. London, UK: Routledge.

Rahman, R. (1979). *Islam,* 2nd ed. Chicago.

Sadr al-Din al-Qunawi, Muhammad ibn Ishaq. (1949). *I'jaz al-bayan fi tafsir umm al-Qur'an.* Hayderabad al-Dakan Matba'at Majlis Da'irat al-Ma'arif al-'Uthmaniyah.

Saniotis, A. (2018). Understanding Mind/Body Medicine from Muslim Religious Practices of *Salat* and *Dhikr.* Journal of Religion and Health 57 (3): 849-857.

Schimmel, A. (2011). *Mystical dimensions of Islam.* Chapel Hill: The University of North Caroline Press.

Segal, Z.L., Williams, M.G., & Teasdale, J.D. (2002). *Mindfulness-based cognitive therapy fordepression: a new approach to preventing relapse.* New York: Guilford Press.

Sells, M. A. (1996). *Early Islamic mysticism: Sufi, Qur'an, mi'raj, poetic and theological writings.* New York: Paulist Press.

Shihadeh, A. (2005). From Al-Ghazali to al-Razi: 6th/12th century developments in Muslim philosophical theology. *Arabic Sciences and Philosophy 15*, 141 179.

Shirazi, Sa'di. (2003). *The Bustan of Sa'di: the Orchard.* Islamabad: Alhamra.

Simkin, D. R. & Black, N. (2014). Meditation and mindfulness in clinical practice. *Child, Adolescence Psychiatric Clinical, 23* (3), 487-534.

CHAPTER FIVE

USING QUR'ANIC DIVINE SIGNS IN PSYCHOTHERAPY AND COUNSELLING:
Introducing Ayah-Therapy Foundations and Techniques

Filius F. Iakhin, Olga S. Pavlova

Introduction

Many directions of psychotherapy and counseling use metaphors, symbolic images, iconic figures, therapeutic stories, and parables as methods of clinical intervention. In some schools of psychotherapy, such as symbol-drama, analytical psychology, psychosynthesis, and art therapy, they became the main techniques of therapy. Some psychoanalytic schools, psychodrama, gestalt therapy, existential analysis, and schema therapy also actively use them in clinical practice. Even in cognitive behavioral therapy, which is characterized by the dominance of cognitive and behavioral interventions, the professionals do not ignore the advantages of integrating metaphors, parables, and instructive stories into therapy (Otto, 2000; Stott, 2010; Kovpak, 2019).

One can find something common in these techniques: some worldly things, events (real or imaginary), and sensual images point to the ideal contents of the human psyche and the environment and, using them as a therapeutic intervention can alleviate the clinical symptoms of mental problems or serve as a resource for deep positive changes in personality.

Nevertheless, because all schools and branches of world psychotherapy have elaborated their specific terminology, it is rather problematic to specify a common term signifying the main functional component of these interventions. However, we presume that such an all-encompassing concept exists: these mental phenomena are comprehended in a very ambiguous but inclusive concept of "symbol." Despite the differences in terminology and comprehension of this concept, we believe that the reason for such a wide application of the symbols in clinical practice is the multilateral interconnection of the symbols and the mental sphere of a person and its importance for mental processes.

In practical clinical activity, it is important to remember that despite the universalism of symbols, a large part of them turn out to be culture-bound phenomena. In relation to religious people, they refer to deep layers of their worldview. In this regard, in counseling and therapy, the client's ethnic, religious, racial, regional, and other characteristics are to be considered (Pavlova, 2018). Thus, the application of symbols in Islamic counseling and psychotherapy should not be implemented while ignoring the Islamic understanding of what the symbols are that determine the core meanings and foundations of their religious worldview and spiritual life.

The term "symbol" both in Muslim sources and Islamic Studies literature, is mainly used in the context of the permissibility and limits of the symbolic (allegorical) interpretation of the Qur'anic text and belongs to the sphere of *tafsir* - the Islamic science of Qur'anic exegesis (Buck, 2017). However, this aspect of the problem of symbolism in Islam is rather distant from the issues of Islamic counseling and psychotherapy and is beyond the scope of this chapter.

Nevertheless, due to numerous references in the Qur'an, Islamic literature reveals the content of another concept that has a broader meaning than the symbol and symbolism, but in many ways encompasses all characteristics of the symbols, including their interconnection with mentality, psychological and spiritual life, that is "ayah," what can be translated into English as "divine sign" or "miraculous sign."

This chapter is aimed at revealing the potential of using "divine signs" introduced in the Qur'an in the provision of religiously oriented psychological assistance to Muslims. It sets the prospects of developing the method of "ayah-therapy" based on the application of these divine signs. To achieve these goals, we analyzed some approaches to the concept of a symbol (sign) in psychology and philosophy, and the theory and practice of applying symbols in psychotherapy and counseling. Understanding that divine signs (*ayat*) have the deepest connection with the inner world of man and a comprehensive impact on his intellectual and spiritual development, along with the integration of the techniques that are applied in secular clinical practice, allowed us to introduce some methods for using the divine signs presented in the Qur'an as symbolic images in the practice of counseling and psychotherapy for Muslims.

Literature review

The concept of "symbol" has many aspects, and it is no wonder that many works devoted to symbols and symbolism in different fields of knowledge are available: philosophy, cultural studies, religious studies, anthropology, arts, psychology, linguistics, semantics, etc. It is impossible and unnecessary to make an extensive review of numerous sources within the framework of this chapter, and some fundamental ideas on symbols provided in the philosophical, psychological, and religious literature will be presented later.

In psychology, a huge amount of stuff on the role of symbols in the human psyche, methods, and techniques for using symbols in clinical practice has been accumulated. Nevertheless, like many other concepts in psychology, no one has managed to elaborate a universally accepted understanding of the notion of symbol and give its comprehensive characteristics and definition. Significant differences in methodology, even in the paradigm that defines the fundamentals of any school of counseling and psychotherapy, determine the apprehension of this concept and understanding of the role and extent of using symbols in clinical practice. Newly published works on symbolism in psychotherapy only go beyond the framework of a given school after trying to find common understanding and develop a generally accepted concept (Goodwyn, 2016).

In this regard, any attempts to review and summarize the theory and practice of using symbols in various schools of psychotherapy should be welcome. Among such efforts made by Russian authors, we would like to mention the research by Tsybulya V.I., who described the functions of symbols in psychotherapy, analyzing the ideas of prominent authors belonging to different areas of psychology and psychotherapy (psychoanalysis, analytical psychology, existential-humanistic psychology, etc.) (Tsybulya, 2012). In the article by another Russian author, Veraksa A.N., the cognitive and emotional functions of symbol are revealed, and their role as a special tool for orientation in situations of uncertainty is considered (Veraksa, 2013).

In Islamic literature, the name of ibn Qayyim al-Jawziyya should be mentioned, as in his prominent works, he made much effort to draw Muslims' attention to contemplations over the signs of Allah - the Qur'ān and His creations (Jawziyya, 2013). Malik Badri, an outstanding Islamic psychologist of modern time, devoted much of his famous work "Contemplation: An Islamic Psychospiritual Study" to reflections on divine signs as a tool for religious and spiritual self-improvement (Badri, 2018).

However, research on Islamic models of counseling and psychotherapy that have been made recently did not pay specific attention to the methods and techniques of using divine signs in clinical practice.

Underpinned by the fact that the application of symbols (understood in a broader meaning that encompasses the position of schools and areas of psychology that do not contradict Islam) is one of the acknowledged and rather effective tools of psychotherapy and counseling, the need to develop the initiative of using symbols in Islamic discourse as divine signs (symbolic images, stories, parables) seems to be of great importance for the development of theory and practice of Islamic counseling and psychotherapy.

Symbols in psychology and psychotherapy: a general review

As mentioned above, the concept of "symbol" is akin to psychology. A lot of authors from various areas of psychology used this term, and though they followed their comprehension, they, nevertheless, did not move far from the essential feature of symbol as an expression of something that explicated broader meanings than a simple designation, an indication of a thing or phenomenon (The Latest Philosophical Dictionary, 1999).

The word "symbol" was understood by S. Freud as the images of dreams in the unconscious, which were given a certain universal meaning (Freud, 2006). E. Fromm considered symbols as "visual images of words denoting any idea, feeling or thought" or rituals in which inner experience is indicated not by a word or image but by action (Fromm, 2009). For R. May, symbols and myths were an expression of individual or collective conscious and unconscious experience, a result of a dynamic connection between the subjective and objective poles, based on a living, active mutual influence, and exchange (May 2001).

Developing his ideas of collective unconsciousness, C. G. Jung went even further: according to him, every mental phenomenon can become a symbol if one assumes that it means something other than the phenomenon itself, eluding direct knowledge (Jung, 2018. p.14). For Jung "symbol" means a certain concept (term) or image, which along with its commonly used meaning, has a special additional meaning that carries something indefinite, unknown.

Russian researcher Tsybulya V.I. states that "a symbol in psychotherapy can be any sensually tangible (or internally imaginable) phenomena, provided that they are considered by the therapist as having or embodying a psychological meaning that matters for the goals of therapy" (Tsybulya, 2012). As a result of his review of approaches to symbol in various schools of psychotherapy, he listed such functions of the symbol as determining the meaning of a symptom or a problematic situation, generating the meaning, reflecting and understanding the meanings of Being, integrating, generating of experiences; explication of experiences; reacting (responding); organization and managing the therapeutic process;

forecasting; structuring of mental processes; suggestion (Tsybulya, 2012).

This diversity in the understanding of the symbol and its functions within psychology is not accidental. It does not point directly to the underdevelopment of psychological knowledge, but it proceeds from the complexity of the psyche in its relationship with the surrounding environment - nature and culture. Here, we cannot evade an excursion into the history of philosophical understanding of symbol since this concept was initially elaborated and developed within the framework of philosophy, attracting the close attention of thinkers from different historical periods of philosophy. And what is worth mentioning is that philosophical ideas about the symbol almost always permeated the mental sphere, so the symbols were regarded as immanent and indispensable tools for apprehension, cognition, and thinking, affecting human mindset, emotions, or behavior.

Symbol in philosophy: a historical excursus

A brief overview of the history of philosophical concepts of symbols, one can start with the Platonic tradition, according to which symbols were considered an expression of some higher essence, providing a transition from the rational world to the irrational world. They are interpreted as meaningful images, the decoding of which requires using an intuitive method of cognition (Afanasiev, Kozhukhovskaya, 2005).

Qualitatively, new meanings were given to symbols in Neoplatonism, which had taken the category symbol as one of the fundamental concepts of the whole philosophical system. Neoplatonists thought both human knowledge and the essential fundamentals of the outside world to be symbolic and in their closest relationship (Afanasiev, Kozhukhovskaya, 2005). For them, the world consisted entirely of symbols created by the creative deity and projected by him into various spheres of human life. Thus, symbols were considered "divine symbols" that a person would perceive as a correspondence between the external and internal - natural phenomena and their essence (Yakovleva, 2010). According to one of the prominent representatives of Neoplatonism - Porphyry of Tyre, through dreams and symbols, a person receives knowledge about the Divine Will (Yakovleva, 2010).

One of the "fathers" of early Christianity, A. Augustine, instead of the Greek term "symbol," used a Latin concept of a sign (*signum*), which is the same for natural and cultural phenomena. Augustine proposed a well-known definition: "A sign is a thing that generates in thinking, in addition to its sensual appearance, also something else" (Christian Doctrine, Augustinian Library, 1997). However, it is highly likely that it was not his main goal to reveal the connections between the sign and the designated object. Using the concept of traces (*vestigium*) as a type of sign, Augustine argues that this profane world bears the seal of the Creator Himself. Each thing is a kind of trace (*vestigium*) of God, Who endows it with a form that gives things the qualities of integrity, immutability, and continuity (Giraud, 2016). The created world is regarded as a sign of God (La Doctrine chrétienne, Bibliothèque augustinienne, 1997, p.475), and His Wisdom is manifested in everything in the form of a basic law and its essence: Divine Wisdom speaks to man through certain traces imprinted by it in everything created (Giraud, 2016). Thus, the sensory world full of traces appears, according to Augustine, as the Wisdom of God addressed to man.

In Augustine's opinion, man follows the path of his salvation, striving and approaching God through unraveling, interpreting, and reading traces (*vestigium*) and signs (*signum*) by which God speaks and designates Himself in His Scriptures and the surrounding world. In order to be at peace with oneself and with others, and most importantly with God, it is necessary, first of all, to be attentive and understand these signs (Giraud, 2016).

As we can see, in late antiquity and early Christianity, authors considered created nature, including man himself, as a certain set of signs, symbols that help comprehend Divine Wisdom and Will trying to gain peace of mind.

In the Middle Ages, the concept of a symbol was passed through transformation: religious symbols got "sanctity" that made them inaccessible, and even forbidden, for understanding and interpretation (Yakovleva, 2010). In the Renaissance, symbols became predominantly an aesthetic category, as an instrument of knowledge and creation of beauty (Afanasiev, Kozhukhovskaya, 2005).

A modern approach to the problem of symbols was started by I. Kant in his "Critique of the Power of Judgment" (Kant, 1994). According to Kant's view, man's ability to fully and objectively explore and talk about his Self, about his psyche, soul, and consciousness, i.e., the inner world, is limited. These phenomena can only be thought of symbolically. However, it is none other than the symbol that allows a person to be the subject of knowledge, even in relation to what is not given to him in direct experience and does not depend on him. As Kant thought, our reflections about God could only be symbolic, and for him, the symbol of the morally good was the beautiful (Kant, 1994). Thus, the symbol retains its important epistemological function, albeit limited by a certain framework.

Later, in the depths of neo-Kantianism, symbols were given a specific role: all types of human mental and spiritual activity (language, myth, art, religion, science, etc.) were encompassed within the integrative concept of symbolic forms of culture. For E. Cassirer, a symbol is a product and tool of cognition, which is a sensually expressed, pure, and free invention built by cognition to master the world of sensual experience (Cassirer, 17).

Structuralism (Levi-Strauss and others) shifted from Cassirer's concept of symbolic forms to the ideas of symbolic systems that modeled the world. For structuralists, the phenomena of culture are some systems of various symbols and signs, which are the external expression of the Self, and the symbol is a product of the expression of the structures of the unconscious (Radugin, 2001)—no more, no less. Psychologism is above all.

In the philosophical thought of the Soviet period, based on the dialectical approach, a rather deep and comprehensive critical analysis of the existing approaches to the problem of the symbol was carried out. Summarizing the meaning of symbol for man, a prominent Soviet Russian philosopher A.F. Losev writes: "... having a symbol of a thing, we, in essence speaking, have an infinite number of different reflections, or expressions, of a thing that can express this thing with any accuracy and with any approximation to a given function of a thing" (Losev, 1976). Another author Svasyan K.A. notes the same role of the symbol: "Modeling the world in symbolic forms, a person masters it, masters it up to the control of phenomena" (Svasian, 1980). Other philosophers of the Soviet period -

142

Mamardashvili M.K. and Pyatigorsky A.M. - drew attention to another characteristic feature of a symbol: it indicates something unknown at the present moment; in other words — it performs a signal function (Mamardashvili, Piatigorsky, 1997). Thus, once again, philosophers came to some conclusions with deep psychological meaning.

As we can see, philosophical thought provides for an idea of symbol as a multifaceted phenomenon of human existence, performing some crucially important functions: epistemological, heuristic, integrating, and what cannot also be ignored - religious. By using symbols, man cognizes the world around him, experiences challenging uncertainty and the unknown, gets amazed at what he has learned, receives certain experiences, and integrates everything that symbols directly or indirectly are related to into his inner life.

Such deep meanings and functions of the symbol, which are of great psychological significance, also prove the possibility and necessity of using symbols in psychotherapy and counseling. Muslim clients are no exception. However, the sources of their symbols are not profane.

Qur'anic symbols as Divine signs

For a believer, symbols from religious sources acquire a religious meaning. The use of symbols in clinical practice for Muslims should be carried out within the framework of the monotheistic Islamic paradigm, keeping in mind the Islamic understanding of what symbols mean in relation to the core meanings and foundations of their religious worldview and spiritual life. And that needs our answers to which phenomena in nature, history, and culture from the Islamic point of view are given special meanings that show Muslims how to approach their Creator and better understand Divine qualities, strengthen their faith, and gain peace of mind.

The Holy Qur'ān reveals them and directly calls these phenomena *"ayah"* - a sign of Allah. The word *"ayah"* (in the plural - *"ayaat")* in the Arabic language, first of all, denotes the smallest structural unit of the Qur'an, that has an independent meaning and is part of the corresponding sura of the Qur'an. At the same time, in the Qur'an the word "ayah" is used not only in relation to the Qur'anic text. It also relates to various phenomena mentioned in the Qur'an that are in nature, culture, history. Some stories and parables are also called "ayah." The word of "ayah" in the translations of the Qur'an into English is denoted by the word "signs." According to Islam, the signs of Allah are what He created, revealed for the understanding of people in the world around (nature, culture) and in man himself, or some events, images, or allegories in the Qur'anic stories (parables) that He presented as protreptic, exhortative examples to learn and perceive for one's benefit.

The Qur'an, from ayah to ayah, reveals the quintessence and functions of Divine signs:

"We will show them Our signs in the universe and within themselves until it becomes clear to them that this ˹Qur'ān˺ is the truth. Is it not enough that your Lord is a Witness over all things?" (41 Fussilat: 53).

"There are ˹countless˺ signs on earth for those with sure faith, as there are within yourselves. Can you not, see?" (51 Adh-Dhariat:20–21).

Ibn al-Qayyim al-Jawziyya, an outstanding Islamic scholar of the 14th century, in his work "Fawaid" points out that Allah calls on people to learn about Him in two ways: to watch His manifested signs - His creations, and to contemplate over the signs that are perceived by hearing and reason - that is to say - over the Qur'anic text (Jawziyya, 2013, p.44). At the same time, manifested signs (creations) sustain the Qur'anic ayat, which in turn refer to the creations of Allah as evidence (Jaawziyya, 2013, p. 46).

The Qur'an directly calls on people to consider certain signs existing in the surrounding world, in the body and inner world of man, as the creations of God, and perceive and cognize them as Divine signs. The Holy Book reveals the bonds of human souls with the signs of Allah and denotes their significant role in the human psyche, mental processes, behavior, and personal development. It is no wonder that many signs in the Qur'an are referred to in close interrelation with cognitions, emotions, and motivation. According to the Qur'anic ayaat, man should be mindful of signs so that recalling and ideating them and comprehensive reflection on them are the effective means of strengthening faith, intellectual abilities, rationality, and assertiveness:

With it He produces for you ˹various˺ crops, olives, palm trees, grapevines, and every type of fruit. Surely this is a sign for those *who reflect*. And He has subjected for your benefit the day and the night, the sun, and the moon. And the stars have been subjected by His command. Surely in this are signs for those *who understand*. And ˹He subjected˺ for you whatever He has created on earth of varying colours.[1] Surely in this is a sign for those *who are mindful*. (16 An-Nahl:11–13).

It is no coincidence that Ibn Qayyim al Jawziyya specifies the following features, speaking of signs:

Nothing points to another so completely as creations point to the attributes of their Creator, the qualities of His perfection, and the meanings of His names. The variety of creations determines the diversity and multiplicity of indications. These indications are directed both to the mind of a person, and to his feelings, and to nature, and to thinking (Jawziyya, 2016, p. 957).

The interrelation between natural signs as symbolic images and man's mental, spiritual activity is often times emphasized in the Qur'an. For example, the names of natural phenomena and objects that are spoken about in the Qur'anic text became the titles of a number of suras (13 "Thunder," 16 "The Bee," 24 " Light," 27 "Ants," 29 "The Spider," 53 "The Star," 54 "The Month," 57 "Iron," 89 "The Dawn," 91 "The Sun," 92 "Night," 93 "Morning Hours," 95 "Fig Tree," etc.). Each of them comprehends God's appeal to the inner world of man. Allah's oaths by natural phenomena (day, night, sun, month, etc.) in the Holy Qur'an stress the importance of issues to which man's attention is drawn, primarily to his monotheistic beliefs, spirituality, and good morality.

We can see it in full in the first ten ayaat of the Qur'anic sura "The Sun," where the Divine oaths by celestial bodies (sun, moon, earth) are followed by a direct oath by the human soul and incitement to make efforts on its refinement: "And by the soul and ˹the One˺ Who fashioned it, then with ˹the knowledge of˺ right and wrong inspired it! Successful indeed is the one who purifies their soul, and doomed is the one who corrupts it!" (91 Ash-Shams: 7-10).

Some Qur'anic ayaat encompass almost everything created by Allah, starting from the moment of the emergence of space and time, which are the primordial and ultimate entities of the surrounding world that can be covered by human consciousness:

Indeed, in the creation of the heavens and the earth and the alternation of the day and night, there are signs for people of reason. ˹They are˺ those who remember Allah while standing, sitting, and lying on their sides, and reflect on the creation of the heavens and the earth ˹and pray˺, "Our Lord! You have not created ˹all of˺ this without purpose. Glory be to You! Protect us from the torment of the Fire. (3 Ali 'Imran:190–191).

Thus, the Qur'anic text, through signs (the creation of heaven and earth, the change of night and day) refers to the fundamental, *a priori* forms of human existence and reasoning - space and time, and then straightforwardly names those whom these ayaat addressed: they are people who are guided by sound mind and must reflect on these signs, apperceiving the ultimate meanings of their existence.

In our opinion, these ayaat, in their own way, reveal the quintessence of the methods of intervention and goals of therapy developed in different schools of psychotherapy: cognitive-behavioral therapy (development of rational, functional thinking, emotional self-regulation), analytical psychology (understanding the meaning of symbols), existential (acquisition of the meaning of life), humanistic psychology (realizing interior motives, self-acceptance with all the shortcomings, finding the true "Self"), etc.

Some symbolic images are not called "signs" in the Qur'anic text, but they are presented as short parables-examples point to something that greatly exceeds their initial meaning:

Surely Allah does not shy away from using the parable of a mosquito or what is even smaller. As for the believers, they know that it is the truth from their Lord. And as for the disbelievers, they argue, "What does Allah mean by such a parable?" Through this ˹test˺, He leaves many to stray, and guides many. And He leaves none to stray except the rebellious... (2 Al Baqarah: 26).

The Qur'an emphasizes that both signs and parables are exemplified to influence the cognitive functions and attitudes of man, prompting him to reflect and pursue knowledge: "These are the parables We set forth for humanity, but none will understand them except the people of knowledge" (29 Al 'Anqabut: 43); "We set forth such comparisons for people, ˹so˺ perhaps they may reflect" (59 Al Hashr: 21).

Thus, for Muslims, the signs and parables presented in the Qur'an have more than simply symbolic meaning. By the Qur'anic text itself, they are intended to affect mental processes and states, including religiously motivated ones. It proves that their application in dealing with the psychological problems of Muslims can be beneficial.

Methods of using Qur'anic signs in clinical practice with Muslims

For Muslims, the ayaat from the Qur'an are meant to be some kind of treatment by definition: "We send down the Qur'ān as a healing and mercy for the believers, but it only increases the wrongdoers in loss" (17 al "Isra": 82). And it is important to note that this ayah is placed in close vicinity to the ayah well-known to Islamic psychology professionals: "They ask you ˹O Prophet˺ about the rūḥ (spirit)..." (17 al "Isra": 85), and that points to structural and meaningful interconnection between these ayaat and their subjects.

Further, we will introduce some ways of integrating symbolic images (signs), stories, and parables from the Qur'an into the clinical practice with Muslim clients. The universal and religiously encouraged way of using them in clinical practice that comes right from the provisions of the Qur'an and the Sunnah of the Prophet is a reflection on the ayaat (signs). Malik Badri considers the therapeutic value of Islamic meditation as a process that integrates the cognitive, emotional, and spiritual aspects of the psyche. An important object of reflection is the creation of Allah as His signs (Badri, pp.53-63).

Ibn Qayyim al-Jawziyya also writes about the importance of reflection on created signs for gaining deep meanings:

> Through reflection, people find in the created world indications of the uniqueness of Allah, the attributes of His perfection, the truthfulness of His messengers, the upcoming meeting with Him. They look at this world, seeing its transience, frailty, and shortcomings, and at Eternal Life, seeing its duration, eternity, sublimity... (Jawziyya, 2016, pp. 957-958).

Thus, contemplation (meditation) on signs can be taken as a universal therapeutic method for working with Muslim clients. But it needs some specification and particular techniques to be elaborated. To expand the ways of applying specific techniques for working with symbolic images from the Qur'an in clinical practice, we would address the experience of using symbols in some schools of psychotherapy.

Roberto Assagioli, the founding father of psychosynthesis, pointed to three ways of dealing with symbols:

- Suggesting the client use certain symbols of a general nature (symbols of nature, animal symbols, human symbols (mother, father, knight, heart, birth, growth, death, resurrection, etc.), objects created by man, religious and mythological symbols, abstract symbols (numbers, geometric symbols).
- Work with symbols that spontaneously arise in the client in the course of therapy (as it was done in analytical psychology by C. Jung).
- An intermediate way: At first, a symbol is proposed, and then the client is free to develop a derived series of symbols on this basis (Assagioli, p.152).

Assagioli suggested introducing symbols to clients, respecting their background and features (psychological, cultural, age, etc.), and keeping in mind the current process and goals of therapy, and he presented the following three methods:

- Simply name the symbol or briefly describe it (as a rule, in relation to simple symbols, for example, geometric ones, or symbols of a universal nature, such as mother, father, child).
- Through observation by presenting a picture or image, suggesting drawing them (it is recommended to use in relation to more complex symbols).
- With the help of visualization, when the client is asked to visualize, to conjure up an image of a symbol (Assagioli, p.152).

The school of positive psychotherapy founded by N. Pezeshkian elaborated a methodology of applying parables and instructive stories in clinical practice (Pezeshkian, 2013, pp. 25, 36-40). They are assembled according to the goals of therapy and aimed at awareness of internal and interpersonal conflicts and their resolution, overcoming resistance to change, as well as expanding the vision of new life goals.

These methods are adjusted in working with Qur'anic symbols (signs), considering the goals of therapy, the demands and personal characteristics of the client, the content of his interpersonal relationships, and the level of internal and external religiosity.

Let us share some specific techniques used in the practice of providing psychological assistance to Muslims in Russia.

1. Reflection on Qur'anic ayaat containing symbolic images

In the context of the client's request and the therapeutic situation, a specific image is taken from the Qur'an, or a translation of the ayaat where it is mentioned is quoted. The client is invited to share thoughts, sensations, and feelings that arise when in contact with the Qur'anic symbols, reflect on the meanings of the text or the symbol itself, asking reflection-activating questions. For example, in family counseling for spouses, you can use ayaat 187 from Sura 2 "The Cow": "... Your wives are a garment for you, and you are a garment for them."

Working with this symbol helps to transform the existing stable dysfunctional beliefs regarding the family and marriage in general and change the negative understanding of specific aspects of the marriage and family relations of clients, prompting them to strive for the ideal image of married life and relations of spouses described in this verse.

You can also invite clients to draw images of each other in appropriate clothing to the extent that the creation of images corresponds to the canons of Islam and the beliefs of clients to conduct a joint discussion of the drawn.

2. Visualization of images

The visualization method is applied by simply imagining the appropriate image or their combination (for example, mountains, caves, rivers, streams, the appearance of vegetation, the revival of the earth after rain, the movement of clouds). First, the client is informed that the Qur'an mentions the corresponding image as a sign, admonition, or warning. Next, the client is invited to close his eyes and present the corresponding image as fully as possible.

For example, one of the images repeatedly mentioned in the Qur'an is a cave (even the whole sura 18 is called "The Cave"). An analysis of the Qur'anic verses shows that the cave is seen as a symbol of security, shelter, and protection from the danger that Allah Almighty gives. This is proved by the expressions that are used in this sura: " when those youths took refuge in the cave", " take refuge in the cave", so that it is a place for refuge.

The cave as a refuge is mentioned not only in this sura of the Qur'ran. For example, Sura 16, The Bee, ayah 81 says: "And Allah has provided you shade out of what He created, and has given you shelter in the mountains..." Also, in ayaat 40 of sura 9 The Repentance it is said: "While they both were in the cave, he (*Muhammad (peace be on him)*) reassured his companion (*Abu Bakr*), "Do not worry; Allah is certainly with us."

Thus, several times in the Qur'an, the cave is spoken of as a refuge, shelter, a place of security from various troubles of the world around and gaining peace of mind.

Further, being in the cave is mentioned along with the Grace of Allah, facilitating the matter, the existing situation: in the prayer of the youth from the cave: " "Our Lord! Grant us mercy from Yourself and guide us rightly through our ordeal." and in the words: "Your Lord will extend His mercy to you and accommodate you in your ordeal. The very presence in the cave is surrounded on all sides by safety: they are in the middle, and the sun does not burn them. However, from the east and west, it sanctifies the cave, creating the necessary microclimate. They turn from side to side, and this does not allow the biological and chemical bonds of their bodies with the earth to be set, preventing the processes of decomposition (Iakhin, 2020). Moreover, even the very sight of young men and a dog at the entrance, sleeping with their eyes open, serves as their protection from uninvited guests: " Had you looked at them, you would have certainly fled away from them, filled with horror".

And most importantly, this security is associated with Almighty Allah: it is He who gives both external security and inner peace.

Whereas the cave is mentioned in the Qur'an in the context of refuge and security, this image is used when working with clients experiencing anxiety, fears, feelings of defenselessness, hopelessness, etc.

3. *Visualization of a number of Qur'anic images, parables, and stories*

The client is invited to visualize with closed eyes (preferably in a relaxed state) listening to passages read by the counselor in continuous text from the Qur'anic ayaat, where symbolic images are mentioned, translated into the language that the client understands (maybe a whole sura, part of it or a separate Qur'anic parable or story), alternating with other ayaat, which are aimed at religious perfection, spiritual and moral development. Also, a counselor can select and read a certain set of ayat that contain symbolic images that, based on the text of the Qur'an, are aimed at strengthening faith, increasing rationality, achieving inner peace, overcoming anxieties, fears, anger, and other negative emotions, etc.

For example, one can take the Qur'anic image of a shadow, which is given an important symbolic meaning in the Qur'an (a symbol of material existence and the existential helplessness of a person without the will and assistance of the Creator, a symbol of humility and subordination to Allah), pick up all the ayat where the shadow is mentioned in a certain context, and read the text to the client.

Qur'anic stories about prophets and other positive figures, which have important spiritual and psychological meanings that correspond to a specific therapeutic situation, can also be as a whole text. For example, a client experiencing difficulties in self-realization, with a lack of activity, interest in life, or relationship with any kind of authorities, can listen to the stories about the prophets Suleiman, Musa (peace be upon them), Zul-Qarnayn; on problems with shame, fear of rejection - stories about Maryam, the prophet Yunus (peace be upon him), etc.

4. *Listening to audio recordings*

As a home task, the client is invited to record on a voice recorder the reading of the translation of the Qur'anic ayat in his own voice, as a rule, already worked on during the meeting with the counselor, and then listen to this recording daily, preferably in a calm environment and using visualization. It is also recommended that after 5-7 days of listening (until the next meeting with the counselor), record the same ayat again, comparing one's psychological states and expressions, including the characteristics of speech and voice, during the first and second recording.

This technique allows the client to work with symbolic images outside of meetings with the counselor, activating and accelerating the necessary therapeutic processes and tracking the changes in mood and feelings. During the next session, the results of working on this task, its impact on the thoughts and emotional state, and the reflections are discussed.

Thus, with this approach, we have the integration of psychotherapeutic techniques based on symbolic Qur'anic images: on the one hand, the work with symbols itself has a healing effect, which is confirmed by common therapeutic practice, and on the other hand, for a believing Muslim, images taken from the sacred text of the Qur'an , will have a special spiritual symbolic meaning, due to which the therapeutic effect is enhanced and the client's resistance is reduced. We would call this method "ayah-therapy" as it is mainly based on using ayaat from the Qur'an.

With the informed consent of clients, the possibility of using Qur'anic symbolic images in clinical practice with non-Muslim clients is not ruled out since most of these symbols are universal in nature and do not by themselves carry a religious connotation. If the client is a non-Muslim but religiously neutral or has atheistic beliefs, the question of whether the images are signs of God or simply symbolic images of nature may be taken out of the discussion in therapy. In the absence of the consent of the client, work with these images should be excluded.

It is also necessary to pay attention to one important aspect of using symbols in providing psychological assistance to Muslims. According to Islam, not a single symbolic image, whether it is a phenomenon of nature and culture, a sign, an example, or a role model, cannot be recognized as a source of strength and energy, independently influencing the state of people, their health or mental well-being, the actions they perform. It should proceed from the fact that only certain images and phenomena, understood and realized as signs of Allah, can exclusively by His Will become a resource for positive transformations in man: contemplation of signs and reflection on them is beneficial only with the permission of Allah. A different perception of the symbols can be recognized as "shirk" (polytheism, including giving partners to God in guidance and healing), one of the most serious sins according to Islamic institutions.

Conclusion

At the end of this chapter, we find it necessary to draw the following conclusions.

1. The application of symbols in their various manifestations is an important technique in a number of schools of psychotherapy and counseling since symbols perform several significant therapeutic functions.

2. Philosophy provides an idea of a symbol as a multifaceted phenomenon of human existence, performing the critical functions: epistemological, heuristic, and integrative. Through symbols, man cognizes the world around him and himself, experiences challenging uncertainty and the unknown, gets amazed at what he has learned, receives certain experience, and integrates everything that symbols directly or indirectly are related to in his inner life.

3. For a believer, natural symbols are a book of nature written by God, signs in which he can see and discover divine qualities. The discovery and understanding of these signs and the feelings experienced in connection with this experience are a way of getting closer to God and gaining peace of mind.

4. The Qur'anic provisions about the signs of Allah, parables, and stories contained in the Qur'an are aimed (by virtue of the indications of the Qur'anic text itself) at the development of man's cognitive functions (thinking, knowledge, comprehension), intellectual abilities, strengthening his faith and religious beliefs. That points to the possibility and necessity of their application in clinical practice with Muslim clients by analogy with the use of symbols and parables in the relevant areas of psychotherapy (direct presentation and discussion of symbols, visualization, description, image, etc.).

5. Applying symbols in providing psychological assistance to Muslims should be carried out in compliance with the Islamic foundations: no symbol, even considered as a sign, has an independent effect on the human soul (psyche), and any of its healing, positive effects happen exclusively with divine permission.

References

Afanasyev, V.E., Kozhukhovskaya, L. S. (2005). Features of symbolic structures in journalistic texts. *Theoretical and methodological aspects of communication: a collection of scientific works of the Department of Intercultural Economic Communication of the Belarusian State Economic University. Vol. 1.* Minsk: RIVSH; 2005. Pp. 14–23. URL: http://edoc.bseu.by:8080/handle/edoc/63299 (in Russ.)

Al-Jawziyya, I. Q. (2016). Degrees of those who follow the path "We worship only You and ask only Your help." Per. from Arabic, approx. A. Dzhelilov. M.: Eksmo, Umma. (in Russ.)

Al-Jawziyya, I. Q. (2013). Fawaid=Useful instructions. Rep. ed. Sheikh Bakr ibn 'Abdullah Abu Zeid; translated from Arabic E. Sorokoumova. M.: Umma. (in Russ.)

Assagioli, R. (2016). Psychosynthesis. Principles and techniques. *Institute of General Humanitarian Studies.* (in Russ.)

Badri, Malik (2018). *Contemplation: An Islamic Psychospiritual Study.* (A. Lu'lu'a, Trans.). Mahya Yayıncılık. (Original work published 2018).

Buck, C (2017). *Islamic Approaches to Symbolism.* -URL: //https://www.academia.edu/34170280/_Islamic_Approaches_to_Symbolism_2017_

Cassirer, E. *An Essay on Man.* –URL: https://archive.org/stream/ErnstCassirerAnEssayOnMan/Ernst+Cassirer+-+An+essay+on+man_djvu.txt

Cassirer, E. *Philosophie der symbolischen Formen.* –URL: https://archive.org/details/philosophieders00cass/page/n13/mode/2up *(in Germ.)*

Christian Doctrine, Augustinian Library (BA) (1997). *11/2. Paris: Institute of Augustinian Studies; (Doct. christ., II, 1, 1, trans. Fr. Isabelle Bochet).* p. 626. (in French)

Freud Z. (2006). Lectures on introduction to psychoanalysis. Per. with him. M.: LLC "Firm STD".

Fromm, E. (2009). The forgotten language. Now or maybe? Per. s English M.: AST. (in Russ.)

Giraud Vincennes. Signum and vestigium in St. Augustine. –URL: http://metaparadigma.ru/augustin-signum/(in Russ.)

Goodwyn, E. D. (2016). Healing symbols in psychotherapy: A ritual approach. *Routledge/Taylor & Francis Group.* New York – London.

Iakhin F. F. (2020). Symbols and meanings of the Koranic sura "The Cave" in the interpretation of C. G. Jung and Islamic understanding: a comparative analysis of the story of the young men from the cave. *Islam: personality and society. 1/20,* 2020. pp. 53-62. (in Russ.)

Jung, K. (1995). *Psychological types. St. Petersburg: Yuventa; M.: Progress-Univers. (in Russ.)*

Jung, K. (2018). *Man and his symbols. Per. I.N. Sirenko; S.N. Sirenko; N.A. Sirenko. M.: Medkov S.B., Silver threads. (in Russ.)*

Kant, I. (1994). Critique of the ability to judge. In 8 t. T. 5. M.: Choro, 1994. (in Russ.)

Kovpak, D. (2019) Lessons of wisdom. Parables, tales and stories from a psychotherapist. St. Petersburg: Peter; 2019. (in Russ.)

Losev, A. F. (1976). The problem of symbol and realistic art. M.: Art; 376p.

Mamardashvili M. K., & Pyatigorsky A. M. (1997). Symbol and consciousness. Metaphysical considerations about consciousness, symbolism and language. M., School "Languages of Russian Culture". (in Russ.)

May, R. (2001). The courage to create: An essay on the psychology of creativity. Per. from English Lviv: Initiative; M.: Institute of General Humanitarian Studies; 2001. (in Russ.)

Otto, M.W. (2000). *Stories and metaphors in cognitive-behavior therapy Cognitive and Behavioral Practice. Vol. 7(2)*, Spring 2000, Pages 166-172. https://doi.org/10.1016/S1077-7229(00)80027-9

Pavlova, O. S. (2018). Psychological counseling of Muslims: analysis of foreign sources. *Modern foreign psychology;* 7(4): 46–55. doi:10.17759/jmfp.2018070406. (in Russ.)

Pezeshkian, N. (2013). Merchant and parrot. *Eastern stories in psychotherapy*. Per. with him. L.P. Galanza. M.: Academic Project; Paradigm; 2013. (in Russ.)

Radugin, A.A. (2001). Culturology. M.: Center. 304 p.

Svasyan, K. A. (1980). The problem of symbol in modern philosophy (Criticism and analysis). Yerevan: *Publishing House of the Academy of Sciences of the ArmSSR*. (in Russ.)

Stott, R. (2010). *Oxford Guide to Metaphors in CBT. Building Cognitive Bridges* (Oxford Guides to Cognitive Behavioral Therapy): Oxford University Press, USA; Illustrated edition (1 July 2010)/ Paperback: 249 pages

The Clear Qur'ān. Translation of the Holy Qur'an into English by Dr. Mustafa Khattab. -URL: https://Qur'ān.com/

The Latest Philosophical Dictionary (1999). – *URL: https://gufo.me/dict/philosophy/ (in Russ.)*

Tsybulya, V. I. (2012). Functions of symbols in psychotherapy. *Counseling Psychology and Psychotherapy;* 20(2): 158–173. (in Russ.)

Veraksa, A. N. (2013). Symbol as cognitive tool of mental activity. *Psychology in Russia. Vol. 6*, (1). –URL: //http://psychologyinrussia.com/volumes/?article=2075.

Yakovleva, M. V. (2018). Basic theoretical approaches to the study of symbolism in the social and humanitarian fields of knowledge. Bulletin of Udmurt University. *Series Philosophy. Psychology. Pedagogy.* 2010;1:18–23. (in Russ.)

CHAPTER SIX

INTEGRATING THANVI'S COUNSELING TECHNIQUES IN THERAPIES

Amber Haque

Introduction

Although many early Muslim scholars contributed to psychology and counseling, the published works are mainly credited to scholars from the Arab world (Haque, 2004). This issue led the author to explore the works of Muslim scholars around the globe, which resulted in an edited book titled *Islamic Psychology Around the Globe* (Haque & Rothman, 2021). In this book, Thanvi was mentioned among hundreds of scholars who have contributed significantly towards what is termed *'ilm-an-nafs* or knowledge of the self (*nafs*). The *nafs* comprise the body, soul, and intellect (*'aql*), with the soul having its own spiritual heart. The person dies when the soul (*rūḥ*) or the spiritual entity inside the body leaves.

While commonly used with all populations, the mainstream counseling techniques lack addressing the spiritual heart, which is the soul's crucial element, and therefore, are ineffective with Muslims. It is *Tawhid*, which is the guiding principle in Islam and conceptualizes the universe as a dynamic and unified system where all is connected, including the spiritual realm. (Al-Faruqi, 2000). While some early Muslim scholars addressed the cognitive aspects or *'aql* in addressing psychological issues, most focused on addressing the *qalb* (spiritual heart), which can be the source of all illnesses (Haque, 2004).

Ashraf Ali Thanvi wrote extensively about human nature, spiritual ailments, and therapies from Islamic perspectives. His methodologies are relevant for Muslims everywhere, as Islam views human nature as universal. Thanvi's contributions precede modern counseling theories and practices like many other Muslim scholars of the past. Besides integrating his techniques to work with Muslim clients, his approaches can also be a resource for cultural sensitivity training. After giving a brief overview of Thanvi's views on personality, psychological disorders, and healing, the chapter addresses Thanvi's therapeutic objectives, methods, and the steps used in counseling.

Ashraf Ali Thanvi (1863-1943)

According to Ajmal (1987), Thanvi was easily the most outstanding Islamic scholar and a Sufi Saint from pre-independence India. He was born and died in a village in Uttar Pradesh, a province in northern India, and his knowledge and influence on others earned him the title of *Ḥakīm al-Ummah* (Wise Man of the Nation). Thanvi wrote more than 800 manuscripts, books, and treatises focusing entirely on human personality and treatments of psycho-spiritual disorders (Ajmal, 1987; Rizvi, 1962).

Like many previous Muslim scholars, Thanvi's views on human personality, psychological disorders, and healing were from Islamic perspectives. He considered the physical aspects secondary to the spiritual as humans comprise both body and soul. His writings are full of descriptions of the heart (*qalb*), soul (*nafs*), and intellect (*'aql*) and explanations of how cleansing the soul and the development of spirituality can prevent and overcome psychological disorders. Unlike many scholars, Thanvi focused on curing illnesses because he practiced counseling with his disciples and maintained close contact with them for years. He described psychological disorders as organic or functional and believed that while organic disorders need medicine, functional disorders can benefit from psychotherapies. Thanvi's clients came from diverse backgrounds: religious scholars, physicians, other professionals, government servants, and ordinary people.

Functional disorders originate in the heart

Thanvi writes that the most crucial organ in the human body is the heart, mentioned in the Qur'ān in 137 places, and whatever emotions arise in the heart are followed by the rest of the bodily organs. For example, if the heart desires to see something, it does not order the eyes to see it, but the eyes start their work as soon as the desire takes seed in the heart. If the heart wants to go somewhere, it will not order the feet to move, but the feet will start their work immediately. The term "heart," in this context, refers to the spiritual heart or the heart of the soul that can connect with the divine. If the spiritual heart is pure, it is characterized by peace, joy, and contentment. If it is not pure, a person will suffer from diseases of the heart, like anger, anxiety, malice, etc. These diseases are the mother of all diseases from which other diseases stem.

The spiritual heart has two choices: moving toward the *nafs*, potentially generating an undesirable or maladaptive sequence of behaviors, and thought processes, or by using *'aql*, raising itself to a higher level by turning toward the *rūḥ* and developing qualities that define a true Muslim who submits to Allāh. Therefore, the heart is the master of the body, and if one wants to change one's world, one must begin working on one's heart and not on the external world. In his book, *Peace of Heart*, Thanvi mentions 15 types of hearts from the Qur'ān and discusses their exegesis; 10 of the 15 are discussed below.

1. The hardened heart: "Then, after that, your hearts were hardened and became as stones or even worse in hardness" (2:74). Thanvi explains that a human's heart is like the earth. When the earth is not cultivated for a long time, and a person does not toil on it, it becomes hard and stops producing because it has not been put to work. Similarly, the heart is hardened when the individual neglects spiritual needs, and the Qur'ān mentions that such hearts can surpass the hardness of a rock.

2. The rusted heart: "The reason for weak faith is the rusted heart that causes people to see truth as stories" (83:13-14). The evil deeds of humans and their sins make their hearts rusted. A hadith mentions that when a person commits an evil act, a black spot is created in the heart, but the black spot is removed if the person repents. However, if the sins are repeated, the black spot keeps increasing and engulfs the entire heart. The Qur'ān also asserts that those who hide God's oneness have rusted hearts (2:273).

3. The crooked heart: "Those whose hearts are deceitful; they are in search of mischief (*fitna*) and try to put meaning to the words, but their true intentions are known to God only." (3:70) Those whose hearts are twisted are searching for mischief and try to give some distorted meaning to the scriptures.

4. The sealed heart: "After him, we sent other messengers to their people, and the messengers came to them with clear proofs. However, the people would not believe in what they had rejected before. This is how We seal the hearts of the transgressors" (10:74). The sealing of the hearts is for those who keep repeatedly sinning to the point that their hearts are completely blackened, and the person is not attracted to do anything good. It is also true for those who deny God's existence, and due to their continued persistence in it, the heart loses its capacity to see the truth.

5. The blind heart: "For indeed, it is not the eyes that are blind but the hearts" (22:46). This verse refers to the fact that while one can see from the eyes but fails to ponder from the heart, the inner sight is closed. A heart becomes blind when one's life is spent in heedlessness, and one cannot see the difference between good and evil. This is the same as if the person is blind.

6. The heart empty from faith (Iman): "When Allāh's Oneness is mentioned, the hearts of those who deny the hereafter shrink with aversion, but when other gods are noted, they are filled with joy" (39:45). A heart without faith is saddened when God's name is taken, and the hereafter is discussed. "Faith has not yet entered your hearts" (49:14). The hearts filled with faith melt when God's name is taken and accepts the scriptures from the book without question.

7. The contented heart: "In the remembrance (*dhikr*) of Allāh, do hearts find peace" (13:280). The contented heart remembers God because nothing else, including wealth, name, or fame, can give true peace to humans.

8. The unmindful heart: "They have hearts they do not understand with, eyes do not see with, and ears they do not hear. They are like cattle, even less guided. Such people are entirely heedless" (7:179), referring to the sense perception of humans and thus they are unable to note the signs of nature. They are like animals, busy eating and socializing in their circle of animals. All their senses are used but only for worldly pleasures. Exegetes explain that the animals are even better than humans in the sense that they come to their master when called and stop when reprimanded. Humans often cannot use their spiritual capabilities as they have lost them because of their heedless hearts.

9. The heart that trembles: "True believers are those whose hearts flutter with the name of God, and when verses of God are read to them, they increase in their faith (*Iman*)" (8:20). Those who have faith their hearts tremble with fear and love when God's name is called, and when the scripture is read to them, their faith increases even more.

10. A blessed or guided heart: "One day when wealth and offspring cannot benefit except for those who bring a blessed heart" (26:88-89). This quality refers to the heart that is free of denial of God. It is also a heart that is free from associating others with God.

Factors affecting the heart and solutions

In his book, *Sukoon-e-Qalb*, Thanvi mentions the main factors affecting the heart are as follows:

1. Turning away from the Qur'ān or not maintaining a steady relationship with the Qur'ān by reading, understanding, and following the injunctions given in it.

2. Turning away from the *dhikr* or remembrance of Allāh because it is through *dhikr* that one can easily connect with Allāh and He has absolute power over everything (41:54), can intervene between a person and their heart (8:24), inscribe faith in the heart (58:22), put a veil on a person's heart (6:25), and even seal their hearts (2:17).

3. Following the desires of the body but neglecting the soul and the hereafter (*akhirah*).

4. Focusing excessively on entertainment and unnecessarily wasting time.

Thanvi emphasized that the hardness of the heart could be mainly attributed to not following the principles of Islamic law and guidance (Shariah), and it could also be a punishment from Allāh. Here, Shariah refers to whether one's earning is halal, whether time spent is halal, if one follows interpersonal relationships in the prescribed ways, etc. He advised his clients to analyze their own problems.

If any of the above four deficiencies exist, Thanvi prescribes that one can take the following steps:

1. Examine where one falls short, seeking advice from the counselor, if necessary.

2. Form a relationship with the Qur'ān by reading and reflecting.

3. Keep the company of the pious, as one can learn from them.

4. Make regular supplication (*dua*) to protect oneself from the hardness of the heart, as dua is the weapon of the believers and facilitates a strong connection with Allāh.

5. Offer extra prayers because they can increase God-consciousness (*taqwa*).

It is worth noting that early Muslim scholars like Ghazali wrote of similar steps in his book 38, a section in his famous work titled *The Revival of the Religious Sciences (Ihya Ulumaddin)*; but this author did not find any such references in Thanvi's works. While it is known that many early scholars were influenced by the writings of their predecessors, the referencing system did not exist then as it is now. Knowledge was not considered the property of one person and was shared commonly by one another. Thanvi, however, wrote his own exegesis of the Qur'ān, gave explanations, and developed treatment of clients' problems based entirely on the Qur'ān and Hadith. We will see below how Thanvi outlined his unique treatment plan for the clients very concretely, unlike his predecessors, most of whom did not practice counseling.

Narrating the story of Prophet Abraham, Thanvi writes that when Abraham was given a revelation, he was also asked by God to cleanse his heart. Abraham then replied to God that the water could not reach the heart, so how could it be cleaned? God replied that the heart is cleansed when one cries and shows humility and repentance to God. When one repents, the heart's blackness is wiped out, and the wickedness is removed, and when one cries in front of God, the person's heart is cleansed of all sins. In his book, *Amelioration of the Heart*, Thanvi discussed more than 300 topics related to the spiritual heart, *nafs,* and *'aql*, all drawn from the Qur'ān and Sunnah, and used his therapies to work on the struggles between *nafs*, heart, and intellect.

Therapeutic Objectives

The first and primary therapeutic objective for Thanvi was for the client to develop an insight into the dynamics of heart, soul, and intellect. He emphasized that understanding to create a balance among these three metaphysical elements is essential for the heart's purification. The second objective was to stay in touch with the counselor until the problems were resolved. The third objective was to develop the client's self-will and effort to achieve good moral character, as it is only through these personal qualities that improvement in the client's condition is possible. Thanvi pointed out that it is not the religious rituals but enhanced knowledge, thoughts, and actions that make a difference in the client. The fourth objective was to understand overt and covert divine laws because gaining overt knowledge alone is insufficient for change. Only through the hidden meaning can one attain higher realities and improve one's psychological state. The fifth objective was to change the client's thoughts and actions. Thanvi reminded readers/clients that finding peace should not be objective because it is not in one's hands to find peace. However, peace will automatically follow if one can change one's thinking and do righteous actions by following the traditions of Prophet Muhammad (PBUH).

Therapeutic Methods

Thanvi used many methods seen today in modern psychology and counseling. Grounded in spiritual psychology, his methods were also culture specific.

1. *Client-centered approach.* Thanvi's writings focused on each client's unique problems, and he worked with them individually or in groups that discussed common issues. Thanvi took up each imperfection of the client separately and guided them toward a cure. He expected the client to meditate on the nature of one's weakness

and the suggested therapy. This approach is discussed in a case study below.

2. ***Directive approach.*** Thanvi counseled his clients based on cultural expectations and asked them to repeat their lessons. While teaching, he always advised his students to study beforehand and only move ahead if the concepts were clear. Afterward, the students had to repeat what they understood. People from the Indian subcontinent and the Middle East come from collectivistic cultures and expect a directive rather than a non-directive approach used in mainstream psychotherapies.

3. ***Reading and communication.*** Thanvi gave reading materials on the struggles between the heart and soul and advised clients to read the scriptures and make supplications from the Qur'ān and Sunnah. Thanvi believed that if the client's problems were not serious, they could be treated by reading materials, and the clients did not need to see a therapist face to face. He asked his clients to keep a diary of thoughts, write them freely on paper, follow the counselor's advice, and communicate regularly with letters. The case study shows how his clients valued free expression, which helped them develop insight into their problems and understand everyday issues. This approach helped establish deep relationships between him and his clients.

4. ***Having complete faith in the counselor and persevering in the treatment for the cure.*** Thanvi emphasized that for a positive outcome, it was necessary that they should have complete faith in their counselor (see qualities of a Muslim counselor given below) and persevere in the treatment for the cure. He focused on cleansing the heart and helped his clients measure progress through their thoughts and actions. The thoughts and actions were recorded in dairies and discussed with the counselor. Additionally, the client was free to terminate the sessions if not satisfied with the counselor. Thanvi did not set time limits with his clients, as every case could be unique, and he dealt with some cases for years. Each session would also vary depending on the situation and may last for a few minutes or longer. There is no description of his works about the length of each session other than depending on the individual need.

5. ***Murāqaba* (Mindfulness).** *Murāqaba* is a way to develop in-depth insight into one's spiritual heart and relationship with God. It helps

one understand one's surroundings, eliminate undesirable characteristics, and create positive ones. In *Murāqaba*, one can see that the thoughts are circular and can negatively influence one's thinking. The vicious circle of thoughts can be broken by entering a higher circle by taking a spiritual counselor or a guide who can discriminate between thought impulses and dispel the client's sources of doubt. *Murāqaba* can be of two types: (1) *takhliyah*, or self-analysis to obviate one's moral weaknesses, and (2) *tahliyah*, self-analysis to strengthen one's virtues and thus make one's vices weak to ultimately make them die out.

In his book on Thanvi, Khawaja (1999) outlines the various types of *Murāqaba* suggested by Thanvi:

- Seeking Divine intimacy by getting used to privacy with Allāh (in obedience to Him).

- Envisioning Allāh during prayers or having an idea that Allāh is watching during prayers.

- Imagining while reciting the Qur'ān that one is sitting in the presence of Allāh as a student sits before his teacher.
- Being grateful to Allāh for one's subsistence and provisions
- Protecting the *nafs* from doing evil deeds and thinking of punishment in the hereafter.
- Conscious of Allāh's constant watch and grip for the wrongdoings.
- Thinking of one's creation from the earth and the return to it enabling one to be humble.
- Entrusting everything to Allāh's care and submitting completely to His will.
- Thinking of one's and everyone else's mortality except Allāh's and envisioning His light (*Nur*) with one's inner eyes.
- Thinking of oneself as a traveler in the path to reach the destination and not be negligent or careless over one's activities that would impede smooth travel to the desired goal.
- Creating incentives to traverse the path carefully and not be lethargic or indifferent at any time.

- Thinking of one's death, being in the grave, and finding contentment over good deeds and punishment for bad deeds inside the grave.
- Comparing the present transitory life to the eternal life after death and the consequences thereof based on actions in this world.
- Thinking of infliction of pain and torment in the afterlife for one's own evil deeds in this world.

6. *Moral approach.* Thanvi asked his clients to repent from all sins as a condition for peace. He emphasized that repeating the same sins and dealing negatively with others will never open the doors of peace and quoted this verse from the Qur'ān, "Leave all sins, open and secret" (6:120). He asked his clients to cry in their prayers and reminded them, "Just like a tiny spark of fire can blow away heaps of gunpowder, two drops of tears in front of God can wipe away a lifetime of sins." He asked his clients to remember their sins and wrongdoings and reminded them that the rewards come from facing difficulties with patience. He reminded them that problems and calamities are tests of faith, the challenges in life decrease arrogance, and helplessness takes us closer to God. He also reminded that sadness could be a gift of God as it helps in life's training and treatment of the soul. A practicing Muslim is reminded of the verse. "And certainly, We shall test you with something of fear, hunger, loss of wealth, lives and fruits, but give glad tidings to the patient ones." (2:152). The Qur'ān teaches that many of God's prophets were put through severe tests, suffered from grief and sorrow, but persevered in their belief and trust in Allāh. There are lessons in these stories for the Muslims, and the anecdotes are commonly used in Islamic-oriented therapies.

Thanvi wrote *Talimat-e-Ashrafiya,* a collection of couplets and poems instructing clients with spiritual counseling. While most couplets were in Urdu, some were in Persian, as it was the lingua franca before British colonization and widely used in North India. Here are a few examples of Thanvi's advice to his clients:

On being an Ascetic

Neither shun the world nor its pleasures
Shun sinfulness and heedlessness

However much your ego and Satan incite you
Never shun remembering (the Lord) and submitting (to Him)

Struggles and Solutions

Do not fear struggles, be resolute and face them
Embarking upon the journey is not difficulty
Stepping out and starting the journey is difficult
Strive hard for it makes you reach the goal
To initiate (the journey) is difficult
To achieve (the target) is not difficult

The Key to Happiness in Both Worlds

O seeker of goodness of both worlds
Be always mindful of two things
Neither temperament should prevail over intellect
Nor intellect should prevail over Divine law

Qualities of a Muslim Counselor

Thanvi's spiritual model imposes strict conditions on counselors, eliminating those who do not fit the criteria and qualifications necessary for successful counseling outcomes. He outlined the essential qualities of a Muslim counselor as follows:

1. Fundamental knowledge of religion (*deen*) and the habit of following the Sharia laws in personal life.

2. A willingness to seek knowledge from other Muslim scholars, especially those considered to be among the Ulema.

3. Not claim perfection or have greed because such characteristics show attachment to this world.

4. Not be allergic to the company of knowledgeable spiritual guides (*Shuyukh*) or Muslim scholars (*Ulema*).

5. Not be shy to point out the clients' deficiencies and not leave them with their condition. This must be done with love and concern for the clients.

6. Habitual of making *dhikr* and *shughal* (other types of Allāh's remembrance) because there will be no benefit or blessing (*barakah*) in education without them.

7. In the company of a Muslim counselor, the client's love for Allāh should increase, and their love for the world (*duniya*) should decrease.

8. Compared to ordinary people, more practicing Muslims are attracted to Muslim counselors.

Other qualities of a Muslim counselor are to accept the client's statement of the problem and find solutions. There should be an emphasis on action and reminders that emotions might mean appropriate measures were not taken at the right time. The counselor should clarify a reward system for the client to meet therapy goals and set more specific goals after improvements of initial plans. The counselor would ask the client for evidence if the client's report seemed inaccurate. The counselors may differ from the client but should give reasons and evidence to support their position.

Thanvi's Ten Steps in Counseling

The following applications are stepwise, but overlap is possible. The number and duration of sessions vary depending on the client's needs and progress. At the end of each session, the counselor asks the client to repeat everything they learned, including their assignments. Reading materials are shared on every topic. Journaling is the primary assignment, asking clients to write about their problems and underline the main points. The counselors are directive, asking clients what they did and critical of what they did not do or did wrong. The counselor provides ongoing spiritual guidance based on client's needs. The focus in counseling is encouraging the client to change and develop morally. Open but short communication between counselor and client is encouraged in person or remotely. The counselor instructs the client that changing the *nafs* is a major struggle (*jihād*) with immense rewards from Allāh.

1. ***Client Counselor matching.*** The prerequisite for successful counseling outcomes is client-counselor matching. This is true for the alignment of beliefs and the mutual respect that client and counselor should have for one another. Before step one, the client should research the counselors who match (or nearly match) Thanvi's criteria for a Muslim counselor mentioned above. The counselor and client discuss the importance of mutual trust and willingness to

continue therapy until problems are resolved. The service fee is negotiable between the counselor and the client.

2. *Client responsibilities.* The client is responsible for choosing a counselor with care. After mutual matching, the client agrees to stay with the counselor for at least two months after beginning therapy and realizes that one cannot attain purity without much toil and struggle. To progress, the clients must strive and fulfill their responsibilities including not giving up on therapy and putting complete trust in Allāh. *Dhikr, shughal,* specific book reading, and keeping the company of pious people as their company can facilitate spiritual development. These activities are in addition to the individualized treatment plan the counselor gives to the client. Clients must set aside a specific time for writing personal notes, and the counselor allows them to write as they wish and give topics that might get them started. The client should write as specifically about the problem as possible, underline the words and phrases that are the essence of the issues, or write in the margins.

Muhasaba, or self-reckoning, after five daily prayers or at least every night and communicating with the counselor about one's condition of the *nafs* and its progress is essential. Clients must keep communication with the counselor open and regular, at least every 3-4 days. They are encouraged to communicate in writing but are allowed personal visits as needed. If the client reports making progress, the counselor gives encouragement. The client is instructed that counseling will not result in miracles, vision of God, or salvation on Judgment Day. Additionally, therapy is not magic and religious incantations would not yield direct material benefits.

3. *Knowledge of the Levels of nafs.* The counselor instructs clients about the various levels of *nafs* and their interplay with the *qalb, rūḥ,* and *'aql.* A client suffering from a negative spiritual condition because of the blaming *nafs* and thinking of oneself as a loser hoping that there is no punishment from Allāh, is instructed that while fear of punishment from Allāh is one aspect of slavery, the other aspect is putting trust in Him as a loving God, who does not deprive His seekers of His mercy. The client is asked to hope for a reward rather than thinking about not being punished. The use of *'aql* in looking at Allāh's merciful qualities and hoping for a positive outcome is essential in therapy. For clients complaining about not doing anything

to receive Allāh's mercy are encouraged to think of themselves in lowly terms and to do more, and not give up trying as Allāh's mercy rains on those who try. While this is a cognitive approach using *'aql*, it also works on the *nafs* by making one feel humble and training the *nafs* to be faithful to Allāh. These instructions make the client understand the metaphysical world and maintain a balance among these three concepts, which is essential for the heart's purification.

4. *Knowledge of spiritual diseases of the heart.* The counselor discusses the 15 types of hearts mentioned in the Qur'ān and the factors leading to their illnesses. The counselor gives assignments for reading with instructions to write daily notes on the struggles of thoughts and behaviors. The client underlines or highlights the most disturbing circumstances and writes questions to discuss in the next session with the counselor. A client with hard-heartedness towards others is instructed to practice the opposite behavior, e.g., politeness. A client is always asked to be in the company of pious people and reminded that no one could benefit the client more than their own efforts. For clients who complain of their hearts not being filled with strong *Iman,* are reminded to follow the fundamentals of *Iman* as mentioned in the Qur'ān, i.e., "O believers! Have faith in Allāh, His Messenger, the Book He has revealed to His Messenger, and the Scriptures He revealed before. Indeed, whoever denies Allāh, His angels, His Books, His messengers, and the Last Day has clearly gone far astray" (4:136). Regarding obsessions or *waswas*, clients are instructed that if *waswas* arise in the heart by themselves, they are harmless and should be ignored, and clients should engage in some productive work. However, creating negative self-thoughts is a sinful act. A hadith is narrated that indicates; Allāh forgives thoughts that are not acted upon.

5. *Covert and overt divine laws*. A client acknowledges the basic principles of Islam that stem from its belief in Allāh as the only Creator and Sustainer of the Universe and *tawhid* as the guiding principle, where all is connected, including the spiritual realm. The purpose of human life is to worship Allāh, which would lead to harmony and peace in this world and success in the hereafter. Clients are referred to the Qur'ān and Sunnah for moral guidance. The client is told that Allāh is aware of all we do, and while it is possible to deceive other human beings, one cannot deceive the Creator. The

emphasis is on developing *taqwa* or piety and a commitment that pleasing Allāh is the goal in the way the prophet prescribed.

6. *Following Sharia or Islamic law in personal life.* The counselor explores the importance of *Sharia* and how it is connected to Allāh's divine laws and pleasure. It is emphasized that rituals or prayers alone cannot enhance a person's condition unless the client is willing to change the circumstances that create the problems. The value of enhanced knowledge combined with improved thoughts and actions is discussed. Examples shared include client's knowledge of what is forbidden, discouraged, allowed, recommended, and obligatory in Islam. The client is asked whether one's income is lawful (*halal*) without which one's prayers may not be accepted, whether one performs all obligatory acts, including daily prayers, paying zakat, observing fast, etc., one's interpersonal ways of dealing, usage of one's time, etc. The client is instructed to align their thoughts and actions with Islamic beliefs and practices. The client is reminded of the verse in Surah Al-Raad, "Verily Allāh will not change the condition of a people until they do not change what is in themselves," referring to the negative conditions or that which are against Islamic laws.

7. *Self-diagnosis.* The client is asked to use *Muhasaba* or self-reflection on the condition of their spiritual heart and examine where they fall short. Clients learn to do this exercise after five daily prayers or at least every night. Each progress or shortcoming is written in notes and communicated to the counselor with the client's own feelings. For example, if there is arrogance in the client, they need to self-examine if there were any thoughts or actions during the day when they felt superior to others in any way. The advantage of this method is that it can be done anytime and without the counselor and can be more accurate if honestly documented and communicated to the counselor in writing. This also works as baseline data that can be compared with time. Self-diagnosis will depend on the presenting problem and the client is guided as necessary. They are reminded that peace is not the objective of therapy; it will automatically follow by changing the thoughts and actions aligned with the prophetic way of life.

8. *Prescriptions for the nafs.* The counselor gives a specific treatment based on each client's unique problem. For example, for

lack of faith, the counselor may ask the client to repent to Allāh (*tawbah*, perform extra prayers, do *dhikr* as prescribed in hadith, etc.). For jealousy, the counselor may ask the clients to ask for forgiveness from the person with whom they are jealous, pray for their happiness, and attempt not to repeat this mistake. For arrogance, one is asked to show humility in various ways, think of others as potentially better, cry in front of Allāh, etc. For backbiting, the client is reminded to think about the punishment stated in the hadith that it is the same as eating the flesh of one's own brother's dead body, ask for forgiveness from the person to whom one has complained about, pay a pre-determined fine with money, offer pre-determined non-obligatory prayers as repentance, and in future, think before saying anything.

For clients wishing to see others respect them, they are asked to think of one's faults so that the feelings of self-aggrandizement will go away. Clients who feel themselves better than those who do not pray are reminded that the one who prays does not have to be better than the one who does not pray because those who do not pray may have another good act, while those who pray may have a sinful act, making the non-praying person better overall. Secondly, it is possible that due to the praying person's immoral actions, he or she may become a non-praying individual and vice versa. However, praying is a gift from Allāh, and not praying is a spiritual disease, and one should thank Allāh for the gift and pray for those who do not pray.

These issues highlight the significance of humility and a reminder that instead of focusing on the faults of others, one needs to concentrate on one's spiritual condition. The trap of thinking of oneself as better than others take away humility, love, and respect for others. On issues of spousal relations, Thanvi asked to focus on taming one's *nafs* because it is impossible to do good deeds without developing a healthy soul. Thinking of others as potentially better people can solve many interpersonal problems.

9. ***Prescription of Duas.*** While clients can make prayers as they wish, they are encouraged to make dua of the prophets and those given in the Qur'ān, especially as relevant to conditions of the *nafs* and *qalb*. The counselor prescribes *duas* from a book called, *Munajat-e-Maqbool* or *The Answered Whispers,* compiled by Thanvi and drawn from *Al-Hizb al-Azam* (The Great Prayer Book) by Mulla Ali-al-Qari

(d. 1602). While such *duas* are good anytime, they can be more effective if made after performing ablution and extra non-obligatory prayers.

For grief and sadness, the prescribed dua is, "O Allāh, I seek refuge in You from grief and sadness, from weakness and laziness, from miserliness and cowardice, from being overcome by debt, and from being overpowered by other people. When asked how to remain fixed on Allāh's remembrance, the recommended dua is the one narrated by Prophet Mohammed, "*Ya Muqallebal Qulub, Thabbit Qalbi 'alaa Deenik,*" (O Turners of the hearts, make my heart steady on Your *deen*). Also, "Our Lord, do not let our hearts swerve after You have guided us and grant us mercy from Your presence. Indeed, you are the most generous Grantor. Our Lord, we have wronged our souls. And if You do not forgive us and grant us mercy, we certainly shall be among the losers." "O Allāh, purify my heart from hypocrisy, my deeds from ostentation and pretension, my tongue from lies, and my eyes from wrongful glances. You know what the eyes deceptively glance at and what the hearts conceal." "O Allāh, bestow my soul its *taqwa*. Purify it, for You are the best of those who can purify it. You alone are its guardian and master." "O Allāh, open our hearts with Your remembrance, complete Your blessings on us through Your Grace, and make us among Your pious servants." Praying helps one concentrate on *dhikr* and *shughal* and reminds one to remember Allāh. Remembrance of Allāh is also not only by tongue but by actions and following the Qur'ānic injunctions as closely as possible.

10. Termination. There is no termination in therapy as it is in the secular model, but when the client's condition is improved, and direct services are not needed, therapeutic communication can stop. The client and counselor may keep in touch about the client's condition to prevent relapse. Spiritual guidance and company, especially the counselor's prayers, are blessings.

What not to expect from therapies

The culture in the subcontinent at Thanvi's time and even today is that spiritual counseling can result in many benefits, including miracles, inner knowledge, a vision of God, and even salvation on Judgment Day. Thanvi reminded that therapy is not magic and

173

religious incantations cannot yield direct material benefits. To progress, the clients must strive and fulfill their responsibilities.

Thanvi also cautioned about using dream interpretations in counseling. He wrote that while being pleased with good dreams is okay, dreams can be deceiving. Dreams can be a positive omen only if they encourage one to do good deeds and follow the Sunnah of the Prophet. However, being accepted by Allāh does not depend on dreams but on actions in the wakeful state. When his clients narrated experiences of seeing or visualizing someone who had died or shared experiences of what may be going on in a transgressor's grave, Thanvi cautioned in considering them accurate because these are a veil and distraction and reminded that despite being superior to all pious Muslims, the Prophet's companions rarely reported such supernatural events. There is also no guarantee of special status for someone visualizing such events, as similar experiences may occur to non-believers.

Conclusion

Thanvi is little known outside the Indian Subcontinent but carries a large following in Urdu-speaking circles worldwide. This is mainly because his manuscripts were written in Urdu, and only a few were translated into English. His contributions to Islamic counseling came long before the techniques offered by modern counseling, yet there are commonalities in them, except that his focus is on the spiritual elements. His explanation of the different types of hearts is unique and detailed, and he prescribed treatments based on individual needs. His insistence that his clients understand both the covert and overt divine laws and practice Sharia in their personal life is challenging, which he contends is essential for success. He clearly outlined therapeutic objectives and methodologies based on Islamic principles and cultural needs. The qualities needed of a Muslim counselor are demanding but Islamic in approach. Thanvi cautioned us of what not to expect from therapies, as was the case of local culture, and outlined the role of the client, giving them much responsibility and conditions to improve. It is hoped that research on his works will continue.

References

al Fārūqī, I. R. (2000). *Al Tawhid: Its Implications for Thought and Life.* International Institute of Islamic Thought, Herndon, VA. (Faruqi, 2000)

Ajmal, M. (1987). Sufi Science of the Soul. In Hossein Nasr, Islamic Spirituality, 531-553. Routledge and Kegan Paul, London.

Haque A. & Rothman, A. (2021). Islamic Psychology around the Globe. Pp. 396. International Association of Islamic Psychology, Seattle: USA.

Haque, A. (2004). Psychology from Islamic Perspective: Contributions of Early Muslim Scholars and Challenges to Contemporary Muslim Psychologists. *Journal of Religion and Health, 43 (4)*, 357-377.

Khwaja, A. A.)1999). Maulana Ashrafi Ali Thanvi: His views on religious and moral philosophy and Tasawwuf. Kitab Bhawan, New Delhi.

Thanvi, A.A. (n.d.). Sukoon-e-Qalb. 200 pages. Maktab Inamiya Publishers, Karachi, Pakistan.

Thanvi, A. A. (n.d.). Tarbiah as-Salik. 1736 pages. Zamzam Publishers, Karachi, Pakistan. Thanvi, A. A. (n.d.). Ashraful Jawab, 609 pages, Umar Faruq Publishers, Karachi, Pakistan.

Thanvi, A. A. (n.d.). Bawadir-un-Nawadir, 865 pages, Umar Faruq Publishers, Karachi, Pakistan.

Thanvi, A. A. (n.d.) Beheshti Zewar (for women). 240 pages, Umar Faruq Publishers, Karachi, Pakistan.

Thanvi, A. A. (n.d.) Beheshti Zewar (for men). 699 pages, Umar Faruq Publishers, Karachi, Pakistan.

Thanvi, A. A. (n.d.). Islah-e-Dil (Amelioration of the Heart). 297 pages, Umar Faruq Publishers, Karachi, Pakistan. World Psychiatry Association (2016).

CHAPTER SEVEN

INTEGRATION OF ISLAMIC SPIRITUALITY IN THE TREATMENT OF GRIEF AFTER PERINATAL LOSS

Venus Mahmoodi, Lindsay White, Zarnab Virk, and Anna Akhavan

Introduction

A woman's *reproductive story*—or envisioned transition to parenthood—is often crafted over a lifetime and shaped by personal as well as cultural expectations, fantasies of motherhood, and hopes for her unborn child. Focus on this narrative sharpens during pregnancy and, in part, the reproductive story bonds the mother-to-be with her developing child from a very early stage of pregnancy, possibly preconception (Diamond & Diamond, 2016; Jaffe et al., 2011). Sociologically, pregnancy serves as a 'rite of passage,' transforming a *woman* into a *mother* and conveying special status (Côté-Arsenault et al., 2009). Spiritually, the condition of growing a human being in one's body and the lived experience of pregnancy can have sacred significance (Molina, 2019). More specifically, within Islam, Muslim women connect motherhood with religious connection and obligation, becoming a part of their spiritual identity (Schleifer, 1996). The physical and emotional sacrifices of a woman bestow her the honored status of the mother within Islam while also providing her with the opportunity for spiritual and religious growth (Schleifer, 1996).

Unfortunately, not all pregnancies produce the expected outcome, namely, the birth of a healthy baby; many parents experience adverse pregnancy outcomes, such as miscarriage, stillbirth, therapeutic abortion, and neonatal death (DiMarco et al., 2002). Perinatal loss is a summary term for these different outcomes and denotes the unintended demise of an anticipated child between conception and the first 28 days postpartum (Barfield, 2011). These losses may mark the end of a pregnancy and a devastating break in a woman's reproductive story.

The most common forms of perinatal loss are during pregnancy, including miscarriage and stillbirth. Miscarriage refers to fetal death before the 20th week of gestation, while stillbirth occurs in the later stages of pregnancy, when a fetus dies before or during birth, having reached at least 22-28 gestational weeks or weighing a minimum of 1000 grams (Quenby et al., 2021; Froen et al., 2011). Environmental considerations, such as air pollution, and maternal factors, such as the mother's age or nutritional, physical, and psychological health, may contribute to the risk of perinatal loss (Quenby et al., 2021). Obstetric complications during pregnancy and delivery may also increase risk; however, the cause of a perinatal loss is often unknown (CDC, 2022).

Individuals might imagine their ability to conceive and carry a pregnancy to be a biological certainty, but literature on reproductive health contradicts this assumption, estimating that one in five recognized pregnancies fail (Bennett et al., 2005; Côté-Arsenault, 2003; Diamond & Diamond, 2016; Kobler et al., 2007; The World Health Organization [WHO], 2019). Additionally, nearly one in four women may experience a perinatal loss in their lifetime (Diamond & Diamond, 2016). Global epidemiological data estimate that 23 million women experience a miscarriage annually (Quenby et al., 2021), and approximately 1% of pregnancies end in stillbirths, about 2 million globally each year (Centers for Disease Control and Prevention [CDC], 2020; Mayo Clinic, 2021). Nuanced differences in definitions and lack of consistent reporting suggest the total proportion of pregnancies lost could be even higher than estimated.

Despite the high prevalence, perinatal loss is still treated as a taboo subject globally, contributing to social stigma and isolation (WHO, 2019).

As is the case with other types of loss or death, an intense period of grief may follow the experience of a perinatal loss. Factors such as proximity to the due date, parental age at the time of loss, the unexpectedness of the death, and being a first-time parent may all contribute to the acuity of perinatal loss grief symptoms and course of bereavement. Pregnancy loss can leave a prolonged, adverse psychological imprint on a mother's life, especially when the mother is unable to grieve or her loss is not acknowledged by family or society, a phenomenon known as disenfranchised grief (Doka, 1989). As bereaved mothers have observed, a perinatal loss is a perceived theft of the future, robbing them of their imagined role as a mother, leaving instead a sensation of empty arms following the death of their baby (Diamond & Diamond, 2016; Jaffe et al., 2011; Leon, 1990).

Due to the intensity of symptoms, many women mourning a perinatal loss would benefit from psychotherapy to improve functioning and heal from grief. Given that both pregnancy and loss are often connected to spiritual identity for Muslim women, integrating religious and cultural concepts into the grief process can help mitigate symptoms more effectively. Integrating Islamic religious and spiritual values into psychotherapy treatment helps mental health providers facilitate bereaved Muslim mothers' meaning-making process and grief recovery following a pregnancy loss. This integration process begins with understanding the rulings from the Qur'ān and Sunnah (prophetic traditions) about motherhood and the status of motherhood, rulings about personhood (when the soul enters the body), judgments about miscarriage and Islamic rites, and how the Prophet Muhammad (peace be upon him; pbuh) addressed grief. After understanding the rulings from the Qur'ān and Sunnah, a crucial step is weaving these religious beliefs into treatments addressing Muslim mothers' grief, allowing for therapy to become a holding space where patients find comfort and hope.

The purpose of this chapter is to provide a comprehensive review of Islamic concepts pertaining to pregnancy loss and their integration into treating symptoms of grief and profound loss. The chapter begins with a description of grief, bereavement, its

CLINICAL APPLICATIONS OF ISLAMIC PSYCHOLOGY

treatments, and Islamic views on grief, loss, and bereavement. The chapter also discusses perinatal loss in Islam. The focus will then shift to religious concepts utilized in grief psychotherapy when treating Muslim patients suffering after perinatal loss, which will be illustrated with case examples. The chapter does acknowledge the lack of research in this area and that this approach is based on clinical practice with Muslim women who experienced pregnancy loss seeking treatment from a Muslim therapist skilled in Islamic psychology.

Grief and Perinatal Loss

Grief is a natural, non-pathological response to a significant loss. Symptoms of normal, uncomplicated grief include lack of pleasure, decreased motivation, sadness, tearfulness, and inability to focus, in many ways, emulating a depressive episode. These symptoms are specific to the loss, however, and tend to remit within six months to one year after the death as the bereaved experiences increased acceptance, positive emotions, and return to daily functioning (Bonnano et al., 2001). Unfortunately, approximately 15% of cases take a chronic course in which symptoms are prolonged and remain intense over time, known as complicated grief (Bonanno & Kaltman, 2001). In cases of complicated grief, the bereaved experiences symptoms resembling depression, but unlike normal grief, the acuity and disruption to functioning do not diminish with time. Some people experience the same—or heightened—symptom intensity even years after the initial loss, particularly if acute grief goes unprocessed and unacknowledged.

Perinatal loss is associated with a high incidence of complicated grief. In one study surveying parents grieving a pregnancy loss, 30% of the sample demonstrated atypical mourning patterns, scoring higher on grief measures 1-year or 2-years post-loss than they did at their initial 2-month post-loss assessment (Lin & Lasker, 1996). Further complicating the mourning process and clinical presentation, about 15-25% of bereaved mothers experience deleterious effects on their mental health following a perinatal loss (Bennett et al., 2005). In addition to prolonged grief, women who have suffered a perinatal loss are at heightened risk for depression, anxiety, and post-traumatic stress (Badenhorst & Hughes, 2007; Gold et al., 2016; Kersting & Wagner, 2012; Murphy et al., 2014). In the short term, pregnancy loss may require a woman to undergo invasive medical procedures to remove the fetus from the womb, which can cause mistrust of her body and exacerbate a perception that her body has failed, contributing to feelings of shame and guilt (Diamond & Diamond, 2016). Long-term, not only are mothers grieving a perinatal loss four times as likely to exhibit clinically significant levels of depression nine months post-loss, but they are also seven times as likely to exhibit high levels of post-traumatic stress (Gold et al., 2016).

Notably, an encounter with death can inspire existential questions, and mourners often turn to spiritual counselors for support or assistance with culturally meaningful rituals and funerary practices before they present to therapy (Doka & Morgan, 1993). While attempts to make sense of loss in spiritual terms can strengthen faith for some, for others, newfound doubt can deepen grief and prompt existential struggle, contributing to psychospiritual distress (Doka & Morgan, 1993). One possibly protective facet of spirituality is its relationship with meaning-making. In a study investigating normative grief patterns in a broad sample of parents mourning the death of a child, participants who endorsed belief in death as God's will, among other spiritual themes, were less likely to exhibit maladaptive grief symptoms (Lichtenthal et al., 2010).

Social factors can also play a significant role while mourning and, particularly, whether the bereaved moves through normative grief or develops complicated grief. Bereaved mothers may withdraw socially, disconnecting from friends with living children (Côté-Arsenault et al., 2009). Although these cultural rituals and religious practices often facilitate the mourning process by connecting the bereaved with a social network, no such prescriptions exist for cases of pregnancy loss (Cacciatore, 2013; Capitulo, 2005; Kobler et al., 2007).

The transitional nature of pregnancy and the inherent ambiguity of its loss may contribute to the lack of sociocultural acknowledgment and taboo status. Perinatal loss exists at an unusual crossroads of life and death, in which the mother may be the only person with any knowledge of or connection to the deceased (Diamond & Diamond, 2016; Froen et al., 2011; Jaffe et al., 2011; Quenby et al., 2021). Until recently, stillbirths were granted only a death certificate, symbolically disregarding the baby's existence (Jaffe, 2011). Even in the hospital setting, pregnancy losses were historically dismissed as 'non-events' (Capitulo, 2005, p. 30; Kobler et al., 2007; Koopmans et al., 2013). Only in the last three decades has there been a concerted effort to standardize acute psychosocial response to pregnancy loss in nursing. This pervasive marginalization characterizes the disenfranchised grief a mother may feel following perinatal loss, which leaves her to mourn alone, struggling to make sense of the loss while in psychological and spiritual distress (Lang et al., 2011).

Psychotherapy and Perinatal loss

Most bereaved individuals can recover from normative acute grief symptoms without formal intervention from a therapist. Those experiencing heightened distress and complicated grief do require additional support, namely psychotherapy or even medication, depending on symptom severity. Regardless of the grief type, interventional format, or theoretical orientation, therapists can create a holding space in which the bereaved can feel comfortable sharing details of their loss as well as processing their thoughts and emotions. When the loss is acknowledged, and space is provided for mourning, even complicated grief symptoms subside after treatment.

Although there is limited research on interventions for perinatal loss and bereavement, there are a few randomized control trials (RCTs) that provide evidence for the effectiveness of therapy for grief after perinatal loss (Johnson et al., 2016; Johnson et al., 2022; Kersting et al., 2013; Wenzel, 2017). One of the largest and earliest RCTs used an online version of cognitive behavioral therapy (CBT) to treat symptoms of post-traumatic stress and prolonged grief following pregnancy loss by targeting acute symptoms (e.g., tearfulness, negative thoughts) (Kersting et al., 2013; Wenzel, 2017). Results of the RCT showed significant reductions in these symptoms and improved functioning of the bereaved women (Kersting et al., 2013). Theoretically, cognitive behavioral therapy (CBT) challenges maladaptive thinking patterns characteristic of bereaved mothers experiencing grief related to pregnancy loss by using cognitive restructuring techniques and mindfulness practices while encouraging behavioral activation to combat social withdrawal (Wenzel, 2017).

Interpersonal psychotherapy is another modality shown to effectively treat acute distress from pregnancy loss, with recent studies demonstrating a decrease in grief symptomatology in a cohort of 274 participants (Johnson et al., 2016; Johnson et al., 2022). Conceptually, this intervention aims to decrease social isolation by fostering a bereaved mother's social support network. Simultaneously, IPT emphasizes psychoeducation and skills building to facilitate exploration of distress stemming from pregnancy loss (Johnson et al., 2022).

Clinical practice and case studies also support psychodynamic psychotherapy for the treatment of distress following pregnancy loss (Markin & McCarthy, 2020). Psychodynamic techniques prioritize the creation of a therapeutic holding space for the intense emotions associated with the loss seeped in empathy. Attachment-based approaches focus on rewriting the reproductive story to maintain a connection with the deceased baby while also using the mother's attachment style to offer her support that aligns with her need for care (Kleiman, 2017). While each treatment model proposes a different therapeutic focus, common themes of empathy, empowerment, and flexibility appear in these approaches for grief and associated distress after a perinatal loss (Leon, 2015).

Islam and motherhood

The importance of motherhood in Islam plays a significant role in the high levels of distress experienced by Muslim women after a pregnancy loss. Therefore, before discussing pregnancy loss in Islam and treating grief symptoms, we need to address how motherhood is conceptualized within Islam. There are several conceptualizations of the motherhood role in Islam: the responsibility and obligations associated with motherhood, the innate qualities of mothers to fulfill those responsibilities, the change in social and spiritual status, and the opportunity for a deeper spiritual connection to Allah. Interwoven in the spiritual identity of Muslim motherhood is a sense of religious obligation to build family and community and their sense of personal responsibility in relation to Allah's will (Schleifer, 1996). Many Hadiths (Prophet sayings and behaviors) focus on the rewards women receive due to the sacrifices they make to care for a child, including changes in their identities, physical wellbeing, mental health, and social relationships, which speak to the external responsibilities of motherhood. And this is further reinforced by Islam, where mothers are bestowed with the responsibility for their children and imbued with innate qualities necessary for the effective fulfillment of this role (Hamdan, 2009), which speaks to the internal drive towards compassionate caretaking. Taking into consideration both inner and outer dimensions of motherhood, the reproductive story of a Muslim woman integrates her obligations to her Lord, cultivates the innate traits that will make her a good mother, and uses motherhood to develop her spiritual connection with Allah.

The first conceptualization focuses on the obligations of motherhood and identifying her responsibilities in fulfilling those obligations. In a Hadith Qudsi, Allah tells His servants that by completing their obligations to Him, they will draw nearer to Him (Bukhari, 6502). Therefore, by completing just her religious obligations to her children, a mother can obtain proximity to Allah. The obligations of motherhood are addressed in the following Hadith about the division of responsibilities for each member of society:

The Prophet (pbuh) said: Each of you is a guardian and is responsible for his ward. The ruler is a guardian, and the man is the guardian of the members of his household; and the woman is a guardian and is responsible for her husband's house and his offspring; and so each of you is a guardian and is responsible for his ward (Bukhari, 5200).

The Prophet (pbuh) highlights the role of mothers as being responsible for their households and their children, meaning they must ensure their children have their basic needs met and are nurtured physically and emotionally (Hamdan, 2009; Schleifer, 1996). They may either fulfill these responsibilities on their own by providing a caring, safe environment of nurturance, including meeting emotional, physical, and educational needs, or they may have caregivers who fulfill these tasks, as even seen at the time of the Prophet (pbuh) (i.e., using wet nurses to breastfeed young children). The Hadith Qudsi continues by acknowledging that a servant who goes beyond their minimal obligations will draw even nearer to Allah and build a deep connection with Him (Bukhari, 6502). This means that a Muslim mother who goes beyond her basic obligations and responsibilities in the care of her children for the sake of Allah will receive the ultimate reward of the Afterlife, proximity to Allah.

The second conceptualization of motherhood is connected to the innate qualities a woman has been gifted by Allah to fulfill her duties of motherhood. Allah provides Muslim women with these qualities to enable them to fulfill her responsibilities more willingly, despite knowing the challenges associated with pregnancy, labor, and delivery, and caretaking responsibilities (Schleifer, 1996). To have a well-adjusted, emotionally healthy child, mothers need to encompass two traits: mercy and generosity. Mercy is a trait intimately connected with motherhood as the word for womb in Arabic is *al-rahm* comes directly from Allah's name *Al-Rahman*, meaning The Most Merciful (Bukhari, 5988). The mercy between a mother and her child has been brought to this world from Allah to illustrate His Mercy to His servants; yet it is a powerful reminder of how Allah's mercy is manifested on the earth, an act of love and deep connection.

Allah's messenger (pbuh) said: Allah created on the same day when He created the heavens and the earth, one hundred parts of mercy. Every part of mercy is analogous to the space between the heavens and the earth, and He, out of this mercy, endowed one part to the earth and it is because of this, the mother shows affection to her child (Muslim, 2733).

'Umar ibn al-Khattab (may God be pleased with him) said: "Some prisoners were brought to the Prophet (pbuh), and there was a woman among the prisoners who was searching (for her child). When she found her child, she embraced him and put him to her breast. The Prophet (pbuh) said to us, 'Do you think that this woman would throw her child in the fire?' We said, 'No, by Allah, not if she can prevent it.' The Prophet (pbuh) said, 'Allah is more merciful to His slaves than this woman is to her child.'" (Agreed upon; Bukhari, 5999).

These Hadiths illustrate the mercy that is bestowed in women to show their children and that this mercy is a God-given trait. This trait is integral for a Muslim woman to fulfill her obligation of motherhood and can often be appreciated as a way to connect deeper with Allah.

The second innate trait of mothers is generosity. Mothers show their generosity through their time, providing sustenance and supporting their families. Although their obligations might state that they are only responsible for the basic care of their children, generosity means that they complete these tasks with *ihsan* (done with excellence). This means that even though these are not obligations, a mother might choose to breastfeed her child for two years, spend her time feeding and caring for her child, and financially support her family. Because in Islam, Muslim women are not obligated to spend money on their families, any money she spends on her husband and children is a charitable act and compensated in the Afterlife by Allah.

Another conceptualization of motherhood in Islam is that motherhood raises the social and spiritual status of a woman (Schleifer, 1996). Most Muslims believe that the natural progression in their lives is to marry then have children, which is connected to a sense of religious obligation (Schleifer, 1996).

Whoever obeys God and the Messenger will be among those He has blessed: the messengers, the truthful, those who bear witness to the truth (martyrs), and the righteous – what excellent companions these are! (Qur'ān, 4: 69).

The interpretation of this verse speaks to the relationship that martyrs have with Allah, and this is the same status given to women who die from childbirth (Schleifer, 1996). An oft-cited Hadith speaks about the high status of mothers in Islam: narrated by Abu Huraira, when the Prophet (pbuh) was asked by a man, "Who is most deserving of my good company?" The Prophet (pbuh) said, "Your mother." The man asked, "Then who?" The Prophet (pbuh) said, "Your mother." The man asked again, "Then who?" The Prophet (pbuh) said, "Your mother." The man asked again, "Then who?" The Prophet (pbuh) said, "Your father" (Sahih Bukhari, 5626). This hadith emphasizes the status of mothers over fathers and the importance of treating mothers with care and respect because of the sacrifices and challenges they undergo in their care for their children (Schleifer, 1996). The status change is one associated with her role within society and the rights she has over her children, but also the status she has with Allah in fulfilling her role as a mother.

The final conceptualization is associated with the inner dimensions of spiritual connectedness through motherhood. Each stage of building a family has its own reward for her Afterlife, from trying to conceive and pregnancy to childbirth and caretaking of the child. In the Qur'ān, there is an acknowledgment of the physical hardships that are experienced by a woman and attached to that a spiritual reward in the Afterlife (31:14). It is her "exclusive opportunity" to obtain Allah's pleasure by knowingly taking on something that has been proven to be physically, emotionally, and spiritually taxing (Schleifer, 1996, p. 51). Setting up His servants for successful, Allah has placed these biological inclinations and innate qualities to drive her desire for building a family. It is the culmination of the three other conceptualizations of motherhood: the obligations of motherhood, innate traits of mothers, and the station of mothers. In this hadith, the Prophet (pbuh) acknowledges how these three different conceptualizations lead to rewards and saving from the Hellfire.

Aisha (may God be pleased with her) related: "A woman by the name of Jameelah came to me with her two daughters. She asked me for charity but found nothing with me except a date, which I gave her. She divided it between her two daughters and ate nothing herself; then, she got up and left. After this, the Prophet (pbuh), came, so I narrated this story to him; he said: "He who is involved (in the responsibility) of (nurturing) daughters and is generous to them, will have them as a fortification for himself against the Hellfire." (Bukhari, 499)

To summarize, in this section, we present the conceptualizations of motherhood in Islam and how each part is connected to the mother's spiritual connection with Allah. Both the outer and inner dimensions of motherhood lead to an internalization of the motherhood role as a direct connection to Allah. Yet, when the reproductive story is interrupted due to a miscarriage or stillbirth, the loss is associated with the premature physical severing of the fetus from the mother's body and the disappointment for the inability to fulfill her religious obligations and missing out on the immense rewards associated with motherhood. The hopes and dreams, the sense of responsibility to be a mother for Allah's pleasure, the yearning to mother due to the mercy and generosity in her heart, and the need for a spiritual connection with Allah through motherhood are lost. Therefore, a loss can cause immense distress for a Muslim mother, especially when her identity as a mother is intimately connected with her spiritual identity as a Muslim.

Islam, Death, and Grief

When a Muslim dies, rituals are associated with preparing the body for burial. There is a ritual washing (*ghusl*) of the body by the deceased's family member or trusted person, after which the deceased is enshrouded with a white cloth (Hedayat, 2006). During this time, family members might recite the Qur'ān or pray on behalf of the deceased while awaiting burial. At the burial site, the Imam performs the *Janāzah* (funeral) prayer with those present, and the body is buried. Following the burial of the deceased, family and friends continue reciting Qur'ān and prayers on behalf of the deceased, which allows for continuity of the relationship after death. Other practices on behalf of the deceased include giving charity in their name and performing the pilgrimage (hajj and umrah). These prescribed and recommended rituals help families process their emotions and cope with the aftermath of their loss (Hedayat, 2006).

In Islam, grief and bereavement are well-recognized sequelae following a death. In the Qur'ān, the word *huzn* is used multiple times to describe grief and bereavement. Within the Qur'ān and the Sunnah, there are numerous descriptions of loss and death followed by experiences of grief. The Prophet Muhammad (pbuh) experienced the loss of his father prior to birth, his mother at age six, his uncles, his wives, his children, his companions, and his home. Through his experiences and those of the other Prophets, Muslims learn how to grieve. When the Prophet's (pbuh) first wife died, he expressed the love he had for her and acknowledged the important role she had in his life, including being the first believer in Islam. When his son, Ibrahim, died in his arms, he cried and expressed his sorrow and gratitude to God. A description of this hadith will be provided later in the chapter when discussing perinatal loss. When Prophet Yaqub's (Jacob) son, Yusuf (Joseph), was separated from him, he cried so much that he went blind (Qur'ān, 12:84). Muslims are allowed to grieve as long as it is not detrimental to their physical, psychological, and spiritual wellbeing. Extreme responses such as wailing accompanied by self-mutilation or harm are not allowed and are highly discouraged (Sahih Bukhari, 1294). Other aspects of grief within Islam involve communal connectedness through visits from family and friends. Muslims are encouraged to visit the family of the deceased and provide care by offering meals, empathy, and support and performing religious practices on behalf of the deceased (Hedayat, 2006).

The Islamic bereavement approach focuses on acceptance of God's decree (*qadr*), reliance on God (*tawakkul*), patience (*sabr*), and religious coping using practice and spirituality (Akanni, 2016; Kristiansen & Sheikh, 2012; Mehraby, 2003). *Qadr* is the understanding that some aspects of life are pre-determined, including wealth, children, birth, and death. In the Qur'ān, death and grief are described as part of life in the world and can be a way to develop proximity with God. The Qur'ān states, "You believers will surely be tested in your wealth and yourselves, and you will certainly hear many hurtful words from those who were given the Scripture before you and from the polytheists. But if you are patient and mindful of Allah—surely this is a resolve to aspire to" (Qur'ān, 3: 186). This verse is clear that Muslims can expect challenges, trials, and tribulations, and by observing patience, acceptance, and God-consciousness, they will overcome these challenges with God's help. In the Qur'ān, God provides reassurance that He will help Muslims through the tribulations in life (Qur'ān, 2:214); and God will never place a trial or a tribulation that a person cannot bear (Qur'ān, 2:156). Imam Al-Ghazali, a prominent scholar of Islam, spoke of acceptance of the *qadr* as being the first step in processing the consequences of grief and loss (Akanni, 2016). The Qur'ān provides context and helpful framing around the loss to acknowledge that whether there is grief or joy, the Muslim is accepting of His plan (Mehraby, 2003).

The two other aspects of the framework are *tawakkul* and *sabr*. *Tawakkul* is often described as reliance on God or absolute faith in God's plan. In the Qur'ān it states,

If you ask them who created the heavens and the earth, they will reply "Allah". Say: "Do you think then that, if Allah be pleased to afflict me, those you called upon besides Him could relieve my affliction or that if He be pleased to show me mercy, they could withhold His mercy?" (Qur'an 39: 36-37)

"If God touch thee with affliction, none can remove it but He, if He touch thee with happiness, He hath power over all things. He is Irresistible (watching) from above His worshippers, and He is the

Wise, Acquainted with all things" (Qur'an 6: 17-18).

These verses focus on the *yaqin* that God will provide relief from the afflictions and challenges that a Muslim might experience, and it is only through their true faith in God that their grief will be eased (Akanni, 2016). Muslims are also told in the Qur'ān that if they are patient during their grief and tribulations, God will reward them greatly in this world or in the Hereafter (Qur'ān, 41:35). Patience is a virtue that can provide reframing of the loss and building up resilience as well as attaining God's blessings and mercy (Qur'ān, 2:156). Multiple verses speak of receiving God's mercy, compassion, and blessings for exhibiting patience and true faith in the aftermath of a loss (Qur'ān, 2:156 & 9:51). When these reminders are provided for Muslims, they feel connected to Allah and are able to effectively move through their grief.

Integrating these concepts with grief counseling is essential for bereaved Muslims to move through their grief. Moving through one's grief means that a person can process their emotions, thoughts, and experiences following the loss or death. As previously discussed, most people move through their grief without the need for professional support, but often this is applicable to those with adequate social support, who have spaces to express their emotions and who can fulfill their basic needs. However, if a person is struggling with their grief or experiencing complicated grief, then these concepts will need to be integrated within a psychotherapeutic setting, ideally with a clinician that has a background in Islamic psychology. Furthermore, in an Islamic context, integrating both religious concepts and evidence-based practice is preferable to ensure spiritually- and culturally competent treatment for Muslim women undergoing perinatal loss.

Muslims, Perinatal loss, and Grief

To understand perinatal loss among Muslim women and how the previously discussed religious concepts need to be integrated in their grief process, the discussion needs to focus on personhood in Islam and its influence on religious practices. A well-accepted majority of scholars views personhood (ensoulment of the fetus or beginning of life) as occurring 120 days after conception (Ahaddour, 2021; Al-Matary & Ali, 2014; Shaikh, 2003, p. 121; Shaw, 2014), whereas a small minority believes it to be 40 days after conception (Ahaddour, 2021). The specific number has been inferred based on the Qur'anic verses 23:12–14, which explain fetal development chronologically in the following stages: *nutfa* or drop; *'alaqa* or blood clot; *mugdha* or lump (Ahaddour, 2021). As a result, Islamic bioethics (based on the majority view) indicate that pregnancy terminations can be only permissible before 120 days of conception (Ahaddour, 2021; Ayed & Ayed, 2018; Shaikh, 2003, p. 119; Shaw, 2014). Seeking an abortion after 120 days warrants consultation with a religious scholar. In Islam, if a fetus dies after 120 days post conception, all the funeral rites are performed as described previously. The baby is given a name, the *ghusl* is performed, and the *Janāzah* prayer is performed. This can be validating for Muslim mothers because their babies have a proper burial, a place for them to visit to recite prayers, and acknowledgment of the loss by the community. In contrast, if a fetus dies prior to 120 days, there might be some confusion about the status of the fetus's personhood, given the differences in opinion. Given that the majority of Muslim scholars accept 120 days as the dominant opinion on when personhood occurs, it is more likely that the fetus would not be considered a person by the community. The consequence of this decision means that the fetus is buried without the requirement of being named or having the funeral rituals performed. For many Muslim women, this experience can feel invalidating and isolating, putting them at higher risk for developing complicated grief.

The Islamic grief approach for perinatal loss is similar to what was previously outlined in the grief and bereavement section. However, a few Hadiths provide some guidance on the grief process related to perinatal loss for Muslims. One of the most important Hadiths is when the Prophet (pbuh) expresses his grief while holding his young son, Ibrahim, as he was dying. The Prophet (pbuh)'s companions saw him weeping silently when he finally died. His companion asked him about his tears, and the Prophet (pbuh) said, "The eye sheds tears, and the heart grieves, and we only say what pleases our Lord, and we are saddened by your separation, O Ibrahim." (Bukhari, 1303). From this Hadith, Muslims learn how to mourn appropriately, especially the loss of a very young child or fetus, due to the ambiguous nature of the loss and the untimeliness of the death. The Prophet (pbuh) expressed his grief with tears, and he (pbuh) also remained connected to God through that process, only doing what he believed was pleasing to God. This Hadith is particularly important because perinatal loss often leads to disenfranchised grief, which may lead women not to express their emotions. However, this Hadith provides an important framework for women to express their grief while remaining connected to Allah.

Another important Hadith to consider is one that rewards the patience of the bereaved mother. In the Hadith, the Prophet (pbuh) said, "By the One in Whose Hand is my soul, the miscarried fetus will drag its mother by the umbilical cord to Paradise if she (endured patiently and) sought the rewards (of God for her loss)" (Ibn Majah, 1609). This hadith provides mothers with the promise of reunification in the afterlife and even a means of salvation by rewarding her for enduring her loss with *sabr* and accepting the *qadr*. The expectation is that the mother mourns the loss of her baby by expressing her sadness and, with patience, as outlined in the previous Hadith, to receive the reward of reunification. In Islam, patience means that a Muslim endures hardships with *tawakkul* and strong faith, expresses gratitude for the blessings in their life, accepts that life has its challenges, and avoids despair and losing hope (Parrott, 2020).

Integrating Islamic Concepts in Grief Psychotherapy for Perinatal Loss

Scholars are continuing to develop the best definitions for Islamically-integrated psychotherapy. York (2018) defines it as, "The integration of Islamic teachings, principles, philosophies, and/or interventions with Western therapeutic approaches" (p. 3). Whereas Keshavarzi, Khan, Ali, and Awaad (2021) developed a model called Traditional Islamically-Integrated Psychotherapy, defined as "an integrative model of mental health care that is grounded in the core principles of Islam while drawing on empirical truths in psychology." Utilizing these definitions, Islamically-integrated psychotherapy integrates key concepts in Islamic spirituality that help Muslims reframe the experience of trials and tribulations, explore conceptualizations of motherhood and grief in Islam, and integrate these with Western psychological concepts.

There is strong evidence that integrating Islam into

psychotherapy is highly effective in the treatment of depression and anxiety (Saged et al., 2022). Saged et al. (2022) showed that by integrating psychotherapy with seeking forgiveness and building trust in Allah in the treatment of depression and anxiety, patients felt more comfortable within the therapy setting, which, in turn, reduced symptoms significantly. Therefore, it is highly likely that integrating religious concepts and practices within the therapeutic frame can be used to treat acute grief due to perinatal loss. Strong religious beliefs have been shown to correlate to a decrease bereavement symptom and improve acceptance of perinatal loss (Allahdadian & Iraipour, 2015). Cowchock et al. (2010) reported a significant positive effect of religion in high-risk bereaved women; the more potent the individual beliefs, the lower the score of hopelessness and grief on psychometric tests. Additionally, studies on religious-spiritual coping, trauma, and optimism have found that higher religiosity is positively associated with positive religious coping, which leads to optimism (Ai, Peterson, & Haung, 2009).

Religious and conventional coping mechanisms can be effective tools in managing acute distress in communities of faith, including Muslims (Abu-Raiya & Pargament, 2015). Coping can occur by using the concepts described earlier to help with reframing negative thoughts and emotions, while also building stronger faith in God (Achour, Bensaid, & Nor, 2016). Among indigenous coping strategies, effective techniques include *muraqaba, tafakkur,* and *tadabbur.* *Muraqaba* is defined as either meditation or contemplation, a presence-focused approach that allows for inner observation of one's body, mind, and spirit (Isgandarova, 2018). *Tafakkur* and *tadabbur* are types of muraqaba, with *tafakkur* focusing on reflection on the creation and *tadabbur* focuses on the remembrance of God. Therefore, religious acts such as reciting *Qur'ān*, *dhikr* (remembrance of God), supplication, the five daily prayers, and contemplation are all religious practices that Muslims have found support in helping them cope with acute distress (Lorenz, Doherty, & Casey, 2019).

Another important consideration in grief work is meaning making (Uren & Wastell, 2002). When a woman is able to make meaning of the tragic loss of her baby, she is better equipped to process her grief and trauma and understand the possible lessons she gains from the loss. More specifically, integrating Islam into grief psychotherapy can help provide an opportunity to reframe the meaning of motherhood and perinatal loss, reconceptualize events as being part of God's plan, and instill hope for the future. When meaning is derived from a religious or spiritual context, it has more value because there is something greater, namely God, that the bereaved can connect to, especially if there is the possibility of reunification in the afterlife, as is the case with Islam. The therapeutic space is created for the therapist and patient to acknowledge and validate the loss while drawing on their faith in God's mercy and that everything is ultimately in His control. This can be done through sharing stories of the Prophet (pbuh) and how he overcame his grief after multiple profound losses, as described earlier.

There are no studies that focus on perinatal loss within the Islamic context, nor are there studies that focus on integrating Islam in grief psychotherapy for perinatal loss. However, drawing from clinical practice, the first author provides some considerations when exploring Islamic psychotherapy for bereaved perinatal women. One of these factors focuses on the timing of fetal death during the pregnancy, which can determine whether there is a promise of reunification in the afterlife. If the fetus dies after 120 days, the funeral rituals can be an effective tool in the healing process by providing a concrete mourning ritual. As well, most of these mothers had the opportunity to take pictures of and spend time with their deceased babies in the hospital following labor and delivery. While this is not the experience of all women who experienced perinatal loss after 120 days, those who have these experiences, anecdotally, describe them as being very helpful as they continue through the grief process. For these women, the promise of reunification also contributed greatly to improved moods and effective grief processing.

Unfortunately, women who experience a miscarriage prior to 120 days may face confusion or disenfranchised grief because the fetus is not recognized as a person and funeral rites are not performed, especially because there is no certainty of reunification in the afterlife. When these women present to therapy in distress, the focus of Islamic psychotherapy might be on God's will, reliance on God, and most importantly, God's mercy. Emphasis on God's mercy in therapy helped some women move through their grief more easily, even without certainty of reunification.

An Islamic Psychology Approach for Perinatal Loss

As evident in previous sections, ample evidence suggests psychotherapy is effective for bereavement related to perinatal loss. Cognitive behavioral, interpersonal, and psychodynamic psychotherapies have been found to support women through their grief. Furthermore, the literature suggests that cultural and religious contexts play a significant role in the trajectory of grief. For Muslim women, in particular, incorporating religious concepts, instilling hope of possible reunification, and managing acute symptoms in the context of evidence-based approaches can significantly improve their grief after perinatal loss. However, there is currently no framework available for Muslim women who seek psychotherapy for grief due to perinatal loss.

In 2020-2021, the number of stillbirths and miscarriages increased after women avoided medical offices due to fears of COVID-19 infection, especially prior to the development of the vaccine (DeSisto et al., 2021). There are no specific statistics for Muslim women, but anecdotally, the first author saw a fifty percent increase in perinatal loss psychotherapy cases of Muslim women during the pandemic. These women sought therapy from a Muslim therapist with expertise in reproductive psychology, specifically pregnancy loss. Drawing on her expertise in the psychology of perinatal loss and knowledge of religious concepts salient to the treatment of grief and motherhood, the author, in practice, devised a preliminary approach to integrating Islamic spirituality in grief psychotherapy following pregnancy loss.

This approach begins with allowing the patient to tell her story, the narrative of her hopes and dreams related to the pregnancy, her reproductive story, and details of the loss. The patient shares the name of the child, if funeral rites were performed, and any current support from family and friends. The therapeutic focus then shifts to teaching the patient to utilize religious and conventional Western coping strategies to manage symptoms of acute grief, intense emotions, and acute distress. Some of these coping strategies focus on *muraqaba*, which can be done in conjunction with religious practices or independently, as well as grounding (distraction),

CLINICAL APPLICATIONS OF ISLAMIC PSYCHOLOGY

challenging negative thought patterns, and doing pleasant activities. Once her emotions are well-managed, therapy can guide the patient to explore her spirituality by identifying how she sees her relationship with God, her conceptualization of motherhood, and her hope in reunifying with her child.

After managing the acute symptoms of grief, the focus shifts to identifying key Islamic spirituality concepts (*Qadr, Yaqin,* and *Tawakkul*) and how they might influence the patient's grief process. These concepts are important for building and maintaining a strong relationship with God. Patients with experiences of profound loss, like fetal demise, seek out spiritual support, but their spirituality might be affected in different ways. Some women feel more connected with God after pregnancy loss, while the loss prompts others to question God's plan.

Discussions in the therapeutic space focus on the patient's understanding of the pre-determined decree (*Qadr*), certainty in God's plan (*Yaqin*), and reliance on God (*Tawakkul*). When a patient is struggling with the death of a fetus or a full-term baby, the therapist can assess her connection with God by asking open-ended questions (e.g., tell me about how this loss has influenced your *iman* (faith), how has the loss impacted your *ibadah* (religious practices), how do you feel about Allah since the loss). The therapist should understand whether the patient feels connected or disconnected from God by asking these questions and identifying changes in religious practice. A strong therapeutic rapport can help patients feel comfortable sharing details of these changes in their connection with God, given that many Muslims might feel shame about disclosing these details.

Case Stories

To illustrate this discussion, the authors share the stories of three Muslim women who experienced pregnancy loss during the pandemic. The first story focuses on Maryam (pseudonym), a 30-year-old married woman who had experienced three separate miscarriages, each at six weeks. Maryam struggled with the *qadr* and questioned if she was meant to have children. In this story, how religious concepts are integrated into her treatment is highlighted. Maryam and her husband considered utilizing Assisted Reproductive Technologies (ARTs) to conceive due to her recurrent miscarriages.

However, Maryam felt uncertain about pursuing ARTs due to worries about upsetting God's plan for her, and she expressed frustration at God about the possibility of using ARTs. What was written in her *Qadr*? Did she have belief in Allah's plan for her? How can she rely on Allah but also pursue the means available to her to achieve conception? These questions were explored in the sessions. Although the therapist has some background in these concepts through her own religious studies, a religious scholar was consulted to clarify how these religious concepts applied in the circumstances of Maryam's life. The religious scholar provided details of which ARTs are permissible for couples to use to conceive a child and how to understand *Qadr* and *Tawakkul* in the context of her life. He clarified that Muslims do not know what is written for them, but they need to use religious practice (e.g., *istikharah* (prayer of guidance), *mushwirah* (consultation), *dua* (supplication) to remain connected with God to identify her next steps (i.e., starting or stopping ARTs). Maryam expressed frustration at not knowing God's plan for her but was also curious about how she might proceed. After much emotional processing, consultation with the religious scholar, and utilizing coping strategies to manage her anxiety, Maryam chose to pursue ARTs to conceive despite not knowing with certainty that she would have a successful pregnancy. Her trust in Allah was strengthened, allowing her to tolerate the unknown of the possibility of pregnancy. In each session, Maryam checked in about her thoughts and emotions about ARTs and her progress through treatment, to determine if she is making the best choice for her and her family.

The next part of the approach focuses on the concept of motherhood in Islam. Muslim women feel a strong connection to the identity of motherhood due to the immense reward outlined in the Qur'ān and Sunnah. Their struggles during pregnancy and postpartum are equated to martyrdom for the sake of God. Motherhood may confer high status within society as well as within spiritual ranks for Muslim women. After pregnancy loss, some Muslim women feel they have lost their opportunity to become a mother, which, they believe, impedes their ability to receive those rewards and status. The focus of psychotherapy for these women is to look at how pregnancy loss can still allow these women to connect to motherhood and its status. First, the discussion focuses on identifying the woman as a mother because, in psychodynamic texts, women often identify as a mother even early in pregnancy (Brandon et al., 2011; Winnecott, 1956). So even if there is an early loss, women can still identify as mothers. For women who experienced a loss after 120 days, there are discussions of reunification and that her child is safely cared for by Prophet Abraham, which further reinforces mother's identity (Bukhari, 7047).

This concept is highlighted in the case of a 32-year-old married woman (Sarah) with two children, who presented to therapy after having experienced a pregnancy loss at 16 weeks, just days shy of 120 days. Because the loss occurred before 120 days, Sarah's husband was adamant that the child was not considered a person and refused to acknowledge the baby as part of their family. Sarah was devastated by this loss. Sarah's identity of motherhood was intimately connected to her identity as a Muslim woman. In her struggle with pregnancy, postpartum, caring for her two children, and experiencing a miscarriage, she often disliked her experiences of motherhood. Therefore, Sarah often felt guilty and angry with herself for experiencing these emotions because she felt she should enjoy every aspect of motherhood.

In the therapy session, Sarah's fetus was acknowledged. Sarah was asked about the name and sex of the child, which she shared with the therapist. Once her baby was acknowledged, the conversation focused on the ambiguity of her daughter's personhood and the mercy of God, meaning the possibility of being a person and reuniting in Heaven. These concepts reinforced Sarah's motherhood to her daughter. The therapist also provided education about dialectics, feeling different emotions about a particular experience, experiencing both gratitude for being a mother and for disliking aspects of it, and validating her contradictory emotions.

The final component of the approach is rooted in the hope of reunification. For women experiencing losses after 120 days, there are Hadiths that describe how the fetus reconnects with the mother. In one narration, the mother is pulled into heaven with the umbilical cord (Ibn Majah, 1609). In another narration, the mother receives reassurance from the Prophet Muhammad (pbuh) that her child is safely under the care of Prophet Abraham, awaiting its mother's arrival (Bukhari, 7047). Instilling this hope in a woman of faith after undergoing a pregnancy loss has a profound effect on her mental wellbeing. There might still be anger, frustration, sadness, and guilt following the death of the fetus. However, once these emotions are processed and validated, the mother is ready to acknowledge the hope of the future. Unfortunately, many women experience bouts of re-grief around specific milestones, like the due date, learning of the pregnancy, and other important dates. However, this is considered a normative experience and does not negate the previous work done to decrease symptoms of grief.

Laila (pseudonym) was a 28-year-old Muslim woman who experienced a full-term stillbirth. She experienced years of infertility prior to conceiving this child. During labor, there were some complications that resulted in the death of the baby. Laila had a strong religious identity and struggled with acute symptoms of grief, including tearfulness, anger, sadness, and guilt over the outcome. Her treatment began by processing her emotions and providing her with tools to manage her emotions effectively, utilizing conventional therapeutic tools like deep diaphragmatic breathing, journaling as well as religious coping, including *dua* (supplication) and *dhikr* (remembrance of God). After managing her acute symptoms, therapy focused on instilling hope and building a strong identity around motherhood. Laila shared pictures of her son and the poems she wrote for him, evidence of her strong connection to her son and the importance of the role of motherhood in her life. By remaining connected to him through poetry, pictures, and religious practices in his honor, she gave herself some concrete tasks that would help her through her grief. She also looked forward to reuniting with him in the afterlife.

For all three women, meaning making, rooted in their religious identity, represented the final step in processing their grief. Exploration focused on their resilience and how they could move through an experience that they did not feel they could overcome. The therapist also acknowledged and validated the strength it took for them to undergo a subsequent pregnancy without the certainty of success. For all three, the conceptualization of their relationship with God was at the center and a means to increase their *yaqin* in God's plan for them. Therapy created a safe space to explore ruptures and repairs in this relationship, free from feelings of shame or guilt surrounding doubt, overall strengthening this relationship, which held importance for all three women.

Conclusion

Perinatal loss is a profoundly distressing and traumatic event for all women. For Muslims, experiences of perinatal loss often directly correlate with their Muslim identity and spiritual connection with Allah. When treating women suffering from acute or complicated grief, integrating an Islamic approach can effectively mitigate symptoms and provide patients with the tools needed to remain connected with their faith while moving through their grief. Important concepts like *tawakkul*, *sabr*, and *yaqin* (certainty) are integral components to helping these Muslim women move through their grief because each speaks specifically to their spiritual connections. By acknowledging their reliance and certainty in God while enduring the loss with patience, Muslim women can cultivate a deeper relationship with God, make meaning of their loss experience, and decrease symptoms of grief. This is done by creating a space of emotional and spiritual holding for the patient by the clinician, building an environment to safely share deep emotional distress while sharing the load with the therapist. Within an Islamic context, the therapist is a *khalil* to the patient, a close and dear companion who supports her as she navigates one of the most devastating losses in her life.

There is no research focused on integrating Islamic concepts within psychotherapy for Muslim perinatal loss patients, but the approach presented in this chapter has been effective in supporting Muslim women experiencing miscarriages and stillbirth by acknowledging the loss, providing coping strategies to manage acute distress, and making meaning of the experiencing within an Islamic spiritual context. After undergoing treatment with this framework, patients reported experiencing improved daily functioning, improved connection with God, and decreased symptoms of grief. Patients also experienced hope after some months of work, with some occasional repeat experiences of grief during important milestones. For some, that hope was realized through a subsequent pregnancy, while for others, it was connected to finding ways to support their local communities, build better relationships with themselves, and continue building their connection with Allah. Studies are needed to determine the mechanisms of change and effectiveness across populations of Muslims; however, this review of the literature with clinical examples provides a starting point that has yielded significant success among the Muslims with whom this model was utilized.

References

Abu-Raiya, H. (2014) 'Western Psychology and Muslim Psychology in Dialogue: Comparisons Between a Qur'anic Theory of Personality and Freud's and Jung's Ideas', Journal of Religion and Health 53(2): 326–338.

Abu Raiya, H., & Pargament, K. I. (2010). Religiously integrated psychotherapy with Muslim clients: From research to practice. Professional Psychology: Research and Practice, 41(2), 181.

Adib, S. (2004). From the biomedical model to the Islamic alternative: A brief overview of medical practices in the contemporary Arab world. Social Science and Medicine, 58, 697-702.

Ahaddour, C. (2021). Ethical issues at the beginning of human life: Towards a contextualized Islamic understanding of prenatal diagnosis and termination of pregnancy. *Louvain* studies.

Ai, A.L., Peterson, C., & Huang, B. (2003). The effects of religious-spiritual coping on positive attitudes of adult Muslim refugees from Kosovo and Bosnia. The International Journal for the Psychology of Religion, 13, 29–47.

Alaradi, M., Hutti, M. H., & Chaffin, N. (2021). Arab Muslims' perceptions of perinatal loss care in the United States of America. *Health & Social Care in the Community.*

Allahdadian, M., & Irajpour, A. (2015). The role of religious beliefs in pregnancy loss. *Journal of Education and Health Promotion,* *4,* 99–99. https://doi.org/10.4103/2277-9531.171813

Al-Matary, A., & Ali, J. (2014). Controversies and considerations regarding the termination of pregnancy for Foetal Anomalies in Islam. *BMC Medical Ethics,* *15*(1). https://link.gale.com/apps/doc/A539598525/AONE?u=colu mbiau&sid=bookmark-AONE&xid=032e2117

Ayed, M., & Ayed, A. (2018). Fetal and newborn palliative care in Islam-when to be considered: A review. *Case Rep Lit Rev,*

2(4), 100019.

Ayubi, Z. (2021). Authority and epistemology in Islamic medical ethics of women's reproductive health. *The Journal of Religious Ethics*, 49(2), 245–269. https://doi.org/10.1111/jore.12350

Badenhorst, W., & Hughes, P. (2007). Psychological aspects of perinatal loss. Best Pract Res Clin Obstet Gynaecol, 21(2), 249-259. https://doi.org/10.1016/j.bpobgyn.2006.11.004

Behjati Ardakani, Z., Navabakhsh, M., Tremayne, S., Akhondi, M. M., Ranjbar, F., & Mohseni Tabrizi, A. (2021). The impact of third-party reproduction on family and kinship. *Journal of reproduction & infertility*, 22(1), 3–15. https://doi.org/10.18502/jri.v22i1.4990

Bennett, S. M., Litz, B. T., Lee, B. S., & Maguen, S. (2005). The Scope and Impact of Perinatal Loss: Current Status and Future Directions. Professional Psychology: Research and Practice, 36(2), 180-187. https://doi.org/10.1037/0735-7028.36.2.180

Black, B. P., Wright, P. M., & Limbo, R. K. (2015). Perinatal and pediatric bereavement in nursing and other health professions. Springer Publishing Company.

Bonanno, G. A., & Kaltman, S. (2001). The varieties of grief experience. Clin Psychol Rev, 21(5), 705-734. https://doi.org/10.1016/s0272-7358(00)00062-3

Bowlby, J. (1969). Attachment and loss. Basic Books.

Brandon, A. R., Pitts, S., Denton, W. H., Stringer, C. A., & Evans, H. (2009). A history of the theory of prenatal attachment. *Journal of prenatal & perinatal psychology & health: APPPAH*, 23(4), 201.

Cacciatore, J. (2013). Psychological effects of stillbirth. Semin Fetal Neonatal Med, 18(2), 76-82. https://doi.org/10.1016/j.siny.2012.09.001

Capitulo, K. L. (2005). Evidence for healing interventions with perinatal bereavement. MCN Am J Matern Child Nurs, 30(6), 389-396. https://doi.org/10.1097/00005721-200511000-00007

Carter, D., & Rashidi, A. (2003). Theoretical model of psychotherapy: Eastern Asian-Islamic women with mental illness. Health Care for Women International, 24, 399-413.

Catlin, A. (2018). Interdisciplinary Guidelines for Care of Women

Presenting to the Emergency Department With Pregnancy Loss. MCN Am J Matern Child Nurs, 43(1), 13-18. https://doi.org/10.1097/NMC.0000000000000399

Centers for Disease Control and Prevention. (2020, August 13). *Pregnancy and infant loss*. Centers for Disease Control and Prevention. Retrieved July 14, 2022, from https://www.cdc.gov/ncbddd/stillbirth/features/pregnancy-infant-loss.html

Côté-Arsenault, D. (2003). Weaving Babies Lost in Pregnancy into the Fabric of the Family. Journal of Family Nursing, 9(1), 23-37. https://doi.org/10.1177/1074840702239489

Côté-Arsenault, D. P. R. N. C. F., Brody, D. R. N. C. M. F. A. M. S., & Dombeck, M.-T. P. D. R. N. (2009). Pregnancy as a Rite of Passage: Liminality, Rituals & Communitas. Journal of Prenatal & Perinatal Psychology & Health, 24(2), 69-87.

Cowchock, F. S., Ellestad, S. E., Meador, K. G., Koenig, H. G., Hooten, E. G., & Swamy, G. K. (2011). Religiosity is an important part of coping with grief in pregnancy after a traumatic second trimester loss. Journal of Religion and Health, 50(4), 901-910.

Cowchock, F. S., Lasker, J. N., Toedter, L. J., Skumanich, S. A., & Koenig, H. G. (2010). Religious beliefs affect grieving after pregnancy loss. J Relig Health, 49(4), 485-497. https://doi.org/10.1007/s10943-009-9277-3

Diamond, D. J., & Diamond, M. O. (2016). Understanding and treating the psychosocial consequences of pregnancy loss.

Diamond, D. J., & Diamond, M. O. (2017). Parenthood after reproductive loss: How psychotherapy can help with postpartum adjustment and parent-infant attachment. Psychotherapy (Chic), 54(4), 373-379. https://doi.org/10.1037/pst0000127

DiMarco, M. A., Menke, E. M., & McNamara, T. (2001). Evaluating a support group for perinatal loss. MCN Am J Matern Child Nurs, 26(3), 135-140. https://doi.org/10.1097/00005721-200105000-00008

Doka, K. J. (1989). Disenfranchised Grief. Lexington Press.

Doka, K. J., & Morgan, J. D. (1993). Death and spirituality. Baywood Pub. Co.

Ellis, A. (2000) 'Can Rational Emotive Behavior Therapy be

Effectively Used with People Who Have Devout Beliefs in God and Religion? Professional Psychology: Research and Practice 31(1): 29–33.

Fonte, J., & Horton-Deutsch, S. (2005). Treating Postpartum Depression in Immigrant Muslim Women. Journal of the American Psychiatric Nurses Association, 11(1), 39–44. https://doi.org/10.1177/1078390305276494

Freud, S., Riviere, J., Strachey, A., Strachey, J., & Sigmund Freud Collection (Library of Congress). (1924). Collected papers. The International Psycho-analytical Press.

Froen, J. F., Cacciatore, J., McClure, E. M., Kuti, O., Jokhio, A. H., Islam, M., Shiffman, J., & Lancet's Stillbirths Series steering, c. (2011). Stillbirths: why they matter. Lancet, 377(9774), 1353-1366. https://doi.org/10.1016/S0140-6736(10)62232-5

Ghaly, M. (2014). Islamic bioethics: The inevitable interplay of "texts" and "contexts." *Bioethics, 28*(2), ii–v. https://doi-org.tc.idm.oclc.org/10.1111/bioe.12081

Gold, K. J., Leon, I., Boggs, M. E., & Sen, A. (2016). Depression and Posttraumatic Stress Symptoms After Perinatal Loss in a Population-Based Sample. J Womens Health (Larchmt), 25(3), 263-269. https://doi.org/10.1089/jwh.2015.5284

Hamama-Raz, Y., Hartman, H., & Buchbinder, E. (2014). Coping with stillbirth among ultraorthodox Jewish women. Qualitative health research, 24(7), 923-932.

Hamdan, A. (2008). Cognitive restructuring: An Islamic perspective. Journal of Muslim mental health, 3(1), 99-116.

Hamdan, A. (2011). *Nurturing eeman in children*. International Islamic Publishing House.

Hogan, N. S., & Schmidt, L. A. (2002). Testing the grief to personal growth model using structural equation modeling. Death Stud, 26(8), 615-634. https://doi.org/10.1080/07481180290088338

Husain, A., & Hodge, D. R. (2016). Islamically modified cognitive behavioral therapy: Enhancing outcomes by increasing the cultural congruence of cognitive behavioral therapy self-statements. International Social Work, 59(3), 393-405.

Isgandarova, N. *Muraqaba* as a Mindfulness-Based Therapy in Islamic Psychotherapy. *J Relig Health* **58**, 1146–1160 (2019). https://doi.org/10.1007/s10943-018-0695-y

Jaffe, J., Diamond, M. O., & American Psychological Association. (2011). Reproductive trauma: psychotherapy with infertility and pregnancy loss clients (1st ed.). American Psychological Association.

Johnson, J. E., Price, A. B., Kao, J. C., Fernandes, K., Stout, R., Gobin, R. L., & Zlotnick, C. (2016). Interpersonal psychotherapy (IPT) for major depression following perinatal loss: a pilot randomized controlled trial. Arch Womens Ment Health, 19(5), 845-859. https://doi.org/10.1007/s00737-016-0625-5

Johnson, J. E., Price, A. B., Sikorskii, A., Key, K. D., Taylor, B., Lamphere, S., Huff, C., Cinader, M., & Zlotnick, C. (2022). Protocol for the Healing After Loss (HeAL) Study: a randomised controlled trial of interpersonal psychotherapy (IPT) for major depression following perinatal loss. BMJ Open, 12(4), e057747. https://doi.org/10.1136/bmjopen-2021-057747

Kain, V. J. (2021). Perinatal palliative care: Cultural, spiritual, and religious considerations for parents—What clinicians need to know. *Frontiers in Pediatrics*, *9*, 149.

Kavanaugh, K., & Hershberger, P. (2005). Perinatal loss in low-income African American parents. J Obstet Gynecol Neonatal Nurs, 34(5), 595-605. https://doi.org/10.1177/0884217505280000

Kavanaugh, K., & Robertson, P. A. (1999). Recurrent perinatal loss: a case study. Omega (Westport), 39(2), 133-147. https://doi.org/10.2190/X65F-ENLV-VALG-F7AG

Kersting, A., Dolemeyer, R., Steinig, J., Walter, F., Kroker, K., Baust, K., & Wagner, B. (2013). Brief Internet-based intervention reduces posttraumatic stress and prolonged grief in parents after the loss of a child during pregnancy: a randomized controlled trial. Psychother Psychosom, 82(6), 372-381. https://doi.org/10.1159/000348713

Kersting, A., & Wagner, B. (2012). Complicated grief after perinatal loss. Dialogues Clin Neurosci, 14(2), 187-194. https://www.ncbi.nlm.nih.gov/pubmed/22754291

Kleiman, K. R. (2009). Therapy and the postpartum woman: notes on healing postpartum depression for clinicians and the women who seek their help. Routledge. Table of contents only http://www.loc.gov/catdir/toc/ecip0813/2008012586.html

Kobler, K., Limbo, R., & Kavanaugh, K. (2007). Meaningful moments. MCN Am J Matern Child Nurs, 32(5), 288-295; quiz 296-287. https://doi.org/10.1097/01.NMC.0000287998.80005.79

Koenig, H. G. (2018). Chapter 11 - Evidence-Based Religious Interventions. In H. G. Koenig (Ed.), Religion and Mental Health (pp. 255-277). Academic Press. https://doi.org/https://doi.org/10.1016/B978-0-12-811282-3.00011-2

Koenig, H. G., & Larson, D. B. (2001). Religion and mental health: evidence for an association. International Review of Psychiatry, 13(2), 67-78. https://doi.org/10.1080/09540260124661

Koopmans, L., Wilson, T., Cacciatore, J., & Flenady, V. (2013). Support for mothers, fathers, and families after perinatal death. Cochrane Database Syst Rev (6), CD000452. https://doi.org/10.1002/14651858.CD000452.pub3

Lang, A., Fleiszer, A. R., Duhamel, F., Sword, W., Gilbert, K. R., & Corsini-Munt, S. (2011). Perinatal loss and parental grief: the challenge of ambiguity and disenfranchised grief. Omega (Westport), 63(2), 183-196. https://doi.org/10.2190/OM.63.2.e

Lasker, J. N., & Toedter, L. J. (1991). Acute versus chronic grief: the case of pregnancy loss. Am J Orthopsychiatry, 61(4), 510-522. https://doi.org/10.1037/h0079288

Leon, I. G. (1990). When a baby dies: psychotherapy for pregnancy and newborn loss. Yale University Press.

Leon, I. G. (2015). Pregnancy and loss counseling. Fertility counseling: Clinical guide and case studies, 226-238.

Lewis, C., Latif, Z., Hill, M., Riddington, M., Lakhanpaul, M., Arthurs, O. J., Hutchinson, J. C., Chitty, L. S., & Sebire, N. J. (2018). "We might get a lot more families who will agree": Muslim and Jewish perspectives on less invasive perinatal and paediatric autopsy. PLoS ONE, 13(8), e0202023.

Lichtenthal, W. G., Currier, J. M., Neimeyer, R. A., & Keesee, N. J. (2010). Sense and significance: a mixed methods examination of meaning making after the loss of one's child. J Clin Psychol, 66(7), 791-812. https://doi.org/10.1002/jclp.20700

Lin, S. X., & Lasker, J. N. (1996). Patterns of grief reaction after pregnancy loss. Am J Orthopsychiatry, 66(2), 262-271. https://doi.org/10.1037/h0080177

Luthringer, M., & Marziale, J. Grief, Bereavement, and Coping with Loss (PDQ®): Supportive care-Health Professional Information [NCI].

M. (2015, April 2). The Future of World Religions: Population Growth Projections, 2010-2050. Pew Research Center's Religion & Public Life Project. https://www.pewresearch.org/religion/2015/04/02/religious-projections-2010-2050/

March of Dimes. (2017, October 2017). Ectopic Pregnancy. Retrieved July 12 from https://www.marchofdimes.org/complications/ectopic-pregnancy.aspx

Markin, R. D., & McCarthy, K. S. (2020). The process and outcome of psychodynamic psychotherapy for pregnancy after loss: A case study analysis. Psychotherapy (Chic), 57(2), 273-288. https://doi.org/10.1037/pst0000249

Markin, R. D., & Zilcha-Mano, S. (2018). Cultural processes in psychotherapy for perinatal loss: Breaking the cultural taboo against perinatal grief. Psychotherapy (Chic), 55(1), 20-26. https://doi.org/10.1037/pst0000122

Mayo Foundation for Medical Education and Research. (2021, October 16). *Miscarriage*. Mayo Clinic. Retrieved July 14, 2022, from https://www.mayoclinic.org/diseases-conditions/pregnancy-loss-miscarriage/symptoms-causes/syc-20354298

McCarthy, F. P., Lutomski, J. E., & Greene, R. A. (2014). Hyperemesis gravidarum: current perspectives. Int J Womens Health, 6, 719-725. https://doi.org/10.2147/IJWH.S37685

Mohamed, B. (2018, Jan 3). New estimates show U.S. Muslim population continues to grow. Pew Research Center. Retrieved July 28, 2022, from https://www.pewresearch.org/fact-tank/2018/01/03/new-estimates-show-u-s-muslim-population-continues-to-grow/

Mohamed Hussin, N. A., Guàrdia-Olmos, J., & Liisa Aho, A. (2018). The use of religion in coping with grief among bereaved Malay Muslim parents. Mental Health, Religion & Culture,

21(4), 395-407.

Molina, N. (2019). Motherhood, spirituality, and culture. Routledge,

Murphy, S., Shevlin, M., & Elklit, A. (2014). Psychological Consequences of Pregnancy Loss and Infant Death in a Sample of Bereaved Parents. Journal of Loss and Trauma, 19(1), 56-69. https://doi.org/10.1080/15325024.2012.735531

Nuzum, D., Fitzgerald, B., Evans, M. J., & O'Donoghue, K. (2021). Maternity healthcare chaplains and perinatal post-mortem support and understanding in the United Kingdom and Ireland: An exploratory study. *Journal of Religion & Health, 60*(3), 1924–1936. https://doi-org.tc.idm.oclc.org/10.1007/s10943-020-01176-4

Park, J. (2003) 'Unheimlich Maneuvers: Enlightenment Dolls and Repetitions in Freud', The Eighteenth Century 44(1): 45–68.

Petro, S. J. (2015). Drawing Close to the Brokenhearted: Pastoral Responses to Parents Grieving Stillbirth. J Pastoral Care Counsel, 69(1), 13-18. https://doi.org/10.1177/1542305015572961

Puscheck, E. (2011, June 8, 2018). Early Pregnancy Loss. Retrieved June 22, 2022, from https://reference.medscape.com/article/266317-overview

Quenby, S., Gallos, I. D., Dhillon-Smith, R. K., Podesek, M., Stephenson, M. D., Fisher, J., Brosens, J. J., Brewin, J., Ramhorst, R., Lucas, E. S., McCoy, R. C., Anderson, R., Daher, S., Regan, L., Al-Memar, M., Bourne, T., MacIntyre, D. A., Rai, R., Christiansen, O. B., Coomarasamy, A. (2021). Miscarriage matters: the epidemiological, physical, psychological, and economic costs of early pregnancy loss. Lancet, 397(10285), 1658-1667. https://doi.org/10.1016/S0140-6736(21)00682-6

Ramezani, S., Khosravi, A., Motaghi, Z., Hamidzadeh, A., & Mousavi, S. A. (2017). The effect of cognitive-behavioural and solution-focused counselling on prevention of postpartum depression in nulliparous pregnant women. J Reprod Infant Psychol, 35(2), 172-182. https://doi.org/10.1080/02646838.2016.1266470

Saged, A.A.G., Mohd Yusoff, M.Y.Z., Abdul Latif, F. *et al.* Impact of Qur'ān in Treatment of the Psychological Disorder and Spiritual Illness. *J Relig Health* 59, 1824–1837 (2020).

https://doi.org/10.1007/s10943-018-0572-8

Saged, A. A. G., Sa'ari, C. Z., Abdullah, M. B., Al-Rahmi, W. M., Ismail, W. M., Zain, M. I. A., & alShehri, N. B. A. B. M. (2022). The Effect of an Islamic-Based Intervention on Depression and Anxiety in Malaysia. *Journal of religion and health, 61*(1), 79-92.

Serour, G. I. (2013). Ethical issues in human reproduction: Islamic perspectives*. *Gynecological Endocrinology, 29*(11), 949–952. https://doi-org.tc.idm.oclc.org/10.3109/09513590.2013.825714

Shaikh, S. (2003). Family planning, contraception, and abortion in Islam: undertaking Khilafah. In *Sacred rights: the case for contraception and abortion in world religions*. D.C. Maguire, ed. Oxford: Oxford University Press: 102–128.

Shaw, A. (2014). Rituals of infant death: Defining life and Islamic personhood. *Bioethics, 28*(2), 84–95. https://doi-org.tc.idm.oclc.org/10.1111/bioe.12047

Shinwell, E. S., & Shinwell, A. R. (2008). Reorientation of care in the NICU: a Jewish perspective. Semin Fetal Neonatal Med, 13(5), 314-315. https://doi.org/10.1016/j.siny.2008.04.025

Sotillos, S. B. (2021). Bridging Psychologies: Islam and Secular Psychotherapy. Spiritual Psychology and Counseling, 6(2), 95-99.

Stroebe, M., & Stroebe, W. (1991). Does "grief work" work? J Consult Clin Psychol, 59(3), 479-482. https://doi.org/10.1037//0022-006x.59.3.479

Stroebe, M. S., Schut, H. A. W., events, C. l., health, m., Utrecht, U., & psychologie, A. K. (1999). The Dual Process Model of coping with bereavement: Rationale and description. Death Studies, 23(3), 197 - null. https://doi.org/Urn:Nbn:Nl:Ui:10-1874-384090

Stroebe, W., Stroebe, M., Abakoumkin, G., & Schut, H. (1996). The role of loneliness and social support in adjustment to loss: a test of attachment versus stress theory. J Pers Soc Psychol, 70(6), 1241-1249. https://doi.org/10.1037//0022-3514.70.6.1241

Sutan, R., & Miskam, H. M. (2012). Psychosocial impact of perinatal loss among Muslim women. BMC Women's Health, 12, 15. https://doi.org/10.1186/1472-6874-12-15

The World Health Organization. (2019). Why we need to talk about losing a baby. The World Health Organization. Retrieved July 8, 2022, from https://www.who.int/news-room/spotlight/why-we-need-to-talk-about-losing-a-baby

Uren, T. H., & Wastell, C. A. (2002). Attachment and meaning making in perinatal bereavement. *Death studies*, *26*(4), 279–308. https://doi.org/10.1080/074811802753594682

Wall-Wieler, E., Roos, L. L., & Bolton, J. (2018). Duration of maternal mental health-related outcomes after an infant's death: A retrospective matched cohort study using linkable administrative data. Depression and Anxiety, 35(4), 305-312. https://doi.org/10.1002/da.22729

Wenzel, A. (2017). Cognitive behavioral therapy for pregnancy loss. Psychotherapy (Chic), 54(4), 400-405. https://doi.org/10.1037/pst0000132

Winnicott, D. W. (1956). Primary maternal preoccupation. *The maternal lineage: Identification, desire, and transgenerational issues*, 59-66.

Zeanah, C. H., Danis, B., Hirshberg, L., & Dietz, L. (1995). Initial adaptation in mothers and fathers following perinatal loss. Infant Mental Health Journal, 16(2), 80-93.

CHAPTER EIGHT

A SHORT INTRODUCTION TO 'ILM AL NAFS AND NAFS PSYCHOTHERAPY:
The Language of Dreams

Mustafa Merter, Nursena Balatekin, and Lütfiye Söğütlü

Introduction

One of the paradoxes of Western psychology is its lack of a unitary and comprehensive model of the human psyche. Therefore, a structural and dynamic model of the psyche and the nafs is needed. 'Ilm Al Nafs and Nafs Psychotherapy Training Program in Istanbul, Turkey, presents a unique, all-encompassing model and practice of psychology that differs from secular psychology. The subtle constituents of nafs sciences include categories of unconscious, multi-level nafs structure, discrete states of consciousness, and their relationship with the spiritual heart.

A nafs psychotherapist at 'Ilm Al Nafs completes the learning analysis process and comprehensively understands the nafs. This is important because knowing the structure of nafs provides therapists with a road map for approaching human reality. In 'Ilm Al Nafs, the therapy process cannot occur without a map and codex outlining the laws. This is defined by Islamic knowledge levels of *ayn al-yaqīn* and *haqq al-yaqīn* (Lone, 2020). *'Ilm al-yaqīn* (apprehension

211

through science) is completed through *'ayn al-yaqīn* (witnessing through visualizing). However, to have a sense of *'ayn al-yaqīn* (witnessing through visualizing), nafs psychotherapists study the interpretation of dreams of the counselees. The most efficient way to accomplish this is through dream analysis. 'Ilm Al Nafs founded the theory of nafs psychotherapy, but merely learning the theory of 'Ilm Al Nafs is not enough to practice, as one must undergo learning analysis. In other words, to know the other person, one must first know oneself, so the candidates at 'Ilm Al Nafs are trained to know themselves in-depth before they can start seeing the counselees. Psychologists who want to practice nafs psychotherapy undergo a rigorous admissions process before embarking on a 3- to 4-year learning analysis, including dream analysis and studies in 'Ilm Al Nafs. After the 2nd year of the learning process, the candidates can see counselees under supervision. The candidates also attend group psychotherapies in addition to the personal learning analysis process.

It is important to note that nafs psychotherapy can be applied to people of any belief system. However, the psychotherapist who practices nafs psychotherapy must be a Muslim to interpret the notions of the 'Ilm Al Nafs and follow the practices and steps before and during the sessions (like ablution and prayers). It is an integral part of being a nafs psychologist to practice Islam and internalize the values and requirements of the Islamic faith.

Brief Theoretical Framework of 'Ilm Al Nafs

The origins of Western psychology can be traced back to the 17th and 18th centuries. Freud, his followers, and his opponents' interpretations of the "self" and the "psyche" produced many structural and dynamic models, such as Jungian's (Stein, 1998) "spherical" structural and dynamic models and Assagioli's (2000) "egg diagram," for unconscious categories, and the introduction of a higher self. There is, however, no satisfactory, clear, and comprehensive approach to "psyche" and "unconsciousness" (Hillman & Ventura, 2018). Research has shown that current psychotherapies are limited to addressing the needs of the counselees, and as a result, approaches from ancient resources, such as mindfulness, have grown in interest in recent years. In contrast, psychological approaches with no spiritual foundations attempt to integrate this ancient knowledge to offer comprehensive healing services. For instance, Ken Wilber's "The Spectrum of Consciousness" (Scotton et al., 1996) gives interesting information about functions of the psyche like "modes of knowing," "reality perception," "time/space relation," "shadow," but still lacks an accessible structural model. In addition to this, Charles Tart's "States of Consciousness" (Tart, 1975) is an excellent book about the dynamism of consciousness. However, it is still limited by being unable to explain the whole structure. Although there is a vast amount of research and approaches in psychology, psychopathology cases are still on the rise (Twenge, 2008, 2013, 2017). Psychology must, therefore, reconsider its approach to human beings and investigate earlier sources. Indeed, psychology's assertions can be found in the Qurʾān, the Holy Sayings of Prophet Mohammed (saw), and Sufi wisdom, the exegesis of ancient sources. It is possible to connect modern psychology's premises with many divine precepts, and Western psychology can benefit from them. Otherwise, it ends up like the analogy of blind men differing in defining an elephant based on tactile experience (See Rumi's poem, *The Blind Men and the Elephant*). These "partly truths" should be integrated into the nafs' structure and dynamism by referencing divine precepts and Qurʾān. For example, in ʿIlm Al Nafs, the Jungian concepts of animus and anima could be compared to Allah's Holy names of *Jamal* and *Jalal* (Murata & Schimmel, 2010).

In Western psychology, *unconsciousness* is defined as a subconsciousness that claims humans for their nature in terms of pleasure principles, drives, and libido. According to this, a human can only partially suppress the "evil" part of oneself. The Qurʾanic symbolism, on the other hand, describes "inner hell" as the dark, narrow, and fearful existential universe. However, the essence of humanity is not evil, chaotic, or polymorphic. These negative aspects of human creational potential are present only in the lower levels of the personal unconscious (*asfal al-safilin*). Although the Jungian concepts of central self and collective unconscious allow us to approach a more comprehensive understanding of the psyche, they must be more comprehensive to explain the higher realms of human grandeur.

Higher human consciousness and the multi-level

existential nafs structure (see Figure 1) have enabled us to discover the missing third dimension of humanness (in psychology). The Qur'an reveals that humans have an evil potential in *asfal al-safilin*, but their nature (fitra) is created in *ahsan al-taqwim*. Therefore, there is a higher unconscious as well. The *hal* (state) of *gaflet* exists when a human is on the bottom levels of his existence (unawareness). *Gaflet* is an Ottoman-Turkish expression that means being awake and engaging in this-worldly pursuits without attending to one's spiritual duties, which is, to be heedlessly sleeping. These notions were manifested in Sufi practice (Wishnitzer, 2014). We must rid ourselves of this abominable existence to progress to higher levels, as stated in the Holy Saying of Prophet Mohammed (saw): "Die before you die." So, we understand Soren Kierkegaard's tragic unachieved goal when he spoke of the "existential leap" (Kierkegaard, 1992, p. 335).

All humans start their journeys from the basic existential level of the nafs structure, which is nafs (*nafs al-ammara*). This is a stage between the "lowest of the low" and the higher stages. In other words, there are two opposite attractions to the nafs al-ammara; one is the influence of darkness, and the other is luminous and merciful. There are

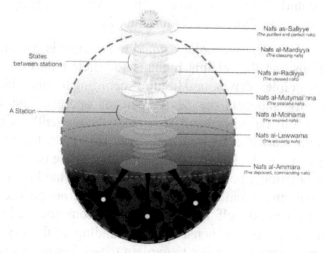

States between stations

A Station

Nafs as-Safiyye
(The purified and perfect nafs)

Nafs al-Mardiyya
(The pleasing nafs)

Nafs ar-Radiyya
(The pleased nafs)

Nafs al-Mutymaï'nna
(The peaceful nafs)

Nafs al-Molhama
(The inspired nafs)

Nafs al-Lewwama
(The accusing nafs)

Nafs al-Ammara
(The depraved, commanding nafs)

Figure 1

(Merter & Arslan, 2020)

214

nafs-i-ammara, states: lower subtle states and higher subtle states. In Sufi terminology, these states are called "*hal*", and hundreds are cited by different authors (Tart, 1975). Mevlana Jalaluddin Rumi's Masnavi is like a treasure box for these subtle/discrete states of human highness. The word "hal" is mentioned in the Qur'an in Surah Hud (11:43), along with having the holy word "bale." By studying the hals in dreams, 'Ilm Al Nafs reaches parts of the psyche that CBT or psychoanalysis do not. According to Jung, the psyche has shadows: the central self, the anima, the animus, and personas (life roles) (Jung, 2009), but this does not involve a holistic and integrated model. However, contrary to Western psychology, the individual is not trapped in his nafs-i-ammara. This view by Western psychology imprisons human beings to an existential level, nafs-i-ammara, as it ignores the higher levels of human existence. Humans, on the other hand, have an infinite capacity to evolve (*tekamul*). Human nafs weaknesses are a part of being human, but not its essential nature. As stated in the Qur'ān, the essential nature has the potential for perfection: "Certainly, we created man in the best manner" (95:4). The more we learn about the nafs, the more we realize its significance (Morris and Burrell, 2005). The transition from nafs-i-ammara, ammara, to *nafs-e kamila* in this structure results in a number of radical changes, which are well summarized in Morris' book.

Nafs Psychotherapy

Individuals with sufficient ego integrity and stability to consider long-term therapy can receive nafs psychotherapy, according to 'Ilm Al Nafs, after excluding acute and chronic psychotic conditions and addiction detoxification.

The first session is usually where counselees come to the therapist with intense feelings. In these cases, the therapist remains passive and allows the counselee to talk. Regardless of the condition of the counselee, in the first session, the therapist gathers information about the mental status examination, the history of the disease, and the background and family history. While taking a family anamnesis, therapists screen not only psychopathology but also family dynamics, such as the styles of family relationships and the most striking features. Nafs psychotherapy mainly relies on the technique of dream analysis. The dream analysis process will be explained further in detail. Lastly, during the therapy process, specifically in the termination phase, the therapist guides the counselee to *infāk*. If the counselee finds a meaningful way of realizing self-potential and serving others, it improves resilience and prevents relapse.

The first session is usually where counselees come to the therapist with intense feelings. In these cases, the therapist remains passive and allows the counselee to talk. Regardless of the condition of the counselee, in the first session, the therapist gathers information about the mental status examination, the history of the disease, and the background and family history. While taking a family anamnesis, therapists screen not only psychopathology but also family dynamics, such as the styles of family relationships and the most striking features. Nafs psychotherapy mainly relies on the technique of dream analysis. The dream analysis process will be explained further in detail. Lastly, during the therapy process and specifically in the termination phase, the therapist guides counselee to *infāk*. If the counselee finds a meaningful way of realizing self-potential and serving others, it improves resilience and prevents relapse.

Therapy Agreement

A therapy agreement is made with the counselee before beginning therapy. Time is an essential factor affected by the counselee's current situation, therapy motivation, etc. Sometimes, the therapy process is completed in 15 sessions and other times, it takes years. As a result, counselees should be aware that the process could take up to two years on average. Initially, sessions are scheduled once a week; in rare cases, two meetings are scheduled weekly. In addition, in some rare cases, two or three times a month are used. The counselee is asked to be punctual about the therapy hours.

Another important briefing is on the type of psychotherapy that the therapist practices. A short psychoeducation is given about the 'Ilm Al Nafs and its differences from other schools. Although the psychology of the nafs takes its basic approach from Islam and Sufism, religion is not necessarily communicated during therapy.

The nafs psychotherapy process lets a person know them, perform purification of nafs, and feel the Lord (if one believes), but after that, it is a choice of direction that is up to the counselee. However, if the counselee is already a believer, the therapist may offer suggestions such as performing Umrah, supererogatory prayers, awareness of *infâk* and *ishar*, the morality of *futuwwat*, and Sufi readings.

Therapy Motivation and Intention

In general, people seek psychological help because of pain or confusion that they can no longer bear alone. The first reason to come to therapy may be anxiety, depression, neurosis, or addiction, and the first goal of therapy is to eliminate this pain. At the end of this warm-up and mutual acquaintance period, if things go well, the first complaints are resolved to a certain extent, and the situation is evaluated together with the counselee. For example, if the target is the treatment of depression if the causes of depression are understood, and if life conditions have changed with psycho-social interventions, depression may not return after psychotherapy ends. However, even after the target symptoms have resolved, it is helpful to ask the following question in the dialogue: "If you were coming to therapy for the first time, what would your complaint be?" The answer is critical. If the person expresses his deeper pain while confronting himself, it means he wants to express it. In this case, a longer and more in-depth journey of self-knowledge may be recommended.

Sometimes, people may come to therapy without severe symptoms, but this can bring existential questions. The questions may relate to death, meaning, intimacy, and loneliness. In such situations, therapists often see the person experiencing both the attraction of the lower and the upper unconscious. To explore the dynamics of the lower and upper unconsciousness, dream analysis is the primary practice in nafs psychotherapy.

Dream Analysis in Nafs Psychotherapy

The analysis of dreams is the most critical component of nafs psychotherapy. Dream analysis helps the counselee become aware of this nature and assures him that there is a healthy, essential central self beyond insufficiencies, sorrows, and pathologies. Pathology is

217

the excessive identification of one with one's roles in life. However, dream analysis helps the counselee identify with roles.

A phenomenological approach to dreams is required. The therapist does not give meaning to symbols but asks questions to help the counselee make free associations and recall-related memories of the dreams. The therapist and the counselee try to figure out what the dream's director (Allah) is trying to say. The therapist says to the counselee that he should imagine himself on a theater balcony, sitting side by side with the therapist, ready to witness the play that will be realized on the stage. Different scenes, actors, and sometimes tragedies or comedies happen there. The dream examines the *hals*, weaknesses, and strengths of the counselees. The therapist discusses each symbol and figure in the dream with the counselee. Finally, deciphering the counselee's world language is the therapist's goal.

There are two approaches to dream analysis: objective and subjective. First, in the objective dream analysis, the therapist follows a phenomenological approach, asks the counselees about associations for a given symbol, and tries to understand the meaning of the dream objects. For instance, in the objective analysis process, the therapist may ask the client, 'What kind of world is this? or 'What do you think is the main message that the scenarist intended to give us?' 'Does this scene remind you of anything?' The reason is that the presentation of the scene in the dreams represents the counselee's perspective of the world. Dream comes from the inner world, so the inner world influences the counselee to interpret the outer world. The therapist and counselee find connections between the counselee's associations and memories and bring them to consciousness. This unites the inner and outer worlds.

Second, in the subjective dream analysis, the therapist claims that all the figures in the dreams are different aspects of the counselee. These could be his personas, shadows, or higher potentials. The therapist continues with questions. For example, the therapist asks, ' All the figures in the dreams are part of you. Do you think you have any part of yourself acting or feeling the same as the person in the dreams acts or feels?'. After that, when they detect how the dynamics of his parts work, the therapist guides the counselee to find those parts of himself in consciousness. Here, the therapist sticks to the associations of the counselee and tries to create meaningful perspectives on the current situation by questioning and bringing counselees' associations together.

In the end, the therapist asks the counselee to name the figures in the dream to separate themselves from the subpersonalities, shadows, or different personas. It is prominent for the counselee to understand that his shadows or personas are part of him but cannot define his whole self. His authentic self is beyond his nafs. Naming his different parts helps the counselee identify and realize them daily. It also allows him to observe himself and distinguish between his good and evil sides. The therapist then asks the counselee to name their dream. Finally, the therapist distinguishes the male and female figures and tries to see the inner structuring of Jalal and Jamal potential. The female figures symbolize jamal, and the male figures symbolize the jalal tendency of the counselee. Tawhid (immanent unicity) results from the union of the nafs and qalb or the marriage of the Jamal and the Jalal. The Tawhid *hal* guides the counselee through the process of individuation. After a brief reflection, the therapist investigates the "*hals*" this analysis elicits in the counselee. Aside from self-correction while identifying shadows, the fantastic aspect of this dream work is the curing potential of the previously mentioned discrete states (*hals*).

The counselee must be aware of his shadows and recognize the limitless potential of his beautiful nature. Counselees are assisted in developing metacognitive skills to accomplish this by dream analysis. Counselees begin to understand their inner worlds by discovering the dynamics of their different personas. They start to consider themselves from higher existential levels and higher selves. In other words, this is like the one observing his life playing on the stage from the theater's balcony, as mentioned above. Thus, they see some personas and shadows there. Then, they become able to realize their different parts in daily life. Since they know that their personas and shadows are not defining them, they take control over their personas and the shadows. Instead of following shadows without awareness, they start to rule them, so they ascend the nafs al-ammara.

These are only the basic steps that are applied in nafs psychotherapy. It consists of many more concepts, applications, and theories. 'Ilm Al Nafs does not intend to replace modern psychology altogether. Indeed, 'Ilm Al Nafs is open to utilizing modern psychology's findings and therapy technics. For instance, for problems of the middle unconscious, utilizing CBT can be very useful. 'Ilm Al Nafs offers some critical insights into a psyche model that is a lot more encompassing. There are a few consequences of the multi-level nafs structure and its dynamism; however, much research remains to be done. At this point, we may ask if this exile in the basement level of Nafs's structure is our fatal destiny. The answer comes in the ayah وَهَدَيْنَـٰهُ ٱلنَّجْدَيْنِ (Qur'an 90:10).

In conclusion, a few clinical implications exist of having a Multi-level Psyche Concept and its dynamics. Initially, it instills hope in the infinite potential of a human being. Humans are not "thrown" into a ridiculous world and condemned to misery. Second, psychopathology is given new fundamentals. For instance, humans appear to be miserable victims of their anger, sadness, anxiety, guilt, and shame, but this can be relative and transcended when viewed from a higher level (mushahada). Third, the importance of ethics becomes more visible and vivid. The concepts of heaven and hell come alive for the individual, and the perception of heaven and hell based on the afterlife embraces the perception of heaven and hell for the time being. It becomes a question of the present, of the here and now. More experts are shifting from intervention to prevention, suggesting that the current treatment techniques lack holistic prevention. Finally, psycho-hygiene becomes critical to avoid the deeper levels of dark existence. Moral behaviors are defined as psycho-hygiene. Finally, there is hope for more responsible behavior regarding ecological disasters (Qur'an 30:41).

Case Report

Generalized Anxiety Disorder (GAD) and Nafs Psychotherapy

Therapy begins with a primary "reason for referral." We ask the person who comes to us for the first time who referred him to us first and how he found us. The next question is, "What issues made you come to me?". Sometimes, people find it difficult to answer this question and give superficial reasons. In this case, the therapist draws a circle on a whiteboard; in this circle, the "burdens of life" are written so that the counselee can see them. After that, they are given different scores for each burden. Every person is burdened by different "weights" throughout his life, and therapy aims to lighten these weights or learn to live and exist with them. When things are going well when the person's initial reasons for coming are no longer relevant, this circle is periodically redrawn, and the question, "What would be the reasons if you were coming to me for the first time today?" is asked. If palliative, trivial causes are suggested, the question of whether to end therapy is considered. In the meantime, if practical, exemplary dream lessons have come, the person may have learned to use the dream "key" by now. In other words, contact with the "governor" has been established, and the evolution has begun. With an appropriate process, therapy can be finished. However, in a new crisis, therapy can begin again. The point to be considered here is transfer dependency. If such dependence is felt, it should be analyzed, and if necessary, the therapy should be terminated. Every human being is a realm without a fixed treatment plan.

When the case below was evaluated, it was thought that the counselee might be a candidate for nafs psychotherapy after the first meeting. The counselee was informed about the psychology of the nafs, and the therapy process started upon the counselee's approval. The counselee's thoughts about the dream, one of the primary materials of nafs psychotherapy, were asked, and the importance of dreams in nafs psychotherapy was explained. He was also instructed on how to record dreams.

Diagnosis: GAD and comorbid depression

The counselee is a 32-year-old male mechanical engineer who is married and has a child. He had apathy and anhedonia. His complaints began ten years ago, following the death of a friend. He had the feeling that something terrible was about to happen. He also had anxiety, exhaustion, difficulty focusing, aggression, and nervousness. He had previously received psychiatric treatment with Paroxetine at a dose of 10mg/day, which was then increased to 30mg/day. His complaints subsided after a year, and he stopped using drugs. His complaints were resolved approximately 3.5 years after the initial medical treatment. He sought treatment again and was given Paroxetine. His psychiatrist then tried various medications to induce remission. Sertraline, fluoxetine, duloxetine, venlafaxine, lorazepam, and risperidone. About three years ago, he began cognitive-behavioral therapy (CBT) and medication. He had stopped taking his medication three months before coming to see us, and his symptoms had returned. He complained of depression, unhappiness, loss of appetite, constant tension, anxiety, an inability to focus, an inability to rest, and sleeping difficulties.

The Family Background

There is no history of alcohol or substance use, head trauma, physical illness, accident, or medical operation. In his family history, the counselee had a 22-year-old sister who was a student. His mother was 52 years old, a primary school graduate, and a housewife. His father was 55, a high school graduate, and a tradesman. The parents had an arranged marriage, and there was no consanguinity between them. There was no family history of any other mental or neurological disease.

Mental Status Examination

The counselee was conscious, focused, and cooperative. His self-care was about average. He was making direct eye contact. During the examination, his attention was normal. His state of mind was anxious and depressed. His actions were aligned with his thought content, surroundings, and mood. His intelligence and memory were both normal. His abstract thinking, judgment, and the evaluation of reality were complete. The speech was both spontaneous and purposeful. The speech rate and format were both normal. He had a habit of going into detail about his complaints. There were anxiety-related psychomotor manifestations. There were no suicidal thoughts or plans. The Beck Anxiety Inventory (BAI) score was 32, and the Beck Depression Inventory (BDI) (Ulusoy, Sahin, and Erkmen, 1998) score was 24. According to the DSM-5, the counselee was diagnosed with generalized anxiety disorder and major depression.

The counselee was transferred to the out-counselee treatment facility. Paroxetine (a medication used as an SSRI under antidepressants) was started at a dose of 10 mg/day, which the counselee had previously used and reported seeing the most benefit from. After discussing treatment goals with the counselee and obtaining his or her consent, psychotherapy has started upon approval. The sessions were scheduled for one hour, once a week.

Therapy Process

The four dreams of the counselee are indicated in the case study. The analysis of the second dream has more detailed information than the others.

<u>Opening Dream (The first dream that the counselee brings sessions)</u>

1st Dream:

> '*I was working on a large project in my study room. My name is on the project, and I believe the project has an impact on my health. There is a different situation on the table. On the table, is an indicator that shows my current strength and the strength required to complete this project. According to the indicator, the project will require another third of its current strength to be completed. I begin to consider that the required power is not particularly great, but rather how to obtain it. Meanwhile, the door opens, and one of my close friends enters, smiling and saying, "You know what to do."'*

The dream scene that the counselee told was described by the therapist. The therapist said to the counselee that he is on a project that affects his health, and he needs strength. While he is thinking about how to get this power, a guiding friend steps in. Then the therapist asked: What do you think about the reason behind this dream? What could be the cause of the dream? Then the counselee started bringing associations. After, the counselee smiled and said, "The dream describes my current situation, and I guess that friend is the person who found you and directed me to you and I think this therapy process will help me understand my healthy lifestyle and myself this time." After this interpretation, the therapist and counselee continue the subjective interpretation of the dream. Based on the symbols in the dream and what these symbols mean to the counselee, the counselee is asked to finally summarize the subjective interpretation and name the symbols and the dream.

<u>The Dream of Transitioning to Resistance Against Disease</u>

2nd Dream:

> '*I am in a big city and watching out from the window of a prison. Suddenly, a cruel commander and his soldiers come and kill*

223

those who resist them. Then they take those who do not resist but are afraid of being sent to a worse prison. I was in a state of surrender at the time, neither resisting nor being afraid and hiding. I told the soldiers' commander, "I can cook very well; if you want, take me to your commander." They force me to cook in order to test me. The commander enjoys the food, and I am assigned to the commander's mansion as a cook. Meanwhile, I believe that "I have saved my life" and that "I will gain the trust of these cruel people, poison them, and save the city."

As mentioned earlier in the article, there are two interpretations of the dream in dream analysis: objective and subjective. In the objective interpretation, the counselee's perception, as reflected by the dream scene, is discussed. The associations and associations in his personal story are discussed phenomenologically. In the objective interpretation stage, the therapist describes the dream: "In the dream, there are people whom a cruel commander in the middle of a war persecutes. While standing helplessly, a person also finds a way out in surrender." The therapist asks the counselee: "What do you think that means? Does this remind you of anything? Why did such a dream come about now?' The counselee's interpretation: 'There are serious problems between my boss and me and other employees; there is mobbing to all of us. I used to be in constant conflict, but I have found it useless lately. Now I'm gathering evidence of this situation and considering suing him. He trusted me more during this period because I did not conflict with my boss.' He added with a laugh: 'Of course, I do not intend to poison; I will just file a lawsuit.'

In the second stage, there is subjective interpretation. The counselee sees all the people in the dream as his reflection. For example, it is questioned which side of the counselee is that cruel commander. The subjective interpretation of the dream was very interesting. He had thought for years that he would never be able to get rid of this disease, but now he has declared war on the commander, that is, his disease (he associated with the interpretation), which he has symbolized as his sick and cruel side. He employs a variety of strategies. Furthermore, he was moving forward without fear, in complete surrender and calm.

Finally, the counselee is asked to name the dream and the people in the dream. While doing this, he is asked to give the first name and adjective that comes to mind. The aim here is to increase the permanence of the dream interpretation in the counselee's mind, to enable him to distinguish the emerging aspects from himself, and to support him in recognizing it as a role. In addition, based on the given nouns and adjectives, it is asked if any other points should be mentioned. Every association creates a new meaning and accesses the client's unconscious.

On the Path to Individuation, Bid Farewell to the Inner Mother and Father with an Inner Family Dream

3rd Dream:

> 'While walking through a vast valley, I come across my parents. They begin to walk together. My father praises the valley's beauty. My mother mentions that it will soon be dark and that they must return home. The road splits as we walk home, and my father points the way to our house. We turn towards the road indicated by the father, and I have the sudden impression that I no longer live with my parents. "It's no longer my house; I'm going to have my own house,". My mother is a little upset and refuses to leave, but eventually agrees. I return and take a different route home.'

There was no psychiatric disease in the counselee's mother or father's family history. Further interviews revealed that he was raised by a protective and anxious mother and an authoritarian father who struggled with anger management. Many inner family dreams preceded this dream during the therapy; these dreams were mostly dreams of confrontation with the inner mother and father. When the dreams of confrontation were over, dreams of individuation began to come, and this was the most striking and impressive dream of separation. Our counselee had become estranged from his inner mother and father, whom he described as his anxious and angry sides.

New Anima and a New Personality

4th Dream:

> 'I am holding a baby girl dressed in pink. There are people I do not recognize around me, but the atmosphere is serene. I am in charge of looking after the baby. The baby emerges from my arms, and she gazes out the window at the deep blue lake.'

The conflicts and confrontations fade away gradually, and the unconscious is resolved. The baby girl represents the new anima that accompanies him as well as a new personality.

Additional Notes: The BDI and BAI were used again in the fourth session of the counselee's nafs psychotherapy. BDI: 18 BAI: 27. Because the counselee was feeling better and did not want to take more medication, the dose was not increased. It was re-evaluated at the end of the tenth month as BDI: 4 BAI: 6. The drug was tapered and discontinued at the end of the 12th month at the counselee's request. The therapy was stopped at the end of the 14th month.

References

Assagioli, R. (2000). *Psychosynthesis: A collection of basic writings.* Synthesis Center.

Gion, C. (1962). *Angst Und Schuld Als Grundproblem Der Psychotherapie.* Hans Huber.

Hillman, J., & Ventura, M. (2018). We've Had a Hundred Years of Psychotherapy—And the World's Getting Worse. İçinde *The Political Self* (ss. 189–206). Routledge.

Jung, C. G. (2009). *The Red Book: Liber Novus.* W.W. Norton & Company.

Lone, J. M. (2020). A Comparative Study of Ramanuja's and Sirhindi's Epistemological Views. *Journal of Indian Council of Philosophical Research, 37*(3), 433–450.

Montague, R. (2007). *Your brain is (almost) perfect: How we make decisions.* Penguin.

Morris, J. W., & Burrell, D. B. (2005). *The reflective heart: discovering Spiritual intelligence in Ibn Arabi's Meccan illuminations.* Fons Vitae Louisville, KY.

Murata, S., & Schimmel, A. (2010). *The Tao of Islam: A sourcebook on gender relationships in Islamic thought.* State Univ. of New York Press.

Mustafa, M. (2014). Nefs Psikolojisi. Kaknüs Yay.

Stein, M. (1998). *Jung's map of the soul: An introduction.* Open Court Publishing.

Tart, C. T. (1975). *States of consciousness.* EP Dutton New York.

Textbook of transpersonal psychiatry and psychology. (1996). İçinde B. W. Scotton, A. B. Chinen, & J. R. Battista (Ed.), *Textbook of transpersonal psychiatry and psychology.* New York, NY,

US: Basic Books/Hachette Book Group.

Twenge, J. M. (2008). Generation me, the origins of birth cohort differences in personality traits, and cross-temporal meta-analysis. *Social and Personality Psychology Compass, 2*(3), 1440–1454.

Twenge, J. M. (2013). Teaching generation me. *Teaching of Psychology, 40*(1), 66–69.

Twenge, J. M. (2017). *iGen: Why today's super-connected kids are growing up less rebellious, more tolerant, less happy--and completely unprepared for adulthood--and what that means for the rest of us.* Simon and Schuster.

Ulusoy, M., Sahin, N. H., & Erkmen, H. (1998). Turkish version of the Beck Anxiety Inventory: psychometric properties. *Journal of cognitive psychotherapy, 12*(2), 163.

Wishnitzer, A. (2014). Into the dark: power, light, and nocturnal life in 18th-century Istanbul. *International Journal of Middle East Studies, 46*(3), 513–531.

CHAPTER NINE

SPIRITUALLY FOCUSED ASSISTANCE (SFA) PROGRAM:
An Islamic Protocol for Religious Cognitive Behavioral Therapy (RCBT)

Mohammad Omar Salem and Khalid Elzamzamy

Introduction

A vast body of literature supports the fact that religion and spirituality are associated with positive physical and mental health outcomes. Patients who report religious and spiritual beliefs and practices have been found to have less depression, anxiety, suicide attempts, and substance use disorders (Koenig, 2018). Religion and spirituality may equip patients with hope, meaning, and purpose. Studies have shown that religious patients not only find meaning and coping in religion but also want their treating clinicians to incorporate religion into their therapy (Larimore et al., 2002; Hefti, 2011). Studies examining the incorporation of religion into psychotherapy showed that integrating religious domains into therapy improved outcomes for religious patients when compared to standard modalities (Hefti, 2011; Propst et al., 1992).

A range of spiritual strategies may be incorporated into therapy with religious clients or clients who are open to integrating religion and spirituality into their care. The integration of religion and spirituality in therapy is a step towards integrative therapeutic approaches, and it complements traditional approaches such as medications and mainstream therapeutic modalities. The integration of religion and spirituality is based on an ontological understanding of human beings that goes beyond the reductionistic mind-body dichotomy or biopsychosocial formulation to include spiritual and ethical ontological dimensions to human existence. Religious and spiritual strategies may be utilized in an eclectic fashion where the therapist integrates elements that best match the unique needs of a given client. In this chapter, the "Spiritually Focused Assistance" (SFA) program will be detailed and elaborated. This will be followed by a discussion of a range of other spiritual strategies that may be utilized.

Spiritually Focused Assistance (SFA) Program

The "Spiritually Focused Assistance" (SFA) [pronounced as safa or ṣafā] is an Islamically adapted protocol for religious cognitive behavioral therapy (RCBT). The program was developed by Dr. Mohammed Omar Salem, who presented it in its initial format at a joint meeting of the Transcultural sections of the Royal College of Psychiatry (RCPsych) and the World Psychiatric Association (WPA), which was held in Coventry, UK in 2003. The protocol was informed by Dr. Salem's extensive expertise, work in multiple regions across the Muslim world with patients across their lifespan, and his prowess in Islamic spiritual literature. Since then, he has been conducting workshops to train mental health professionals in this program. In the earlier stages of implementing this protocol in a hospital setting (a substance use treatment facility), multiple parameters showed the efficacy of the intervention, including length of hospitalization, dropout rates, and relapse rates (Salem & Ali, 2008).

Overview

The SFA protocol is flexible and may be tailored to the patient's needs. The protocol has far-reaching applications across various psychopathologies, including trauma- and stressor-related disorders, anxiety disorders, depressive disorders, maladaptive personality traits, personality disorders, substance use disorders, and chronic health problems. The SFA protocol may not apply to patients with impaired reality testing, such as psychosis and severe OCD.

The SFA protocol is a growth-oriented model that focuses on supporting and activating the patient's healthy schemata while relying on the religious resources of the patient, supplemented with self-help material and accessible religious sources. Therapists from all training backgrounds may be able to incorporate elements from the SFA program in their practice. However, the program is denominationally specific. In other words, it requires that both the therapist and the patient share the same spiritual and religious orientation and affiliation.

Protocol *Structure*

The SFA protocol comprises sixteen (16) "stations," each representing a specific theme. This station-based structure was inspired by the Islamic spiritual literature that described the path toward spiritual growth using terms such as *madārij* and *ma'ārij*, both of which mean steps or stations. The stations evolved and developed in response to clients' needs as the protocol was implemented in various settings. The stations were mapped around overarching themes. First, some stations are related to working with time-related experiences: 1) Past (Forgiveness, Gratitude); 2) Present (Present time orientation, Reliance on Allāh); 3) Future (Hope, Optimism). Two stations are considered mood regulation stations: Serenity, Pleasure, and Happiness. Three stations are centered around reactions "when bad things happen": Afflictions, Surrender, and Acceptance. Two stations address existential themes: nature of life, making the Hereafter one's main concern. Finally, three stations address issues related to self-communication: intra-, inter-, and ultra-personal communication. These stations are used as templates for the 'topic of the day' themes during CBT sessions. This protocol is expected to run between 8-20 sessions, depending on the patient's needs and the target symptoms. Each session or a group of sessions may be dedicated to one theme of these stations. The stations are interrelated, and their sequence may be flexible and customized to meet the patient's needs. The SFA protocol may also be used as a standalone approach in other spiritually-based interventions.

Each station has two main ingredients, namely psychoeducation and practical applications. Psychoeducation includes an interactive and reflective activity aiming at defining the theme of the station, offering scriptural supportive references, including storytelling, and demonstrating the clinical utility. Practical applications include both cognitive and behavioral components. Cognitive components are reinforced through utilizing self-help material in between sessions (see below for further details on religious self-help). On the other hand, behavioral components may include practical acts of worship (reciting the Qur'ān, Dhikr, praying), relaxation techniques, physical activity, social engagement, and environmental modifications. The feedback and outcome of the station will be reviewed at the beginning of the following station as part of the agenda of CBT sessions.

The stations of the SFA protocol are as follows:

1. Spiritual Surrender التسليم الكامل لله

2. Serenity السكينة والطمأنينة

3. Gratitude and Appreciation الشكر والامتنان

4. Acceptance الرضا والقبول

5. Hope الأمل

6. Optimism التفاؤل

7. Afflictions الابتلاءات

8. The Nature and Purpose of This Life

9. Making The Hereafter One's Main Concern

10. Forgiveness العفو والتسامح

11. Present-time orientation العيش في حدود الحاضر

---

12. Reliance on Allāh التوكل على الله

---

13. Happiness and Pleasure السعادة واللذة

---

14. - 16. Communication Stations: Intra-personal
Communication (self-evaluation); Inter-personal
communication (with people); Ultra-personal
communication (inspiration)

Spiritual Surrender التسليم الكامل لله

Absolute surrender to Allāh is a central concept in Islamic teachings
and a foundational station in the SFA protocol. Surrender to Allāh,
which is the literal meaning of the word 'Islam', means
unconditionally giving oneself to Allāh. On the surface, surrender
may have negative connotations linked to giving up on one's
freedoms and autonomy. However, the subjective experience of
surrendering to Allāh is characterized by an enhanced state of being
and well-being.

Surrender has multiple manifestations in a client's life. The
degree to which a client demonstrates surrender will manifest in the
client's acceptance of Allāh's destiny for them and their abidance by
the teachings and doctrines set by Allāh. A clinician may initiate this
station by exploring a client's attitude toward surrender to Allāh and
by identifying strengths and challenges in the client's state of
submission and surrender. Important areas to explore include
obstacles to surrender and facilitators of submission. Obstacles and
facilitators relevant to the station of surrender include certain areas of
personal weakness & temptations, environmental and social factors,
habitual behavioral factors, cognitive factors, and spiritual,
metaphysical factors.

Scriptural References

وَمَنْ يُسْلِمْ وَجْهَهُ إِلَى اللَّهِ وَهُوَ مُحْسِنٌ فَقَدِ اسْتَمْسَكَ بِالْعُرْوَةِ الْوُثْقَى وَإِلَى اللَّهِ عَاقِبَةُ الْأُمُورِ
(لقمان : 22)

"Whoever willingly submits/surrenders his face to God, while
excelling in good deeds, has truly grasped the firmest handhold.

233

For to God alone is the ultimate end of all affairs." (Qur'ān, 31:22)

Application / Homework (Cognitive and Behavioral)

- Behavioral: Obstacles to surrender are identified and recorded. For each problem area, a behavioral plan is set (e.g., to avoid cues of certain temptation). The homework will aim at self-monitoring for identified problematic areas
- Cognitive: Self-help bibliotherapy to enhance surrender will be assigned (e.g., appropriate stories of Prophets and narratives of past and contemporary righteous figures highlighting their surrender to Allāh's Will under difficult situations and bitter tests and the ultimate positive outcome).

Serenity السكينة والطمأنينة

Serenity is a human experience that involves a positive mood state, thoughts, and emotions. It is intertwined with tranquility, gratitude, contentment, and deep inner peace. Serenity is also closely related to the first station of "surrender." The religious roots of serenity entail a sense of connectedness to God, focused attention to and awareness of this connection while keeping other realities distinct and in perspective (*al-hudur ma' Allāh wa ihmal al-aghyar*), and an ability to accept situations that cannot be changed, trusting in His Wisdom, with complete surrender to His Will.

From a practical clinical sense, the station of serenity is a "mood regulation" station composed of two main ingredients: 1) a detachment from negative emotional experiences and surroundings and 2) a revival/activation of the sense of connectedness to Allāh as a secure haven. Detachment, which is the first step in attaining serenity, entails detachment from external events and 'disidentification' from disruptive and negative mood states. In 'mental disidentification', the client observes and monitors his/her thoughts as mere thoughts that occurred in their mind from the perspective of an objective or detached observer. This leads the individual to identify less with their thoughts. The second step in attaining serenity entails finding an inner secure haven (personal cloud) that can be accessed even during emotional turmoil. Ideally, the individual practices reaching this inner haven on a regular basis in order to be accessible in times of emotional distress or during stressful life events. When the individual finds this inner space, they experience tranquility and freedom from external and internal disruptions. The therapist's task is to engender serenity by facilitating the development of those particular components of serenity. The therapist may supplement this station by teaching the client relaxation and breathing techniques to facilitate an initial relaxed state that fosters a space where the client can focus on their connectedness to God and reduce their preoccupation with the outside world. The activation of the connectedness to God may be facilitated by rehearsing relevant *dhikr* (words of remembrance), verses, or prayers that reinforce the awareness of and connectedness to God. Muslim scholars, such as Ibn al-Qayyim (2008, p. 206; 2006, p. 134; 1972, p. 230) and al-Ghazali (2006, pp. 85-87) refer to this process as "the presence of heart with God" (*hudur al-qalb ma' Allāh*). Examples of verses that may foster such a state of heart presence include:

Scriptural References

قل إن الأمر كله لله

"Indeed, the whole [of every] affair belongs to God [alone]".
(Qur'ān, 3:154)

قال لا تخافا ، إنني معكما أسمع وأرى

"He said: Have no fear. Indeed, I am with you both. I hear and I see." (Qur'ān, 20:46)

والله يسمع تحاوركما إن الله سميع بصير

"For God hears your discourse with each other. Indeed, God is all-hearing, all-seeing." (Qur'ān, 58:1)

قل الله ، ثم ذرهم في خوضهم يلعبون

"Say [to them all]: God! Then leave them in their indulgence, playing!" (Qur'ān, 6:91)

الَّذِينَ آمَنُوا وَتَطْمَئِنُّ قُلُوبُهُم بِذِكْرِ اللَّهِ أَلَا بِذِكْرِ اللَّهِ تَطْمَئِنُّ الْقُلُوبُ

"Those who believe, and whose hearts find serenity in the remembrance of Allāh. Verily, in the remembrance of Allāh do hearts find serenity." (Qur'ān, 13:280)

Application / Homework (Cognitive and Behavioral)

- Regular doses (personal sessions) of *dhikr* (with full presence of the heart)
- Regular doses of salah (with full presence of the heart): The homework will add to the obligatory prayers additional supererogatory (*nafl*) prayers and night prayers (Qyiam) in a manner that is consistent with the Sunna.
- Regular doses of reflection (with full presence of the heart)
- Regular practice of the technique.

Gratitude and Appreciation الشكر والامتنان

Appreciation and gratitude have been recently recognized as important elements in positive psychology and positive psychotherapy (Cunha et al., 2019; Emmons & Stern, 2013; Emmons & Crumpler (2000). This station aims to inspire positive cognitions that can evoke positive emotions, which defeat and replace negative ones. This is based on the notion that "opposing emotions cannot co-exist together."

In Islamic Psychology, the main source of all gifts is Allāh. Examples of the countless gifts from Allāh include but are not limited to answered prayers that bring about goodness and protect against harm and evil, and blessings across all domains including, health, family, wealth, faith, knowledge, safety, and well-being. The gratitude record is an important section in the "Faith Diary," which will be elaborated further in a later section. A regular habit of journaling in the gratitude record about new gifts and blessings should be emphasized. Clients should be reminded that among Allāh's bounties is His Mercy, which He extends through a medium of significant human figures, such as parents, family members, and friends.

Scriptural References

236

وَآتَاكُمْ مِنْ كُلِّ مَا سَأَلْتُمُوهُ وَإِنْ تَعُدُّوا نِعْمَةَ اللَّهِ لَا تُحْصُوهَا إِنَّ الْإِنْسَانَ لَظَلُومٌ كَفَّارٌ

Thus has He given you of all that you have asked Him. And were
you to endeavor to count the blessings of God, never could you
enumerate them. Indeed, the [disbelieving] human being is a
relentless wrongdoer and utterly ungrateful. (Qur'ān, 14:34)

وَإِذْ تَأَذَّنَ رَبُّكُمْ لَئِن شَكَرْتُمْ لَأَزِيدَنَّكُمْ

And when your Lord proclaimed, 'If you are grateful, I will
certainly give you more (Qur'ān, 14:7)

قال النبي صلى الله عليه وسلم : "من لا يشكر الناس لا يشكر الله عز وجل".

The Prophet, may Allāh's peace and blessings be upon him, said,
"He who does not thank people does not thank Allāh".

Application / Homework (Cognitive and Behavioral)

The client is asked to keep a regular diary titled "gratitude
record," recording all significant favors and gifts offered to
him by God and people, including answered prayers to get
things done (benefit) or to get away from harm. The gratitude
record is an important section in the "Faith Diary," which will
be elaborated further in a later section.

Acceptance الرضا والقبول

In response to prolonged distressing life events or difficult life
circumstances, clients may struggle with accepting reality and
coping with it. This station of "acceptance" focuses on
developing an ability to accept situations that cannot be
changed by fostering surrender and trust in God's wisdom.
Acceptance of situations that are beyond one's control is an
alternative to exerting energies in the pursuit of unachievable
goals. The client's focus is to be re-directed mainly to what is
changeable. From a religious perspective, acceptance is
closely linked with a state of "patience." In Islamic teachings,

experiencing patience in difficult, uncontrollable situations is promised a great Divine reward. Moreover, there is even a higher reward for demonstrating "satisfaction and acceptance" towards God's destiny, a rank above and beyond patience.

Scriptural References

فَعَسَى أَنْ تَكْرَهُوا شَيْئًا وَيَجْعَلَ اللَّهُ فِيهِ خَيْرًا كَثِيرًا

It may be that ye dislike a thing, and Allah brings about through it a great deal of good." (Qur'ān, 4:19)

قل لن يصيبنا إلا ماكتب الله لنا

Say, Never will anything afflict us, but that which God has written for us. (Qur'ān, 9:51)

مَا أَصَابَ مِن مُّصِيبَةٍ فِي الْأَرْضِ وَلَا فِي أَنفُسِكُمْ إِلَّا فِي كِتَابٍ مِّن قَبْلِ أَن نَّبْرَأَهَا ۚ إِنَّ ذَٰلِكَ عَلَى اللَّهِ يَسِيرٌ"

No calamity occurs on earth or in yourselves without being in a Record before We bring it into being. This is certainly easy for Allāh. (Qur'ān, 57:22)

ما أصابك لم يكن ليخطئك، وما أخطأك لم يكن ليصيبك

"Whatever has come to you (afflicted you/befallen you) would never have missed you, and that whatever has missed you would never have come to you." (Sunan Abi Dawud)

يا غلام إني أعلمك كلمات: "احفظ الله يحفظك، احفظ الله تجده تجاهك، إذا سألت فاسأل الله ، وإذا استعنت فاستعن بالله، واعلم: أن الأمة لو اجتمعت على أن ينفعوك بشيء، لم ينفعوك إلا بشيء قد كتبه الله لك، وإن اجتمعوا على أن يضروك بشيء، لم يضروك بشيء إلا بشيء قد كتبه الله عليك؛ رفعت الأقلام، وجفت الصحف" ((رواه الترمذي وقال حديث حسن صحيح)) .

Ibn Abbas (May Allāh be pleased with them) said: One day, I was riding behind the Prophet (ﷺ) when he said, "O boy! I will instruct you on some matters. Be watchful of Allāh (Commandments of Allāh), He will preserve you. Safeguard His Rights, He will be ever with you. If you beg, beg of Him Alone; and if you need assistance, supplicate to Allāh Alone for help. And remember that if all the people gather to benefit you, they will not be able to benefit you except that which Allāh had foreordained (for you); and if all of them gather to harm you, they will not be able to afflict you with anything other than that which Allāh had pre-destined against you. The pens had been lifted and the ink had dried up". (Al-Tirmidhi)

Application / Homework (Cognitive and Behavioral)

- Acceptance and the circles of control: To help the client differentiate the controllable from the uncontrollable aspects of a situation, you might offer them a piece of paper titled "circles of control." Draw two circles on the page: "things under my control" and "things not under my control." The clients should think of their concerns and write each concern in the correct circle. As part of this process, the therapist helps participants explore the consequences of trying to control the uncontrollable in terms of anxiety and loss of energy that can be invested in changing things under their control.
- Acceptance and problem solving: Spotting the controllable, the client is encouraged to actively pursue all reasonable avenues for systematically solving problems. It should be their habit to actively address situations that can be changed positively and cope with them in a fighting spirit.

Hope الأمل

Hope is the feeling of wanting something to happen and believing it will be done God-Willing. Hope is an essential agent in Religious Coping.

The station of "hope" and evoking hope in clients is a very important therapeutic intervention and a central element of healing. Some perceive inspiring hope as the practitioner's first and foremost duty toward clients. Studies have shown positive associations between hope and a range of outcomes, including life goals, happiness, less distress, superior coping skills, improved recovery from physical injuries, and less burnout at work (Herbert, 2011).

Hopeful individuals possess positive thinking that reflects a realistic sense of optimism (Goleman, 1996) and the belief that they can produce routes to desired goals (Ciarrochi et al., 2007). Such individuals perceive obstacles as challenges to overcome and can utilize their optimism to plan alternatives to achieve their end goal (Luthans et al., 2010). Studies have found that hope positively correlates with life satisfaction and serves as a buffer against negative and stressful life events (Valle et al., 2006). Thus, individuals high in hope tend to show better athletic, academic, occupational, and health outcomes (Luthans et al., 2010). Hope has been conceived as a "consistent" trait, e.g., being hopeful most of the time, and as a "dynamic" state, e.g., feeling hopeful at a given moment.

Clinically, the degree of hope can be measured on a (0-10) scale, where (0) indicates feeling completely hopeless, and (10) indicates feeling very hopeful. The therapist aims to increase the degree and consistency of hope until the client fosters a more consistent trait of hope.

Scriptural References

يَٰبَنِىَّ ٱذْهَبُواْ فَتَحَسَّسُواْ مِن يُوسُفَ وَأَخِيهِ وَلَا تَأْيْـَٔسُواْ مِن رَّوْحِ ٱللَّهِ ۖ إِنَّهُ لَا يَأْيْـَٔسُ مِن رَّوْحِ ٱللَّهِ إِلَّا ٱلْقَوْمُ ٱلْكَٰفِرُونَ

And do not despair of God's mercy. For, most surely, none despairs of God's mercy except the disbelieving people (Qur'ān, 12:87)

وَمَنْ يَقْنَطُ مِنْ رَحْمَةِ رَبِّهِ إِلَّا الضَّالُّونَ

"Who would despair of the mercy of their Lord except the misguided?" (Qur'ān, 15:56)

.يُرِيدُونَ أَنْ يُطْفِئُوا نُورَ اللَّهِ بِأَفْوَاهِهِمْ وَيَأْبَى اللَّهُ إِلَّا أَنْ يُتِمَّ نُورَهُ وَلَوْ كَرِهَ الْكَافِرُونَ

They wish to extinguish Allāh's light with their mouths, but Allāh will only allow His light to be perfected, even to the dismay of the disbelievers. (Qur'ān, 9:32)

وَلَا تَهِنُوا وَلَا تَحْزَنُوا وَأَنْتُمُ الْأَعْلَوْنَ إِنْ كُنْتُمْ مُؤْمِنِينَ ۞ إِنْ يَمْسَسْكُمْ قَرْحٌ فَقَدْ مَسَّ الْقَوْمَ قَرْحٌ مِثْلُهُ وَتِلْكَ الْأَيَّامُ نُدَاوِلُهَا بَيْنَ النَّاسِ وَلِيَعْلَمَ اللَّهُ الَّذِينَ آمَنُوا وَيَتَّخِذَ مِنْكُمْ شُهَدَاءَ وَاللَّهُ لَا يُحِبُّ الظَّالِمِينَ

Do not falter or grieve, for you will have the upper hand if you are ˈtrueˈ believers. If you have suffered injuries, they suffered similarly. We alternate these days among people so that Allāh may reveal the believers, choose martyrs from among you—and Allāh does not like the wrongdoers (Qur'ān, 3:139-140)

حَتَّى إِذَا اسْتَيْأَسَ الرُّسُلُ وَظَنُّوا أَنَّهُمْ قَدْ كُذِبُوا جَاءَهُمْ نَصْرُنَا فَنُجِّيَ مَنْ نَشَاءُ.

And when the messengers despaired and their people thought the messengers had been denied help, Our help came to them. We then saved whoever We willed. (Qur'ān, 12:110)

Application / Homework (Cognitive and Behavioral)

- Hope enhancement strategies include sharing and recalling past successes, hope-based goal mapping exercises, examining possible pathways to problem-solve and reach the targeted goals, identifying positive resources, and positive self-talk.
- Reframing: help the clients reframe distressing situations in ways that instill hope.

Optimism التفاؤل

Optimism is the feeling that the future, or something in the future, will be good or successful.

"وإنما تطيب الحياة بالأمل والتفاؤل، والمتفائل يقرأ الأحداث على أحسن الوجوه ويرى الخير حتى من خلال الشر وشعاع الشمس من خلال الغمام، ونور الفجر من وسط الظلام". محمد صالح المنجد

"Rather, life is beautified with hope and optimism. The optimist reads events in the best way and sees good even through evil, sees the sun rays through the clouds, and sees the light of dawn from the midst of darkness." M. Salih Al-Munajjid

Optimists fall into two groups: passive optimists and dynamic optimists. Passive optimists tell themselves positive messages about the future, such as "everything will be fine," while expecting other people and entities to solve the problems. On the other hand, dynamic optimists take an active stance and an empowering approach that facilitates success by focusing on opportunities. Islam encourages dynamic optimism and is against pessimism. Pessimists, passive optimists, and dynamic optimists all selectively focus their attention on certain dimensions and interpretations of reality that match their underpinning orientation. Optimists interpret their experiences differently than others, and these thoughts and interpretations translate into positive actions, emotions, behaviors, and motivations. On the other hand, pessimists focus on problems, pains, and pitfalls. It is as though where the pessimist sees problems, the optimist sees challenges and opportunities. By focusing on constructive, joyful, open-ended aspects of life, the optimist spots more solutions and feels more motivated to overcome obstacles. Dynamic optimism promotes happiness, success, and mental and physical well-being (quote Seligman),- and seems to turn a person into a magnet for good outcomes.

Scriptural References

قال رَسُولُ اللَّهِ صلى الله عليه وسلم: " قَالَ اللَّهُ أَنَا عِنْدَ ظَنِّ عَبْدِي بِي ".

Allāh's Messenger said, "Allāh said, 'I am to my slave as he thinks of Me".

النَّبِيَّ ـ صلى الله عليه وسلم ـ كان يُعْجِبُهُ الْفَأْلُ الْحَسَنُ وكان يحب الاسم الحسن

"The Prophet (ﷺ) used to like good signs" ... and "he liked a pleasing name."

النَّبِيَّ صلى الله عليه وسلم كَانَ إِذَا بَعَثَ عَامِلاً سَأَلَ عَن اسْمِهِ فَإِذَا أَعْجَبَهُ اسْمُهُ فَرِحَ بِهِ

وَرُئِيَ بِشْرُ ذَلِكَ فِي وَجْهِهِ وَإِنْ كَرِهَ اسْمَهُ رُئِيَ كَرَاهِيَةُ ذَلِكَ فِي وَجْهِهِ وَإِذَا دَخَلَ قَرْيَةً سَأَلَ عَنِ اسْمِهَا فَإِنْ أَعْجَبَهُ اسْمُهَا فَرِحَ بِهَا وَرُئِيَ بِشْرُ ذَلِكَ فِي وَجْهِهِ وَإِنْ كَرِهَ اسْمَهَا كَرَاهِيَةُ ذَلِكَ فِي وَجْهِهِ رُئِيَ

When the Prophet sent out an agent, he asked about his name. If it pleased him, he was glad about it, and his cheerfulness on that account was visible in his face. If he disliked his name, his displeasure on that account was visible on his face. When he entered a village, he asked about its name, and if it pleased him, he was glad about it, and his cheerfulness on that account was visible on his face. But if he disliked its name, his displeasure on that account was visible on his face.

Application / Homework (Cognitive and Behavioral)

The client reviews and tries to apply these concepts in his/her life. In case of conflicts or difficulties, the main reference for rectification would be to go back and to stick to the above religious concepts.

Afflictions الابتلاءات

Experiencing a degree of pain and suffering is inevitable in this life. From a religious and spiritual point of view, afflictions and tribulations serve multiple purposes. Afflictions may serve to expiate one's sins, to increase one's good deeds, and to elevate one's rewards and rank in the Hereafter. Such spiritual notions give meaning to challenging life events. Another core Islamic notion with regard to afflictions is the glad tidings brought forth in the Qur'ān where Allāh promises, "Indeed, with hardship comes ease. Indeed, with hardship, comes ease" (Qur'ān, 94:6). The verse indicates that Allāh will make a way out for the afflicted person. It also reassures that the more severe the tribulation, the closer one is to assistance and relief. This station is relevant to individuals experiencing traumatic situations and, as a result, struggle with hopelessness and helplessness.

Scriptural References

وَلَنَبْلُوَنَّكُم بِشَيْءٍ مِّنَ ٱلْخَوْفِ وَٱلْجُوعِ وَنَقْصٍ مِّنَ ٱلْأَمْوَالِ وَٱلْأَنفُسِ وَٱلثَّمَرَٰتِ وَبَشِّرِ

ٱلصَّٰبِرِينَ

And We will surely test you with something of fear and hunger and a loss of wealth and lives and fruits, but give good tidings to the patient (Qur'ān, 5:155)

سيجعل الله بعد عسر يسرا

God shall bring about, after hardship, ease. (Qur'ān, 65:7)

أَحَسِبَ النَّاسُ أَن يُتْرَكُوا أَن يَقُولُوا آمَنَّا وَهُمْ لَا يُفْتَنُونَ. وَلَقَدْ فَتَنَّا الَّذِينَ مِن قَبْلِهِمْ فَلَيَعْلَمَنَّ اللَّهُ الَّذِينَ صَدَقُوا وَلَيَعْلَمَنَّ الْكَاذِبِينَ

Do people think once they say, "We believe," that they will be left without being put to the test? We certainly tested those before them. And Allāh will clearly distinguish between those who are truthful and those who are liars. (Qur'ān, 29:2-3)

Application / Homework (Cognitive and Behavioral)

To work for easing the hardship through the following religious principles and practices:

- Regular praying الدعاء
- Plenty of seeking forgiveness (*istighfar*)
- Avoiding sins
- Awaiting Allāh's relief, which is a form of worship.
- Other possible ways that can ease the hardships include seeking social support and problem-solving.

The Nature and Purpose of This Life

Understanding the temporality of this worldly life is an important experiential theme. Our life in this world, whose pleasures are restricted and short-lived, is meant to be a journey towards an everlasting life hereafter. The purpose of creation for all men and women for all times has been one: To know and worship God.

﴿ وَمَا خَلَقْتُ ٱلْجِنَّ وَٱلْإِنسَ إِلَّا لِيَعْبُدُونِ ﴾[الذاريات: 56]

"And I did not create the jinn and mankind except to worship Me"

Knowing and worshiping God is achieved through following his messages revealed to His Prophets, which answer humanity's existential questions. These messages and Divine doctrines also detailed how to lead a happy life. They repeatedly emphasized that this life is a test and a transitory phase to an eternal afterlife.

Recognizing the abovementioned worldview provides a proper direction and minimizes the impact of stressors on the individual. Considering the temporality of this life provides mature coping strategies that facilitate acceptance of hardships and increase resilience in the face of life stressors. Accordingly, such a worldview reduces worries about future uncertainties and sadness about past losses.

Scriptural References

قُلْ مَتَاعُ الدَّنْيَا قَلِيلٌ وَالآخِرَةُ خَيْرٌ لِمَنِ اتَّقَى

Say, 'The enjoyment of this world is little, and the Hereafter is better for he who fears Allāh...' (Qur'ān, 4:77)

إِنَّا جَعَلْنَا مَا عَلَى الْأَرْضِ زِينَةً لَهَا لِنَبْلُوَهُمْ أَيُّهُمْ أَحْسَنُ عَمَلًا * وَإِنَّا لَجَاعِلُونَ مَا عَلَيْهَا صَعِيدًا جُرُزًا

We have indeed made whatever is on earth as an adornment for it, in order to test which of them is best in deeds. And We will certainly reduce whatever is on it to barren ground. (Qur'ān, 18:7-8)

مَا أُوتِيتُمْ مِنْ شَيْءٍ فَمَتَاعُ الْحَيَاةِ الدُّنْيَا وَزِينَتُهَا وَمَا عِنْدَ اللَّهِ خَيْرٌ وَأَبْقَى أَفَلَا تَعْقِلُونَ

Whatever you have been given is no more than the enjoyment and adornment of this worldly life. But what is with Allāh is far better and more lasting. Will you not then understand? (Qur'ān, 28:60)

وَيَوْمَ تَقُومُ السَّاعَةُ يُقْسِمُ الْمُجْرِمُونَ مَا لَبِثُوا غَيْرَ سَاعَةٍ كَذَلِكَ كَانُوا يُؤْفَكُونَ

And on the Day the Hour will arrive, the wicked will swear that they did not stay more than an hour. In this way they were always deluded. (Qur'ān, 30:55)

Application / Homework (Cognitive and Behavioral)

- Bibliotherapy: chapters on "contempt of the worldly life" in Al-Ghazali's *Ihya' 'ulum al-din* and other self-purification literature.
- The client is asked to re-formulate and review his life concerns in light of the limitations of this earthly life.

Making The Hereafter One's Main Concern

Our departure from this world is inevitable, and as the Hereafter is for eternity, it must be duly considered, given due attention, and remain in perspective as the ultimate goal for every Muslim. Death is not the end of our lives, but the beginning of our real life. Because our future fate is being decided on the basis of our present performance, we can either make use of our opportunities on earth to ensure a well-deserved place for ourselves in Paradise, or we can throw them away and condemn ourselves to punishment in Hell. The Qur'an states: "God has created death and life to test which one of you is best in conduct." (67:1)

Death marks the end of the testing period for all human beings. However, death only means a change of residence, for the soul never dies. Thus, man's life is divided into a brief stay in this world and an eternal life in the next world. When the time comes for the Last Day, God will destroy this world and replace it with a permanent, everlasting world. All human beings will be resurrected and brought before the Almighty to be judged. Those who have done good deeds in the world they have left behind will be rewarded. Their reward will be paradise, unimagined joy, happiness, and peace.

Our departure from this world is inevitable, and as the Hereafter is for eternity, it must be duly considered, given due attention, and remain in perspective as the ultimate goal for every Muslim. Death may occur at any moment; thus, we should be prepared to meet Allāh in the best state.

The belief in the Hereafter naturally has a great influence on the life of a believer. When the believer knows that God is watching all one's actions, our behaviors will be more responsible, tolerance to hardships will be increased, and the associated positive cognitions will attract healthy emotions and better adjustment to the transitory outside world.

Scriptural References

فَلَا تَعْلَمُ نَفْسٌ مَّا أُخْفِيَ لَهُم مِّن قُرَّةِ أَعْيُنٍ جَزَاءً بِمَا كَانُوا يَعْمَلُونَ

No soul can imagine what delights are kept in store for them as a reward for what they used to do. (Qur'ān, 32:17)

وَإِذَا رَأَيْتَ ثَمَّ رَأَيْتَ نَعِيمًا وَمُلْكًا كَبِيرًا

And if you looked around, you would see bliss and a vast kingdom. (Qur'ān, 76:20)

سَابِقُوا إِلَى مَغْفِرَةٍ مِّن رَّبِّكُمْ وَجَنَّةٍ عَرْضُهَا كَعَرْضِ السَّمَاءِ وَالْأَرْضِ أُعِدَّتْ لِلَّذِينَ آمَنُوا بِاللَّهِ وَرُسُلِهِ ۚ ذَٰلِكَ فَضْلُ اللَّهِ يُؤْتِيهِ مَن يَشَاءُ ۚ وَاللَّهُ ذُو الْفَضْلِ الْعَظِيمِ

Compete with one another for forgiveness from your Lord and a Paradise as vast as the heavens and the earth, prepared for those who believe in Allāh and His messengers. This is the favor of Allāh. He grants it to whoever He wills. And Allāh is the Lord of infinite bounty. (Qur'ān, 57:21)

إِنَّ الَّذِينَ آمَنُوا وَعَمِلُوا الصَّالِحَاتِ كَانَتْ لَهُمْ جَنَّاتُ الْفِرْدَوْسِ نُزُلًا. خَالِدِينَ فِيهَا لَا يَبْغُونَ عَنْهَا حِوَلًا

Indeed, those who believe and do good will have the Gardens of Paradise as accommodation. where they will be forever, never desiring anywhere else. (Qur'ān, 18:107-108)

"قَالَ اللَّهُ عَزَّ وَجَلَّ أَعْدَدْتُ لِعِبَادِيَ الصَّالِحِينَ مَا لَا عَيْنٌ رَأَتْ وَلَا أُذُنٌ سَمِعَتْ وَلَا خَطَرَ عَلَى قَلْبِ بَشَرٍ".

247

The Prophet, PBUH, said: Allāh, the Exalted and Glorious, said: I have prepared for My pious servants which no eye (has ever) seen, no ear has (ever) heard and no human heart has ever perceived those bounties leaving apart (those bounties) about which Allāh has informed you.

Application / Homework (Cognitive and Behavioral)

- Contemplate and envision all afterlife stages from the time of death to al-barzakh to the Last Day then to the final eternal destination (Al-barzakh is defined as a bridge across time and space, and it is the period between a person's death and their resurrection on the Day of Resurrection).
- Bibliotherapy: The book Al-Tawahhum by Imam Al-Harith Al-Muhasabi might be a helpful tool in the above contemplation exercise, and it may be used in sessions with clients or assigned as homework.

Forgiveness العفو والتسامح

This station of forgiveness refers to a range of thoughts and behaviors, including releasing resentments toward others, restoring, or repairing relationships, mending emotional wounds, or releasing an offending party who caused an injury from potential retaliation. Resentment may exacerbate emotions of anger, fear, and sadness and interfere with the person's ability to work through the positive steps necessary for maintaining recovery. Thus, resentment can have a poisonous effect on a person's spiritual and psychological life. On the contrary, forgiveness appears to be correlated with a decrease in depression and anxiety (Coyle & Enright, 1997). It is an important psycho-spiritual intervention that may contribute to interpersonal and psychological healing.

Scriptural References

"فَاصْفَحِ الصَّفْحَ الْجَمِيلَ"""

"Therefore, pardon, with the fairest pardon" [Qur'ān, 18:85]

"وَلْيَعْفُوا وَلْيَصْفَحُوا ۗ أَلَا تُحِبُّونَ أَن يَغْفِرَ اللَّهُ لَكُمْ ۗ وَاللَّهُ غَفُورٌ رَّحِيمٌ"

"But, rather, let them pardon and overlook. Do you not love that God should forgive you? Indeed, God is all-forgiving, mercy-giving." [Qur'ān, 24:22]

وَالَّذِينَ يَجْتَنِبُونَ كَبَائِرَ الْإِثْمِ وَالْفَوَاحِشَ وَإِذَا مَا غَضِبُوا هُمْ يَغْفِرُونَ

who avoid major sins and shameful deeds, and forgive when angered (Qur'ān, 42:37)

الَّذِينَ يُنفِقُونَ فِي السَّرَّاءِ وَالضَّرَّاءِ وَالْكَاظِمِينَ الْغَيْظَ وَالْعَافِينَ عَنِ النَّاسِ ۗ وَاللَّهُ يُحِبُّ الْمُحْسِنِينَ

Those who donate in prosperity and adversity, control their anger, and pardon others. And Allāh loves the good doers. (Qur'ān, 3:134)

Application / Homework (Cognitive and Behavioral)

- Encourage clients to forgive and help them get rid of negative emotions and restore broken relationships.
- To contemplate the high reward of forgiveness in the Hereafter.

Present-time orientation العيش في حدود الحاضر

The station focuses the client's attention and energy on the present moment, aiming to minimize the impact of the pains of past and future fears and worries. This is done by enriching a client's trust in God and His Wisdom. We do not live in the past or the future; we live only in a moving point called the Presence. This station also aims to address any "learned helplessness" that could obstruct such forward movement in life with a fighting spirit. This also includes good time management. Therefore, remaining mindfully in the present moment is encouraged to overcome negative thoughts and emotions.

Scriptural References

"خذوا ما أتيناكم بقوة"

Take hold of all that We have given you with utmost power!
(Qur'ān, 2:63)

"كنتم خير أمة أخرجت للناس ، تأمرون بالمعروف وتنهون عن المنكر وتؤمنون بالله"

You are the best Community ever brought forth for humankind:
You enjoin what is right. And you forbid what is wrong. And
you believe in God. (Qur'ān, 3:110)

المؤمن القوي خير وأحب إلى الله من المؤمن الضعيف

The Prophet, PBUH, said: A strong believer is better and dearer
to Allāh than a weak one (Sahih Muslim)

"احرص على ما ينفعك واستعن بالله ولا تعجز"

The Prophet, PBUH, said: Strive to seek that which will benefit
you, seek help from Allāh, and do not feel helpless. (Sahih
Muslim)

Application / Homework (Cognitive and Behavioral)

- Abide by a regular timetable for daily activities.
- Avoid distractors: There are so many distractors that can
  negatively impact efficient time management. Examples
  include social media, smartphones, TV, video games, and
  people. Distractors take away one's focus from important
  matters in life. Practical directives include time management
  strategies and self-monitoring of involvement with
  distractors.

Reliance on Allāh التوكل على الله

During negative emotional conditions, such as depression, certain
maladaptive thinking patterns are common such as "I am no longer
able to cope," "life is too difficult for me," "there is no way out," and
"no one is there for me." This station aims to counter such

maladaptive thinking patterns by instilling reliance on Allāh (*tawakkul*). Relying upon Allāh means to hand over one's affairs to Him while summoning Allāh's might, power, and capability. It is through knowing Allāh and His attributes that a client realizes that with the help of Allāh nothing is difficult or impossible and that Allāh is always there to assist those who trust Him. This station also instills a realization that Allāh knows a person's interests better than the person him/herself.

Scriptural References

وَمَنْ يَتَّقِ اللَّهَ يَجْعَلْ لَهُ مَخْرَجًا. وَيَرْزُقْهُ مِنْ حَيْثُ لَا يَحْتَسِبُ وَمَنْ يَتَوَكَّلْ عَلَى اللَّهِ فَهُوَ حَسْبُهُ إِنَّ اللَّهَ بَالِغُ أَمْرِهِ قَدْ جَعَلَ اللَّهُ لِكُلِّ شَيْءٍ قَدْرًا

And whoever fears God, He shall make for him a way out. Moreover, He shall provide for him from where he has never conceived. Thus, whoever relies on God, then He is sufficient for him. God shall, indeed, attain His purpose. Truly, for all things God has apportioned a due measure. (Qur'ān, 65:2-3)

أَلَيْسَ اللَّهُ بِكَافٍ عَبْدَهُ

"Is not God enough for His servant?" (Qur'ān, 39:36)

Application / Homework (Cognitive and Behavioral)

- Every morning and evening, recite the following supplication with full heart presence and contemplation (7 times):

حَسْبِيَ اللَّهُ لا إِلَهَ إِلاَّ هُوَ عَلَيْهِ تَوَكَّلْتُ وَهُوَ رَبُّ الْعَرْشِ الْعَظِيمِ

Allāh is sufficient for me. There is none worthy of worship but Him. I have placed my trust in Him, He is Lord of the Majestic Throne. (Recite seven times in Arabic.)

- Bibliotherapy: reading real-life stories of people who demonstrated tawakkul (Al-Hazmi, 1994). Also, reading life stories of people who gave up things for the sake of Allāh and were rewarded with something better (Al-Hazmi, 1990).

Happiness and Pleasure السعادة واللذة

Humans, as well as other organisms, engage in rewarding behaviors. The pleasurable feelings associated with these behaviors provide positive reinforcement, and thus, the behavior is repeated. Rewards can be natural as well as artificial, such as drugs. This station aims for the therapist to assist the client in exploring, identifying, and regularly practicing a range of pleasurable behaviors. These behaviors may include physical activity, gardening, social activities, or traveling. In addition, spiritual experiences may provide high-quality pleasurable effects. The positive affective states associated with spiritual experiences would turn the brain's pleasure center to new cues of pleasure. Re-channeling and re-directing the pleasure reward response to these positive experiences would expand the pleasurable choices of the client.

Scriptural References

قال أحدهم : إلتمس اللذة في ثلاث : في الذكر وعند السجود وعند قراءة القرآن، فإن لم تجد الحلاوة فاتهم نفسك

"It was said: seek pleasure in three: in dhikr, in sujud, and Qur'ān recitation. If you can't find joy in these, then you must question yourself"

Ibrahim ibn Adham, may Allāh have mercy on him, said, "If the kings and their sons knew what we experience of spiritual pleasure and happiness, they would fight us for it with their swords."

"True faith and true worship have light and sweetness that God casts into the hearts of whomever He wills of His servants" Al-Banna

---

"What has he found who has lost God? And what has he lost who has found God?" — Ibn 'Ata' Allāh Al-Iskandari.

Application / Homework (Cognitive and Behavioral)

- Assist the client in exploring, identifying, and regularly practicing a range of pleasurable spiritual behaviors aimed at spiritual development and purification of the heart. Examples of such activities include Prayer, dhikr, Qur'ān recitation, contemplation, and being in the companionship of righteous people.
- Assist the client in exploring, identifying, and regularly practicing a range of other pleasurable behaviors such as gardening, physical exercise, social activities, and travel.

(14-16) Self-Communication Stations:

14) Intra-personal Communication (within self) (self-evaluation)

This station deals with one's self-concept and self-esteem. The station examines the distance and relationship between one's true-self, ideal-self, and false (social) self. This careful examination will aid in developing self-development strategies that match the client's needs.

Scriptural References

مَن كَانَ يُرِيدُ الْعِزَّةَ فَلِلَّهِ الْعِزَّةُ جَمِيعًا ۚ إِلَيْهِ يَصْعَدُ الْكَلِمُ الطَّيِّبُ وَالْعَمَلُ الصَّالِحُ يَرْفَعُهُ ۚ وَالَّذِينَ يَمْكُرُونَ السَّيِّئَاتِ لَهُمْ عَذَابٌ شَدِيدٌ ۖ وَمَكْرُ أُولَٰئِكَ هُوَ يَبُورُ

Whoever seeks honor and power, then ˹let them know that˺ all honor and power belong to Allāh. To Him ˹alone˺ good words ascend, and righteous deeds are raised up by Him. As for those who plot evil, they will suffer severe punishment. And the plotting of such ˹people˺ is doomed ˹to fail˺. (Qur'ān, 35:10)

وَلَا تَهِنُوا وَلَا تَحْزَنُوا وَأَنتُمُ الْأَعْلَوْنَ إِن كُنتُم مُّؤْمِنِينَ

Do not falter or grieve, for you will have the upper hand if you are believers. (Qur'ān, 3:139)

بَلِ الْإِنْسَانُ عَلَى نَفْسِهِ بَصِيرَةٌ * وَلَوْ أَلْقَى مَعَاذِيرَهُ

In fact, people will testify against their own souls, despite the excuses they come up with. (Qur'ān, 75:14)

عن النبي صلى الله عليه وسلم قال: " الكيس من دان نفسه، وعمل لما بعد الموت"

The Prophet (ﷺ) said, "A wise man is the one who calls himself to account (and refrains from doing evil deeds) and does noble deeds to benefit him after death."

حديث: "إنَّ اللهَ تعالى يُحِبُّ مَعاليَ الأُمورِ ، و أشرافَها ، و يَكرَهُ سَفْسافَها"

The Prophet, PBUH, said: Allāh loves things that are sublime and hates the insignificant matters

Application / Homework (Cognitive and Behavioral)

- Monitor any defective self-schemata and try to correct
- Examine the distance between the true-self and the false (social) self (how genuine are one's reactions to others).
- Examine how close the true-self is to the Ideal-self? Set realistic goals (Consider one's abilities, limitations, and how realistic one's goals are).

Inter-personal communication (with people)

This station focuses on a range of social relationships and interpersonal affective states. The therapist assists the client in exploring relationships with family, relatives, friends, neighbors, and colleagues to identify difficulties in initiating and maintaining relationships and difficulties with boundary-setting and social roles. The clinician aims to instill positive pro-social and adaptive communication skills and equip clients with tools to handle criticisms and hostilities.

Scriptural References

وَالْكَاظِمِينَ الْغَيْظَ وَالْعَافِينَ عَنِ النَّاسِ وَاللّهُ يُحِبُّ الْمُحْسِنِينَ"

Those who donate in prosperity and adversity, control their anger, and pardon others. And Allāh loves the good doers. (Qur'ān, 3:134)

قَالَ رَسُولُ اللهِ صلى الله عليه وسلم: إِنَّ الرَّجُلَ لَيُدْرِكُ بِحُسْنِ خُلُقِهِ دَرَجَةَ الْقَائِمِ بِاللَّيْلِ.

The Messenger of Allāh, may Allāh bless him and grant him peace, said, "A man who is known for his good character has the same degree as someone who stands at night in prayer."

قال رسول الله صلى الله عليه وسلم "أكمل المؤمنين إيمانا أحسنهم خُلقا"

Messenger of Allāh (ﷺ) said, "The believers who show the most perfect Faith are those who have the best manners."

قال صلى الله عليه وسلم: "إِنَّ مِنْ أَحَبِّكُمْ إِلَيَّ وَأَقْرَبِكُمْ مِنِّي مَجْلِسًا يَوْمَ الْقِيَامَةِ أَحَاسِنَكُمْ أَخْلَاقًا"

The Messenger of Allāh said: "Indeed the most beloved among you to me, and the nearest to sit with me on the Day of Judgment is the best of you in character."

Application / Homework (Cognitive and Behavioral)

Review and develop social skills around getting on with people: Family, Relatives, Friends, Neighbors, and Colleagues. Work on any difficulties in initiating or maintaining relationships. Cope positively with criticism and advice. Appropriate use of a sense of humor facilitates positive communication. Issues related to assertiveness and self-confidence should be addressed and resolved.

16) Ultra-personal communications (inspiration)

This station focuses on communicating with Go, reflecting on inner and intuitive abilities, and connecting with the parapsychological and unseen realms. God talks to us in Qurʾān; we talk to God by prayer and Dhikr. God likes us to call him and ask him for the smallest needs and big goals. He sees us and hears us and reminds us whenever we mention him. He offered us two important windows in communication with the world of the unseen: the prayer of Istikhara and the true visions in dreams. Whenever we thank Him for some of His gifts, He increases and blesses them.

This station fosters more use of faculties of the spiritual heart and right brain over the critically thinking logical left brain. The station fosters a wide range of reflections, inspirations, and dream work with great reliance on the Faith Diary.

Scriptural References

فَاذْكُرُونِي أَذْكُرْكُمْ وَاشْكُرُوا لِي وَلَا تَكْفُرُونِ

Remember Me; I will remember you. And thank Me, and never be ungrateful. (Qurʾān, 2:152)

وَإِذَا سَأَلَكَ عِبَادِي عَنِّي فَإِنِّي قَرِيبٌ ۖ أُجِيبُ دَعْوَةَ الدَّاعِ إِذَا دَعَانِ ۖ فَلْيَسْتَجِيبُوا لِي وَلْيُؤْمِنُوا بِي لَعَلَّهُمْ يَرْشُدُونَ

When My servants ask you about Me: I am truly near. I respond to one's prayer when they call upon Me. So let them respond to Me and believe in Me, perhaps they will be guided. (Qurʾān, 2:186)

وَإِذْ تَأَذَّنَ رَبُّكُمْ لَئِن شَكَرْتُمْ لَأَزِيدَنَّكُمْ ۖ وَلَئِن كَفَرْتُمْ إِنَّ عَذَابِي لَشَدِيدٌ

And when your Lord proclaimed, 'If you are grateful, I will certainly give you more. But if you are ungrateful, surely My punishment is severe.' (Qurʾān, 14:7)

قَدْ سَمِعَ اللَّهُ قَوْلَ الَّتِي تُجَادِلُكَ فِي زَوْجِهَا وَتَشْتَكِي إِلَى اللَّهِ وَاللَّهُ يَسْمَعُ تَحَاوُرَكُمَا ۚ إِنَّ اللَّهَ سَمِيعٌ بَصِيرٌ

Indeed, Allāh has heard the argument of the woman who pleaded with you concerning her husband and appealed to Allāh. Allāh has heard your exchange. Surely Allāh is All-Hearing, All-Seeing. (Qur'ān, 58:1)

أَنَّ رَسُولَ اللَّهِ صلى الله عليه وسلم قَالَ " لِيَسْأَلْ أَحَدُكُمْ رَبَّهُ حَاجَتَهُ حَتَّى يَسْأَلَهُ الْمِلْحَ وَحَتَّى يَسْأَلَهُ شِسْعَ نَعْلِهِ إِذَا انْقَطَعَ "

The Messenger of Allāh (ﷺ) said: Let one of you ask his Lord for his every need, until he asks Him for salt, and asks Him for the strap of his sandal when it breaks."

Application / Homework (Cognitive and Behavioral)

Activate the Faith Diary to record all your communications with Allāh SWT. Be careful of your words and deeds because He is watching you. This will enhance your awareness of His Presence. Love Him because of His continuous care and countless gifts He is offering you.

See below for further discussion on faith diary/dream diary.

Other Spiritual Strategies in Psychotherapy

The Role of Clergy in the multidisciplinary team

The role of religious clergy, such as an Imam or a chaplain, in incorporating spiritual interventions into the daily life of clients as part of a multidisciplinary approach to treatment may enhance the overall well-being of patients in inpatient and outpatient settings (Florell, 1973; Parkum, 1985). We recommend that a chaplain or an Imam be included as members of the multidisciplinary team that looks after patients in various hospital settings. Trained Imams or chaplains are well-equipped to support the clinical team (psychiatrist, psychologist, social worker) in conducting a holistic evaluation and providing spiritual interventions as part of the client's treatment plan. This role complements traditional medical care. The spiritual assessment and subsequent counseling offered by the Imam aim at faith revival. Spiritual interventions offered by clergy include cognitive aspects (spiritual beliefs) and behavioral components (spiritual practices). Spiritual practices are focused activities to foster spiritual qualities that can yield positive emotional states. This includes acts of worship, such as prayer, contemplation, and fasting, and acts of kindness and charity, such as caring for others.

Spiritual Support Groups

In 1998, a group comprised of a psychiatrist (Author MOS), psychiatric nurses, and hospital chaplains at the Medway Maritime Hospital in the UK planned and implemented a Spiritual Support Group (SSG) that ran weekly for over two years. The group started with a pilot 8-week group and later extended and expanded based on positive outcomes and demand from staff and patients. We recommend incorporating weekly SSGs in the inpatient and outpatient settings. The groups can be facilitated by clinical team members alongside a chaplain or an Imam. Patients with acute psychotic symptoms may not be suitable candidates for such groups due to impaired reality-testing. The themes discussed were tailored and designed to tolerate a multi-faith population in a UK hospital setting and address a range of patient needs. Examples of these themes include:

- The meaning of life
- Hope and despair
- Making meaning of suffering and tribulations
- Human self-worth, dignity, and self-esteem
- Anger, forgiveness, and reconciliation
- Guilt and self-forgiveness
- Rejection, loss, and acceptance
- Death and afterlife

Group participants may also suggest themes they would like to discuss in sessions. We recommend that sessions conclude with a debriefing among team members. SSG aims to satisfy patients' spiritual needs by incorporating a spiritual component into the dynamics of a group therapy setting, using supportive, cognitive behavioral, and existential techniques. The SSG aims for members to develop and strengthen their inner resources and coping skills to live more hopefully and purposefully and to make meaning of their distressing events (Salem, 2003).

Religious Self-Help

We recommend incorporating a range of self-help strategies in working with religiously oriented clients. Below are examples of such strategies.

Religious Journaling (The Faith Diary): a highly recommended self-help intervention is spiritual journaling by keeping a faith diary. Clients are encouraged to regularly journal on all aspects of their spiritual journey and experiences and to review their diaries from time to time. The faith diary can be divided into sub-sections such as gratitude, lessons, Divine messages, prophetic and intuitive dreams, etc.

In the "gratitude" section, clients should record all gifts they acknowledge, including answered prayers. They also may reflect on blessings they are grateful for across all domains, including health, family, wealth, faith, knowledge, safety, and well-being. It should be regularly reviewed with the addition of new significant gifts.

In the "lessons "section, the client observes the consequences of his/her obedience to Allāh and how it facilitates his achievements in the best way. On the other hand, the client can also see the bitter consequences of his/her sins (Al-Hazmi, 1990; Al-'affani, 1996; Khattab, 1990, 1978; Al-Iskandari, 2001).

In the "Divine messages" section, clients record certain religious experiences that they feel they were intended for at a particular moment. Examples include coincidental hearing or reading some sacred verses that reflect on or answer their concerns at that particular moment. Also, beyond coincidence, experiences with religious significance are recorded. Such reflection on religious experiences reinforces faith revival.

259

In the "dreams" section, clients are advised to document all aspects pertaining to dreams with religious connotations. The importance of dreams has been emphasized in the Islamic Holy Scriptures (Qur'an and Hadith). Twenty-four verses of the Holy Koran discuss dreams in five chapters. Also, around 100 prophetic accounts refer to dreams and dreaming. According to Islamic teachings, one important subtype of dreams is called Ru'ya, meaning truthful dreams or visions, dreams of Divine origin and either glad tidings from God or premonitions. The warning dream is a message to the dreamer to warn him/her of some impending threat or danger, or to prepare him/her for bad news. Such dreams are valued religious experiences and should be recorded regularly.

Since dreams tend to be forgotten, clients are encouraged to record them for regular reflection and possible correlation with future events. It is also believed that the earlier the dream is narrated or reported, the more accurate the interpretation will be. Dream diary entries should include important dream content, namely, characters, emotions, setting, social interactions, activity, objects, success/failure, misfortune/good fortune. Important "descriptive elements and modifiers" should also include color, size, age, etc. (Hall, & Van de Castle, 1966). Entries should be dated and given a title indicating their content. When one records and reflects on their dreams, they may develop their personal dream language based on the frequently occurring symbols in their dream (Salem, 2010; Elzamzamy & Salem, 2020).

Religious biblio-therapy: Clients are encouraged to incorporate a daily dose of reading religious and spiritual literature that is selectively chosen to meet the client's clinical needs. This may be in the form of reciting daily sections from the Qur'ān, reading books and articles on self-purification, and listening to audiobooks and book commentaries.

Spiritual contemplation and prayer: a daily dose of supererogatory prayers and contemplation may be recommended by clinicians. Night-time prayers may be especially helpful.

Scripture memorization: Selected Qur'anic verses may be memorized to be available to the client to recite and ponder upon in relevant situations. Various verses may aid in coping with difficult and distressing situations, may provide a source of motivation and hope, may help with meaning-making, or may be a source of strength through storytelling. These verses can be written on flash cards or displayed on posters at home or at work to enhance their effects and improve their recall.

Praying for patients and with patients

Praying for others, including patients, is part of the Islamic tradition. Numerous papers explored patients' requests for prayers from their treaters and how treaters should respond to such requests (Anandarajah & Mennillo, 2007; Christensen et al., 2018). Integrative physician Dennis Gersten (1997), in his office, just before seeing a patient, tries to remember to dedicate the session to God by enhancing his awareness of God and asking for His help and guidance through the session. Clinicians may pray for clients' healing and recovery outside of sessions and may do so in session upon clients' request. Praying for someone without their knowledge is a favored deed in Islam and a source of answered prayers.

Religious community support

A religious community may be a source of psycho-spiritual strength and resilience. Clients affiliated with a religious community and find strength in that affiliation may be encouraged to engage with the community by enriching their social network and seeking social support in times of distress and crisis.

Conclusion

Many clients with mental health problems respond poorly to mainstream modalities of treatment. One potential reason for this resistance is the need for more cultural appropriateness of certain interventions and the poor incorporation of significant elements of human existence, such as spirituality. Building on the literature that demonstrated higher efficacy of religiously integrated interventions with religious clients, this chapter offered a wide range of spiritual interventions that may be incorporated into therapy with Muslim clients. The proposed SFA protocol primarily utilizes cognitive and behavioral strategies derived from traditional Islamic sources. Stations are flexible and comprehensive, covering a wide variety of spiritual interventions. Although existing literature does support the main lines of interventions proposed in this chapter, further research is needed to demonstrate the efficacy of specific interventions for specific disorders. Naturalistic and comparative studies can be used for that purpose.

References

Al-'affani, S. H. (1996). *Al-Jaza' min jins al-'amal* [Retribution matches the deeds]. Maktabat Ibn Taymiyya.

Al-Ghazali, A. (2006). Kitab al-Arba'in fi Usul al-Din. Jeddah: Dar al-Minhaj.

Al-Hazmi, I. A. (1990). *Man taraka shay'an l-Allāh 'awwadahu Allāh khairan minh* [Whoever gives up something for Allāh, Allāh will reward them with something better]. Dar al-Shareef.

Al-Hazmi, I. A. (1994). *Al-Faraj ba'd al-shidda wa-l-diq* [Relief after distress and hardship]. Dar al-Shareef.

Al-Iskandari, M. M. (2001). *Wa-huwa yatawalla al-salihin* [And He protects the righteous]. Dar Ibn Hazm.

Anandarajah, G., & Mennillo, R. (2007). Responding to a Patient's Request to Pray. *American Family Physician, 76*(1), 133-134.

Christensen, A. R., Cook, T. E., & Arnold, R. M. (2018). How should clinicians respond to requests from patients to participate in prayer? *AMA Journal of Ethics, 20*(7), E621-629.

Ciarrochi, J., Heaven, P. C., & Davies, F. (2007). The impact of hope, self-esteem, and attributional style on adolescents' school grades and emotional well-being: A longitudinal study. *Journal of Research in Personality, 41*(6), 1161-1178.

Coyle, C. T., & Enright, R. D. (1997). Forgiveness intervention with postabortion men. *Journal of consulting and clinical psychology, 65*(6), 1042.

Cunha, L. F., Pellanda, L. C., & Reppold, C. T. (2019). Positive psychology and gratitude interventions: A randomized clinical trial. Frontiers in psychology, 10, 584.

Elzamzamy, K., & Salem, M. O. (2020). Dreams and Their Role in Islamically Integrated Mental Health Practice. In Keshavarzi. H., Khan, F., Awaad, R., Ali, B. (Eds.), *Applying Islamic Principles to Clinical Mental Health Care: Introducing Traditional Islamically Integrated Psychotherapy.* Routledge.

Emmons, R. A., & Crumpler, C. A. (2000). Gratitude as a human strength: Appraising the evidence. Journal of social and clinical psychology, 19(1), 56.

Emmons, R. A., & Stern, R. (2013). Gratitude as a psychotherapeutic intervention. Journal of clinical psychology, 69(8), 846-855.

Florell, J. L. (1973). Crisis-intervention in orthopedic surgery: Empirical evidence of the effectiveness of a chaplain working with surgery patients. *Bulletin of the American Protestant Hospital Association, 37*(2), 29-36.

Gersten, D. (1997). Are you getting enlightened or losing your mind?: A spiritual program for mental fitness. Harmony.

Goleman, D. (1996). *Emotional intelligence: Why it can matter more than IQ.* Bloomsbury Publishing.

Hall, C. S., & Van de Castle, R. L. (1966). *The content analysis of dreams.*

Hefti, R. (2011). Integrating religion and spirituality into mental health care, psychiatry, and psychotherapy. *Religions, 2*(4), 611-627.

Herbert, M. (2011). *An exploration of the relationships between psychological capital (hope, optimism, self-efficacy, resilience), occupational stress, burnout, and employee engagement* (Doctoral dissertation, Stellenbosch: Stellenbosch University).

Ibn al-Qayyim, M. A. (1972). Bada'i' al-Fawa'id (vol. 3). Cairo: Maktabat al-Qahirah.

Ibn al-Qayyim, M. A. (2006). Al-Wabil al-Sayyib. Damascus: Maktabah Dar al-Bayan.

Ibn al-Qayyim, M. A. (2008). Madarij al-Salikin (vol. 1). Riyadh: Dar Taybah.

Khattab, M. S. (!978). *'Adalat al-sama'* [Heaven's Justice]. Dar al-I'tisam.

Khattab, M. S. (1990). *Tadabir al-qadar* [Destiny's measures]. Dar Qutayba.

Koenig, H. G. (2018). *Religion and mental health: Research and clinical applications.* Academic Press.

Larimore, W. L., Parker, M., & Crowther, M. (2002). Should clinicians incorporate positive spirituality into their practices? What does the evidence say? *Annals of Behavioral Medicine, 24*(1), 69-73.

Luthans, F., Avey, J. B., Avolio, B. J., & Peterson, S. J. (2010). The development and resulting performance impact of positive psychological capital. *Human resource development quarterly, 21*(1), 41-67.

Parkum, K. H. (1985). The impact of chaplaincy services in selected hospitals in the eastern United States. *Journal of Pastoral Care, 39*(3), 262-269.

Propst, L. R., Ostrom, R., Watkins, P., Dean, T., & Mashburn, D. (1992). Comparative efficacy of religious and nonreligious cognitive-behavioral therapy for the treatment of clinical depression in religious individuals. *Journal of consulting and clinical psychology, 60*(1), 94.

Salem, M. O. (2003, July). The Spiritual Support Group Medway Maritime Hospital Experience. In *Royal College of Psychiatrists Annual Meeting.*

Salem, M. O. (2010). Function of dreams: An integrated approach. Journal of the Islamic Medical Association of North America, 42(1)

Salem, M. O., & Ali, M. M. (2008). Psycho-spiritual strategies in treating addiction patients: experience at al-Amal hospital, Saudi Arabia. *Journal of the Islamic Medical Association of North America, 40*(4).

Valle, M. F., Huebner, E. S., & Suldo, S. M. (2006). An analysis of hope as a psychological strength. *Journal of school psychology, 44*(5), 393-406

CHAPTER TEN

ISLAMICALLY INTEGRATED STRATEGIES FOR ADDICTION TREATMENT:

Al Ghazali's 'Ilm-un-nafs, RCBT, MI, and the Stages of Change

Sarah Mohr and Latifat I. Ahmed

Introduction

The current public health crisis of addiction and Muslims

Why is it relevant, important, and urgent to discuss addiction treatment at all? While drug and alcohol use has been a problem since the beginning of civilization, most of the world, and particularly the United States, has seen a rapid rise in drug-related deaths, as well as wider problems of dereliction and loss of quality of life, productivity, and health and happiness. The number of overdoses due to the lethal opioid fentanyl has continued to spike over the last ten years, increasing in speed during the pandemic. The Trump administration declared the opioid epidemic a public health emergency in 2019, prior to the pandemic, and with the onset of the pandemic, the death toll exceeded 100,000 in twelve-months for the first time on record.

Not surprisingly, in spite of the prohibition on intoxicants in Islam, the Muslim community is not immune (Moghahed, 2021).

Additionally, increased stigma in Muslim communities has led to a reluctance to seek help by many which has contributed to the hidden nature of the crisis. It has been popular wisdom that Muslims suffer drug and alcohol-related problems at a much lower rate than the general population, at least in the US. However, increasingly the Muslim community is being impacted by substance use disorders (SUDs), leading to a growing call among Muslims for attention to the problem. Additionally, some Muslims are beginning to question if the Islamic tradition can offer unique solutions to the crisis of addiction that will both help the wider public and be a source of blessing for the Muslim community as Muslims have an opportunity to be of service to those suffering from the devastation of the drug epidemic.

Islamic Prohibition on Intoxicants

As stated already, the crisis of addiction has impacted communities all over the United States and around the world. Muslims have a unique position in the conversation about addiction because of the traditional prohibition against intoxicants in the Islamic religion. As background, the Qur'an is the written verbatim word of God for Muslims, revealed in graduality during the twenty-three-year period of the prophetic mission of Muhammad (PBUH), and it is the first source of Islamic law (Nasr, 2017). The second source of Islamic law is the Sunnah, which is the spoken words, acts done, and confirmations given by the Prophet Muhammad (PBUH) (Usmani, 1998). These two sources collectively form the foundation of Islamic law, ethics, theology and are established as revelations that form the basis of legislation in Islam. Thus, any discussion on intoxicants and their impact on the human psyche (soul), according to Islam, must begin from these two sources and transcend to others whose evidence is obtained from them.

These legislations were revealed with God's understanding of human nature, and one of such is that of intoxicants. The word *khamr* refers to intoxicating substances in general and linguistically means *concealment, to cloud* and *cover the understanding*. Therefore, any drink or substance which conceals the mind's ability to think and judge normally is called *khamr* (Ammar, 2016). The Qur'an is silent on drugs and narcotics specifically, but its prohibition on *khamr* is well known; In the Holy Qur'an, it is explicitly expressed in the following words:

You who believe, Intoxicants and gambling, idolatrous practices, and [divining with] arrows are repugnant acts- Satan's doing- shun them so that you may prosper. With intoxicants and gambling, Satan seeks only to incite enmity and hatred among you, and to stop you from remembering God and prayer. Will you not give them up? Obey God and Obey the messenger, and always be on your guard; if you pay no heed, bear in mind that the sole duty of the Messenger is to deliver the message clearly [5:90–92].

These verses became the final verses on intoxicants which established the Islamic prohibition of intoxicants. The Prophet Muhammad (PBUH) also clearly prohibited *khamr* in his words stated:

Ibn 'Umar, may Allah be pleased with him, reported that the Messenger of Allah (PBUH) said: 'Every intoxicant is khamr (wine) and every intoxicant is Haraam (unlawful). Whosoever drinks wine in this world and dies whilst having consumed it and not having repented from it will not drink it in the next world [i.e., in Paradise] (Muslim 4963).

In the scholarly exegesis of the verses on *khamr,* we learn that intoxicants became prohibited in stages. There were three stages to its prohibition. When the Messenger of God migrated to the Madinah, the city in which Islam became established after his migration, the people were consuming alcohol and gambling, and naturally, they asked him what Islam had to say about these matters given that they just embraced a new faith. God revealed the first verse on alcohol as His Messenger does not say anything about the religion on his own accord and whim. "... Say, 'In them is a great sin and some benefit for men." (2:219). With this, the people went on consuming intoxicants as it wasn't clearly prohibited. Another time, one of the emigrants was leading his companions in prayer and mixed-up verses in his recitation. Thereafter, God revealed a tougher statement, "... Approach not the prayer when you are in a drunken state until you know what you utter." (4:43). Then the people would drink before the time of prayers so they would be sober whilst in prayer until the verses 5:90-92 (quoted above) of the Qur'an were revealed and finally established the prohibition of *khamr* which happened due to an incident were the people became drunk in a feast and began boasting about each other's statuses and the supremacy of their tribe over the other, an act which is evidently obscene in the religion and prohibited leading to one of them striking another with a bone to his nose. The immediate action after that final revelation on intoxicants was revealed, the Muslims abandoned all intoxicants and rendered it forbidden to consume and not just consumption but sitting in the midst of those who consume it, buying it, brewing it as the Prophet clearly stated:

Ten matters related to *khamr* are cursed. *Khamr* itself is cursed. Whoever drinks it, its server, seller, buyer, brewer, who asks for it to be brewed, whoever carries it, whomever it is carried to and whoever consumes its price. (Ibn Majah 3380)

Through the concepts of abrogation (Louay, 2012), the first two prohibitions on *khamr* are no longer considered in Islamic law but remained recited in the Qur'an, thus legal punishments in Muslim majority countries on whoever consumes intoxicants as it is prohibited in the religion. For narcotics and other drugs like hashish, there were no clear statements on them in the Qur'an and Sunnah. Many Muslims today take that as a basis for their consumption. However, the dominant opinion among scholars is that because during the time of the revelation on intoxicants, what the people knew as intoxicating substances were alcohol extracted from grapes, dates, honey, wheat, and barley as narcotics and other drugs weren't known in the Arab world. However, the basis of prohibition of these drugs lies in the statement given by the Prophet as well as his companion; "Every intoxicant is *khamr,* and every intoxicant is unlawful." (Muslim 4963)

From all these, the prohibition of intoxicants is so clear and well established for every Muslim that any substance that intoxicates the mind, preventing it from sound reasoning, is an intoxicant and therefore forbidden to consume. Furthermore, with the gradual interdicting of alcohol as shown in the revelations, it became a beacon of light for Muslim practitioners (also practitioners of contemporary psychology) to appreciate Islam's deep understanding of human nature and addiction and further understand its impact on the human soul thus illuminating the idea of Islamically integrated methods for treatment (Ali, 2014).

Al Ghazzali's ʿIlm-un-nafs

The concept of man, 'who he is?' 'what makes a being?' has been a phenomenon that has sparked curiosity in the minds of thinkers, philosophers, and scholars of all times. Western scholars have researched this idea for long and developed studies on the behavioral pattern of man- the differences in the characteristic patterns of thinking, behaving, feeling, and personality traits in order to understand how these intricacies and complexities together form a whole (Razak & Haneef, 2017).

However, a common critique of Western studies is that they fall short of bringing about a holistic understanding of the uniqueness of man. Many people critique some Western or contemporary psychologies that tend to believe man is a biological entity only. This idea stems from the scientific and materialistic view, which emphasizes empiricism and explains that to gain the true understanding and reality of a thing, it has to be experienced and defined solely by the senses (Utz, 2011). Thus, many contemporary psychologies consider man and the entire universe to exist without any divine influence, i.e., the 'no God' ideology, and that has immensely influenced the various methods, research formulas, treatments, and remedies on mental behaviors. For example, beliefs that alcohol and drug addiction are hereditary/biological behavior and, as such, primarily physical disorders, are biologically related and dependent only on material causes (Sahu & Sahu, 2012).

In contrast, Islamic psychology centers its paradigm on the belief of the spiritual uniqueness of man and includes as axiomatic in all fields of thought the fundamental beliefs in the unseen. Thus, the verse at the very start of the Qurʾān, oft recited:

This is the scripture in which there is no doubt, containing guidance for those who are mindful of God, who believe in the unseen, keep up the prayer, and give out of what We have provided for them (Qurʾān, 2:2).

Islamic theology thus explains that while mankind indeed does not possess knowledge of the unseen because it is strictly a divine attribute, this lack of knowledge does not throw into question its actual existence. Islam emphasizes the belief in the unseen as part of its fundamental belief system and structure of the religion. Ancient as well as modern scholars have made discoveries and research around this phenomenon seeking to establish the makeup of man as not only genetic and biological but also spiritual and possessed of its own existentialities. This belief also has led to the secondary belief that errors in the treatment of the self and soul manifest in the form of physical agonies, ailments, and sufferings (Haque & Keshavarzi, 2014).

According to Islamic psychology, man is not just a physical being living in a physical world but a spiritual being journeying in a physical world, and his final return is to the hereafter- life in the *barzakh* (grave) and finally paradise/hell (Utz, 2011). Much work has been done in the last 60 years on the Islamic concept of the self that has recentered Islamic views. Islamic psychologists generally believe, based on historical sources, revelation, and tradition, that the spiritual makeup of man is of four elements- nafs (lower self), ʿaql (rational self), rūḥ (spirit), and the qalb (heart) (Rothman & Coyle, 2018). According to this school of thought, these parts of the self-work together and play a role in one's physical behaviors, manners, and actions. Thus, according to this theory, a being cannot only be physically dis-eased but can also be spiritually dis-eased. It follows that treatment and remedies are not often physical alone, they can also be spiritual (Sudan, 2017).

Most modern thinkers who write about this view of the self use the work of Imam al Ghazzali as a primary source, reference, and authority upon which they base their views. For example, Dr. Laleh Bakhtiar's work, known by some as the mother of Islamic psychology, predated and influenced much of the more recent work on the Qur'ānic psychology of the self and drew heavily on Al Ghazzali (Bakhtiar, 2002; Bakhtiar, 2019). Other thinkers who have drawn on Al-Ghazzali include Rothman and Coyle (2020), Keshavarzi and Haque (2013), and many others, as Al-Ghazzali stands among Muslims as a giant in theories of both theology and the study of the psyche. Rothman and Coyle (2020), in their grounded theory study of Muslim mental health practitioners, state that their findings reflect the influence that Al-Ghazzali's theories had on their study participants and that much of the clinical work being done by Muslims draws on his thinking. Additionally, the work toward building the model of Islamically integrated psychotherapy, including

Traditional Islamically Integrated Psychotherapy (TIIP), pioneered by Dr. Hooman Keshavarzi, Dr. Fahad Khan, and Imam Bilal Ali of the Khalil Center, draws much of its theoretical inspiration from Al-Ghazzali's theories and writings (Keshavarzi, Khan, Ali, & Awaad, 2021).

Al-Ghazzali's understanding of the self, then, is pivotal in the work being done on Islamic psychology, a burgeoning global movement that is based in part on the above-mentioned emphasis on the failure of Western psychology to adequately address the power of the unseen, both within the human person and in the phenomenal and noumenal worlds. Not surprisingly, for a variety of reasons, the work on Islamically integrated models for addiction treatment, in terms of the body of literature available to the public in English, has appeared even more recently than the work on Islamic psychology generally. This recent development can be explained in a variety of ways, not the least of which is the stigma attached to addiction among Muslims, but also the growing awareness among Muslim mental health practitioners that in the face of the raging drug epidemic, Islam and Islamically integrated approaches offer unique and important solutions that have vast potential for alleviating the suffering of a wide range of people.

One of the applications of Al-Ghazzali's work that has appeared in the literature is his concept of the six-stage purification of the self he mentions in the *Mukthasar*, his self-abridgment of his longer work *Revival of the Religious Sciences* (Al-Ghazzali, 2014). This six-stage process includes many pieces which have the potential for drug treatment. However, it is largely unexplored in the literature, partly due to the lack of literature on Islamically integrated drug treatment and partly due to the newness of Islamically integrated psychology generally.

The six stages are as follows:

Musharata ("shart" stipulation): to make a contract or agreement with oneself toward meeting the identified goals.

Muraqabah ("raqab" guard): to guard or reflect over one's actions.

Muhasabah ("hisab" account): to take an ongoing self-account of one's actions.

Muaqabah ("aqabah" punish): to consequent oneself for failing to keep up with the self-agreement or contract.

Mujahadah ("jihād" strive): to strive to overcome the desire of the lower nafs

Muataba ("atab" repent): to regret making an error and vowing not to make the same mistake(s). (Al-Ghazzali, 2014, p. 427-430; Keshavarzi & Haque, 2013, p. 242)

In terms of drug treatment, it becomes readily apparent upon minimal reflection how these stages of self-purification could aid people suffering from addiction in addressing their woes.

RCBT: Religiously Integrated Cognitive Behavioral Therapy

To change direction slightly for a minute, another component of Islamically integrated psychotherapy has been, as the name suggests, the integration of Islam with more Western approaches. It has been increasingly developed in the literature that many Western approaches were actually practiced historically in mental hospitals established by Muslims hundreds of years prior to their inception in Europe and North America. One of these techniques, pioneered by Muslim physicians such as Al-Balkhi, is Cognitive Behavioral Therapy (CBT) (Badri, 2013).

Part of the push in Islamic psychology, aside from incorporating Islamic theology and philosophical models of the self, has been to call for culturally sensitive models of clinical practice. Research has shown in a number of studies that Muslims respond better to interventions that center Muslim identity and reflect an understanding of the core beliefs common to most Muslims (Tanhet & Young, 2022). In light of this, interventions have been assessed as to their congruence with Islamic beliefs, and one of the interventions that has been consistently identified is Cognitive Behavioral Therapy (CBT).

CBT is an evidence-based intervention that was developed

originally by Aaron Beck that was based on the idea that "dysfunctional thinking (which influences the patient's mood and behavior) is common to all psychological disturbances."(Beck, 2011, p. 4) Since Beck pioneered the idea in the 1950s and 60's CBT has been empirically tested with a wide variety of psychological disorders, including depression, anxiety, panic disorder, eating disorders, personality disorders, and substance abuse, to name a few of a lengthy list (Beck, 2011, p. 4). In fact, it seems, according to the research, that there are a few psychological disturbances that do not respond well to CBT. CBT has also been shown to ameliorate a wide range of medical problems with psychological components, including chronic back pain, migraine headaches, insomnia, obesity, hypertension, and many others (Beck, 2011, p. 4).

CBT practice involves the therapist coming up with a cognitive conceptualization of the client and then assisting the client to modify dysfunctional thought patterns in order to change behaviors and emotions. One of the key features of CBT, in contrast to other therapeutic interventions, is its directive and structured nature. From the beginning, CBT is a transparent and intentional collaboration between therapist and client that aims to transform the fundamental way clients frame and perceive their reality quickly and proactively. As part of this transparency, it is a basic belief of CBT practice that is intentional, directive, and structured. Beck describes the logic behind this saying:

Most patients feel more comfortable when they know what to expect from therapy, when they clearly understand what you want them to do, when they feel that you are a team, and when they have a concrete idea of how therapy will proceed, both within a session and over the course of treatment (Beck, 2011, p.1). Many of these features of CBT are uniquely suited to Muslim populations.

The broader movement to develop religiously integrated clinical practice has included the concept of Religiously Integrated CBT (RCBT), a modification of CBT that makes interventions more spiritual and religious in language and orientation (Pearce et al., 2015). Because it is seen as reflecting the preference for directive approaches that many Muslims have named in studies of culturally sensitive clinical interventions for Muslims, a variety of mental health practitioners have explored the potential for RCBT to provide structure for clinical practice by and for Muslims. One well-known example in the literature is the article by Hodge and Nadir (2008) which discusses the possibilities for RCBT with Muslim populations, including suggesting possible modifications, which include Islamic concepts. If we understand CBT as thought modification, changing dysfunctional thoughts towards healthier ones, RCBT makes these modifications within a religious frame.

RCBT as Addiction Treatment Intervention

As stated above, CBT has been shown to be an effective intervention for the treatment of substance use disorders (Morin, Harris, & Conrod, 2014). CBT is most well-known for its use in relapse prevention (RP) (Marlatt & Donovan, 2005; Marlatt & Gordon, 1985). RP has additionally been adapted to Mindfulness Based Relapse Prevention (MBRP), a form of CBT that could easily be understood as RCBT (Bowen, Chawla, & Marlatt, 2010). CBT has also been used to treat substance use disorders through the Community Reinforcement Approach, which was piloted in the 1970s (Hunt & Azrin, 1973), and the Guided Self-Change model (GSC), a form of brief intervention that emphasizes motivational enhancement (Sobell & Sobell, 1993). All of these interventions utilize CBT as their foundational framework.

RCBT has significant potential as a substance use intervention for Muslims. As already mentioned, MBRP is a form of RCBT that utilizes spirituality to reduce the impact of substance use disorders. Interestingly, mindfulness is increasingly appearing in the literature on Islamic approaches to substance use disorders (Mohr, 2022), including the use of dhikr, considered by many Muslims as a form of mindfulness indigenous to Islam, as a spiritual intervention (Raslan, 2021; Rassool, 2021). Additionally, spiritual approaches to change in the literature on Islamically integrated approaches to SUDs often draw on Al-Ghazzali and Islamic psychology's 'ilm-un-nafs and, particularly, jihād-an-nafs (Adisa & Steiner, 2021; Mohr, 2022). That further exploration of these connections holds much promise for Muslim populations is supported by the research that MBRP, in particular, has a positive effect on substance use in people seeking recovery.

MI as an Adjunct to RCBT

One of the challenges of CBT and RCBT is connected to its greatest weakness: it tends towards the therapist having a high degree of control over the therapeutic process and tends to put the therapist in the driver's seat of change with the client somewhat a passenger. For this reason, Motivational Interviewing (MI) is a useful complement to CBT, as it heavily emphasizes clients as the expert on themselves and resists putting the therapist in the role of fixing or changing clients. Pioneered by Miller and Rollnick in the 1980s, MI stresses the importance of partnership, as does CBT, but with the focus on putting the client in control of the process by allowing them to tap into what is seen as the functionality of their intrinsic motivation for change. Miller and Rollnick (2013) state:

MI involves a collaborative partnership with clients, a respectful evoking of their own motivation and wisdom, and a radical acceptance recognizing that ultimately whether change happens is each person's own choice, an autonomy that cannot be taken away no matter how much one might wish to at times (p. viii).

Thus, rather than CBT's emphasis on changing the client, there is a different logic and approach that sees the client as possessing inherent wisdom that needs to be accessed for change to happen.

MI was originally developed as an intervention for SUDs, although it is now used in the treatment of a wide variety of disorders. Additionally, MI has been integrated into CBT models, including the GSC model mentioned above (Morin, Harris, & Conrod, 2014). The positive benefits of the combination of MI and CBT have been tested in a variety of disorders, including anxiety (Randall & McNeil, 2017) and extensively in the treatment of SUDs (Naar & Nafren, 2017). The idea that using a combination of MI and CBT to treat SUDs is a growing field of study and research, and preliminary results show positive benefits for the combined approach that improve outcomes when compared to either approach alone (Naar & Nafren, 2017).

Synthesis of ideas: RCBT, MI, and Al-Ghazzali's Six Stages for Addiction Treatment

The main theoretical contribution this article seeks to make is to bring together several trends, theories, and facts to propose a specific form of intervention that would reflect an Islamically integrated model for the treatment of SUDs. As mentioned above, Al-Ghazzali's theory of the self is central to Islamic psychology. His six stages of personal change represent an actionable model that can be integrated with evidence-based approaches, including RCBT and MI to aid in SUD treatment for Muslim and non-Muslim populations.

The six stages as mentioned above are musharata, muraqabah, muhasabah, muaqabah, mujahadah, and muatabah. As a starting place to integrate MI with this model, the transtheoretical model of the Stages of Change provides interesting insights as it is both a stage-based model, like Al-Ghazzali's, and a central part of the MI approach. The Stages of Change are pre-contemplation, contemplation, preparation, action, and maintenance, and also include a relapse phase (Prochaska & DiClemente, 1983). The basic understanding of the stages of change model is that there is fluidity and movement between the stages and that it is possible to go from one to another rapidly, and that the progression therefore is rarely linear but rather unpredictable and characterized by flux. Likewise, Al-Ghazzali's stages are not always linear but interdependent.

However, this is not to say there is no sense of progression for either model. Al-Ghazzali's model begins with musharata, the idea of an agreement to meet goals. This aligns closely with the idea of preparation. Muraqabah and muhasabah both align well with the action phase, if the comparison is made to substance use treatment, where behavior change begins. Muaqabah aligns well with ideas of relapse prevention, where there is a recommitment to goals. Mujahadah aligns with the overall process of change, and could be present in all stages of change, as reflected in the literature on Islamic approaches to SUDs. Finally, the stage of repentance, or muataba, can be associated with the stage of maintenance, characterized by the ongoing sustained application of earlier work.

The use of RCBT and MI with clients can be integrated with Al-Ghazzali's stages of change. For example, encouraging clients to move past pre-contemplation and contemplation to preparation can utilize the method of contrasting values. In other words, an MI intervention asking clients who are beginning to explore the negative consequences of SUD: "How does this align with your religious
276

values as intoxicants are prohibited?" RCBT intervention could help a client who has low self-efficacy, or powerlessness as a core belief, by suggesting a modification of an automatic thought of inability to change: "I can do anything with God's help."

If the work begins in pre-contemplation or contemplation, it could be a smooth transition to using the six stages with clients. For example, a counselor could write down the six stages on paper and give them to a client as homework. CBT often incorporates homework, and it is one of the emphasized interventions in CBT models. As RCBT the homework could involve journaling on musharata, muraqabah, and so forth. The MI component of the intervention would be to use the open-ended questions, affirmations, reflective listening, and summarization (OARS) of MI to explore the journaling and improve a client's adherence to goals.

The idea of mujahadah, in particular, holds promise for use among Muslim clients in the treatment of SUDs. Literature on addiction recovery has already begun to explore the potential of Al-Ghazzali's concept of *jihād-an-nafs*, and the idea of striving for self-improvement is central to any successful course of treatment for addiction as well as the success and sustainability of sobriety specifically, or recovery more generally (Adisa & Steiner, 2021; Mohr, 2022). The idea of *mujahadah* has been linked in the literature to 12-Step models, but it could also be utilized in conjunction with CBT-focused recovery groups like SMART Recovery or Life Ring. Simply, the idea of working on oneself to better oneself is one of the core concepts of all forms of psychological treatment and as such, extremely useful. This could be incorporated into the treatment of SUDs both by counselors in treatment settings but also by people in recovery on their own, using CBT models like SMART Recovery in conjunction with the idea of mujahadah.

Future Directions

These ideas are entirely in theoretical form. However, CBT and MI lend themselves well to empirical testing, and there is no reason to think that an RCBT/MI approach tailored to Muslims with Al-Ghazzali's six stages would be difficult to test for efficacy. Thus, studies of these ideas would be the logical next step for these theories. Perhaps, beginning with case studies would be possible sooner, and then with larger-scale studies over time, these ideas could become evidence-based, validated interventions that could inform the treatment of SUDs for Muslims and non-Muslims alike.

Conclusion

The six stages of change comprise an elegant intervention for Muslim clients due to their indigeneity to the Islamic tradition, as well as their congruence with evidence-based models for the treatment of SUDs. Utilizing them as a framework for an approach based on RCBT and MI for Muslim clients has immense potential. The prohibition of intoxicants in Islam, as well as the understanding of the self that Islamic psychology proposes, can work together to form a foundation for Islamically integrated treatment of SUDs. Drawing on the theories of self-change that are indigenous to the Islamic tradition, such as those based on Al-Ghazzali's *'ilm-un-nafs* as it is appearing in the literature, can provide new and needed insights that might well be able to reach people that are struggling to find recovery.

References

Adisa, A. & Steiner, J.A. (2021). *Overcoming addiction: An Islamic approach to recovery: 12 Steps for the Muslim & the Muslim Addiction Recovery Program.* Union City, California: Tayba Foundation.

Al-Ghazali. (2014) *Mukthasar: Ihya ulum ad-din.* (Khalaf, M., Ed. and Trans.) Lympia/Nikosia, Cyprus: Spohr Publishers Limited.

Ali, M. (2014). Perspectives on Drug Addiction in Islamic History and Theology. mdpi, 5, 912-928. 10.3390/rel5030912

Andrade, L. F. S., Alcântara, V. C., & Pereira, J. R. (2019). Communication that constitutes and transforms subjects: communicative action in Jürgen Habermas, dialogical action in Paulo Freire and Organizational Studies. *Cadernos EBAPE.BR, 17*(1), 12–24. https://doi.org/10.1590/1679-395164054

Badri, M. B. (1976). *Islam and Alcoholism.* Brentwood, MD: American Trust Publications.

Badri, M.B. (2013). *Abu Zayd al-Balkhi's Sustenance of the Soul: The Cognitive Behavior Therapy of a Ninth Century Physician.* Herndon, VA: International Institute of Islamic Thought

(IIIT).

Bakhtiar, L. (2002). *Al-Ghazzali: His psychology of the greater struggle*. Chicago, IL: Kazi Publications.

Bakhtiar, L. (2019). *Qur'ānic psychology of the self: A textbook on Islamic moral psychology ('ilm al-nafs)*. Chicago, IL: Kazi Publications.

Beck, J.S. (2011). *Cognitive behavior therapy: Basics and beyond* (Second Edition). New York, NY: The Guilford Press.

Bowen, S., Chawla, N., & Marlatt, G. A. (2010). *Mindfulness-Based Relapse Prevention for the Treatment of Substance Use Disorders: A Clinician's Guide*. New York: Guilford Press.

Freire, P. (2001) *Pedagogy of the Oppressed: 30th Anniversary Edition*. New York: Continuum.

Haque, A. & Keshavarzi, H. (2014). Integrating indigenous healing methods in therapy: Muslim beliefs and practices. *International Journal of Culture and Mental Health, 7* (3), 297-314. http://dx.doi.org/10.1080/17542863.2013.794249

Haleem, M. A. (Ed.). (2005). *The Qur'an*. OUP Oxford.

Hodge, D, R, & Nadir A. (2008). Moving toward culturally competent practice with Muslims: modifying cognitive therapy with Islamic tenets. Social Work. *53* (1),31-41. https://doi.org/10.1093/sw/53.1.31

Hunt, G. M., & Azrin, N. H. (1973). A community-reinforcement approach to alcoholism. *Behavior Research and Therapy, 11*(1), 91–104.

Hutton, M., & Heath, T. (2020). Researching on the edge: emancipatory praxis for social justice. *European Journal of Marketing, 54*(11), 2697–2721. https://doi.org/10.1108/EJM-02-2019-0150

Keshavarzi, H & Haque, A. (2013). Outlining a Psychotherapy Model for Enhancing Muslim Mental Health within an Islamic Context. *International Journal for Psychology of Religion, 23*:230–249. https://doi.org/10.1080/10508619.2012.712000

Keshavarzi, H., Khan, F., Ali, B., & Awaad, R. (2021). *Applying Islamic principles to clinical mental health care: Introducing Traditional Islamically Integrated Psychotherapy*. New York, NY: Routledge.

Khashan, A. (2016). The Qur'ān's Prohibition of Khamr (Intoxicants): A Historical and Legal Analysis for the Sake of

Contemporary Islamic Economics. イスラーム界研究: *Kyoto Bulletin of Islamic Area Studies*, 9, 97–112. https://doi.org/10.14989/210344

Louay Fatoohi. (2012). *Abrogation in the Qur'an and Islamic Law*. Routledge.

Marlatt, G. A., & Donovan, D. M. (2005). *Relapse Prevention: Maintenance Strategies in the Treatment of Addictive Behaviors* (2nd ed.). New York: Guilford Press.

Marlatt, G. A., & Gordon, J. R. (Eds.). (1985). *Relapse Prevention: Maintenance Strategies in the Treatment of Addictive Behaviors*. New York: Guilford Press.

Miller, W. R., & Rollnick, S. (2013). *Motivational interviewing: Helping people change* (Third Edition). New York, NY: The Guilford Press.

Mogahed, D. (2021). Substance Abuse and Addiction in the Muslim Community: Facing Stigma and Seeking Support. ISPU. https://www.ispu.org/substance-abuse-and-addiction-in-the-muslim-community/

Mohr, S. (2022). *Loving the present: Sufism, mindfulness, and recovery from addiction and mental illness*. Oregon: Resource Publications.

Morin, J.G., Harris, M., and Conrod P.J. (2014). A review of CBT treatments for substance use disorders. *Oxford Handbook Topics in Psychology*. https://doi.org/10.1093/oxfordhb/9780199935291.013.57

Naar, S. & Nafren, S. A. (2017). *Motivational interviewing and CBT: Combining strategies for maximum effectiveness*. New York, NY: the Guilford Press.

Nasr. S. (2017). *The Study of Qur'ān*. New York, NY: HarperOne.

Pearce, M. et al. (2015). Religiously integrated cognitive behavioral therapy: a new method of treatment for major depression in patients with chronic medical illness. *Psychotherapy*, 52(1), 56–66. https://doi.org/10.1037/a0036448

Prochaska, J. O., & DiClemente, C. C. (1983). Stages and processes of self-change of smoking: Toward an integrative model of change. *Journal of Consulting and Clinical Psychology*, 51(3), 390–395. https://doi.org/10.1037/0022-006X.51.3.390

Randall, C. L., & McNeil, D. W. (2017). Motivational Interviewing as an Adjunct to Cognitive Behavior Therapy for Anxiety

Disorders: A Critical Review of Literature. *Cognitive and behavioral practice*, *24*(3), 296–311. https://doi.org/10.1016/j.cbpra.2016.05.003

Raslan, M.S. (2021). *The danger of personal drug abuse: Addiction and the breakdown of society*. Imran, A. (Trans). USA: Muktabaturlirshad Publications.

Rassool, G.H. (2021). *Mother of all evils: Addictive behaviors from an Islamic perspective*. Islamic Psychology Publishing.

Razak, M. A. A., & Haneef, S. S. S. (2017). The spiritual dimension of man: An Islamic psycho-spiritual study. *International Journal of Islamic Thoughts (IJITs)*, *6*(2).

Rothman, A., & Coyle, A. (2018). Toward a framework for Islamic psychology and psychotherapy: An Islamic model of the soul. *Journal of religion and health*, *57*(5), 1731-1744.

Sahu, K. K., & Sahu, S. (2012). Substance abuse causes and consequences. *Bangabasi Academic Journal*, *9*(12), 52-59.

Sobell, M. B., & Sobell, L. C. (1993). *Problem Drinkers: Guided Self-Change Treatment*. New York: Guilford Press.

Sudan, S. A. (2017). Principles of Islamic counseling and psychotherapy. *Asian Journal of Management Sciences & Education*, *6*(3), 129-138.

Tanhan, A., & Young, J.S. (2022). Muslims and Mental Health Services: A Concept Map and a Theoretical Framework. *Journal of Religion and Health*, *61*, 23–63. https://doi.org/10.1007/s10943-021-01324-4

Usmani, M.T. (1998). *The Authority of the Sunnah*. Karachi, Pakistan: Kitab Bhavan.

Utz, A. (2011). *Psychology from the Islamic perspective*. International Islamic publishing house.

Quotes from the Qur'ān are drawn from M.A.S. Haleem, A. (2005). *The Qur'an: A New Translation*. Oxford, UK: Oxford University.

CHAPTER ELEVEN

HEALING WITH THE DIVINE NAMES IN THERAPY

Halima Krausen and Rabia Malik

Introduction

In the Sufi tradition, the Divine Names have often been used as practices (Wazifa's) for students on the path. A Divine Name or cluster of Divine Names would be prescribed by the Sheikh or Sheikha as practice to awaken the student's consciousness of God as well as for inner reflection and self-knowing. There are numerous guidebooks with descriptions of the meanings contained within the Names and their potential effects, such as, Al Gazali (1995), Tosun Bayrak (2001). A more recent guidebook by Meyer, Hyde, Muqaddam, Kahn (2011) called Physicians of the Heart is particularly useful in the contemporary context and will be drawn upon in this chapter. It explores in depth both the psychological and spiritual dimensions of the meanings and effects of the Divine Names.

The Divine Names have also started to be used in the therapeutic context by Muslim clinicians. Here they may serve the foremost purpose of psychological growth but also hold the potential for openings to spiritual growth. Depending on what the client is struggling with, attention can be drawn to certain Divine Qualities to explore the client's relationship with these Qualities within themselves and in relationship with God. This can help reveal the individual's experiences as well as blocks and personal limitations in relating to these Divine Qualities and to God in general. This awareness of one's blocks and our own helplessness can be a gateway for turning to God with sincerity and calling upon God's Grace. Meyer et al. (2011) stress that it is important for there to be integration of both the psychological and spiritual dimensions of this process. It is as important to become aware of the typically wounded and alienated state of our ego structures and our identification with this falsely constructed idea of the self (in other words, our personality structure) as it is to become aware of our deeper spiritual essence and potential, and thereby our relationship with the Divine.

This chapter that explores the therapeutic use of the Divine Names is jointly written by Rabia Malik, a psychotherapist based in the UK, and Halima Krausen, a religious scholar and Sheikha based in Germany. Rabia first encountered a more in-depth exploration of the Divine Names in a workshop with Halima and then proceeded to work with her individually to explore them more systematically over a number of years and subsequently started to use them in her therapeutic practice. In this chapter, Halima will provide a theological overview of the Divine Names and their relevance for our self-understanding and our understanding of God. Rabia will then illustrate their therapeutic potential through a case example particularly drawing on the Divine Qualities of Mercy and Forgiveness. We will then conclude with some general pointers, recommendations, and important considerations for practitioners on how the Divine Names can be applied in therapeutic practice.

Qur'ānic References and Theological Considerations of the Divine Names

The Qur'ānic account of the creation and purpose of the human being is expressed in Baqarah 2: 29-34. "And Lo Thy Sustainer said unto the angel: Behold I am about to establish upon earth one who shall inherit it" They said: "Wilt Thou place on it such as will spread corruption thereon and shed blood – whereas it is we who extoll Thy limitless glory, and praise Thee, and hallow Thy name?" (God) answered: "Verily I know that which you do not know." And he imparted unto Adam the names of all things, then he brought them within the ken of the angels and said: "Declare unto Me the names of these (things), if what you say is true." They replied: "Limitless art Thou in Thy glory! No knowledge have we save that which Thou has imparted unto us. Verily Thou alone art all-knowing, truly wise." Said He: "O Adam, convey unto them the names of these (things)." And as soon as (Adam) had conveyed unto them their names, (God) said: "Did I not say unto you, 'Verily I alone know the hidden reality of the heavens and earth, and know all that you bring into the open and all that you would conceal?" And when we told the angels, "Prostrate yourself before Adam!' – they all prostrated themselves, save Iblis who refused and glorified in his arrogance: and thus, he became one of those who deny the truth." (Asad, 2003)

These verses raised different questions for the commentators, ranging from a literal approach to various philosophical and mystical perspectives. The simplest explanation is that Adam, meaning Man, is taught the Names of all existing things or, by implication, language, and conceptual thought. Going one step further and considering the etymology of the word *Ism*, name, which ultimately means personal name, title, and noun, including concepts like the qualities that are expressed in the Divine Names in the Qur'an. A name is thus a means to know something or someone. It alludes to the meaning behind the name, thus opening the way for a relationship. The conclusion from this is that Adam is taught the Divine Names as a way to cultivate a live relationship with the Divine which would ultimately enable him to be a vicegerent on earth.

In systematic theology, traditions from the Prophet Muhammad are considered. He said, "Let your character be as the characteristics of

God Most High", and "God Most High has such-and-such characters", and "he who is characterized by one of them enters paradise". They seem to indicate a more existential connection between the human and the Divine than a mere relationship between the Source of all Being and the cognizant subject. This is expressed in statements like the one by Ibn Arabi (Chittick 1994) who teaches that Adam was created upon the form of the Names and was capable of knowing the Divine Names in a way that the angels did not. In other words, the essence and possibility for full knowledge of the Names is implanted in Adam. A similar thought is expressed more systematically by Al-Ghazali (1995) who points out how each of the traditional 99 most beautiful Divine Names corresponds to a human potential, which is essential for humans to relate to that quality. He recommends meditating on these names, safeguarding against too much anthropomorphism, however, with a warning that there is still an essential difference between the divine and human quality, which is limited in time, space, and scope. Applying this to creation in general, Jalaluddin Rumi finds a poetic expression: "Know that the world of created beings is like clear water, reflecting the Divine Attributes. Their knowledge, justice, kindness, and patience reflect God's, like the heavenly star is reflected in running water. The water flowing in the stream changes many times, but the reflection of the moon and the star in the water remains the same" (Mathnawi Book 6 – 3172).

In connection with the tradition, "Those who know themselves know their Lord," various ways of theologically reflected introspection and self-exploration have been developed in later mystical traditions. Traditionally, the Divine Names are taught in the context of supplication. For example, concerned about one's livelihood, one would call upon God as *ar-Razzaq*, the Provider; searching for guidance or knowledge, one would use the names *al-'Alim*, the Knowing, or *al-Hakim*, the Wise; when forgiveness is sought, it would be with names like *al-Ghaffur* or *ar-Rahim*, etc.

Some scholars objected to looking at the existential connection between God and human from the standpoint of similarity in general, stressing God's incomparability and saying that it is enough to worship God "bila kayfa", without asking how (God is), and discouraging people from asking such questions. However, this is not a satisfactory solution for the human urge to ask about deeper meanings and truths and the existential questions which are closely connected with one's self-esteem and ethical value system and which are, on the other hand, closely connected with one's concept of the Divine: The questions of origin, destination, and the meaning of life. Thus, theology cannot simply be a definition of a binding concept of God (*Aqidah*) but must include any attempt to express the complex relationship with the Source of Being that leaves space for a healthy self-image and self-assessment. Harm can be done by narrowing it down to concepts of divine will, power, and control without considering the reassuring aspects of divine mercy, justice, and care. These latter qualities become particularly necessary in the therapeutic context, where people often come because they have suffered injustice, been wounded, and their faith shattered. Therapy can be a liminal space for transformation, where clients come in existential crisis, disorientated, and in an ambiguous state in need of re-assessing the beliefs they take for granted and the outcomes they had hoped for.

Case example

In the following snapshots, Rabia will reflect on the application of the Divine Names in therapy with a client she will refer to as "S". The case study is an amalgamation of different cases. Elements have been disguised to obscure the client's identity and ensure confidentiality.

Ya Rahman

"S" was a professional woman in her 30's of Pakistani origin who had gone through a separation after two years of marriage. Although she was disappointed and still angry about the separation, she was especially hurt by how alone she felt and let down by friends and family, whose initially sympathetic response was soon followed by impatience and dismissiveness, telling her to get on with her life and have faith and pray. She felt alone and that no one understood her grief and pain.

"S" described herself as coming from a broken home – her father left her mother when she was ten. Her mother had been distraught by the divorce but threw herself into her work, and the family had become disengaged and fragmented. "S's" teenage years had felt lonely, and she described a parental void at home. She turned to the outside world of friends to find some connection and, after a rebellious stage, returned to her faith later in life.

"S" now lived away from her mother but still visited her and still craved understanding and comfort from her. In one session, she recalled saying to her mother, 'You never just ask me how I am'? Her mother had responded by launching into a tirade about how awful things had been for her and how she had managed on her own. "S" would cry when recalling these episodes but would then wipe her tears and say, "I can't expect her to be different". "S" coped by carrying on with her work, which was in the health care profession, but would lament feeling burnt out and that nobody cared for her.

In one particular session, where S again recalled another episode where her mother had met her cry for help with anger and beratement, Rabia encouraged her to stay with her sadness and longing and used guided meditation and embodied processing therapy techniques to explore the layers and underlying roots of her woundedness. Rabia asked her to close her eyes and allow herself to feel her despair, noticing where she felt it in her body and recalling any memories that came up in association with those feelings and physical sensations. She said she felt a deep sadness in her chest and heart and remembered the day her father left her mother. How her mother had run behind him to try and stop him, but he had driven away. As we worked through her feelings and focused on deepening her breathing by breathing from her stomach, her emotions began to regulate, and her state became calmer. Rabia asked if there was anything from this calmer, more grounded she wanted to say to her distraught and deeply hurt self. She said she should not take it personally and that her mother and family were not capable of responding to her emotional needs; instead, she should rely on and turn to God. After the guided meditation, Rabia asked "S" if she had tried turning to God. She started crying and said she felt God did not like her and was mocking her and wondered whether He would really help or let her down, too.

Drawing on Qur'anic verses, Rabia talked to her about how God is Most Merciful and that His compassion is repeatedly emphasized (Qur'ān, 6:54). However, she pointed out that it can be hard for us to imagine God's compassion when we have not experienced compassion from others in our life, and how we often project that unto God, especially experiences we have had of our parents. Rabia suggested that between now and the next session, she try to do *dhikr* and meditate on the Divine Quality of *Rahmah* (Mercy) and notice what it brings up. Dhikr, meditation on the Divine Names, is traditionally done through loud or silent repetition of one of the Names, evoking that Quality and remembering God and our essential Self. The Divine Name can also be held in a contemplative way. Using what she had learned from exploring the Divine Names with Halima, Rabia suggested to "S" that she could reflect on 1. Her experience of compassion from others and towards others, 2. Towards herself, and 3. From God.

"S" started the next session by saying she had tried to do the homework task on *Ya Rahman but* found it hard. She felt so exhausted that it was hard to connect with herself and God at times. She was struggling during the past week as she had hurt her back but noticed that even when she was feeling pain, she kept working and was always pushing herself to keep going. She realized that she never felt *Rahmah* from her mother. It became apparent that her mother had never played a containing role with her and was emotionally hardened. In a frustrated tone, she proclaimed – 'so what, I can't change my parents or my history – what can I do?'. Rabia noticed the tinge of defensiveness and harshness in her voice and pointed out that it is probably this inner voice that kept pushing her and telling her to get on with it. She wondered where this came from and whether "S" was ever able to show kindness, *Rahmah*, to herself. "S" knew the internal voice was just like her mother's voice. She realized she coped by being hard on herself when she was sad, just as her mother did to her. It was hard for her to connect with Rahmah for herself.

At this point in the midst of "S's" frustration, Rabia focused on her own breath, slowing things down and trying to connect with and hold space for Ya Rahman in a quite gentle inward way.

After a few moments of silence, "S" recalled that something touching had in fact, happened whilst doing the Dhikr on *Ya Rahman*. She had bumped into a friend and told her how exhausted she had been feeling and that she didn't feel like cooking. That evening, to her surprise, her friend had turned up with a meal for her that she had prepared. She was touched by this act of kindness. It had brought tears to her eyes as she felt her friend had felt her sadness and need, which "S" was always trying to cover up by being strong. Rabia pointed out to "S" that what her friend did could be a sign of Ya Rahman.

Rabia helped "S" become more aware of God's nearness and intimacy. Feeling this nearness and intimate *Rahmah* - Mercy, softened "S" and enabled her to become more merciful towards herself and others. This softening helped her face with compassion the deep underlying wound of her sadness and her mother's sadness, thus allowing things to start to heal. By learning to accept all of her states with compassion, "S" started to understand and learn from them rather than working so hard to push them away.

Analysis

"S" learned from her mother to push her way through life. Her parents' separation had been traumatic for her, and she had taken responsibility for her mother's sadness. Her mother had never been able to process her own sadness as she had not had a compassionate support system around her. She was socially shunned for being a divorced woman. She had coped and survived by becoming emotionally hardened, even towards her own daughter. This pattern continued to be perpetuated by "S", who was now going through her own separation from her husband. Moreover, "S" projected her self-loathing onto God, leading her to feel that God didn't like her and would let her down.

Meyer et al. (2011) suggest that there are two major wounds that the ego bears, and the way we defend and adapt to these wounds coalesce into our personality structure and patterns that then repeat through life. The first major wound of humiliation or shame is caused by our relationships with other humans, primarily our caregivers and family. Children are often left with a sense of self-blame by taking it upon themselves to fulfill, out of a sense of loyalty, what was lacking in their parents. This can be seen in "S's" case, where the underlying wound is from her father's and mother's traumatic separation and her taking on the feeling of responsibility for her mother. "S's" and her mother's compulsive hard work was driven by a lack of self-worth.

Rizzuto (1981), in her book, the *Birth of the Living God*, gives a psychoanalytic view of how the representation of God is affected by the child's relationship with their father and mother and significant early objects. Meyer et al. (2011) suggest this identification with our sense of self-deficiency that arises from our early experiences with our caregivers actually isolates and separates us from relating to others and blocks us from relating to God. The second deeper layer of wounding they propose is experienced as being caused by our relationship with God. There is a feeling that you have been abandoned by God. This can be clearly seen when "S" says she wants to connect to God but feels God doesn't like her and is mocking her. We often project our experiences onto God, and our woundedness separates us further form the Divine source. The Qur'ān stresses again and again God's Mercy. We begin again and again with the *Bismillah* – In the Name of God, the Most Compassionate, the Most Merciful. Yet many people don't feel connected to God's *Rahmah*.

The Arabic root R-H-M for *Rahmah,* is connected with the meaning of womb and motherly love. An unconditional container that provides and nourishes us to enable the growth of the embryo. When our experiences of others, and of our mothers in particular, who in fact should be our first experience of Rahmah, are not so Merciful because of their own wounding, then it can obstruct our faith in God's Mercy. Meyer et al. (2011) in *Physicians of the Heart* give the following description of Al Rahman.

Ar Rahman is endless love. It is the infinite, unconditional reality of love. God's essence necessarily includes this quality of love. *Ar-Rahman* might be imagined as the inner self of God, an infinite container that is incredibly compassionate, kind, and tender. It is the sun of loving compassion that is endlessly shining. *Ar-Rahman* includes all the other divine Names. It is the source of all: it is the gate that opens into all God's qualities and an inner secret of each one. The root meaning comes from the word Rahm, 'womb'. In human beings, this quality is naturally felt in relation to pregnancy. Allah provides human beings a womb to be born into and through which to have the realization of the love that is at the very foundation of all that exists. Invocation of *Ya Rahman* is a healing remedy for all who feel disconnected from God and for those marked by a wound of self-loathing.

This Loving Mercy is what enables our ability to 'be with', to tolerate and integrate our experiences, to learn, heal, and grow. It was important for "S", in spite of the lack of *Rahmah* that she felt from her mother, to experience her call for God's Mercy being answered through her friend. Such events, in the context of doing *dhikr* of the Divine Names, increase our faith in a benevolent universe and in a God who is responsive to our needs. They also increase our trust in others, and they increase our faith in our interconnectedness with God. We come to trust that He Hears and Sees us. It was also symbolic that kindness came in the form of food, which fulfills a basic need and becomes an embodied experience. The *Rahmah* was literally tasted. This experience provided an opening that could be built upon, enabling "S" to develop compassion for herself and to trust in God's Compassion.

There is growing awareness and some excellent work being done on the importance of Compassion in healing by therapists such as Tara Brach (2020), who comes from the Buddhist tradition and has devised a technique called RAIN. An acronym for Recognize, Accept, Inquire and Nurture. Also, Gabor Mate, who uses Compassionate Enquiry in working with trauma (2018). Both stress that self-compassion is needed to help process and integrate painful feelings and traumatic experiences to release underlying false beliefs and shame that keep people locked in harmful patterns. Compassion is a quality that is stressed in all religions, and so these approaches also fit nicely with the Islamic framework. However, using the Arabic terms such as Al Rahman for Mercy make it even more resonant for Muslim clients as it resonates with daily practices and prayers. Also, the Arabic etymology of Mercy and its connection with the word for womb creates particular images that can be helpful and resonant, and so these techniques can be modified and developed further to fit with the psyche of Muslim clients. In addition, in our approach, we encourage the client to call upon the Divine Source, and we draw on the network of 99 Names and Qualities of God that are rooted in the Islamic framework and cosmology.

Ya Ghafūr

As the course of the work unfolded and after some months "S" and her husband resumed contact and had begun talking to see if they could reconcile. She wanted to work on their relationship, but she felt so let down by him and was struggling to forgive him for some of the things that went wrong in their relationship and that she held against him. He had acknowledged the wrong he had done to her and had tried to change things, but every time she was triggered by him, her hurtful feelings would resurface. She felt that these feelings were holding her back from moving forward with their relationship. I told her about the names of Allah for forgiveness and how it was interesting that there were three Divine Names associated with forgiveness. Al Ghaffār – the one who forgives again and again, Al Ghafūr – the one who forgives to the essence, or in other words, to the underlying heart of the matter and Al 'Awfu – who wipes away the traces.

Rabia suggested to "S" that they try a meditation using guided imagery to see what comes up. After talking her through relaxation, Rabia asked her to recall her relationship with her husband and focus on what she felt and where she felt the pain in her body. "S" located it in her heart. Rabia asked her to focus on the pain in her heart and to let whatever memories and feelings that emerged in association with it come up. She cried as she recalled the many times that she felt on her own and disconnected from her husband. She felt she couldn't be vulnerable to him and always had to be strong. In particular, she recalled how she had miscarried and felt her husband was not there for her in her grief. I asked her to recite the names *Ya Ghafūr, Ya Raheem* and imagine them as a healing balm for her wound. After a few minutes, Rabia could observe her crying receding and her state calming as her distress decreased. Rabia then asked her to do diaphragm breathing more deeply into her stomach and allow whatever other memories came up to come up from a deeper place within. "S" said she saw her dad leaving her mother and how distraught her mother was. "S" also felt distraught and abandoned by her father but felt she had to be strong for her mother, who was emotionally broken. She saw that ten-year-old girl who vowed to be strong and never let herself be so desperate for a man. Rabia asked her to be with that little girl and sit beside her and asked her to tell her younger self whatever she wanted to tell her as the woman she is now. "S" told her younger self that it was ok, it was not her fault, and that she didn't need to be strong for everyone else. It was ok to cry and be sad, and her parents had their own difficulties that they couldn't overcome. After some more deep breathing, Rabia asked her to visualize her father and her husband before her and to really look at them, noticing how she felt. "S" said she felt a deep sadness for them and for herself and for all their failings. Rabia then asked her to turn away from them and see if she could feel herself turn toward God's light and let that light shine unto her face and body. Over the next few minutes staying with this visualization, Rabia could see "S's" state visibly change, the sadness dissipated, and she seemed lighter. Rabia then asked "S" to turn back towards the men in her life and to tell her what she saw now. She said she saw herself and her husband standing on Jabal Al Rahmah (where they had been on Haj), and she felt more compassion and openness towards him from a place of strength and that they were both held in God's Mercy. Finally, Rabia asked her what she would want to say to her husband now, and she said, 'Be my partner, help me, I need you, I want to love you'.

Analysis

The theme of forgiveness frequently comes up in therapeutic work. People are often told from a religious perspective that they 'should forgive' (Qur'ān, 42:40), and while it is no doubt beneficial, it is a delicate process of learning and letting go that should not come from a place of suppression or be forced. The verse in the Qur'ān, where Adam and Eve ask for forgiveness, suggests a conscious awareness of their mistake (Qur'ān, 7:23). Each person needs to become aware of their responsibility eventually. "S's" husband had accepted some responsibility for the ways that he had let her down, but she was finding it hard to let go and forgive him, especially when she was re-triggered by his behavior. Meyer et al. (2011) have a chapter on the Family of Divine Forgiveness in *Physicians of the Heart*, where they describe how the three Divine Names for forgiveness correspond to three progressively deeper levels of forgiveness. They suggest that *Al Ghaffār* has a continuous and repetitive quality, and in accordance with this, God forgives us again and again. Likewise, in relationships, we are often required to forgive one another again and again. Whereas *Al Ghafūr* has a quality of penetrating right into the essence of a thing. Meyer et al. (2011) describe it as,

> *Al-Ghafūr* is the essence of forgiveness because it reveals the depth of the divine heart. *Al Ghafūr* means to forgive all the way into the deepest possible place, all the way to the ground floor. It

is divine forgiveness that penetrates into the most repressed secrets in our hearts. Its presence allows us to accept that there is forgiveness even for the worst crime we have ever committed in our life, or the worst crime ever done to us. P 51

During the guided meditation, "S" got closer to the essence of what hurt her most when she recalled feeling let down by her husband when she miscarried. Deeper still, she recalled the hurt from her father leaving her mother and then even deeper, realizing that her parents' breakup was not her fault and that she did not need to compensate for it by being strong for her mother. Slowly, through this process, a greater capacity for self-compassion was being awakened in her. Then, utilizing an image from Meyer et al.'s chapter (2011), where they describe *tawbah* as turning away from perceived defects and shadows to face Divine perfection, Rabia suggested to "S" that she face God's light before turning back toward her father and husband, with whom she was hurt and angry. Rabia was struck by the image that emerged of her and her husband standing on the mount of *Jabal Al Rahmah* – a highly symbolic place of the reunion of Adam and Eve and all souls on the Muslim Pilgrimage, the Hajj. By turning away from the shadow and towards God, the compassion that arose in her was through God and not her own ego. This is important because when we forgive from our ego, it is from a partial position and place of our limited understanding. But when we call on God to forgive us, it is from a vaster position of the Most Compassionate. By "S" feeling held in God's Mercy and Forgiveness, she was able to move beyond the cycle of blame and express her need for connection and desire for love with her husband.

Steps for practice.

1. Exploring underlying psychology: We suggest that it is important to first uncover and explore the underlying wounding the clients bring and the overlying ego structure, defenses, and patterns that are particular to them in order to avoid spiritual bypassing in calling upon the Divine Names. This engagement is vital for the client to feel understood and to instigate the process of healing. Various mainstream approaches are useful for this. In particular, embodied processing techniques (such as somatic experiencing (Levine, 2010; Van Der Kolk, 2015) are useful for uncovering multi-layers of

wounding, as well as inner child work and guided imagery meditations using the breath to regulate and ground the process. Peter Levine (2008) points out how the breath regulates our autonomic nervous system, and this can help us access our deeper or true self. In the Islamic framework, it can help us connect to the Nafs al Mutmainah. This can be seen in the above snapshots when as the process deepens and "S" is encouraged to breathe more deeply from her abdomen and to ground, her insights gain clarity and more objectivity. In *Physicians of the Heart,* Meyer et al (2011) suggest that this uncovering of our wounding and defenses can bring us to an awareness of our own helplessness in the patterns that we compulsively play out and live and prepare us to turn to God in sincere surrender, calling out in need.

Now it is possible to draw more specifically on the Islamic framework and the practice of doing *dhikr* of the Divine Names.

2. Calling Upon God by choosing a Divine Name: Through the exploration of this preliminary process the client becomes more receptive and open, and a Divine Name may emerge spontaneously for the client and or therapist that feels like a quality that is needed to heal and reset the balance. In the first snapshot "S" from a more regulated place realizing her family's limitations in meeting her needs, spontaneously said she wanted to connect more with God. The quality of Mercy, *Rahmah* is generally a good place to start from and is emphasized as a key quality of the Divine. Yet this quality is also very often distorted by a more judgmental and fearful notion of God. In the second snapshot *Ya Ghaffur* felt called for, as "S" tried to work through and let go of her underlying wounds triggered by her relationship with her husband.

The therapist can encourage the client to call upon God sincerely to remove the blocks and limits they face by focusing on such Divine Qualities. Through *Dhikr* – remembrance and reconnection with the Divine Source.

3. Dhikr: There are numerous studies emerging on the benefits of dhikr for treating stress, anxiety, and mental health (Nosrati et al., 2021 provide a systematic review of studies).

In the Qur'ān, it says, 'Remember Me and I will remember you.' (2: 152)

Through the practice of *dhkir,* the recollection of God and our soul-nature is activated, and the Divine Name can be drawn into our most wounded places like a healing balm.

Wardah Abbas (2020), in her article on: "How *dhikr* transformed my body and mind", describes *dhikr* as, *Dhikr* literally means "*remembrance*". In Islamic spirituality, dhikr is known as the "Way of the Heart". It is a collective word for several acts of Islamic meditation and worship that transcend the self and the ego-mind and links with the Eternal, beyond time and space. Its objective is the state of pure consciousness, awareness, and presence. *Dhikr* takes many forms; *shukr* (gratitude), *du'a* (supplication), *istigfar* (forgiveness), *Tadabbur* (reflection), *salah* (prayer), *tasbih* (glorification), amongst several others. Using the divine power of *dhikr,* believers shift from mind-based mindfulness to heart-based consciousness, from ego to soul, and thus from confusion and conflict to presence and peace. Through the divine power of *dhikr,* human beings cultivate independence and so reclaim their natural and divine state of security, peace, and confidence, potentially reaching higher levels of spiritual existence.

Dhikr can involve silent or loud repetition of a Divine Name or Names, and clients could be asked to do this regularly to invoke this Quality and to increase their awareness of it in their lives. We also find it helpful to ask them to do *Tadabbur (reflection)* on their: 1. Personal experience of the Divine Quality in relation to others and life experiences 2. How they experience and live this Divine Quality from within themselves, and 3. In relation to God. This process of reflection can reveal their personal experiences and assumptions and increase their yearning and need for God's Grace. If appropriate, the therapist could also ask the client to hold the Divine Name during guided meditation, such as in Snapshot 2 when Rabia asked the client to repeat and hold the names *Ya Ghaffur, Ya Raheem* as she processed her inner wounds.

4. Healing through God's Grace: When the client is not defensive and is brought to a place of surrender – God's Grace can enter. Meyer et al. (2011) point out that, through reconnection to the Divine Source, we can realize the ego's stubbornness in clinging to a fixed idea of itself as isolated and deficient. And through this reconnection, we can

connect to the constant flow of Divine power, coming into influx with the natural generative motion of being and becoming (p 14-15). It is important that the therapist be aware that this process of calling upon the Divine Names is not in their control and to be open to the mystery that unfolds, trusting in what is given by God's Grace. By calling upon God, we call upon a force for change that is more holistic and much vaster than our identification with our ego structure and beyond our comprehension. Having processed underlying wounds and patterns, hopefully, the client is more open and receptive to this and able to turn in their need to God, trusting in his Mercy. This is where our approach varies from more secular-based approaches. From the perspective of the Islamic framework, it is God who heals (Qur'ānic verse 26:79-80). The healing that occurs through God's Grace may work in unexpected ways. In the second snapshot, when "S" is asked to turn to God's Light before returning to her relationships and the men she felt hurt by, she is then enabled to ask for forgiveness of the whole and to see her own and the other's part in the process. An image comes up for her of being reunited with her husband on *Jabal Al Rahma* – The Mountain of Mercy. This highly symbolic place of meeting of souls resonates on a deeper psychological and spiritual level.

Practice Considerations

These snapshots from a case example illustrate how the relationship with God has immense healing potential. While God's essence is incomparable and unknowable to us, the Divine can be experienced. In the Qur'an, it says, "And if My servants ask Thee about Me- behold, I am near; I respond to the call of him who calls, whenever he calls unto Me: let them, then, respond unto Me, and believe in Me, so that they might follow the right way." (2:186)

We can experience something of the Divine Qualities as we also have some human experiences with these qualities. Al Ghazali (1995) says that the potential for all the Divine Names is in each human being; they are like seeds – some of which will sprout and others that won't, all be it in a limited way relative to the Divine in time and space.

Helminski (2020) describes how when the human being remembers God through the Divine Names, it is like opening a channel that inspires glimmers of meanings and feelings contained in each Name. This becomes a lived experience rather than a merely conceptual understanding. He stresses that there is a mystery in the Divine Names. Each Name is imbued with a force and Divine Intelligence that works through us, and that unfolds through dhikr and practice, and thereby the self may become spiritualized (p154-155).

In the context of therapy, the Divine Names can primarily help gain psychological insight, connecting clients with themselves and reflecting their own experiences and habitual patterns regarding specific qualities, such as compassion or forgiveness.

However, they can also give a taste of a deeper connection with God and spiritual insight, which may facilitate breaking out of more limited habitual egoic patterns, re-balancing, and healing. It is important that the opening to draw on the Divine Names, emerges organically from the therapeutic work: either the clients' inclination or wish to connect with God or intuitive inspiration from the practitioner that a certain Divine Quality may be useful or called for, rather than be imposed by the practitioner.

For the practitioner to use the Divine Names authentically, effectively, and ethically, it is important for them to have first explored working with at least some Divine Names themselves under spiritual guidance. This enables them to understand the process of doing dhikr and meditating on a particular Name or Names over a period and appreciate how it can work in psychological and mysterious, and spiritually powerful ways. The spiritual teacher can help guide the practitioner to Names that may be personally resonant for them or for healing more generally. The Divine Names are generally classified into two categories – Jamal, Names of Beauty, and Jalal, Names of Majesty. The Jamal Names can be more safely used for therapeutic purposes as they tend to stress God's immanent and intimate Qualities. These are especially useful in healing and helping build a more trusting relationship with God. *Ya Rahman* is particularly useful in the therapeutic encounter for both practitioner and client as it is essential in the therapeutic relationship and is a good antidote to many clients' pervasive ideas about a punitive God. As stated earlier, *Ya Rahman is* also emphasized in the Qur'ān (6:54).

The Jalal Names – tend to refer to the transcendent and powerful Qualities and need to be used more cautiously.

Chittick's (1994) guidance is helpful here when he stresses that, according to Ibn Arabi, the goal is not to acquire God's attributes for ourselves but to negate our own egocentric attributes. The human being does not come to rival God. On the contrary, his / her self-image is gradually reduced in stature until there is nothing left of his / her egoic desires. Since nothing belongs to them in the first place, once they eliminate their own attributes and efface their own self, they can become a channel for God's attributes. Thus, the greater spiritual awareness the practitioner has, and the more they are able to efface their ego, the greater healing capacity they have. Also, the more practiced they are in meditation, the more they can hold a meditative space for the client. If the client is open to doing loud or silent dhikr, the practitioner may want to show them how to do it and practice this with them. Again, though caution needs to be urged here as the client may feel intimidated and overwhelmed by this practice and as it may cross therapeutic boundaries and create confusion around the practitioner's role, we propose offering a brief introduction to the client to loud or silent dhikr if it seems appropriate for the client. Or the client can connect to the Name in a more meditative way – holding the Name with an inquiring mind and using reflective questions outlined in the section above. This way, the client can practice what they are comfortable with.

It is imperative that the practitioner use the Divine Names ethically and responsibly, as they are powerful. Any practice done in God's Name confers a greater responsibility and, if misused, becomes especially abusive. This is also why it is important for the practitioner to undergo some spiritual training in working with the Divine Names to ensure humility and to develop discernment so that they do not get carried away with their imagination and develop an awareness of how the ego easily inflates and can be in danger of appropriating spiritual experience. The practitioner should, therefore, only use Divine Names that they have had some experience with. They needn't have worked through all the Names but can draw on the guidance of the spiritual teacher and expand their repertoire as and when certain Divine Names manifest in work with clients. As the practitioner's experience and repertoire with the Divine Names increases, they will become better at intuitively identifying what Divine Qualities manifest in the therapeutic work or being called into manifestation.

The limitations of this approach are mainly that if it is imposed on the client and does not resonate for them or does not feel meaningful. In our experience, though, clients often have a deep yearning for connection with God and feeling loved and closer to Him. This strengthens them to face some of the hardships and blocks in their lives. Facing the blocks can, however, be painful and frustrating and may seem like an impenetrable wall. This is why it is important for the practitioner to be strong in their faith and have some personal experience with this process so that they can hold faith in the Divine Source and Qualities and be patient with the unfolding process. If the practitioner does not have this kind of containing, holding, supportive faith, then the practice could turn into a more didactic teaching, which loses its experiential and mysterious emergent quality, which connects the client experientially and autonomously to God as opposed to centering on the practitioner. Most importantly, though, the practitioner needs to remember that their role is primarily a psychological one and that this practice of working with the Divine Names should not form a kind of spiritual bypass that helps the client avoid their painful life experiences and to turn to God as a form of wishful thinking. We would argue that it is by working through the psychological processes and blocks that the spiritual openings that emerge may be integrated into people's lived experiences.

Conclusion

The Divine Names are a deep ocean to explore. In this chapter, we have focused primarily on the deeper psychological self-understanding they can bring us in relation to the Divine as opposed to the vast metaphysical and spiritual dimensions. Any attempt to express the human relationship with the Divine Source of Being is also the basis for the person's self-image and self-assessment regarding their capabilities, task and ontological position, and ethical system of relations to others, which is psychologically revealing and often reflects our image of God. At the same time, calling upon God and the Divine Force in a state of helplessness, surrender, and receptivity can take us beyond our limited egoic self and bring profound change and healing. The lived experience of these dynamic Divine Qualities can bring us personally closer to God, enhancing our love for Him and His creation. Building trust in God, as a God who Sees and Hears us and is Near to us (Qur'ān, 20:46) and is overwhelmingly Merciful (Qur'ān, 6:54, 7:151), is an invaluable therapeutic resource that can help us find meaning in the struggles of life. After all, the Qur'an states that Adam was taught the names by God, suggesting an ability to understand deeper meanings and a knowing taught to Adam by the Divine and therefore is within the human potential (verse).

References

Asad, M. (2003) *The Message of the Qur'ān*. Bristol: The Book Foundation.

Brach, T. (2020) *Radical Compassion: learning to Love Yourself and Your World with the practice of RAIN*. London: Penguin Random House.

Burrell, D., Dahir, N. (1995) *Al Ghazali – The Ninety-Nine Beautiful Names of God*. Cambridge. Islamic Texts Society.

Chittick, W. (1994) *Imaginal Worlds: Ibn al-Arabi and the Problem of Religious Diversity*. Albany: State University of New York Press.

Helminski, K. (2020). *In the House of Remembering: The Living Tradition of Sufi teaching*. London: Threshold Books.

Levine, P. (2010) *In an Unspoken Voice: How the Body Releases Trauma and Restores Goodness*. U.S: North Atlantic Books.

Levine. P. Healing Trauma: *A Pioneering Program for Restoring the Wisdom of the Body*. Canada: Sounds True.

Mate, G. (2018) *In the Realm of Hungry Ghosts: Close Encounters with Addictions*. London: Penguin Random House.

Meyer, W. A., Hyde, B., Muqaddam, F., Kahn, S. (2011) *Physicians of the Heart: A Sufi View of The Ninety-Nine Names of Allah*. San Francisco: Sufi Ruhaniat International.

Nosrati, F. Ghobari-Bonab, B. Zandi, S. Qorhani-Vanajemi, M. (2021). Effects of Dhikr (repetition of Holy Names) on Stress: A Systematic Review. Journal of Pizhūhish dar dīn va salāmat; 7(3):157-171

Rizzuto, A. (1981) *The Birth of the Living God: A Psychoanalytic Study*. Chicago: University of Chicago Press.

Shaykh Tosun Bayrak al-Jerrahi al-Halveti (2001) *The Name and the Named: The Divine Attributes of God*. US: Fons Vitae.

Van Der Kolk. (2015) *The Body Keeps the Score: Mind, Brain and Body in the Transformation of Trauma*. London: Penguin.

Wardah, A. (2020) *How Dhikr Transformed my Body and Mind*. https://medium.com/interfaith-now/how-dhikr-transformed-my-body-and-mind-72bede364a27

CHAPTER TWELVE

TAZKIA THERAPY

Bagus Riyono

Introduction

Tazkia therapy is a holistic psychological healing approach based on Qur'ānic guidance. The unique characteristic of Tazkia therapy is that it is a multidimensional, philosophical, and theoretically rich approach. However, it doesn't mean it is a complex approach but a dynamic and flexible approach to growing the human soul, cognition, emotion, and behavior. Since it is an Islamic approach, Tazkia therapy is firmly attached to believing and trusting Allah, The Almighty and The Most Knowing. However, it is also workable for counselees who have not believed in Allah yet. Tazkia therapy is based on the worldview that all human beings are Allah's creatures that will live forever beyond this worldly life. This worldview believes that all human beings are learning and developing toward the psychological state of a believer who surrenders to Allah's will. Those who do not believe in Allah are perceived as still in the middle of a journey and still in the process of learning.

On the other hand, since life in this world is dynamic, those who already believe in Allah also face the risk of forgetfulness. Tazkia therapy, in this case, is an intervention to remind them to go back to the truth, known in Arabic as *tawba*. The following case illustrates a counselee who already has "iman" but has psychological problems, meaning she suffers from forgetfulness syndrome. The treatment for this case reminds them of the right way to perceive the meaning of life.

The Case of Nurul

Nurul (pseudonym) is a new student at the biggest university in the country. Being a new student in this university is something to be proud of, and most people will be thrilled. However, Nurul reports feeling uneasy lately and spends most of her time alone in her dormitory. At the counseling session, she told me about her life story. Her parents divorced when she was still a little girl. They put her in her grandma's house, and she has been living there until now, raised by her loving grandma. Nurul was a happy teenager, and she didn't feel that her parent's divorce was a big problem because she could still meet them periodically, but not at the same time. Nurul grew up well, and her appearance shows she is a good Muslim. She dressed up in modest clothing and wore a hijab. Initially, she talked about Islamic Psychology and showed interest in studying it more. The way she talks is polite, and humble and she shows sincerity in her curiosity.

Her grandma lives around 365 km from the city where she currently studies. Therefore, she must move and live by herself in the dormitory. She reports that her friends in her department and the dormitory usually go home on holidays or weekends. They go to their parents, and they express cheerfulness when it happens. Nurul felt that she didn't have a home to go on holiday, and she started to think that she was different from her friends because she didn't have a father or mother to go home to. Recently, she realized that grandma's house is not quite a home for her and makes her feel incomplete. This feeling grows day by day, and it is getting worse. She started to question the meaning of life. She began to think she was not having an everyday life and felt lonely every time she reflected on this condition. I asked her, "What was the most disturbing feeling she is experiencing?". She answered that she doesn't understand the purpose of her life anymore. She cannot join her friends when they are having fun, and she doesn't feel like going out with her friends anymore. She thinks that her life has no meaning.

Case Analysis

Nurul's condition is currently not quite severe. However, if she keeps thinking and feeling this way, she could experience depression and become prone to suicidal tendencies. Understanding this condition and considering that she is a practicing Muslim, I then respond to Nurul's confusion by saying, "All human beings will eventually go home and go back to Allah ﷻ. So, the purpose of your life in this world is to prepare yourself so that you will be ready when you go home to Allah ﷻ. That is the most important thing that you should keep in mind. And the problems that you face in your life are not significant as long as you remember that the most important thing for you to do is to keep doing good deeds and useful things so that you will be ready when you meet Allah ﷻ". This message is based on the Qur'ān chapter 2 (Al-Baqarah) verse 62, "Indeed, the believers, Jews, Christians, and Sabians1—whoever ʿtrulyʾ believes in Allah and the Last Day and does good will have their reward with their Lord. And there will be no fear for them, nor will they grieve." Based on this Qur'ānic verse, the principle of mental health is "And there will be no fear for them, nor will they grieve."

Hearing this statement, Nurul seems to realize that this is something she had already known before but recently was clouded by her sadness and confusion. She looks relieved and shows that she understands this reality. She expresses that she is thankful for this session. She went home and felt relieved, free from a heavy burden. In this case, Nurul is an example of those who already have a belief in Allah ﷻ, but her emotion hijacked this belief in Allah ﷻ after realizing that she is different from her friends in terms of family condition. Therefore, based on the Islamic belief system, the therapeutic approach is to remind and bring her back to the essence of life. This approach cannot be done to counselees who do not have this state of spiritual belief. If we do this approach to those who are not ready, it will be classified as spiritual bypassing.

The case of Nurul illustrates the brief method of Tazkia therapy. It seems that it is very simple and short, but it reflects a psychological dynamic that can be explained by a number of theories. What I did to Nurul was not merely to change her

307

behavior or thoughts but also to touch her heart. I picked "home" as the keyword that serves as the window to Nurul's heart. Therefore, I focus on the word "home" that Nurul longs for, to touch her heart and build on it the essential meaning of "home" for the soul. The true and natural home of the soul is heaven, where we will meet Allah.

Defining Tazkia Therapy

The purpose of Tazkia therapy is not limited to the happiness in this worldly life, but it stretches toward eternity, which is the life in the hereafter. This is fundamental as a mindset that will be endorsed throughout Tazkia therapy. The orientation towards eternal life is essential since we focus on the human soul in Tazkia therapy. Since we focus on the human soul, life in this world is temporary and very short. However, this worldly life will determine our happiness in the hereafter. So, our earthly life is a journey, and the destination is our eternal life. The orientation towards life in the hereafter will also influence the happiness in life in this world because it will strengthen our resilience, optimism, hope, and patience in facing any problems. In the case of Nurul, remembering life in the hereafter makes all problems seem trivial and insignificant. Tazkia, or the process of purifying and elevating the soul, will guarantee happiness hereafter, as mentioned in Qur'ān Chapter 20, verse 76.

جَنَّاتُ عَدْنٍ تَجْرِي مِن تَحْتِهَا الْأَنْهَارُ خَالِدِينَ فِيهَا ۚ وَذَٰلِكَ جَزَاءُ مَن تَزَكَّىٰ

"The Gardens of Eternity, under which rivers flow, where they will stay forever. That is the reward of those who purify (Tazkia) themselves". [20:76]

As a terminology, *Tazkia* is from the root words ز ك و ("*zay kaf waw*") that has three dimensions. First, it means pure or to purify; second, it means nourishing; and third, it means to grow or elevate (*Tazkia*). So, we can define *Tazkia* as purely growing. If we think about purification, some elements that must be detached from the heart. So, the process of *Tazkia* has two steps: detaching factors that can cause the heart to be not pure and nourishing and growing in a pure way.

If we learn from the Qur'ānic verses that we collect through the root word ز ك و, we will find 56 verses, and the word ز ك و is mentioned 59 times and 32 of those verses are about zakat. Zakat is the obligation to distribute 2.5% of the wealth if the material possessions reach a certain amount; that is called *nisab*. This implies that the first fundamental element that can contaminate the heart is the love of material possessions that exceed a reasonable amount. In Arabic, this wealth is called *mal,* and the attitude that represents attachment to this *mal* is called *bakhil* (Al-Humazah (104): 2; Al-Balad (90): 6; Al-Fajr (89): 20) Al-Layl (92): (8)). If an individual heart still attaches with this excessive love for material possessions, it would be difficult to move forward in the process of *Tazkia*. This notion is also stated by Imam Al-Ghazali (1993) in his phenomenal book *Ihya' Ulumuddin* as one of the diseases of the heart. The Qur'ānic verse for this issue is as follows:

$$\text{زُيِّنَ لِلنَّاسِ حُبُّ ٱلشَّهَوَٰتِ مِنَ ٱلنِّسَآءِ وَٱلْبَنِينَ وَٱلْقَنَٰطِيرِ ٱلْمُقَنطَرَةِ مِنَ ٱلذَّهَبِ وَٱلْفِضَّةِ}$$
$$\text{وَٱلْخَيْلِ ٱلْمُسَوَّمَةِ وَٱلْأَنْعَٰمِ وَٱلْحَرْثِ ۗ ذَٰلِكَ مَتَٰعُ ٱلْحَيَوٰةِ ٱلدُّنْيَا ۖ وَٱللَّهُ عِندَهُ حُسْنُ ٱلْمَـَٔابِ}$$

"The enjoyment of worldly desires—women, children, treasures of gold and silver, fine horses, cattle, and fertile land—has been made appealing to people. These are the pleasures of this worldly life, but with Allah is the finest destination." [3:14]

$$\text{وَٱلَّذِينَ هُمْ لِلزَّكَوٰةِ فَٰعِلُونَ (4) ... ٱلَّذِينَ يَرِثُونَ ٱلْفِرْدَوْسَ هُمْ فِيهَا خَٰلِدُونَ (11)}$$

"Those who pay 'zakat'; [4] ... Paradise as their own. They will be there forever. [11]" [23: 4&11]

The second step to do *Tazkia* is to control oneself from lust. In this manner, *Tazkia* therapy is the opposite of psychoanalysis because psychoanalysis focuses on fulfilling the libido (sexual lust) in *the pleasure principle* (Freud, 1961a; 1961b). The Qur'ānic verse, when talking about pleasure, always refers to the hereafter in the form of heaven. Therefore, *the Tazkia* approach does not deny pleasure but delays the gratification of pleasure towards the hereafter. At this point, the study about delayed gratification is coherent with the concept of *Tazkia. It* is proven to be a healthy attitude and responsible for healthy personality development (Mischel et al., 1972; Mischel et al., 1989).

The third element of *Tazkia* is to be considerate toward others and respect the rights and privacy of others. The following Qur'ānic verse contains this message:

فَإِن لَّمْ تَجِدُوا فِيهَا أَحَدًا فَلَا تَدْخُلُوهَا حَتَّى يُؤْذَنَ لَكُمْ ۖ وَإِن قِيلَ لَكُمُ ٱرْجِعُوا فَٱرْجِعُوا ۖ هُوَ أَزْكَىٰ لَكُمْ ۚ وَٱللَّهُ بِمَا تَعْمَلُونَ عَلِيمٌ

"If you find no one at home, do not enter it until you have been given permission. And if you are asked to leave, then leave. That is purer for you. And Allah has perfect knowledge of what you do." [24:28]

In this context, the concept of empathy is very fundamental. The attitude to force others to follow our interests is another element that should be washed out of our hearts. This context includes prejudice, stereotyping, and envy toward others because of our differences. In our social life, we must respect differences and learn from each other (Al-Hujurat: 11-13). The acceptable competition is the competition to do good deeds (Al-Baqarah:148).

The tendency to orient our hearts towards these misconducts that will contaminate our hearts is endorsed by *Satan*. Therefore, we should be aware of this temptation and deception from *Satan* and seek refuge in Allah. Since *Satan* is unseen, we cannot control them directly, so must ask Allah to protect us from *Satan's* temptations. Asking for protection from Allah from *Satan's* temptation is another dimension of *Tazkia*. This is a critical discipline because *Satan's* temptation can provoke the other three elements that can contaminate the heart, i.e., love for wealth, lust, prejudice, or envy toward others.

The Process of Tazkia Therapy

In order to be able to do *Tazkia,* we need to develop knowledge from the signs that are revealed by Allah through the Qur'ānic verses, the universe (natural science), and the dynamic of our souls (psychology and social science), as mentioned in Qur'ān Surah Fussilat verse 53 (41:53):

سَنُرِيهِمْ ءَايَٰتِنَا فِى ٱلْءَافَاقِ وَفِىٓ أَنفُسِهِمْ حَتَّىٰ يَتَبَيَّنَ لَهُمْ أَنَّهُ ٱلْحَقُّ ۗ أَوَلَمْ يَكْفِ بِرَبِّكَ أَنَّهُ عَلَىٰ كُلِّ شَىْءٍ شَهِيدٌ

We will show them Our signs in the universe and within themselves until it becomes clear to them that this ˹Qur'ān˺ is the truth. Is it not enough that your Lord is a Witness over all things? [41:53]

The role of the counselor in *Tazkia* therapy is to facilitate the counselee to understand these signs through reason, empathy, and spirituality. When the counselee succeeds in developing empathy, they will obtain wisdom (*hikmah*) (Al-Baqarah (2): 151, An-Nisa (3): 162, Al Jumuah (62): 2). When they become wiser, their soul has grown to a higher level, as mentioned in Qur'ān Al Mujadilah (58) verse 11.

يَـٰٓأَيُّهَا ٱلَّذِينَ ءَامَنُوٓا۟ إِذَا قِيلَ لَكُمْ تَفَسَّحُوا۟ فِى ٱلْمَجَـٰلِسِ فَٱفْسَحُوا۟ يَفْسَحِ ٱللَّهُ لَكُمْ ۖ وَإِذَا قِيلَ ٱنشُزُوا۟ فَٱنشُزُوا۟ يَرْفَعِ ٱللَّهُ ٱلَّذِينَ ءَامَنُوا۟ مِنكُمْ وَٱلَّذِينَ أُوتُوا۟ ٱلْعِلْمَ دَرَجَـٰتٍ ۚ وَٱللَّهُ بِمَا تَعْمَلُونَ خَبِيرٌ

O believers! When you are told to make room in gatherings, then do so. Allah will make room for you ˹in His grace˺. And if you are told to rise, then do so. Allah will elevate those of you who are faithful, and ˹raise˺ those gifted with knowledge in rank. And Allah is All-Aware of what you do [58:11]

The result of *Tazkia* has two faces. The first face is *falah,* which means to succeed through appropriate effort. The success that is promised by the process of *Tazkia* will require effort so that along the way, the individual (counselee) will develop knowledge and skills. By developing skills to be successful, the counselees can secure sustainable success. This means that the counselee can solve their future problems because they have already acquired the skills. This explains why *Tazkia* therapy will minimize relapse because they will become independent.

In the process of *Tazkia* therapy, there are three actors involved. Besides the counselor and the counselee, Allah is always there, and both the counselor and counselee must rely on Allah for insights and blessings. Allah is the One who can change people's hearts. When we say that *Tazkia* therapy touches the heart, it does not mean the counselor alone can do that, but rather the counselor must always be connected to Allah *(dhikrullah)* so that his heart can vibrate through the counselee's heart.

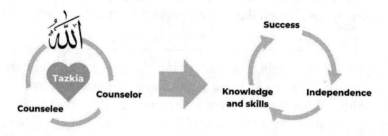

Figure 1. *The Process of Tazkia Therapy*

There are two verses that emphasize the absolute role of Allah in the process of Tazkia, as follows:

أَلَمْ تَرَ إِلَى الَّذِينَ يُزَكُّونَ أَنفُسَهُمْ ۚ بَلِ اللَّهُ يُزَكِّي مَن يَشَاءُ وَلَا يُظْلَمُونَ فَتِيلًا

Have you O Prophet not seen those who falsely elevate (Tazkia) themselves? It is Allah who elevates (Tazkia) whoever He wills. And none will be wronged even by the width of the thread of a date stone. [4:49]

يَا أَيُّهَا الَّذِينَ آمَنُوا لَا تَتَّبِعُوا خُطُوَاتِ الشَّيْطَانِ ۚ وَمَن يَتَّبِعْ خُطُوَاتِ الشَّيْطَانِ فَإِنَّهُ يَأْمُرُ بِالْفَحْشَاءِ وَالْمُنكَرِ ۚ وَلَوْلَا فَضْلُ اللَّهِ عَلَيْكُمْ وَرَحْمَتُهُ مَا زَكَىٰ مِنكُم مِّنْ أَحَدٍ أَبَدًا وَلَٰكِنَّ اللَّهَ يُزَكِّي مَن يَشَاءُ ۗ وَاللَّهُ سَمِيعٌ عَلِيمٌ

O believers! Do not follow the footsteps of Satan. Whoever follows Satan's footsteps, then let them know that he surely bids all to immorality and wickedness. Had it not been for Allah's grace and mercy upon you, none of you would have ever been purified (Tazkia). But Allah purifies whoever He wills. And Allah is All-Hearing, All-Knowing. [24:21]

On the counselee side, before conducting the *Tazkia* therapy session, it is vital to be willing to go through the process. *Tazkia* therapy cannot be forced on any individual without their consent. For those who believe in God and the hereafter, this agreement will involve the willingness to submit to God's will and open their hearts for God's guidance. For those who do not believe in God, at least they will be asked to open their hearts and be willing to have a heart-to-heart conversation honestly and sincerely. The willingness to go through the process of heart-to-heart conversation can be documented in written consent between the counselor and the counselee. It is written in the Qur'ān Chapter 79, verse 18 that this willingness to go through the process of the Tazkia is required, as follows:

$$\text{فَقُلْ هَل لَّكَ إِلَىٰ أَن تَزَكَّىٰ}$$

"And say, 'Would you be willing to purify yourself," [79:18]

Based on the verses above, the counselor in Tazkia therapy helps or facilitates the counselee to do Tazkia and asks for Allah's blessings to allow the counselee to improve. The counselor does not know which counselee will end up with *Tazkia*, so the counselor's job is only to remind and help the counselee to pray with full hope for Allah's help. The counselor should not look down on the counselee because the counselor cannot know the condition of the counselee's heart, as the following verse, *"You never know (O Prophet), perhaps he may be purified,"* (80:3). In other words, the counselor needs to strive throughout the therapy process constantly. In addition, the counselor must always be patient in interacting with counselees and realize that Allah is the only one who can purify the counselor and the counselee.

Before a counselor conducts the therapy, it is required for them to have sufficient knowledge about human beings, especially the dynamics of the *"nafs"* and the universal laws in human life. Three sources of signs or evidence make the foundation of evidence-based knowledge, i.e., the Qur'ānic verses, the natural phenomena, and the dynamics of human souls. Therefore, to become a counselor for Tazkia therapy, they need to study the Qur'ānic messages, natural science, and psychological and social science (Qur'ān, 41:53). This evidence should be coherent with the Qur'ānic messages, meaning that scientific findings that are not coherent with the Qur'ānic messages should be criticized. For example, the current development of neuroscience shows contradictory conclusions. On one side, they concluded that human beings have no soul (Harari, 2016; Crick,

313

1994). On the other side, Barrett (2017) concluded that the study of the brain revealed that human beings are responsible for their own emotions. Barrett's (2017) conclusion is coherent with the Qur'ānic messages, so her empirical study can be used to enrich the theoretical framework of Tazkia therapy. On the other hand, the conclusion that Crick makes (1994) and Harari (2016) are to be criticized by the scientific community, so it is not ready to be integrated for application in Tazkia therapy.

The role of the counselor in Tazkia therapy is as the facilitator and mediator of knowledge that is obtained from Allah through the verses of the Qur'ān. In the Qur'ān, the explanation of this relationship is illustrated with the relationship between Allah, the Messenger, and the rest of human beings. The following is one of the Qur'ānic verses that explains this issue.

كَمَآ أَرْسَلْنَا فِيكُمْ رَسُولًا مِّنكُمْ يَتْلُواْ عَلَيْكُمْ ءَايَٰتِنَا وَيُزَكِّيكُمْ وَيُعَلِّمُكُمُ ٱلْكِتَٰبَ وَٱلْحِكْمَةَ وَيُعَلِّمُكُم
مَّا لَمْ تَكُونُواْ تَعْلَمُونَ ١٥١

"Since We have sent you a messenger from among yourselves—
reciting to you Our revelations, purifying you, teaching you the
Book and wisdom, and teaching you what you never knew."
[2:151]

لَقَدْ مَنَّ ٱللَّهُ عَلَى ٱلْمُؤْمِنِينَ إِذْ بَعَثَ فِيهِمْ رَسُولًا مِّنْ أَنفُسِهِمْ يَتْلُواْ عَلَيْهِمْ ءَايَٰتِهِۦ وَيُزَكِّيهِمْ
وَيُعَلِّمُهُمُ ٱلْكِتَٰبَ وَٱلْحِكْمَةَ وَإِن كَانُواْ مِن قَبْلُ لَفِى ضَلَٰلٍ مُّبِينٍ ١٦٤

"Indeed, Allah has done the believers a great favor by raising a
messenger from among them—reciting to them His revelations,
purifying them, and teaching them the Book and wisdom. For
indeed they had previously been clearly astray." [3:164]

هُوَ ٱلَّذِي بَعَثَ فِي ٱلْأُمِّيِّينَ رَسُولًا مِّنْهُمْ يَتْلُو عَلَيْهِمْ آيَاتِهِ وَيُزَكِّيهِمْ وَيُعَلِّمُهُمُ ٱلْكِتَابَ وَٱلْحِكْمَةَ
وَإِن كَانُوا مِن قَبْلُ لَفِي ضَلَالٍ مُّبِينٍ

"He is the One Who raised for the illiterate people a messenger
from among themselves—reciting to them His revelations (ayat),
purifying them (Tazkia), and teaching them the Book and wisdom
(hikmah), for indeed they had previously been clearly astray—"

[62:2]

From the Qur'ānic verses above, Allah teaches humans to purify their hearts, resulting in "Hikmah" (wisdom). The role of the counselor in Tazkia therapy is to learn first about the "ayat" through the Qur'ān and scientific evidence and convey them to the counselee. Therefore, to conduct Tazkia therapy, the counselor must master the knowledge about the human soul and life through the Qur'ānic verses and scientific evidence. Applying this knowledge, requires some theoretical framework that can translate the messages into practical application. In other words, a counselor of Tazkia therapy needs to have theoretical sensitivity about human nature and human life based on Qur'ānic verses and scientific evidence.

These principles justify that Tazkia therapy is a theoretically rich intervention. However, as we have mentioned in the earlier part of this chapter, Tazkia therapy is also a very empathetic approach in therapy because before the counselor gives advice or treatment, they have to understand first the conditions of the counselor and their level of spirituality. The function of the theories is to help the counselor and the counselee understand the purpose of life so that they can have direction forward in living their life. Tazkia therapy does not stop by making the counselees feel good about themselves or accepting whatever conditions they have. Considering the meaning of *Tazkia*, which is purely growing, the purpose of *Tazkia* therapy is to develop the counselee and counselor to become a better person and closer to Allah. To know what to do to develop oneself, the process of Tazkia therapy needs several theoretical foundations so that there will be a direction and path that can be followed. This path toward the direction can be broken down into workable steps by referring to the theories. We can conclude that Tazkia therapy is an empathetic yet directive intervention.

At least two criteria justify the path that should be taken. First, they have to be coherent between the practical steps and the message of the Qur'ānic verses. The second criterion is that understanding the practical steps and the Qur'ānic verses has to make the individual closer to Allah. The process of acquiring knowledge, combined with the process of *Tazkia*, should result in the acquisition of *hikmah* which can be translated into 'wisdom'.

Tazkia is an ongoing process as long as the individual lives. It is a process ever-growing, but it is also natural if the individual experiences ups and downs during the process of *Tazkia*. So, Tazkia therapy is not a one-shot intervention but like opening the door to elevating oneself. Through Tazkia therapy, the counselee is expected to become independent and capable of developing their knowledge and elevating their soul to become wiser and closer to Allah. For a professional counselor, the condition of the heart can be seen and felt through the counselee's narrative and the body language's appearance. To gain this sensitivity, a counselor needs to master seven theories explaining the human soul's dynamics.

The 7 Theoretical Approaches to Tazkia Therapy

In Tazkia therapy, the heart is the focus of intervention. The heart is the core of human beings that will determine the psychological quality of an individual. As stated by the Prophet Muhammad Shalallahu 'Alaihi Wassalam as follows:

لَا وَإِنَّ فِي الْجَسَدِ مُضْغَةً إِذَا صَلَحَتْ صَلَحَ الْجَسَدُ كُلُّهُ وَإِذَا فَسَدَتْ فَسَدَ الْجَسَدُ كُلُّه أَلَا وَهِيَ الْقَلب

"In the body there is a piece of flesh, and the whole body is sound if it is sound, but the whole body is corrupt if it is corrupt. It is the heart." (Bukhari no. 2051 & Muslim no. 1599)

Imam Al-Ghazali mentioned in his work, *Ihya Ulumuddin,* that medicine is the science of the body to make us healthy and function well in life so that we can perform *"ibadah."* However, we need to develop the science of the heart that will ensure the healthy condition of our souls. A healthy soul is more important than a healthy body because a healthy soul will bring us to heaven (Al-Ghazali, 1993).

The first theory in Tazkia therapy provides a perspective of psychological problems that is more comprehensive than the conventional psychology perspectives. Conventional psychology does not believe in the soul. Some psychologists believe in the soul but do not include it in their theoretical framework. The current widely accepted model combines behavior and cognition, called CBT, but it has not mentioned the heart or the soul. Islamic psychology deals with everything, but our focus is on the soul, and when we talk about the soul, the keyword from the Qur'ānic verses is the *nafs*. In ordinary language, what we mean by the soul is the heart. The heart is more familiar in all cultures and will not be rejected. However, if we use the term soul in a non-religious discourse, there is a possibility of being rejected because not every individual believes in the soul. This is important for communication strategy, but as Islamic psychologists, we will not differentiate between the heart and the soul; in the Qur'ānic verses, the word is *al-nafs* or *al-qalb*. What we mean by the heart does not only cover the feeling. What we mean by the heart here is the core of our consciousness and the core of our existence as living human beings (Theory 1, depicted in Figure 2).

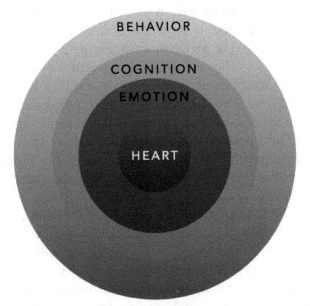

Figure 2. *The heart as the core of human beings (Theory 1)*

The above diagram Figure 2 shows that the core of human beings is the heart. The heart is the one that "creates" emotion. From the heart emerges emotion and cognition, and then it becomes behavior. When an individual has a problem, it is like they have a fire in the house. What is seen by other people from outside is the smoke. The smoke is coming out from the house on fire. If you do not understand the problem, then it seems that the problem is the smoke. And what you will try to do is to blow the smoke away from the house. The smoke here is the metaphor of behavior. What happens if your reaction to this problem is focused on the smoke? Then, once you have succeeded in blowing the smoke away, you think you have already solved the problem. But the smoke will reappear again because it is not the core of the problem. You have to enter the house and find where the fire is because it is the fire that creates the smoke. But of course, before you find the fire, you will deal with the heat from the fire. The heat is the metaphor for the cognition and emotion of this disturbed individual. This heat can take the forms of anger, denial, and unrealistic arguments you must face. However, these emotions and cognition are not the actual cause of the problem.

The problem is in the heart, which is not in peace. As a counselor, you have to be able to sense this unrest in the heart, then embrace it, and inspire it with the correct understanding of the meaning of this life. The above diagram Figure 2 shows that the core of human beings is the heart. The heart is the one that "creates" emotion. From the heart emerges emotion and cognition and then it becomes behavior. When an individual has a problem, it is like they have a fire in the house. What is seen by other people from outside is the smoke. The smoke is coming out from the house on fire. If you do not understand the problem, then it seems the problem is the smoke. And what you will try to do is to blow the smoke away from the house. The smoke here is the metaphor of behavior. What happens if your reaction to this problem is focused on the smoke? Then, once you have succeeded in blowing the smoke away, you think that you have already solved the problem. But the smoke will reappear again because it is not the core of the problem. You have to enter the house and find where the fire is because it is the fire that creates the smoke. But of course, before you find the fire, you will deal with the heat from the fire. The heat is the metaphor for the cognition and emotion of this disturbed individual. This heat can take the form of anger, denial, and unrealistic arguments that you have to face. But these emotions and cognition are not the true cause of the problem. The problem is in the heart, which is not in peace. As a counselor, you have to be able to sense this unrest in the heart, then embrace it, and inspire it with the correct understanding of the meaning of this life.

The next fundamental theory (Theory 2) based on the Qur'ān Surah Al-Baqarah verse 156 is that '*human life is a journey from Allah* ﷻ *to Allah* ﷻ', as depicted in Figure 8.

الَّذِينَ إِذَآ أَصَٰبَتْهُم مُّصِيبَةٌ قَالُوٓاْ إِنَّا لِلَّهِ وَإِنَّآ إِلَيْهِ رَٰجِعُونَ (١٥٦)

"Who, when faced with a calamity, say, "Surely to Allah we belong and to Him we will ʳallʳ return." [2:156]

This basic and fundamental theory is the one that is used in the case of Nurul above. The intervention based on this theory can be effective for individuals who believe in God and hereafter. It is not limited to Muslim, but all individuals who believe in God and hereafter share this understanding.

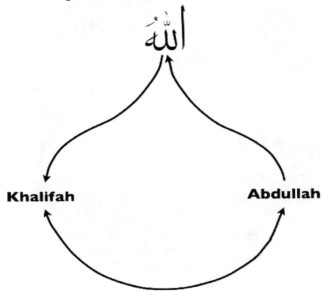

Figure 3. *Life as a journey from Allah to Allah*

In Tazkia therapy, it is very important for the counselor to understand the spiritual condition of the counselee since the heart is spiritual in nature, and according to Imam Al-Ghazâlî (1873) the heart is the home of the soul. So, the first step in Tazkia therapy is to diagnose the spiritual state of the counselee. This ability is subjective in nature, and it will grow along with the experience that counselors have in dealing with different individuals. Mastering these seven theories can help a counselor develop the sensitivity to identify the spiritual level of a counselee. Since these theories are based on understanding the Qur'ānic messages and Hadith, a counselor of Tazkia therapy should always learn the Qur'ānic and the Hadith continuously. By understanding this spiritual state, the counselor can choose what kind of treatment to be applied and how far it can go. For those who do not believe in God and hereafter, the furthest the counselor can go is empathy. This framework can be explained by Theory 3: the theory of the layers of the human soul (Riyono, 2019), depicted in Figure 4.

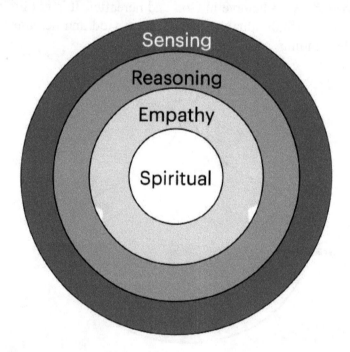

Figure 4. *Theory of the layers of the human soul (Theory 3)*

The theory of layers of the human soul describes that the human soul has four layers, i.e., sensing, reasoning, empathy, and spirituality (Riyono, 2019). This theory is based on the proposition that the soul and body are different entities but connected when humans are conscious (Al-Ghazali, 1873). The outermost layer is sensing, the deeper layer is reasoning and empathy, and the deepest is the spiritual layer. Sensing is the layer *"directly connected to the body or the five senses"* or attached to a human's body, i.e., sight, hearing, taste, smell, and touch. *Reasoning* is the layer that involves cognitive activities in the heart to generate understanding in human beings. It is about intelligence, understanding the meaning, and making conclusions. An Illustration of this process is when we feel the smell of aromatherapy, then we think about its usefulness, so the smell of aromatherapy not just passes through our senses but also into our thoughts. It can be said that sensing is the layer where the soul and body are connected, while reasoning is the layer where the soul and the phenomena in the environment are connected. This connection is conceptual, not a physical connection, meaning that reasoning is the process of understanding the message behind the encounter with the phenomena in human life. So, you could say that reasoning connects the soul and the meaning behind experiences. In practice, when you conclude what you observe or hear, you are using the reasoning layer.

The third layer is empathy, which connects the soul and other human souls. From this layer, human beings can feel various feelings, such as love, compassion, affection, etc. Then, the spiritual, deepest layer is the connection between humans and God. This layer is hard to diagnose because only Allah ﷻ knows the actual condition of this layer. The counselor can never precisely judge this spiritual layer's *imaan* (faith). The diagnosis process is conducted based on the counselee's thoughts, feelings, and behavior, but only Allah ﷻ knows for sure whether the counselee is the truthful or hypocritical one. When the counselee tends to show the characteristics of a hypocrite, there is undoubtedly a disease in his heart.

فِى قُلُوبِهِم مَّرَضٌ فَزَادَهُمُ ٱللَّهُ مَرَضًا ۖ وَلَهُمْ عَذَابٌ أَلِيمٌ بِمَا كَانُوا۟ يَكْذِبُونَ

"There is sickness in their hearts, and Allah ʿonlyʾ lets their sickness increase. They will suffer a painful punishment for their lies." (Q.S. Al Baqarah (2): 10)

If we go back to Nurul's case, we can see the dynamics of her soul from the perspective of layers of the human soul theory. When she met her college friends, which means they had physical encounters, she saw that her friends had places to meet both of their parents. This is when the sensing layer works through her sight. The second layer, reasoning, works when she has the perspective that she does not have a place to go, though she still has her loving grandmother that takes care of her. However, this positive feeling of her grandmother is clouded by a feeling of disconnectedness toward her father and mother that causes her to feel some emptiness in her heart. This problem lies in the level of empathy, which is the connection between souls.

Furthermore, this empathy problem will provoke emotional instability. In conventional therapy (e.g., humanistic therapy, cognitive-behavioral therapy/CBT), the keyword would be 'acceptance,' which means that Nurul is suggested to accept the condition she experienced and adjust to it to feel better. Another approach from conventional therapy might be that she is not alone, and many people have the same problem. Many children are experiencing divorced parents, and they are okay, so Nurul is not supposed to feel bad about that. Another approach in therapy (acceptance and commitment therapy/ACT; Hayes et al., 1999) may say that it is a better condition for their parents to divorce so they will not have fights anymore in front of Nurul. This kind of intervention is limited to the layer of empathy, so they miss the more fundamental meaning of life: the relationship with Allah.

These four layers are not separated from each other. It is like a tree; the deepest layer is the root that will determine the condition of the tree, whether it is healthy or unhealthy. By addressing the spiritual level, Nurul's counselor simultaneously provides a solution to the other layers. When a tree has a problem with its leaves or trunk, even when all these parts are cut down, they can regrow. As long as they still have a healthy root, any psychological problems will be solved. However, if the problem is biological, it will need additional treatment from medical science. As we witness in the winter, trees lose all their leaves, but when spring comes, they rejuvenate.

The fourth perspective of the human psychological dynamic can be illustrated by the theory of meaning (Theory 4, depicted in Figure 5), which explains the dynamics of human motivation (Riyono, 2020). Based on this theory, five energies will motivate human behavior. The first one is "freedom to choose," which, together with the urge, has the internal dynamics of the human psyche. The urge consists of four driving forces, i.e., instinct, need, wants, and revenge. Human freedom to choose is the energy that originates from the four layers of the soul, sensing, reasoning, empathy, and conscience (spirituality). The urge and the freedom compete to influence human emotion, cognition, and behavior. A problem occurs when the urge is more potent than human freedom, which consists of reasoning, empathy, and conscience (spirituality). To deal with this issue, a counselor of Tazkia therapy should help to strengthen the freedom to choose, meaning to strengthen the reason, the empathy, and the conscience to control the urge. Once an individual controls their urge, they will transform into meaning. This transformation is one of the manifestations of growing to a higher level.

In dealing with the environment, an individual will face challenges and incentives. A challenge is a push factor of the environment that demands an individual to respond. The quality of this response will depend on the dynamics of freedom to choose and the urge. Suppose the individual is in a healthy state when the freedom to choose can control the urge. In that case, they will respond to the challenge from the environment and transform it into an opportunity, which will also become something meaningful. The incentive is the pull factor of the environment that will influence the individual emotion, cognition, and behavior. The possibility is similar to the case of a challenge. When the urge dominates an individual, this pull factor will make them suffer and make them see themselves as a victim manipulated by the environment. When an individual already manages the urge, they will treat this pull factor as a milestone to transform themselves toward meaning.

Figure 5. *Theory of Meaning (Theory 4)*

In the process of Tazkia therapy, the direction of the therapy is to free the individual from their urges so that they become independent and able to solve their problems. What to be cautious about in the individual urge is the power of wants and revenge. Wants become problematic when it is excessive and unrealistic. Revenge is always negative. Therefore, it has to be treated with forgiveness. On the other hand, instinct and needs are natural, so they must be treated proportionally. To simplify the issue, this theory describes psychological problems in two ways: one relates to the past (revenge), and the other concerns the future (wants).

The next theoretical framework concerns the reality of the future of human life (Theory 5, depicted in Figure 6). The undeniable fact of human life is that every individual will face uncertainty about their future. When individual is mentally healthy, they will perceive this uncertainty as an opportunity; on the other hand, those who are mentally unhealthy will perceive uncertainty as a threat or a source of anxiety. In the literature on mental health, there is a term called intolerance of uncertainty. IU is the incapability of an individual to endure aversive situations that are triggered by uncertain probability about an event that is likely to occur. Dugas et al. (1998) stated that people with IU cannot effectively deal with problems and use worry as a dysfunctional strategy to cope. This attitude is found to be the beginning of all mental problems (Yuniardi et al., 2018). It is so because when an individual cannot tolerate uncertainty, it means they do not accept the reality of life. We can say that they have unrealistic thoughts and feelings. This unrealistic thought and feeling will create anxiety.

On the other hand, the individuals that can tolerate uncertainty are those who understand the reality of life and are ready to move forward. They see this uncertainty as an opportunity to give them positive future possibilities. This attitude is called "hope" (Riyono, 2022). Hope is a belief that beyond uncertainty, there will be something good. Those with strong hope can tolerate uncertainty and are always grateful for whatever they get because of this belief in goodness. The individuals who do not want to tolerate the uncertainty rely on their expectations. They are not ready to face something that does not meet their expectations. That is why they perceive this uncertainty as something full of risk. They cannot accept facing a condition or situation except the one that they want. While, in fact, what will happen in the future is not always in accordance with what they want. This is why this group of people experiences a lot of disappointment in life. They torture themselves with their wants and expectations and cannot accept the reality of life. From this theory, the process of *Tazkia* is to help them first, accept uncertainty as the reality of life. Second, they need help strengthening their belief and flexibility in accepting any happening in life and trying to see the good side of it. The stronger their belief in the good side of life, the stronger their hope will be.

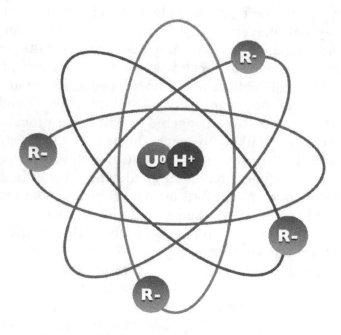

Figure 6. *Theory of RUH (Risk, Uncertainty, Hope; Theory 5)*

The sixth theoretical framework is the anchor theory (Theory 6, depicted in Figure 7; Riyono et al., 2012). You hold on to an anchor to strengthen your hope (Riyono et al., 2012). An anchor is something you trust to tie your hope to. Since hope is a belief about something uncertain, you need to compensate for this uncertainty with something you can rely on. There are four anchors that every human being has, namely the self, others, materials, and virtues. For those who believe in God, they have the fifth, the ultimate anchor, which is God himself. Of these four anchors, the stronger and most sustainable one is the one that is the most reliable, which is the Virtues. When your anchor is your self, you will experience conditions that your self is not reliable, your self can experience confusion, sadness, weakness, and so on. When your anchor is others, you will also face the possibility of unreliability because people change. You might trust others at one time, but at other times, they might betray you and disappoint you. Materials are the weakest of anchors because material possession is an illusion. The belief that money can buy anything is not realistic. There are only certain things that money can buy in this life, and usually, it is also material. Money cannot buy love, peace, and happiness.

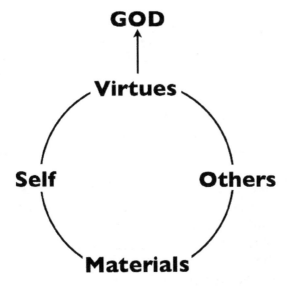

Figure 7. *Theory of Anchor (Theory 6)*

Virtue is enlightening and something that will develop wisdom in an individual. Once you get wisdom that is derived from virtues, nobody can take it away from you. That is why virtue is eternal. Virtue is also universal because true virtue does not depend on culture or location. It is embedded in human nature. When you anchor yourself in virtues, that means you always learn and grow with more wisdom. Anchoring virtues is the ideal state of human personality, and a healthy choice. However, only some individuals realize it and are willing to anchor themselves to virtues. There is a strong temptation to anchor oneself to materials, or self, for those who do not have self-esteem will anchor themselves to others.

From the anchor theory, Tazkia therapy focuses on reorienting the counselees' anchor towards virtues. The counselor first can perform a diagnosis of counselees' problems and identify what is the main anchor of the counselee which could be a material, self, or others. Once this disorientation of the anchor is identified, the counselor can lead the counselee to rethink again about the validity and reliability of their anchor, so the counselee will realize their mistakes. Once the counselee realizes their mistakes, the counselor can introduce the virtues as the option of anchor orientation and help the counselee to internalize this ideal. The counselor also can reflect on past experiences when the individual is anchoring the virtues and maintaining their mental health.

The seventh approach to Tazkia therapy is through a framework called the laws of human life (Theory 7, depicted in Figure 8; Riyono & Budiharto, 2023). This framework is the simplification of the previous theories and takes only the essence and fundamental concepts of them. This framework consists of two sets of concepts, representing the basic condition or reality in human life and the coherent attitudes in response to those realities (Riyono & Budiharto, 2022). There are three realities in human life, i.e., the freedom to choose, the uncertainty of the future, and the vulnerability of human beings. These three realities will create problems if they are not understood and not appropriately responded to. When an individual denies their freedom to decide or act, they will suffer from learned helplessness (Maier & Seligman, 1976). When an individual rejects uncertainty, they will experience a lot of disappointment and anxiety in life (Yuniardi et al., 2018). When an individual rejects the reality that they are vulnerable, they will suffer the numbness of their emotion and become in denial of their true condition (Brown, 2012). Rejecting vulnerability also causes the inability to love and to be grateful, which in the end, they will be unable to fill happiness in their life. The cure for these psychological problems is sets of three attitudes that respond to each condition. To respond with the freedom to choose, the only healthy and reasonable attitude is to take responsibility. The healthy response to all human beings facing uncertainty is strengthening their hope, which is the belief that there will be something good beyond uncertainty. The only logical response to human vulnerability is to become humble. Humility will release the burden of feeling perfect and ease the heart from guilt and shame (Brown, 2012).

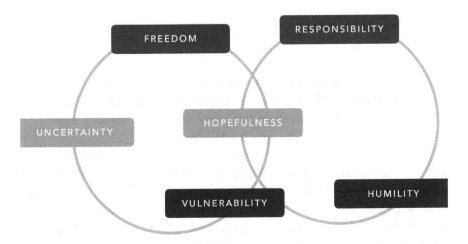

Figure 8. *The law of human life*

According to this theoretical framework, there are two sets of interventions, which should be simultaneously delivered in pairs. The first approach is to remind the counselee that they are able to make decisions by themselves. Simultaneously, the counselor also has to remind the counselee that the logical consequence of this freedom is to be responsible for their choices and decisions. This feeling of responsibility will direct the counselee to make the right decision properly. The second approach is to show evidence about the uncertainty of human life and all aspects of their life. However, the notion of uncertainty must be framed toward the possibilities of good opportunities that can be pursued in the future. By conveying this message, the counselor is planting hope in the counselees' hearts and strengthening the belief in goodness in life. The third point is to remind the counselee of their vulnerability but not to let them down with it, but rather to open their heart to accept others' help sincerely. To be humble means to open their heart to others' contributions and collaborate to solve their problems hand-to-hand. Humility will develop a peaceful feeling in the heart of an individual and will put away worries about not being able to become perfect. To summarize the process of Tazkia therapy, we can refer to the Qur'ānic verses of Surah As-Shams, verses seven to ten.

وَقَدْ خَابَ(٩) قَدْ أَفْلَحَ مَن زَكَّىٰهَا (٨) وَنَفْسٍ وَمَا سَوَّىٰهَا (٧) فَأَلْهَمَهَا فُجُورَهَا وَتَقْوَىٰهَا (١٠مَن دَسَّىٰهَا)

"And by the soul and the One Who fashioned it, then with 'the knowledge of' right and wrong inspired it! Successful indeed is the one who purifies their soul, and doomed is the one who corrupts it." [91:7-10]

These verses of the Qur'ān have seven messages concerning the *nafs* and the process of *Tazkia*: (1) Allah has perfected the creation of the nafs with the necessary potentials; (2) in order to actualize these potentials, Allah provides two tendencies that should be chosen by human beings in the form of *taqwa* and *fujuur*; (3) in order to respond to this test, the human being is endowed with the freedom to choose; (4) the first choice that an individual can take is to do *Tazkia*, which means to purify, to learn, so that they can grow in the path of *taqwa*; (5) there is another available choice that an individual can take without any effort, but this choice will bring the individual toward the path of *fujuur*, which means the path that will bring them down; (6) with the capacity to make an independent decision and the ability to learn, individual has the opportunity to correct their mistakes by performing repentance (*tawba*) and change their choice from *Tadsia* to *Tazkia*, so that they can go back to the right path, which is the path of *taqwa*, (7) this dynamic is always open as long as human is still alive in this world. The understanding of this dynamic is the basic framework of Tazkia therapy.

Conclusion

Tazkia therapy is a Qur'ānic-based intervention aimed at purifying and developing the human soul from the condition of trouble toward a state of peace and happiness. At least there are three actors in the process of Tazkia therapy, i.e., Allah is the designer of human life and who possesses all the power to purify and develop the human soul; the second actor is the counselor, who has learned from the signs with Allah's guidance through the Qur'ān and scientific evidence; the third actor is the counselee who needs more knowledge in facing problems that needs to be helped in understanding themselves in order to develop to become more healthy and better personality.

Tazkia therapy is a process of learning together by relying on Allah's guidance to grow and reach a better state of existence in human life. The general protocol of Tazkia therapy is as follows:

1. The counselor listens empathetically to the counselees' problems.

2. The counselor explores further the possible causes of the counselees' problems.

3. The counselee confirms the core problem that is experienced by the counselee.

4. The counselor asks the counselee what they need to help them solve their problems.

5. The counselor decides where to start by using one of the seven available approaches and customizing with the needs of the counselee.

6. Once the counselor finds the appropriate approach to the problem of the counselee, then he goes deeper through the approach to solve the core of the problem.

7. Based on the selected approach, the counselor directs the counselee's thoughts, emotions, and conscience toward the ideal state.

These protocols can be repeated with other approaches to cover the multidimensionality of the problems and to provide the counselee with options for responding to the problems that they are facing. The counselor can use the available techniques to lead or to reframe the counselee's thoughts and feelings about their problems.

References

Al-Qur'ān translation by Dr. Mustafa Khattab. Retrieved from www.Qur'ān.com

Al-Ghazali. (1993). Revival of religious learning (Ihya' Ulumiddin) translated by Fazl Ul Karim volume 1. Darul Ishaat.

Al-Ghazali. (1873). The Alchemy of Happiness translated by Henry A. Homes. J. Munsell.

Barrett, L. F. (2017). How Emotions Are Made: The Secret Life of the Brain. Houghton Mifflin Harcourt.

Brown, B. (2012). *The Power of Vulnerability: Teachings on Authenticity, Connection and* Courage. Sounds True.

Crick, F. H. C. (1994). *The Astonishing Hypothesis: The Scientific Search for the Soul.* Charles Scribner's Sons.

Dugas, M. J., Gagnon, F., Ladouceur, R., & Freeston, M. H. (1998). Generalized anxiety disorder: a preliminary test of a conceptual model. Behaviour Research and Therapy, 36, 215-226.

Harari, Y. N. (2016). *Homo Deus.* Harvill Secker.

Hayes S. C., Strosahl K. D., Wilson K. G. (1999). Acceptance and Commitment Therapy: An Experiential Approach to Behavior Change. New York, NY: Guilford Press.

Maier, S. F., & Seligman, M. E. (1976). Learned helplessness: theory and evidence. *Journal of experimental psychology: general, 105*(1), 3.

Mischel, W., Ebbesen, E. B., & Raskoff Zeiss, A. (1972). Cognitive and attentional mechanisms in delay of gratification. Journal of Personality and Social Psychology, 21(2), 204–218. doi:10.1037/h0032198

Mischel, W., Shoda, Y., Rodriguez, M.L. (1989). Delay of gratification in children. Science, 244, 933–8.

Riyono, B. (2022). Hope: The Spiritual Dimension of Human Psyche. In print.

Riyono, B., & Budiharto, S. (2023). Constructing a Theory of Life Dynamics as the Foundation of Mental Health: A Study with Qur'ānic "Maqasid" Methodology. In press.

Riyono, B. (2020). Motivasi dan Kepribadian: Perspektif Islam tentang Dinamika Jiwa dan Perilaku Manusia. Al-Mawardi Prima.

Riyono, B. (2019). Sensing Mentality and Cognitive-Spiritual Intervention. Minbar: Islamic Studies, 12(4). https://doi.org/10.31162/2618-9569-2019-12-4-1091-1106

Riyono, B., Himam, F., &Subandi. (2012). In search of anchors, the fundamental motivational force in compensating for human vulnerability. Gadjah Mada International Journal of Business, 14(3), 229–252. Retrieved from http://www.scopus.com/inward/record.url?eid=2-s2.0-84872200325&partnerID=40&md5=a45c1cf5f8aab942e70df edefe94dce9

Seligman, M. E. P. (2011). Flourish: A Visionary New Understanding of Happiness and Well-being. Free Press

Yuniardi, S. M., Freeston, M. H., & Rodgers, J. (2018). Intolerance of Uncertainty and Generalized Anxiety Disorder.

NOTES ON CONTRIBUTORS

Editors

Amber Haque is the Director of Muslim Family Services, ICNA Relief USA, and a non-resident faculty in the Islamic Psychology Diploma Program at Cambridge Muslim College, UK. Previously, he was a full professor and Director of clinical psychology master's programs at UAE University, UAE, and Doha Institute, Qatar, and Associate Professor and Head of the Psychology Department at International Islamic University Malaysia. Dr. Haque earned his Ph.D. in psychology from Western Michigan University and MS in clinical psychology from Eastern Michigan University. Before joining academia, he practiced psychology in Michigan for twelve years. Besides being an academic and administrator, including chair of faculty affairs at UAE University, he was also a visiting scholar at Cornell and UPenn, taught in Bosnia, and served as adjunct faculty at Aligarh Muslim University, India. He served on the editorial board of four and as a reviewer for forty international peer-reviewed journals.

Abdallah Rothman is the Head of Islamic Psychology at Cambridge Muslim College, founder of Shifaa Integrative Counseling, co-founder, and President of the International Association of Islamic Psychology, and visiting professor of psychology at Zaim University Istanbul, International Islamic University Islamabad, and Al-Neelain University Khartoum. He holds an MA and a PhD in psychology and is a Licensed Professional Counselor (LPC) and a Board-Certified

Registered Art Therapist (ATR-BC), licensed in the United States and currently living in the UAE.

Author Bios

Ahmad Nabil Md Rosli is an Assistant Professor of Psychiatry at the Kulliyyah of Medicine, International Islamic University Malaysia (IIUM). After graduating with a Doctor of Psychiatry degree from the University Kebangsaan Malaysia (UKM) in 2017, he is currently practicing at Hospital Tengku Ampuan Afzan (HTAA) and Sultan Ahmad Shah Medical Centre (SASMEC@IIUM) in Kuantan, Malaysia. His passion lies in exploring the intersections of religion, spirituality, culture, and mental health, further honed through accredited training in spiritual care from the Association for Clinical Pastoral Education (ACPE) in Central California, US, in 2019 and 2022. He was invited several times by the Persatuan Dokter Spesialis Kedokteran Jiwa Indonesia (PDSKJI) to deliver academic talks and workshops on spiritual care and mental health. His contributions also extend to scholarly works, with notable chapters in books published by Institut Kefahaman Islam Malaysia (IKIM) and Universiti Islam Malaysia (UIM), showcasing his insights into mental health and Islamic spirituality.

Alizi Alias is a consultant organizational psychologist with over 20 years of working experience in academia and three years of working experience in industry. He has published 14 journal articles and academic book chapters, presented 27 conference papers, four non-academic books and book chapters, and was a regular speaker/trainer in organizational psychology, positive psychology, and Islamic psychology. Alizi Alias graduated from International Islamic University Malaysia (IIUM) with a B. IRKH (Fiqh & Usul Fiqh) and a B.HSc (Psychology). He obtained an MSc in Applied Psychology from the University of Surrey, United Kingdom, and a Ph.D. in Industrial/Organizational Psychology from Universiti Kebangsaan Malaysia (UKM). He taught at IIUM from 1997 to 2018 and spent nine months at the University of Gloucestershire, the UK, as an academic visitor. Apart from IIUM, he lectured on a part-time basis at UKM, UTM, OUM, UNIMY, and Alif Institute London.

Amber Haque – see bio for Editors.

Anahita Akhavan is a 2023 graduate of Columbia University Teachers College's Master of Arts in Clinical Psychology program dedicated to perinatal well-being, especially within marginalized communities. She actively contributes to ongoing research at the pioneering Muslim Perinatal Lab (MPL), led by Dr. Venus Mahmoodi, focusing on the challenges faced by Muslim mothers post-COVID-19 and their broader motherhood experiences. Through this journey, Anahita gained vital research skills, fueling her passion for enhancing the Muslim community well-being. Anahita continues to advance her perinatal mental health knowledge and aspires to promote mental well-being through social media. She envisions future initiatives for accurate mental health education in underserved communities driven by technology's potential for social change. With her solid foundation in MPL, Anahita persists on her journey, dedicated to making meaningful contributions to the well-being of Muslim communities.

Bagus Riyono is currently the president of the International Association of Muslim Psychologists (IAMP). He is also a faculty member of the psychology department of Gadjah Mada University, Indonesia, and head of the Islamic Psychology Study Group (KKPI UGM). In 2011, he earned his doctoral degree in motivation with an Islamic perspective from Gadjah Mada University, Indonesia. In his dissertation, he constructed an integrated theory of motivation consisting of three sub-theories. Currently, he is working on applying his theories in a cognitive-spiritual intervention called Tazkia therapy. His research interests are Tazkia therapy, sensing mentality, anchor personality, human potential, motivation, sensing culture, psychometry, organizational development, family, and parenting.

Fahad Khan is a Licensed Clinical Psychologist with a Doctorate in Clinical Psychology and a master's degree in biomedical sciences. He has also been a student of religious studies in various institutions. He currently serves as the Deputy Director at Khalil Center, providing psychological services while supervising clinical and research work. He teaches undergraduate as well as graduate courses in various academic institutions. His research and writing interests include Muslim mental health and Islamic psychology. He is a fellow of the International Association of Islamic Psychology and serves as a reviewer and editor for various peer-reviewed journals around the world. He is actively involved in professional organizations and has served on many committees and divisions of the American Psychological Association (APA) and the Illinois Psychological Association (IPA). The APA awarded him the 2021 Early Career Psychologist Champion and 2020 Early Career Achievement Awards for his work and dedication.

Filius Iakhin is a member of the Managing Board of the Association Psychological Assistance to Muslims (Russia) and the Head of the Bashkortostan Regional Branch of this Association (Russia, Ufa), Associate Professor at the Institute of Knowledge Integration (IKI) Academy (Tbilisi, Georgia), senior researcher at the Bashkir State Pedagogical University (BSPU) named after M. Akmullah (Russia, Ufa), a private practical/clinical psychologist (counselor). He is a Candidate of Sciences (PhD) in Law from the Dissertation Council of the Moscow State Institute of International Relations (University) (Moscow, Russia, 2004), holds master's degree in psychology from the Bashkir State Pedagogical University (BSPU) (Ufa, Russia, 2022). He also passed licensed long-term conversion training courses on Practical Psychology (2013-2014), Clinical Psychology (2021-2022) in BSPU, certified training courses on Cognitive Behavioral Therapy (2018-2019), Schema-therapy (2019-2021), Islamic Psychology (2020), Multicultural Counseling (2021), Spiritual Pedagogy and Psychology (2020). In 2022, he finished a postgraduate certificate program in Islamic Thought and Knowledge Integration at IKI Academy (Tbilisi, Georgia).

Halima Krausen is a scientific staff member at the Academy of World Religions of Hamburg University. After studying Islamic theology, law, and religious studies, she led the German-speaking Muslim community in Hamburg for twenty years. She is also involved in study circles and lectures in Germany and the UK. Since her student days, she has been active in interfaith dialogue and projects of religious adult education in Germany and abroad. Her publications include book chapters, magazine articles, a series of sermons, and a collection of prayers from Muslim tradition.

Hamid Rafiei-Honar is an Assistant Professor of the Islamic Sciences and Culture Academy and former Vice President of the Islamic Psychology Association (IPA) in Iran. He graduated from Hawzah Elmiyyah of Qom (Islamic Theological Seminary in Qom,

Iran) in the fields of Fiqh and Usul of Fiqh (Methodology of Ijtihad), BA in Psychology and Islamic Studies, MA in Clinical Psychology, Ph.D. in General Psychology from Imam Khomeini Education and Research Institute (IKERI), Iran. He has authored three books and 40 articles in Islamic Psychology, Psychotherapy, and Psychometrics. He has also supervised 50 treatises on developing Islamic scales and psych-education interventions, especially in self-control and self-regulation.

Hooman Keshavarzi is licensed as a psychotherapist with a Doctorate in Clinical Psychology, a master's in clinical psychology, and a Bachelor of Science – specialist psychology track/minor in Islamic Studies. He is currently a visiting scholar at Ibn Haldun University (Istanbul, Turkey), the Program Director of Islamic Psychology at Hamad bin Khalifa University, an instructor at Hartford Seminary, and the founding director of Khalil Center – the first Islamically oriented professional community mental wellness center and largest provider of Muslim mental healthcare in the US. Hooman Keshavarzi has also authored several published academic papers in recognized peer-reviewed journals on integrating Islamic spirituality into modern psychological practice.

Jamilah Hanum Abdul Khaiyom is an Assistant Professor and Clinical Psychologist in the Department of Psychology, Abdul Hamid Abu Sulayman Kulliyyah of Islamic Revealed Knowledge and Human Sciences, International Islamic University Malaysia. She received her Ph.D. in Psychological Medicine from Universiti Putra Malaysia, and her doctoral research was on Group Cognitive Behavior Therapy (CBT) for Patients with Anxiety Disorders. Her research interest is integrating Islamic spiritual elements with cognitive-behavioral and mindfulness interventions in promoting mental health and well-being. She has published over 45 refereed journal articles and ten books/modules. The most recent is *i-ACT for Life*: A Prevention Module Featuring Integrated Elements of Islamic Spirituality and Acceptance and Commitment Therapy (ACT). The module has been digitalized and is being used by the Malaysian population for the management of psychological distress and maintenance of mental health. Because of her active involvement in mental health, she received the Mental Health Advocator Award from the university.

Khadijah Hasanah Abang Abdullah is a psychiatrist and medical lecturer from Universiti Sains Islam Malaysia (USIM). She was awarded a medical degree from The University of Manchester, United Kingdom, and a Doctor of Psychiatry from Universiti Kebangsaan Malaysia. Due to her interest in providing holistic care, she pursued a Diploma in Islamic Psychology from Cambridge Muslim College. She believes that holistic care should include spirituality in the therapeutic process. She practices in both government and private settings in Malaysia. She holds the position of Vice President in Green Crescent Malaysia, a non-governmental organization that promotes mental health awareness and specifically issues related to addiction problems. She has published articles in scientific journals and has been invited as a speaker to various scientific and public events.

Khalid Elzamzamy is an Assistant Faculty and Clinician-Educator Fellow at the Johns Hopkins University School of Medicine. He completed his child and adolescent psychiatry fellowship at the Institute of Living, Connecticut. He received his medical degree from Ain Shams University, Egypt, and completed his adult psychiatry residency at Hamad Medical Corporation in Qatar. He also completed a master's degree in Islamic Studies at Hamad Bin Khalifa University in Qatar. He previously served as a research assistant at Yale University. He is a researcher with the Family and Youth Institute and Khalil Center, USA. He also serves as a faculty member at The Alkaram Institute, USA. His research interests include the integration of religion and spirituality in clinical practice, suicide prevention and postvention, contributions of Muslim intellectuals to psychology and mental health, and Islamic ethics in clinical practice.

Latifat Ahmed is an advocate and a student of knowledge. The common good for all has always been her passion and lifelong dream. For over 12 years, she has been studying Islam and its answers to the world's ills. As a community organizer, she has created programs and policies that have helped bridge the gaps between its members, leading them to lead well-informed and better lives.

Lindsay White completed her bachelor's degree in ancient studies and master's in clinical psychology at Columbia University. She is pursuing her doctorate in clinical psychology with health care emphasis at Pace University. Her work combines interests in parental mental health and innovative treatment methods.

Lütfiye Söğütlü is Associate Professor of Psychiatry at Saglik Bilimleri Universitesi. After graduating from Erciyes University Faculty of Medicine in 2006, she completed her specialty training at Bakırköy Prof. Dr. Mazhar Osman Mental Health and Neurological Diseases Training in 2014. In 2022, he received the title of Associate Professor. Her specialization includes treatment and follow-up of psychotic patients, management of acute psychiatric conditions, sexual dysfunction therapies, cognitive-behavioral therapies in anxiety disorders and depressive disorders, marital therapy, family therapy, treatment and follow-up of adolescent psychiatric patients, evaluation and follow-up of forensic psychiatry cases, outpatient and inpatient substance and alcohol addiction treatment, hypnotherapy, and cognitive behavioral therapy. She has academic studies in depression, anxiety, addiction, trauma, psychotic disorders, and women's mental health. Her field of study is the treatment of these disorders with the Science of Nafs therapy method.

Masoud Azarbayejani is a Professor at the Research Institute of HAWZAH and UNIVERSITY (RIHU), and former President of the Islamic Psychology Association (IPA) in Iran. He graduated from Hawzah Elmiyyah of Qom in Fiqh, Tafsir, Philosophy, and Mysticism. MA in Islamic Theology, MA in Clinical Psychology from RIHU, & PhD. in Philosophy of Religion from Tarbiat Modares University, Iran. He has authored or co-authored 25 books and 60 articles in Psychology of Religion and Spirituality, Islamic Psychology, Philosophy of Psychology, and Islamic Ethics and Education. He has also supervised 50 master's and doctoral dissertations and has contributed to developing three educational programs in psychology and Islam.

Mohamed Hatta Shaharom was trained as a medical doctor and forensic psychiatrist in Egypt, Malaysia, and Australia. He has a Diploma in Islamic Thought, is an Honorary Fellow, The Pacific Rim College of Psychiatrists, Fellow, Academy of Medicine Malaysia and Academy of Professors, Malaysia. He is also a national book award winner 2022. A multi-genre writer who has authored and co-authored more than 45 Malay and English books on psychiatry, Islamic psychology and medicine, international humanitarian relief, poems, short stories, and novels. Held senior posts at Universiti Kebangsaan Malaysia (UKM), CUCMS and Islamic University of Cyberjaya. A visiting professor of psychiatry at University of Cyberjaya and adjunct professor at Universiti Teknologi Malaysia (UTM). Has founded and led a number of non-governmental organizations (NGOs). Former Chairman, Board of Directors (July 2018 - May 2020) of the language and literary institution Dewan Bahasa dan Pustaka, Malaysia.

Mohamed Omar Salem, MBChB, DPM, MRCPsych, FRCPsych, is an Associate Professor. of Psychiatry at Al-Ahli Hospital, Doha, Qatar. His main interests are the religious & spiritual aspects of psychiatry, Islamic psychology, dream research, CBT, and the philosophical and cultural aspects of psychiatry. He is the Middle East representative of the International Association for the Study of Dreams (IASD) and has published several articles in these areas.

Mustafa Merter is a Turkish psychiatrist, psychotherapist, author, and founder of ʿIlm Al Nafs and Nafs Psychotherapy. He was born in 1947 in Istanbul. He received a Swiss Federal High School Diploma in 1969. After, he completed his medical degree in Lausanne Faculty of Medicine in 1975. He worked as an Internal Medicine assistant in Germany and then started his Psychiatry training in Switzerland. He completed his specialization at the Burghölzli Psychiatric Hospital, affiliated with the University Hospital of Zurich. He settled in Turkey in 1987 and practiced his profession as a psychiatrist. Dr. Merter tried to understand psychology by comparing Western Psychology with Sufism. He indicated the concept of "nafs" should be adopted instead of "psyche." He has trained many psychotherapists with his training called Learning Analysis in ʿIlm Al Nafs. He has published two books. Currently, he writes the Psychological Interpretation of the Qur'an.

Nadzirah Ahmad Basri is an Assistant Professor and Clinical Psychologist. She works at the Department of Psychiatry, Kulliyyah of Medicine at the International Islamic University Malaysia, and conducts psychotherapy sessions at the university hospital. A graduate from Kyushu University, Japan, Nadzirah is keen on cross-cultural issues, spirituality, and religiosity. She gives numerous public talks on mental health and well-being and is active in *da'wah* and community activities in local non-governmental organizations. Her research interests lie in women and family's mental well-being, religiosity and spirituality, suicide prevention, and autism spectrum disorder. She was awarded two gold awards from Malaysian universities regarding the experiential learning and mental well-being activities she carried out with the public and her clients at the psychiatry clinic where she works. She lives with her husband and five children in Pahang, a state on the east coast of Malaysia.

Nazila Isgandarova has a Ph.D. from the University of Toronto, a Doctor of Ministry degree in pastoral counseling, marriage, and family studies from Wilfred Laurier University, and a Master of Social Work from the University of Windsor. She is a Registered Psychotherapist at the College for Registered Psychotherapists of Ontario and a Registered Social Worker at the Ontario Social Workers and Social Service Workers. Nazila is the recipient of the Order of Vaughan, the Forum for Theological Exploration research award for her study on domestic violence against Muslim women, the Canadian Association for Spiritual Care Senior Research Award, and the Society for Pastoral Counselling Research Award. Nazila is an Assistant Professor at Emmanuel College of Victoria University in the University of Toronto. Her book, titled Muslim Women, Domestic Violence, and Psychotherapy: Theological and Clinical Issues, was published by Routledge in 2018, and Islamic Spiritual Care; Theory and Practice(s) was published by Pandora Press in 2019.

Nursena Balatekin is a clinical psychologist, psychotherapist, and analyst in Istanbul. She studied Psychology at Uskudar University with a full scholarship and graduated in 2018 with a first degree. She completed her bachelor's degree from Western Kentucky University in Heinrich-Heine-Universität and received a research scholarship from University College London and a graduate scholarship from Sussex University. While on scholarship, she received her master's degree in clinical psychology from Bahçeşehir University. She completed an internship at Hospital de La Paix and NP Brain Hospital, considered one of Turkey's most recognized institutions concerned with mental health. She completed training in learning analysis by Dr. Merter. Also, she received Freudian and Lacanian supervision. She was interested in cognitive neuroscience during her bachelor's degree and received related courses. She ran experiments, did research, and published articles. Currently, she focuses on adolescent and adult psychotherapy in her private practice. As an analyst, she accepts clients, offers courses, and is still working on a novel that describes a therapy story of a patient treated by nafs psychotherapy.

Olga Pavlova is the head of the Department of Cross-cultural Psychology at the Faculty of Social Psychology and Faculty of Psychology and Education at Moscow State University, Russia. She is also an Associate Professor of the Department of Social Psychology, the Higher Attestation Commission for Academic Degrees, and Titles. She has been a Visiting Professor at Universitas Islam Indonesia (Yogyakarta, Indonesia 2019-23), Bolashak Academy (Karaganda, Kazakhstan, 2019), and Associate Professor at the Institute of Knowledge Integration (IKI) Academy (Tbilisi, Georgia, 2021). Founder and Chairman of the Association of Psychological Assistance to Muslims (Russia, 2017-2022). UN expert in education in psychology, social psychology, ethnopsychology, intercultural communication, and psychology of Islam and Muslims. Member of the International Association of Islamic Psychology, the International Association of Muslim Psychologists, and the International Association for the Psychology of Religion. Member of the editorial board of the international scientific journal Psikohumaniora: Jurnal Penelitian Psikologi of the International Journal on Mental Health, Religion, and Culture.

Rabia Malik is a consultant systemic psychotherapist based in London. She has extensive experience working with Muslim clients and community organizations, developing Islamic and culturally appropriate therapeutic interventions and trainings. She was the co-lead at the Marlborough Cultural Therapy Centre for many years, which provided a specialist therapeutic service for minority ethnic clients based in the National Health Service and served as a leading model for community engagement and organizational change. She has published papers on Islamic approaches to therapy and provides freelance training nationally and internationally, as well as supervision to practitioners and therapy to clients. She teaches systemic therapy clinical training programs and has also taught and supervised students on the systemic doctorate at the Tavistock Centre.

Her doctoral research was on the cultural construction of depression among Pakistanis.

Sena Aycan is a licensed psychotherapist with a master's degree in clinical psychology and a bachelor's degree in psychology, specializing in the pedagogy track. She has dedicated herself to working with disadvantaged and vulnerable groups within various governmental and non-governmental organizations throughout her career. Currently serving as a Research and Content Development Fellow at Khalil Center, Sena combines her expertise in psychology with a commitment to creating valuable resources for Muslim mental health. In addition to her work at Khalil Center, Sena actively offers both online and in-person therapy services. Notably, she has been actively engaged in on-site psychotherapy sessions within earthquake-affected areas in Türkiye, extending crucial support to survivors.

Sarah Mohr was born and raised in the SF Bay Area, the traditional territory of the Ohlone people, Sarah has spent the last 25+ years serving persons who are low-income, mentally ill, and substance addicted in her community as a mental health worker. She is a certified drug and alcohol counselor and LCSW. She earned her MSW from CSU, East Bay (2017). She also has a BA in Religion with a minor in philosophy and a minor in women and gender studies from Dominican University (2003) and a master's in religion and psychology from the GTU with a Certificate in Islamic Studies (2009). She is a visiting scholar at the GTU and works full-time in addiction treatment.

Venus Mahmoodi is a clinical psychologist, researcher, professor, and advocate for women's mental health. She is an Assistant Professor of Medical Psychology at Columbia University and a Clinical Psychologist at New York-Presbyterian Hospital, where she provides clinical care to women across the reproductive lifespan in The Women's Program. Dr. Mahmoodi is also adjunct faculty at Teachers College, Columbia University, where she teaches graduate level courses in clinical psychology and mentors students in research. Her research focuses on Muslim women's experience of motherhood, specifically within the perinatal (pregnancy and postpartum) period. In addition to her work at Columbia University, Dr. Mahmoodi serves the Muslim community in NYC by providing workshops on mental health and psychotherapy to perinatal Muslim patients through the Khalil Center, utilizing spiritually integrated techniques. Dr. Mahmoodi completed her Ph.D. at the Pacific Graduate School of Psychology in California and her clinical internship at Mount Sinai Beth Israel in NYC.

Zarnab Virk is a researcher with a master's in clinical psychology from Teachers College, Columbia University, and a bachelor's degree in psychology from Princeton University. She is passionate about expanding mental health research to include underrepresented populations. Her research interests encompass the interplay of religion and spirituality in mental well-being, decision-making and self-regulation, and positive psychology, exploring the factors contributing to human flourishing and resilience. In her free time, she volunteers as a psychological evaluator to document psychiatric symptoms for legal affidavits to support refugees seeking asylum in the U.S.

Zul Azlin Razali attained his Diploma in Islamic Studies and dedicated his early years as an academician to researching and writing on this topic. After multiple academic books and journal articles, he extended his craft into fiction writing. His debut work won a national novel-writing competition. He left his post as an Associate Professor to become a full-time private Psychiatrist. He still writes fiction.

Printed in the USA
CPSIA information can be obtained
at www.ICGtesting.com
LVHW081743280124
769707LV00016B/889